THE AFTERLIFE OF

MALCOLM X

An Outcast Turned Icon's Enduring Impact on America

MARK WHITAKER

SIMON & SCHUSTER
New York   Amsterdam/Antwerp   London
Toronto   Sydney/Melbourne   New Delhi

Simon & Schuster
1230 Avenue of the Americas
New York, NY 10020

First Simon & Schuster hardcover edition May 2025

SIMON & SCHUSTER and colophon are registered trademarks of Simon & Schuster, LLC

Simon & Schuster strongly believes in freedom of expression and stands against censorship in all its forms. For more information, visit BooksBelong.com.

For information about special discounts for bulk purchases, please contact Simon & Schuster Special Sales at 1-866-506-1949 or business@simonandschuster.com.

The Simon & Schuster Speakers Bureau can bring authors to your live event. For more information or to book an event, contact the Simon & Schuster Speakers Bureau at 1-866-248-3049 or visit our website at www.simonspeakers.com.

Interior design by Lewelin Polanco

Manufactured in the United States of America

1   3   5   7   9   10   8   6   4   2

Library of Congress Cataloging-in-Publication Data is available.

ISBN 978-1-6680-3329-6
ISBN 978-1-6680-3331-9 (ebook)

For Alexis

After signing the contract for this book, Malcolm X looked at me hard. "A writer is what I want, not an interpreter." I tried to be a dispassionate chronicler. But he was the most electric personality I have ever met, and I still can't quite conceive him dead. It still feels to me as if he has just gone into some next chapter, to be written by historians.

—ALEX HALEY, *THE AUTOBIOGRAPHY OF MALCOLM X*, 1965

CONTENTS

PART FIVE: EXONERATION: 2017–2021

Prologue

Within days after a point-blank burst of shotgun fire struck down Malcolm X in a panic-filled ballroom two miles to the north, a sign appeared outside the National Memorial African Book Store in Harlem. So many times, Malcolm had preached from that very spot, at 125th Street and Seventh Avenue, cutting a mesmerizing figure in the dark suits that cloaked his tall, slender physique, and the scholar's glasses that framed the handsome face with its fringe of reddish hair, high mocha cheekbones, and intense light eyes. Those street corner sermons drew the most diverse crowds anyone had ever seen in Harlem—shopkeepers and street hustlers, professors and pimps, doctors and junkies, all gathered to hear that resonant voice full of fury, wisdom, and biting humor.

In Harlem, the bookstore was known as "Michaux's," after owner Lewis Michaux, who had started selling books out of a wagon and eventually assembled a collection of 200,000 volumes on all things Black. Among the teeming stacks inside, Malcolm had spent countless hours browsing through the works of philosophers, historians, and poets who helped guide him on his intellectual journey from separatist to pan-Africanist, from narrow dogmatist to globe-trotting searcher. Sometimes he read so late into the night that Michaux locked the doors and let him stay inside. Now Michaux turned to the oral tradition to honor his slain friend, posting a sign outside that mixed homemade verse with a proverb that came down from the Black ancestors:

MAN, IF YOU THINK BRO. MALCOLM IS DEAD,
YOU ARE OUT OF YOUR COTTON PICKING HEAD.
JUST GET UP OFF YOUR SLUMBERING BED,
AND WATCH HIS FIGHTING SPIRIT SPREAD.
EVERY SHUT EYE AIN'T SLEEP
EVERY GOODBYE AIN'T GONE.

Six days after the murder, Ossie Davis delivered a eulogy for Malcolm in front of six hundred mourners at Harlem's Faith Temple Church of God in Christ, at 147th Street and Amsterdam Avenue. The small Pentecostal venue was chosen as neutral ground after Molotov cocktails burned out the Nation of Islam mosque over which Malcolm had presided for a decade, an attack presumed to be an act of retaliation by his followers for what they saw as the NOI's hand in his bloody demise. Malcolm's widow, Betty Shabazz, had called on his friend Davis because she knew Ossie could do the task justice, with his actor's presence and playwright's way with words. But Betty was also looking for someone respected enough by all the dangerous factions pointing fingers in Harlem to keep the event peaceful. Brushing aside the risk that white bosses in the entertainment industry wouldn't approve, Davis accepted the invitation, and offered a tribute that became famous for how he described what Malcolm X meant to Black America. "Malcolm was our manhood," Davis exclaimed, "our living, black manhood!"

Less noticed was a promise of resurrection that Davis held out to his people as he looked down upon the wrought copper casket set on a platform draped in red velvet. They were "consigning these mortal remains to earth, the common mother of all," Ossie declared, "secure in the knowledge that what we place in the ground is no more now a man—but a seed—which, after the winter of our discontent, will come forth again to meet us. And we will know him then for what he was and is—a prince—our own black shining prince!—who didn't hesitate to die, because he loved us so."

Within the year, that princely presence reemerged in the pages of a posthumous autobiography, coauthored by Alex Haley, a ghostwriter who wove a tale of moral redemption out of Malcolm's odyssey from prison to preacher's podium. After the hardcover received surprisingly positive reviews in the white press, *The Autobiography of Malcolm X* became a bestseller as a $1.25 paperback, captivating both Blacks inspired by Malcolm's unreserved message of pride and whites jolted by his blunt perspective on race.

By the fourth anniversary of his death in 1969, Malcolm had become such a folk hero to the Black youth of New York City that they demanded time off from school to honor him. Thousands of collegians and high school students packed events in four of the city's five boroughs, and as far away as Long Island University. At Harlem's fabled Apollo Theater, 1,600 schoolchildren sat through a two-hour program of music and speeches that included the Symphony of New York playing Bach and Ossie Davis reenacting his stirring eulogy.

The events across the city that day were covered for *The New York Times* by C. Gerald Fraser, one of a small group of Black journalists whom the paper had only recently hired to report on developments in Black America previously assigned to white "race beat" reporters. As Fraser explained to the largely white *Times* readership: "Malcolm, since his assassination by three Black Muslims four years ago yesterday in the Audubon Ballroom in Washington Heights, has become something of a legend to youths, many of whom were too young to have known him or have seem him alive. The movement for black unity and black awareness, black consciousness and black pride was developed, in part, out of the speeches of Malcolm and his records and best-selling autobiography. He became a hero because, in the eyes of slum residents, he was the first man they heard who effectively challenged white America."

The celebrations of that "Malcolm X Day," as some were already calling it, stretched to Black urban communities across America. Detroit officials made school optional for the day, and fourteen thousand Black students stayed home. In Boston, a procession of sixty marched through the Black neighborhood of Roxbury and proclaimed their intention to rename a well-known gathering spot "Malcolm X Square." Outside Chicago, students who had taken over a house on fraternity row and renamed it the "Black House" mounted his portrait over a fireplace mantel and captioned it "St. Malcolm." At the University of California at Santa

Cruz, Black students demanded that one the school's seven colleges be named after Malcolm X and devoted to ethnic studies.

At San Jose State College, the day's festivities were organized by Harry Edwards, the Black sociologist who had launched the protest movement that inspired the black-gloved salute at the 1968 Summer Olympics in Mexico City. Edwards had met Malcolm while earning his PhD from Cornell University and christened his movement the Olympic Project for Human Rights (OPHR) in tribute to Malcolm's attempt to bring the plight of Black Americans before the United Nations as a human rights issue. Edwards had even modeled what would become his own signature look—horned-rimmed glasses and a goatee beard—after Malcolm. A reporter covering the San Jose State event asked Edwards why in parts of Black America, Malcolm was already celebrated more than Martin Luther King Jr., who had been cut down by a white assassin's bullet less than a year earlier, in 1968. "It wasn't so much that he led in action as that he inspired action in others, even beyond the grave," Edwards said of Malcolm. "I suspect that won't be so true of Martin Luther King. He's dead."

═══

Thanks to the enduring place of *The Autobiography of Malcolm X* in high school and college classrooms and on library and home bookshelves across America, and to the memorable impact of director Spike Lee's biopic *Malcolm X*, people around the world are familiar with the broad outlines of the extraordinary life that began on May 19, 1925, in Omaha, Nebraska. Malcolm Little was the seventh child of Earl Little, an itinerant Baptist preacher from Georgia, and Earl's fourth by his second wife, Louise Langdon Little, an immigrant from Grenada who like him was also a follower of the Black separatist leader Marcus Garvey.

After members of Omaha's white community looking to punish the Littles for their racial activism attacked their home while Earl was out of town, the family moved first to Milwaukee and then to Lansing, Michigan. There, they were again targeted by a white supremacist group called the Black Legion, who burned their new house to the ground when Malcolm was three years old. At age six, he learned that his father had been found dead on the streetcar tracks he passed on the way into town, a tragedy for which he long suspected the Black Legion was responsible. Struggling to provide for the family on her own, Louise Little sank into mental illness that led to institutionalization and left her children to fend for themselves.

The decade that followed took Malcolm on a dramatic journey from secular descent to religious salvation. Placed in a juvenile home and then with foster families in Lansing, he excelled at his studies but was discouraged by white teachers from pursuing his dream of becoming a lawyer. Disheartened and restless, he dropped out of the eighth grade and went to live with his half-sister, Ella Collins, in Boston. There and then in Harlem, he fell into a world of drug use and petty crime that landed him in a Massachusetts prison at the age of twenty-one. During six years there and at two other prisons, he received news from three of his siblings that they had converted to the Nation of Islam. Under their influence, Malcolm began to study the teachings of the NOI's self-made American "prophet," Elijah Muhammad, who combined calls for racial separatism and personal rectitude with eccentric theories that portrayed whites as genetically engineered "blue-eyed devils."

The young prisoner wrote a series of fan letters to Muhammad, and as soon as he won parole in 1952 he applied to join the NOI and change his name to Malcolm X, in keeping with the sect's belief that followers should shed "slave names" inherited from whites who once owned their ancestors. Rewarding Malcolm's devotion and seeing his promise, Muhammad put him in charge first of the NOI's mosques in Detroit and Philadelphia, and then its largest outpost, Mosque No. 7 in Harlem. Over the next decade, Malcolm became the most visible and dynamic national spokesman for the NOI, giving speeches on college campuses and engaging in debates on radio and television that made him a figure of fascination to many Blacks, and to many whites a feared alternative to the uplifting gospel of nonviolence and racial integration preached by Dr. King.

Then, in the last year of his life, Malcolm's odyssey took another, unexpected turn, one that would transform him into a symbol of political outreach and spiritual growth. He confronted Elijah Muhammad about his history of getting young female assistants pregnant, and Muhammad retaliated by suspending Malcolm from the Nation of Islam in supposed punishment for intemperate remarks he made about the assassination of President John F. Kennedy. After breaking entirely with the NOI, Malcolm made his first pilgrimage to Mecca, converted to the orthodox international version of Islam, and visited the capitals of Africa and Europe.

Returning to Harlem, Malcolm launched his own new political movement with the goal of uniting American Blacks across divides of class and politics and making them see common cause with people of color liberating themselves from white colonial rule around the world. Rightfully fearful that he was being targeted for death from the time of his split with the NOI, he nonetheless kept up a relentless pace of travel, speeches, and interviews in his final year. Then, on the afternoon of Sunday, February 21, 1965, three Black gunmen stormed the stage of the Audubon Ballroom north of Harlem as Malcolm was beginning to give a speech and shot him dead in front of his wife, their four young daughters, and four hundred of his followers—a sudden and brutal end that left millions to mourn the man and the promise of what he could have achieved had he lived longer.

Yet it wasn't the final chapter. This book will tell the story of the extraordinary impact that Malcolm X has continued to have on American culture and politics since the assassination—a mark that in the sixty years after his death arguably far surpassed what he was able to achieve in less than forty years of life. That influence began with the enormous critical and commercial success of *The Autobiography of Malcolm X*, published just nine months after his death. First in hardcover and then in a bestselling paperback edition, the book has sold millions of copies and been named one of the most important books of the twentieth century. It has also continued to fascinate students of Malcolm's thinking into a new millennium, when a previously unknown chapter that was removed from the *Autobiography* and later bought by a private collector at an auction of Alex Haley's estate finally became available to the public after being acquired by New York's preeminent Black history archive.

In the 1960s and 1970s, Malcolm's memory and example provided inspiration to the founders of the Black Power movement, to the poets and playwrights of the Black Arts Movement, and to the first campus advocates of Black Studies. In the world of sports, they had a life-changing impact on three athletes who set an example for the activist-athletes of today: boxer Muhammad Ali; basketball great Kareem Abdul-Jabbar; and John Carlos, one of the two U.S. sprinters who raised those gloved fists at the 1968 Mexico City Olympics. In the 1980s and 1990s, Malcolm found a new generation of admirers and "samplers" among pioneers of hip hop music such as Public Enemy, KRS-One, and Tupac Shakur. The publicity surrounding Spike Lee's 1992 biopic further fueled the revival of interest in Malcolm and drove a surge in sales of "X" merchandise.

In the twenty-first century, the influence of Malcolm X on American politics ranged from the hold he had over the imagination of Barack Obama, the country's first Black president, to the inspiration he provided to the young leaders of the Black Lives Matter movement that in the summer of 2020 produced the largest outpouring of interracial protest in support of racial justice in a generation. Sixty years after Malcolm confuted his reputation for condoning violence by urging supporters to cast ballots before resorting to bullets, his name was even invoked at a Democratic presidential convention. After Kamala Harris replaced Joe Biden at the top of the party's ticket in the summer of 2024, delegates from Malcolm's home state of Nebraska proudly wore T-shirts emblazoned with his image on the convention floor in Chicago and proclaimed him one of their native "icons" during a raucous roll call vote accompanied by a live DJ.

On the political right, meanwhile, Malcolm's calls for Black self-improvement and economic self-reliance have also made him a hero to conservative Black intellectuals, jurists, and policymakers. As a college radical, Clarence Thomas hung a poster of Malcolm in his dorm room, and he continued to feel a sense of kinship as a born-again conservative. "I don't see how the civil rights people of today can claim Malcolm X as their own," Thomas said in 1987, four years before he was appointed to the Supreme Court. Making Malcolm-like appeals for greater personal responsibility in Black communities, Louis Farrakhan, his controversial onetime protégé turned accuser, persuaded hundreds of thousands of Black men to descend on Washington, D.C., in 1995 to declare their commitment to being better domestic partners and fathers.

Sixteen years later, the academic historian Manning Marable produced an exhaustively researched biography that portrayed Malcolm as more radical than the conservatives understood, or than Alex Haley allowed to come across in the *Autobiography*. While winning some of publishing's top prizes, Marable's book was attacked by other devoted students of Malcolm's legacy for its provocative allegations about his personal life. That controversy, in turn, only heightened the interest in another award-winning biography that came out a decade later, by veteran journalist Les Payne, who like both Malcolm and Marable didn't live to see his book published.

In the end, however, the fighting about the would-be keepers of Malcolm's flame only served to demonstrate how much he defied easy categorization. At different times, Malcolm was scoldingly old-fashioned and breathtakingly modern, a preacher of individual responsibility and an organizer of group resistance. He was both a stickler for hardheaded realism and a pioneer of the kind of consciousness-raising that propelled the Black Power movement and later infused the women's rights and gay rights movements. On that early "Malcolm X Day" in 1969, C. Eric Lincoln, the Black scholar who wrote the first major study of the Nation of Islam, speculated about the various things that Malcolm might have become had he lived longer. "The projections of what he was about to do," Lincoln mused, "range from a seat on the board of directors of the Urban League to a Castro-style revolution." As Spike Lee's movie was about to come out, Emanuel Cleaver, the Black mayor of Kansas City, described Malcolm as a man with "ten different personalities and eleven messages to be learned from them."

Malcolm was also ahead of his time as a master of modern media. He was delivering what would become arresting sound bites, viral videos, and memorable memes before those concepts existed. His elegant fashion sense—the conservative dark suits and thin ties; the distinctive glasses, with their horn rims on the top and wire rims on the bottom—evoked the cool of the bebop era then and remain in vogue among artists and intellectuals still. "In the days before Instagram and the proliferation of style as politics, Malcolm understood the power of images," cultural journalist Vikki Tobak pointed out in an essay about a photograph of Malcolm taken by Eve Arnold for *Life* magazine in 1960. Wearing a fedora rakishly tilted over his head, Malcolm sat, as Tobak described it, "in profile, stoic, refined and stylish AF, his hand draped loosely on his neck to frame a ring on his finger bearing the star and crescent moon."

It was an image that premature loss froze in time. Malcolm X and Martin Luther King Jr. were the same age when they were killed: thirty-nine. Like other young icons who didn't outlive that turbulent era—from John F. Kennedy and his brother Robert, to rock legends such as Jimi Hendrix and Janis Joplin—they could ascend into the realm of myth partly because we never had to see them grow old or watch them lose their powers. But in our memories, King will always seem older and more saintly than he was in real life. As a figure of identification and projection, Malcolm will forever stand on the edge between youth and middle age, between daring and discipline, between the psychological attraction of the thrilling bad boy and the stern father.

As much as the still electric effect of the sight and sound of Malcolm X, however, it has been the grim persistence of the racial divide in America that has kept his legacy alive. As scholar C. Eric Lincoln once put it, the explanation for Malcolm's enduring appeal "lies in the simple fact that we have not yet overcome." From the "law and order" code language and "Southern strategy" of the Nixon era; to the racially targeted war on drugs and mass incarceration of the Reagan era; to the unfulfilled liberal promises of the Clinton and Obama eras; to the resurgent white nationalism of the Trump era, Malcolm's unflinching analysis of racial reality has remained recurrently relevant. Today, amid a backlash against affirmative action, so-called diversity, equity, and inclusion programs, and other measures designed to rectify past racial injustice, Malcolm's calls for Black self-reliance have never seemed more urgent. For successive generations of young people, in particular, Malcolm has served as a model not only for what but for how to protest the injustices of each new age—with force and courage, but also with stylishness, erudition, and wit. For Malcolm's admirers, his has remained that most compelling of all voices: one that seems to speak not just *to* you but *for* you.

=====

Stretching over this long time span has also been a murder mystery: Who really killed Malcolm X? This book will also trace that detective story, which began with the capture of a young Black New Jersey resident named Talmadge Hayer minutes after the assassination, as he fled after dropping a .45 caliber pistol inside the Audubon Ballroom. In the days after, two enforcers from the Harlem NOI mosque known as Norman 3X Butler and Thomas 15X Johnson were also arrested. In the middle of the murder trial, Hayer abruptly changed his testimony to swear that the other two weren't involved, but all three were convicted nonetheless and sentenced to life in prison. In the end, Butler and Johnson—who while behind bars embraced orthodox Islam and changed their names to Muhammad Abdul Aziz and Khalil Islam—languished there for a combined forty-two years before they were paroled.

Only in 2020 was the case officially reopened by Cyrus "Cy" Vance Jr., the high-profile Manhattan district attorney, after the D.A.'s office was approached with exculpatory evidence unearthed by the makers of a documentary on Netflix. In the film, a Black freelance journalist named Abdur-Rahman Muhammad is portrayed as identifying holes in the original prosecution case and piecing together proof of who the real killer was and how he had hidden in plain sight. In a twenty-two-month investigation, a special task force appointed by Vance found that numerous pieces of evidence that would have supported Butler's and Johnson's claims of innocence were deliberately suppressed in order to protect the identity of FBI informants and undercover agents working for a secret intelligence unit of the NYPD. While not definitively answering the question that has loomed over the assassination from the beginning—were the FBI or the NYPD somehow in on the Audubon hit?—the probe also offered shocking new proof of how much the feds and the New York police knew about the threats to Malcolm's life before they left him largely unprotected on the day of the murder.

In November 2021, Vance stood before a New York County Supreme Court judge and submitted a forty-three-page motion request-
ing that the convictions of Aziz, now eighty-three, and Islam, who had
died in 2009, be vacated. When the judge declared the two men officially exonerated, the courtroom erupted into loud applause. Docu-
mentarian Abdur-Rahman Muhammad and his producers were there
to witness the emotional scene, and to join Aziz for a celebration outside. "I felt that I was able to get some semblance of justice for Brother
Malcolm X and his family, first and foremost," Muhammad proudly told
reporters, "and second of all, justice for these two men."

Yet that version of the detective story wasn't complete, either. All
along, much earlier and less remembered credit for keeping the questions surrounding Malcolm's murder alive belonged to another, more
unlikely sleuth. He was a shy, soft-spoken white reporter from the
Midwest named Peter Goldman, who developed a personal connection with Malcolm while he was alive, and wrote a deeply reported
book about him after the assassination, long before the prizewinning
biographies. In the late 1970s, Goldman interviewed all three murder
suspects in prison and tried, along with lawyer William Kunstler, to get
the case reopened. Despite those efforts, the wrongful conviction saga
would extend well into a new century—along with the stirring echoes
of Malcolm X's voice that reverberated across six decades of American
history.

PART ONE

CONVICTION

1965–1967

ONE

Death in the Afternoon

To close observers of the Nation of Islam, one of the first death threats came in the form of a cartoon. On March 8, 1964, Malcolm X announced that he was quitting the NOI, where he had served for a decade as minister of the sect's largest outpost, Mosque No. 7 in Harlem, and the most visible spokesman for the leader he long referred to reverently as the Honorable Elijah Muhammad, or "the Messenger of Allah." Four months earlier, Muhammad had suspended Malcolm as punishment for a provocative statement he made after the assassination of President John F. Kennedy. Malcolm was speaking to a rally at the Manhattan Center in New York City nine days after the murder, and in the question period afterward he criticized Kennedy for not having done enough to investigate the killings of Black civil rights martyrs and anticolonial leaders around the world. Kennedy "never foresaw that the chicken would come home to roost so soon," Malcolm quipped, to loud applause from a crowd of seven hundred followers. "Being an old farm boy myself, chickens coming home to roost never did make me sad; they made me glad."

The press interpreted the crack as a heartless suggestion that Kennedy deserved to die, and Elijah Muhammad used the furor as a pretext to put Malcolm in his place. Months of attempts to negotiate a rapprochement between them went nowhere, and now Malcolm was formally announcing his departure from the Nation of Islam and plans to start his own new "black nationalist party." In a statement to the press, he claimed he had no desire to pick fights with Elijah Muhammad or to poach followers from him. Without naming names, however, Malcolm hinted that the real reason for the falling out was not the remark about Kennedy but the Messenger's jealousy. "Envy blinds men and makes it impossible for him to think clearly," he explained. "This is what happened." Malcolm said nothing about the other source of tension that had arisen behind the two men: the questions Malcolm raised privately about Elijah Muhammad's practice of seducing and fathering children with his female assistants, in defiance of the Nation's code of sexual monogamy.

A month after Malcolm's announcement, a cartoon titled "On My Own" appeared in the April 10 issue of the NOI's house newspaper, *Muhammad Speaks*, which was published at its Chicago headquarters and personally approved by Elijah Muhammad before it went to print. The artist was the paper's cartoonist, who called himself Eugene Majied and signed his artwork with that last name. In the cartoon, Malcolm's severed head bounced through a graveyard toward a tombstone etched with the names of notorious traitors: "Judas/ Brutus/ Benedict Arnold/ Malcolm 'Little Red.'" With each bounce, a thought bubble formed over Malcolm's skull.

"I split because no man wants to be Number 2 man in nothing!" read the first thought bubble. "The officials at headquarters fear my public image," read the second.

"The Messenger's family was jealous of me," read the third.

"Even the Messenger . . . Bla . . . Bla . . . Bla . . ." read the last thought bubble.

Decades later, Eugene Majied had left the Nation of Islam, retired to his native South Carolina, and reclaimed his birth name: Eugene Rivers Jr. His son, Boston-based minister Eugene Rivers III, went to visit his father, and asked him about the famous cartoon. Was March 1964 the point at which Malcolm's fate was sealed? the son asked.

No, the elder Rivers responded. The turning point came years before that—by 1959. For several years, envy of Malcolm among Elijah Muhammad's courtiers had been growing when Louis Lomax, a Black reporter and television producer from New York, teamed up with Mike Wallace, the future celebrated host of *60 Minutes*, to produce a five-part series on the Nation of Islam for a nightly local public television program called *News Beat*. Titled *The Hate That Hate Produced*, the series cast the NOI in a menacing light, with Wallace describing the sect as spreading "Black racism" and a "gospel of hate" to a quarter of a million Blacks in fifty cities.

Yet what Wallace showed spoke louder than words. In an opening scene, thousands of NOI followers filled a huge arena, the men dressed in sober dark suits and the women in long white dresses and head-scarves, waiting for the arrival of their leader. Elijah Muhammad had been born Elijah Poole in rural Georgia, Wallace explained. After moving to Detroit, Poole had fallen under the spell of a mysterious Black man named Wallace D. Fard, who claimed to be descended from the Prophet Muhammad and had founded the then tiny Nation of Islam sect. After Wallace Fard Muhammad, as he called himself, disappeared, Poole took over leadership of the Nation and claimed the name Elijah Muhammad. Since then, he had built the NOI into a national movement and attained almost godlike status among his followers, Wallace explained. But when Elijah Muhammad finally arrived at the hall and made his way to the stage, surrounded by bodyguards, he cut an odd-looking figure. He was short and moonfaced, with a large kofia hat encrusted with jeweled crescents and stars perched on his head, and he spoke in a high-pitched lisp. In a one-on-one interview with Louis Lomax, Muhammad seemed even more recessive, his soft voice muffling threats of a coming race war with "plenty bloodshed."

By contrast, the man TV viewers saw introduce Elijah Muhammad was tall and handsome, with an electrifying speaking voice. He was Malcolm X, Wallace explained, the minister of the NOI mosque in New York City and Elijah Muhammad's "ambassador-at-large." In his own one-on-one interview with Lomax, Malcolm was as confident and cogent as the Messenger was shy and mumbling. Asked whether Elijah Muhammad taught his followers to hate white people, Malcolm responded in the language of love. "It's not hate," he told Lomax. "It's not that you hate the source but your love for your people is so intense, so great, that you must let them know what is wrong with them, what is the source of their ills. . . . [Muhammad] teaches black people to love each other."

Originally broadcast in short nightly segments on the local New York public TV station, *The Hate That Hate Produced* proved such a sensation that Wallace re-aired the documentary the next week in its entirety, followed by a panel discussion with mainstream Black leaders that included baseball legend Jackie Robinson and Roy Wilkins, the executive secretary of the National Association for the Advancement of Colored People. From then on, Malcolm X became a nationally recognized figure in white as well as Black America. He began receiving invitations to appear on television and radio talk shows, to speak on college campuses, and to be profiled by national publications. "Much of America came to believe that Malcolm was the Muslims," as one observer put it.

Yet from where the elder Eugene Rivers sat, at NOI headquarters in Chicago, Malcolm's growing celebrity only fed more resentment, no matter how many converts he attracted or how much praise he heaped on the Honorable Elijah Muhammad. From then on, Rivers told his son, Malcolm was bound to become a marked man sooner or later.

Less than two weeks after his resignation from the NOI in March 1964, Malcolm made his own report of a secret murder plot. He accused two former lieutenants at Mosque No. 7—Captain Joseph X, the head of security, and a deputy minister known as Henry X—of using the period of his ninety-day suspension to turn his Harlem followers against him. "As soon as they felt I had been sufficiently isolated, Captain Joseph X then used assistant minister Henry X to spread lies from the speaker's stand that were skillfully designed to make the Muslims think I had rebelled against the Honorable Elijah Muhammad," Malcolm claimed in a statement that was ignored by the white press but covered in the Black-owned *New York Amsterdam News*. "When Joseph felt Henry's poison had turned sufficient number of Muslims against me, Joseph then sent some Brothers from his 'special squad' out to try and kill me in cold blood. Thanks to Allah, I learned of the plot from the very same Brothers he had sent out to murder me."

Despite that scare, Malcolm kept up a frantic public schedule for the rest of 1964. In April, he flew to Saudi Arabia, becoming one of the first Black Americans ever to make the hajj, the pilgrimage of orthodox Muslims to the Islamic holy site of Mecca. On colorful stationery illustrated with drawings of the holy sites, he wrote a long letter sharing his impressions with followers in New York, and signed it with the new name he was given in honor of the pilgrimage: "El-Hajj Malik El Shabazz (Malcolm X)." The followers leaked the letter to Michael "M.S." Handler, a veteran foreign correspondent for *The New York Times* who was now covering the civil rights beat and had become Malcolm's favorite white reporter at the paper. In a front-page story, Handler quoted Malcolm as saying that the trip had caused him to "'rearrange' much of my thought-patterns previously held, and to toss aside some of my previous assumptions"—particularly when it came to his blanket attacks on white people as the source of the world's ills.

"During the past seven days of this holy pilgrimage," Malcolm wrote in the letter, "while undergoing the rituals of the hajj, I have eaten from the same plate, drank from the same glass, slept on the same bed or rug, while praying to the same God—not only with some of this earth's most powerful kings, cabinet members, potentates and other forms of political and religious leaders—but also with fellow Muslims whose skin was the whitest of white, whose eyes were the bluest of blue, and whose hair was the blondest of blonde—yet it was the first time in my life that I didn't see them as 'white' men. I could look into their faces and see these didn't regard themselves as 'white.'"

From Saudi Arabia, Malcolm traveled on to Egypt, Ghana, and a half dozen other African countries that had recently won independence and were banding together in a new alliance called the Organization of African Unity. Upon returning to Harlem, he began laying the groundwork for his own new political movement, which he called the Organization of Afro-American Unity. In a June speech at the Audubon Ballroom, he spelled out an agenda for the OAAU and gave it a slogan. "That's our motto," he declared. "We want freedom by any means necessary." Those last four words would become Malcolm's most famous utterance—and would often be interpreted as carrying a threat of violence. But the rest of the speech made clear that the slogan had been inspired as much by the diplomacy and compromise that Malcolm witnessed among his African hosts as by the anticolonial uprisings that brought them to power.

While trying to get his new political movement off the ground, meanwhile, Malcolm had become mired in an ugly battle with the NOI over control of his home in Queens. At the time he was minister of Mosque No. 7 and starting a family, the Nation had purchased a small brick six-room house in the East Elmhurst neighborhood for them to live. Malcolm maintained that Elijah Muhammad had presented it to him as a gift, but the Nation held the legal deed. Now it was going to court to secure an eviction order, and Malcolm was fighting back by breaking his silence about the Messenger's adultery.

Over the years, a series of teenage NOI female converts had gone to work as secretaries at the Chicago headquarters and became pregnant. Under the Nation's rules for punishing unmarried sex, they were publicly shamed and temporarily banished. Rumors had circulated that Elijah Muhammad might be the father, but Malcolm refused to believe them. But then in the spring of 1963, he was told the stories were true by Muhammad's own son Wallace, who had begun to study the teachings of orthodox Islam in prison and become disillusioned with his father. Malcolm approached several of the women himself, and they confirmed what had happened to them.

Shaken, Malcolm flew to Muhammad's vacation home in Phoenix, Arizona, to confront the Messenger, who made no effort to deny the charges. Instead Muhammad insisted that he was fulfilling his divine destiny, comparing himself to biblical patriarchs who had multiple wives. "I'm David," he told Malcolm. "When you read about how David took another man's wife, I'm that David. You read about Noah, who got drunk—that's me. You read about Lot, who went and laid up with his own daughters. I have to fulfill all those things."

When Malcolm received his suspension several months later, he suspected that Muhammad's anger over being confronted with his sexual misconduct was a factor—but he also thought he could use his knowledge as a bargaining chip. Through Captain Joseph X, Malcolm sent a message to Chicago that he would stay silent if he received a reinstatement hearing. Even when that strategy backfired and Malcolm saw he had no path back, he still said nothing when explaining his reasons for quitting the Nation.

Then two days after Malcolm's resignation speech, the Nation formally demanded that Malcolm and his family vacate the house and give back the furnishings that had been paid for by the NOI. By the time he returned from his trip to Mecca and Africa, Chicago had gone to court to get an eviction order. Gambling that embarrassing Muhammad publicly might get the Nation to back off, Malcolm contacted Mike Wallace, now a reporter for the CBS morning news show, and invited him to the Queens house for an interview. He told Wallace how he had come to learn about the pregnant secretaries, and revealed that there were at least six of them, and that all together they had given birth to at least eight children. He also said he was aware of the risks he was taking in his effort to defend the shamed women and to alert the rest of the NOI flock to the Messenger's hypocrisy.

"Well," Malcolm said, "I very much doubt that any of his followers, who really are aware of what he has done, would continue to follow him."

Wallace took a breath. "Are you not afraid," he asked, "of what might happen to you as a result of these revelations?"

Malcolm's face broke into a nervous smile that suggested he knew full well that his gamble might backfire. "Oh yes," he said. "I'm probably a dead man already."

In July 1964, Malcolm traveled overseas again and spent most of the next five months making appearances in Africa, the Middle East, and Europe. Everywhere he went, he was treated like a dignitary and received by heads of state. He was invited to the second summit of the Organization of African Unity in Cairo, and lobbied delegates to back him in bringing a resolution before the United Nations declaring America's treatment of its Black citizens a human rights violation. But even while enjoying the protection of his African hosts, Malcolm was on high alert.

In a hotel in Nairobi, he ran into John Lewis, the future congressman, who was then chairman of the Student Nonviolent Coordinating

Committee (SNCC), while Lewis was also touring Africa. Malcolm invited Lewis to his room to talk about his United Nations plan. "To see Malcolm X so swept up with such enthusiasm was inspiring, but there was something else I noticed about him both that afternoon and the next, as we continued our conversation in the hotel restaurant," Lewis recalled. "When he went to his hotel room, he took a seat away from both the window and the door, explaining to us that he never sat with his back exposed. He did the same in the restaurant. I wouldn't say he was quite paranoid, but he had a great sense of alarm, a great sense of anxiety. In a calm, measured way he was convinced that somebody wanted to kill him."

Returning to the United States in December, Malcolm became even more brazen in his bid to keep his home by publicizing Elijah Muhammad's adultery. He flew to Los Angeles to persuade two of the assistants who had moved there to file paternity suits. Police there became suspicious of NOI musclemen who seemed to shadow Malcolm wherever he went. The LAPD alerted police in Chicago, his next stop, where patrolmen were placed in a hotel room next to Malcolm's. On February 4, 1965, Malcolm traveled to Selma, Alabama, where he attracted more national headlines by delivering a fiery speech at the historic Brown Chapel AME Church in the company of civil rights leaders who were planning the new voting rights campaign that would lead to the historic march from Selma to Montgomery that spring.

The next week, Malcolm accepted more invitations to speak abroad, this time in England and France. But when he arrived from England at Orly Airport in Paris, he was detained at customs and informed that the French government had declared his visit "undesirable" because of the security threat it posed. French police ushered him into a small office, denied his request to contact the U.S. embassy, then drove him onto the tarmac and put him on a plane back to London. Malcolm spent the unexpected return trip to Britain visiting a working-class neighborhood outside Birmingham, where a BBC camera crew followed him around. Then on Saturday, February 13, he flew back to New York and headed to Queens for a brief visit with Betty and their four young daughters.

At 2:30 that Sunday morning, Malcolm was awoken by the sound of broken glass and the smell of smoke. He emerged from his bedroom to find the curtains and furniture in the living room on fire, set ablaze by two Molotov cocktails that had been hurled through the windows. Throwing a winter coat over his pajamas, Malcolm rushed with Betty to awaken the three daughters—six-year-old Attallah, four-year-old Qubilah, and two-year-old Ilyasah—who slept together in a tiny second bedroom. Then the couple fetched the baby, five-month-old Gamilah, from her crib in a tiny utility room, and led the four girls out the back door and into the freezing cold night air. After taking the girls to a neighbor's house, Malcolm and Betty finally had a moment alone together, and he tried to talk to her about what might be coming. In the past, she had walked out of the room anytime he brought up the morbid subject, but this time she sat quietly and listened. "I just closed my eyes and hung onto everything he said," Betty recalled.

Still wearing his singed overcoat, Malcolm boarded a flight early that morning for a speech in Detroit. When he arrived at the Ford Auditorium, a doctor gave him a flu shot, and he took a long nap before appearing in a rumpled suit that he had grabbed on the way out of the burning house. After apologizing for his appearance, he gave a long but weary speech, still working to shed the angry separatist image that dogged him from his years with the Nation of Islam. "I'm not a racist," he assured the unusually subdued crowd. "I don't believe in any form of segregation or anything like that. I'm for the brotherhood of everybody, but I don't believe in forcing brotherhood on people who don't want it."

By the time Malcolm returned to New York City the spirit of brotherhood was nowhere to be found. A judge had upheld the eviction order from the burned-out house in Queens. His former lieutenants from the Harlem mosque had told the press that Malcolm started the fire himself "for the publicity." At a late-night speech to his followers at the Audubon Ballroom, Malcolm charged that the attack was ordered by Elijah Muhammad himself and vented his outrage at the suggestion that he would put his own family at risk. "My house was bombed by the Muslims," he fumed, "[and] I can't bring my heart to the point where I can be merciful to anyone that low. If anybody can find where I bombed my own house, they can put a rifle bullet through my head."

=====

Torn between fury and fear, Malcolm spent the rest of the week making and unmaking plans at the last minute. He gave a speech at Barnard College but backed out of another one in Mississippi. He made an appointment with his Harlem lawyer, Percy Sutton, the future Manhattan borough president, to draw up a will that would protect any royalties he might get from the autobiography he was writing. At the same time, he called off a trip to upstate New York to spend several days working on the book with his ghostwriter, Alex Haley. Retreating to his new headquarters in the Black-owned Hotel Theresa in Harlem—a small room on the mezzanine floor with an ancient mahogany desk and rusting file cabinets—he summoned one of the few Black reporters working at the time for *The New York Times*, Theodore Jones, for an impromptu interview.

"I know brothers in the movement who were given orders to kill me," Malcolm said, fidgeting with the goatee he had grown in Africa. "I've had highly placed people tell me, 'be careful, Malcolm.' The press gives the impression that I'm jiving about this thing. They ignore the evidence and the actual attempts."

So who was after him? Jones asked.

Malcolm pointed out the window toward the site of Mosque No. 7 a half mile away. "Those folks at 116th Street and that man in Chicago," he said.

Once Elijah Muhammad's name was brought up, Jones asked about those who questioned how much Malcolm had changed since his break from the Messenger.

"I won't deny that I don't know where I'm at," Malcolm admitted, his face suddenly relaxing into a self-deprecating grin. "But by the same token, how many of us put the finger down on one point and say I'm here."

Sometime later, Malcolm added: "I feel like a man who has been asleep somewhat and under someone else's control. I feel what I'm saying now is for myself. Before, it was for and by the guidance of Elijah Muhammad. Now I think with my own mind, sir."

The next day, Malcolm was still in a brooding but philosophical frame of mind when he met with the Black photojournalist Gordon Parks. The two had become friends three years earlier, when Parks followed Malcolm around for several weeks reporting a profile for *Life* magazine.

"Is it really true the Black Muslims are out to get you?" Parks asked.

"It's as true as we are standing here," Malcolm replied. "They've tried it twice in the last two weeks."

"What about police protection?" Parks asked.

"Brother, nobody can protect you from a Muslim but a Muslim—or someone trained in Muslim tactics," Malcolm answered with a rueful smile. "I know. I invented many of those tactics."

Parks reminded Malcolm of what he had been like at the time of the *Life* profile, before the split from the NOI, before his travels abroad, where he had met orthodox Muslims of all colors and whites supporting the anticolonial struggle. In 1963, Malcolm was still spreading the angry gospel of the Messenger, inveighing against the "white devil" and insisting that the only hope for Blacks was total separation of the races.

Parks's reminiscence put Malcolm in a pensive mood, and brought back an encounter with a white admirer that the photographer had witnessed.

"Remember the time that white college girl came into the restaurant— the one who wanted to help the Muslims and the whites get together— and I told her there wasn't a ghost of a chance and she went away crying?" Malcolm said.

"Yes," Parks replied.

"Well, I've lived to regret that incident," Malcolm admitted. "In many parts of the African continent, I saw white students helping black people. Something like this kills a lot of argument. I did many things as a Muslim that I'm very sorry for now. I was a zombie then—like all [NOI] Muslims—I was hypnotized, pointed in a certain direction and told to march. Well, I guess a man's entitled to make a fool of himself if he's ready to pay the cost. It cost me twelve years."

Malcolm tried to turn the conversation to the new, more inclusive movement that he was trying to build, the one he would talk about at a rally at the Audubon Ballroom in two days. "That was a bad scene, brother," Malcolm admitted about his years with the NOI. "The sickness and madness of those days—I'm glad to be free of them. It's a time for martyrs now. And if I'm to be one, it will be in the cause of brotherhood. That's the only thing that can save this country. I've learned it the hard way—but I've learned it. And that's the significant thing."

Still, Malcolm had to acknowledge that he was caught in a perilous bind. The only way to promote his new movement was to keep making well-publicized public speeches, to keep traveling the country and the world, to stay in the newspaper headlines and television broadcasts of the white media. But the more he did that, the more he continued to inflame the jealousies that had played such a large part in his ouster from the Nation of Islam in the first place.

"Now it looks like this brotherhood I wanted so badly has got me in a jam," Malcolm told Parks.

=====

On Friday, February 19, Malcolm spent the evening at the Brooklyn home of novelist John Oliver Killens, who had convened a small group of their mutual friends that included the historian John Henrik Clarke and Clarence Jones, the attorney for Martin Luther King Jr. After splitting with the Nation of Islam, Malcolm had been introduced to Jones by Percy Sutton, Malcolm's lawyer, and the two men had hit it off. Malcolm liked Jones's "irreverence," Jones recalled, and was impressed that the son of a chauffeur and a maid, with a degree from Columbia University, had given up a budding career as an entertainment lawyer to join the civil rights movement. "You're more dangerous than I am," Malcolm would kid Jones—because he was the kind of polished Black professional whom white power brokers liked to think was one of them. For all his loyalty to Dr. King, meanwhile, Jones saw in Malcolm a leader who could break through to less educated and affluent Blacks in a way that the well-born King never could. "I called him the most authentic street Negro in America," Jones recalled.

The discussion at Killen's home was friendly but "heated," Jones recalled, and lasted until one in the morning. When it finally broke up, Jones walked with Malcolm to Malcolm's car and noticed a shotgun in the backseat. Malcolm apologized that, for Jones's safety, he couldn't offer him a ride back to the lawyer's residence in Riverdale, north of Manhattan. Instead, Malcolm summoned another car with three armed guards to take Jones home. He also reminded Jones about the speech he was scheduled to give the following day, which Jones had teasingly told Malcolm he couldn't attend because he planned to be watching Sunday football games on television. At the last minute, however, Jones would have second thoughts and decide to drive to the Audubon Ballroom, and he would be exiting the West Side Highway at 158th Street when the news of what just happened there came across the car radio.

On Saturday, February 20, Malcolm checked himself into an $18-a-night single room at the New York Hilton in midtown Manhattan, leaving Betty and the girls with the neighbor in Queens. He ate dinner alone at the hotel's ornate Old Bourbon Steak House, then went back to his room, unaware that sometime that night hotel security would turn away two Black men who appeared in the lobby and asked for Malcolm's room number. In the morning, he was awoken at eight o'clock by the ringing of the phone in his room. "Better wake up, before it is too late," said an ominous voice followed by an abrupt click on the other end of the line.

Earlier, Malcolm had told Betty that he didn't want her at the speech that day, but now he was feeling anxious and in need of her support. So he called the neighbor in Queens and asked Betty to come to the Audubon Ballroom and bring their girls. Malcolm dressed in a brown suit and tie and waited until the official checkout time of one o'clock to leave the hotel. He had parked his car—a blue Oldsmobile convertible—in the hotel garage, but decided the Olds was too familiar uptown for him to risk driving it all the way to 166th Street and Broadway. So he left the car twenty blocks south and headed for a bus stop.

As Malcolm was waiting for the bus, a car carrying one of his followers, Charles X Blackwell, happened to drive by. "There is the minister, stop and pick him up," Blackwell told the driver, a friend named Fred Williams, who was also chauffeuring his wife to the speech. Malcolm accepted the ride, and together they arrived at Audubon Ballroom at ten minutes to two.

Outside the entrance to the ballroom on 166th Street stood a single policeman, a young white patrolman named Thomas Hoy. Later, both supporters and reporters would demand to know why more cops weren't assigned to the event, but it was Malcolm who had requested the small footprint. He didn't want to scare away new recruits to OAAU, particularly young Blacks who might have had run-ins with the police. He also was counting on a heavy crowd turnout that afternoon for financial reasons, since the last few meetings had been so small that a hat had to be passed twice to pay the ballroom's $125 rental fee. In an effort to remain inconspicuous, two more uniformed patrolmen equipped with walkie-talkies, one of them Black and the other white, had stationed themselves in a small second ballroom adjacent to the main hall on the second floor. A long block and a half away, more than a dozen additional policemen hovered in the vicinity of Columbia Presbyterian Medical Center, the largest hospital in upper Manhattan.

Climbing the stairs to the second floor, Malcolm entered the main ballroom. Hundreds of wooden folding chairs had been set up, facing a raised stage at the front of the room. A flimsy plywood lectern stood at the center of the stage, with a worn baby grand piano to the side. The walls behind the lectern and to the sides of the stage were painted with a faded depiction of rolling hills and trees.

Malcolm made his way to a small dressing room to the right of the stage and waited for the other speakers he had invited to kick off the event. But one after another, the speakers canceled. A Harlem minister had his secretary call to say that he was exhausted after performing a wedding and several baptisms that morning. Malcolm's friend Lewis Michaux, the bookstore owner, got stuck in traffic downtown. Another local official who was supposed to help with fundraising never showed up. As the advertised starting time of two o'clock came and went, Malcolm grew increasingly testy. "I just don't feel right," he said, according to one aide's recollection, and a pulsing vein in his forehead betrayed his inner stress.

When it became clear that there would be no warm-up acts, Malcolm sent his top aide, Benjamin 2X Goodman, out to address the crowd. Goodman walked to the plywood lectern and launched into a windy introduction. He spun out a metaphor about a sea captain steering a ship toward harbor, and another one about a wall so high no one thought it could be climbed.

Finally, just past three o'clock, Malcolm walked out of the dressing room and gave Goodman the signal to step aside.

"Make it plain," Malcolm said.

"I now introduce you to a man who would give his life for his people," Benjamin X told the crowd.

Out in the audience, Betty Shabazz was seated on a bench with her four daughters, who had arrived bundled in snow suits. Betty herself had dressed elegantly for the occasion, as though she was advertising her own liberation from the NOI's severe restrictions on female attire. Her hair was straightened and blown out, and she wore a short-sleeved white blouse over a dark skirt and stylish arm-length leather gloves.

As Betty waited for Malcolm to take the stage, her eldest daughter, six-year-old Attallah, saw her mother's expression grow more and more worried. But now Betty's face melted. "There's my husband!" she uttered in a voice that Attallah immediately recognized. It wasn't a tone of relief or excitement, Attallah recalled, so much as a "coo-ey" noise, a sound of "mushy, all the way love" that emerged from her mother whenever she was around Malcolm, even after seven years of marriage, four pregnancies, and now a fifth one with twins that was already two months along.

At the plywood lectern, Malcolm shuffled through the small stack of note cards in his hands.

"*As-salaam-alaikum*," he began, greeting the crowd with the Islamic salutation that meant "Peace Be Unto You."

"*Wa-alaikam-salaam*," the crowd answered with the traditional response, "And Unto You Be Peace."

All of a sudden, a man stood up in the middle of the crowd and appeared to confront the man seated next to him. "Get your hands out of my pocket!" the standing man shouted. In the back of the hall, acrid smoke started to pour out of a wet sock on the floor. A woman let out a scream, and the two bodyguards who were stationed on the stage with Malcolm climbed down into the audience to investigate the commotion.

Stepping from behind the lectern, Malcolm lifted his arms and appealed for calm. "Hold it . . . hold it . . . hold it," he said.

Several rows back in the crowd, a Black man pulled a 12-gauge shotgun from underneath his overcoat. The man stood up in the aisle, advanced toward the stage, and fired a rapid succession of loud blasts at Malcolm's chest. The force of the shotgun blasts sent Malcolm reeling backward over two folding chairs and onto the floor. As he lay on the floor, two more Black men who had been sitting in the front row rushed toward the stage and fired shots at Malcolm's fallen body, striking him in the arms, legs, and feet. Pandemonium broke out among the four hundred people in the audience, and Betty Shabazz pulled her children to the floor and surrounded them with wooden chairs for cover. "They're killing my husband!" she cried out. "They're killing my husband!"

Charles X Blackwell, the follower who had given Malcolm a lift to the ballroom, was one of the guards who had been assigned to stand on the stage during the speech. When the shouting about the pockets started, he climbed down into the crowd to see what was going on, then heard the sound of gunfire. He turned around to see two Black men racing from the stage toward the back of the ballroom. One of them was a wiry man with a baby face who was firing a .45 automatic pistol into the air to clear people out of the way. Blackwell would also recall seeing a third man duck into the ladies' bathroom on the side of the ballroom, where there was a back door that opened onto a stairway leading down to the street.

The wiry man with the .45 pistol fired in the direction of Gene Roberts, a bodyguard who had been standing at the back of the hall during the speech. Roberts threw a chair at the gunman and knocked him down. Another guard, named Reuben Francis, fired at the gunman as he got up, wounding him in the leg. The gunman limped down the stairs toward the front entrance as more of Malcolm's followers chased after him. On the street outside, the followers knocked the gunman to the ground and started kicking and punching him from all sides.

Meanwhile, on the stage, a small group of intimates surrounded Malcolm's bloody body. Gene Roberts ripped open his dress shirt and the white T-shirt underneath to expose a cluster of bullet wounds across his chest. Roberts kneeled over the body and pulled his face to Malcolm's, trying to administer mouth-to-mouth resuscitation. A young Japanese American activist named Yuri Kochiyama, who had become friendly with Malcolm, cradled his head in her hands. His eyes were closed behind his horn-rimmed glasses, and his mouth, surrounded by the scratchy goatee, was agape. His right arm lay limp along his side, its hand touching his belt buckle, and the left arm stretched out across the floor. Benjamin 2X Goodman drew close and thought he heard a slight gasping sound. But by the time Betty reached her husband and knelt beside him, her gloved hand touching the arm across his chest, no signs of life came from his motionless head. "They've killed him," she sobbed.

A group of Malcolm's followers arrived with a gurney they had commandeered from Columbia Presbyterian, the nearby hospital. They lifted Malcolm's body onto it and transported it down the stairs and onto the street. A cluster of police officers closed in to help push the gurney and keep the frantic crowd at bay. Doctors who were waiting at the hospital entrance cut a hole in Malcolm's trachea in hopes that he might still be able to breathe, then orderlies rushed him to the third-floor emergency room. There, surgeons cut open his chest and tried to massage his heart back to life, but it was too late. After fifteen minutes, a sheet was pulled over Malcolm's head, and a hospital spokesman went to inform the group of followers and reporters who were gathered in a small windowless office down the hall.

"The person you know as Malcolm X is dead," the spokesman said.

Later that day, Malcolm's corpse was transferred from Columbia Presbyterian to Bellevue Hospital on the East Side of Manhattan, where an autopsy report confirmed that he had died of "multiple gunshot slugs and bullet wounds of the chest, heart and aorta." Ballistics tests showed that two different handguns had been involved in the attack, in addition to the shotgun. Questioned about why Malcolm seemed to have so little police protection, top commanders for the NYPD reported that two sergeants and eighteen patrolmen had been present in the general vicinity of the Audubon Ballroom. But they reported that on at least seven occasions, Malcolm had refused offers to station uniformed officers inside his meetings. The commanders wouldn't comment on whether any plainclothes cops were present in the room.

Islamic custom called for burial within twenty-four hours of death, but Betty Shabazz announced that she wanted to wait a week so that dignitaries from around the country and the world could attend the funeral. So from Bellevue Hospital, Malcolm's body was taken in a zippered bag to Unity Funeral Home in Harlem, where it was placed for viewing in a casket with an eggshell velvet lining and a glass covering. After identifying the body in the hospital, Betty vented to the press about why more attention had not been paid to the visible threats to her husband's life. "The police and the press were unfair," she lamented. "They never took him seriously. Even after the bombing of our house, they said he did it himself. Now what are they going to do—say he shot himself?"

By midnight on the night of the murder, the one gunman who had been apprehended at the murder scene was also lying in Bellevue Hospital. In the minutes after the attack, dozens of Malcolm's followers had continued to attack the wiry man with the .45 pistol who was shot in the thigh as he ran out of the Audubon Ballroom. Pushing away Thomas Hoy, the young patrolman stationed in front of the building, the followers pummeled the gunman so badly that they fractured the leg that hadn't been shot. Finally, two more policemen arrived in a squad car and pulled their weapons to make the crowd back off. The cops hustled the gunman into the squad car, as the crowd surrounded the vehicle and rocked it back it forth before it finally managed to pull away. Inside, the young suspect moaned in pain. "My leg, my leg, I'm shot—my leg, my leg," he whimpered.

The policemen took down the man's name as "Thomas Hagan," but they later found out that his real name was Talmadge Hayer. In the squad car, he identified himself as "Tommy"— his family nickname— then slurred his last name in a way that made the cops think he was saying "Hagan." Struck by how young Hayer looked, the cops got out of him that he was twenty-three years old and lived in Paterson, New Jersey. By the time Hayer was in the squad car, he was no longer carrying the .45 automatic pistol, which would later be found inside the Audubon Ballroom where he dropped it. But when the policeman frisked Hayer, they found a .45 handgun cartridge case in his pants pocket that was still holding four unused bullets.

Searching the crime scene late that Sunday, police also discovered a sawed-off shotgun—a double-barreled 12-gauge model sold by the Sears Roebuck catalog company under the label "J.C. Higgins"—wrapped in a coat at the back of the stage inside the main ballroom. Later, Charles X Blackwell would testify that he found the shotgun and another gun—a 9mm German Luger automatic pistol—lying in the tangle of folding chairs about four rows back from the stage. Blackwell said he wrapped the shotgun in his coat and handed it to Reuben Francis, the guard who had wounded Hayer in the thigh. Blackwell claimed that he expected Francis to turn over the evidence to the police, but instead Francis had stashed it behind the stage. Blackwell also testified that he wrapped the Luger in another coat and handed it to a third bodyguard; that gun would never be found.

Beyond Hayer's arrest and the evidence of the three guns used in the assassination, the police didn't have much to go on at first. "Things are so confused right now," the NYPD's chief inspector, Sanford Garelik, admitted to reporters on the night of the murder, "that we don't know who will end up being charged." As the week progressed, pressure mounted on law enforcement to move quickly in assembling a murder case. In what was seen as a retaliatory attack, a firebomb was thrown through the fourth-floor window of Mosque No. 7, sending the building up in flames. Outside the funeral home where Malcolm's body lay in state, a young Black man was arrested carrying a rifle concealed in a canvas case. Meanwhile, rumors spread across Harlem that powerful white forces had played a role in the murder. "This is absolutely the fault of the Police Department," a local Black clergyman told Paul Montgomery, a reporter for *The New York Times*. Outside Lewis Michaux's bookstore, another Black man ominously blamed "the man downtown. Who else would benefit from it?"

The timing hardly seemed coincidental, therefore, when a second murder suspect was arrested just in time to make the front pages of all the
major New York City newspapers on the day before Malcolm's funeral
the following Saturday. The man was a twenty-six-year-old member
of the Harlem mosque named Norman Butler, who had adopted the
name Norman 3X upon joining the Nation of Islam three years earlier.
After arriving at his apartment in the Bronx and taking him in for questioning, police arrested Butler for Malcolm's murder and wasted no
time in feeding details to the press that made him look like a plausible
suspect. Tall and muscular and trained in karate as well as handling
weapons, he was a lieutenant in a Fruit of Islam squad known to rough
up followers who ran afoul of local NOI leaders. Just a month earlier, a
grand jury had indicted Butler for first-degree assault on a former city
corrections officer named Benjamin Brown, who had defected from
the Harlem mosque. Also awaiting arraignment in the Brown case was
another man, who in the following days would be arrested and charged
as the third suspect in the assassination: a fellow member of the Fruit
of Islam enforcement squad known as Thomas 15X Johnson.

Although the press had yet to hear Butler's response to the allegations or specific evidence of his involvement in the murder plot, the
news of his arrest served its purpose. A tense calm prevailed on the day
of Malcolm's funeral. By the end of the week, some thirty thousand admirers had filed past the casket at the Harlem funeral home. On Friday,
a bearded Sudanese cleric who had accompanied Malcolm back from
his trip to Mecca removed the body from the casket, washed it according to Islamic tradition, and wrapped it in a shroud made up of seven
layers of linen. Then the body was returned to the casket and moved
to the Faith Temple Church of God in Christ for the Saturday funeral
service that drew a crowd of three thousand onlookers and included
such dignitaries as Andrew Young, Dr. King's young lieutenant; James
Farmer, the head of the Congress of Racial Equality; Bayard Rustin,
the organizer of the 1963 March on Washington; and Dick Gregory,
the renowned Black comedian.

Apart from Ossie Davis's moving eulogy, the most dramatic moment of the service came when Ahmed Osman, a friend and spiritual adviser of Malcolm's, rose to the pulpit. In the wake of the assassination, the journalist Carl Rowan, then the director of the U.S. Information Agency, had lamented the portrayal of Malcolm as a hero and martyr in newspapers across Africa and the rest of the developing world. Rowan had given a speech to the American Foreign Service Association in Washington in which he described Malcolm as "a Negro, who preached segregation and race hatred, killed by another Negro presumably from another organization that preaches segregation and race hatred." Responding directly to that attack, Osman reminded the mourners that Malcolm had renounced those views after his trip to Mecca, and when he uttered Rowan's name, loud hissing filled the church.

After the eulogies, another Islamic cleric conducted a long prayer service, and Malcolm's intimates filed by the coffin to say their final goodbyes. Dressed in black mourning attire, Betty lifted the veil from her face and sobbed as she pressed her lips to the glass that covered her husband's enshrouded face. Once the pallbearers had carried the coffin outside to a waiting silver-blue hearse, many of the mourners who had gathered outside streamed into the church, hoping to take home a memento such as a program, prayer book, or a flower.

As the crowd thinned, a large Black woman in a head kerchief turned to a white reporter she saw scribbling overheard conversation into a notepad.

"That man didn't teach violence like all the papers say," said the woman, giving her first name as Doris. "He taught me about myself. He taught me that I was more than a Little Black Sambo or Kinky Hair or a nigger."

Fighting tears, Doris asked the reporter: "If I slapped your face, what would your normal reaction be?"

"To hit back," the reporter responded.

"Well, that's what Malcolm told us to do," Doris said. "To defend ourselves. Yet all the papers keep talking about his violence. It makes me sick."

Leading a procession of fifty cars, the hearse carried the casket to

Ferncliff cemetery in the suburban town of Hartsdale, some twenty miles north of Manhattan. Along the route, scores of Black men braved a cold, windy rain to line the streets, some holding their hats over their hearts in tribute. At the gravesite, another visiting cleric said a last prayer, referring to Malcolm X by the orthodox Islamic name that he had taken on his pilgrimage to Mecca and that was now engraved on his plain gray burial stone: Hajj Malik El-Shabazz.

The body was lowered into the ground, and the cemetery's white gravediggers prepared to go to work. But suddenly a group of Malcolm's Black followers stood in their way.

"No white man is going to bury Malcolm," one of the followers said.

"This is a dead man," one of the gravediggers protested. "We're supposed to bury him."

The undertaker from Unity Funeral Home who had overseen the burial tried to intervene. The cars going back to New York City were leaving, the undertaker pointed out, and the followers might be left behind.

"We'll bury him first," one of the followers said. "We'll walk."

When the men started throwing dirt into the grave with their bare hands, the cemetery workers saw they meant business. The white gravediggers dropped their shovels and stood aside, allowing Malcolm's followers to finish the job of burying their hero.

TWO

The Reporters

A cross New York City on the afternoon of the assassination, word of Malcolm X's brutal murder began to reach journalists who would be assigned the task of making sense of it to the world. One of them was Peter Goldman, a thirty-two-year-old newspaperman from St. Louis who had moved to New York to work for *Newsweek* magazine and had become the publication's go-to writer on the civil rights beat. Since the magazine went to the printers on Sunday, Goldman usually worked late into the night on Fridays and all day Saturday. On his day off, he slept late, then went for a long brunch with his wife, Helen Dudar, a feature writer for the *New York Post*. So the two were just getting back to their apartment in Gramercy Park when they heard the news from the Audubon Ballroom on the radio.

Goldman was hardly shocked, given all he knew about Malcolm's bitter falling-out with the Nation of Islam, the death threats against him, and the firebomb attack on his house. But he couldn't help feeling a sense of sadness and loss, despite his natural Midwestern reserve and well-trained journalistic detachment. Unlike most of the white reporters who would write stories about the murder that week, Goldman had gotten to know Malcolm X personally. He had conducted at least five lengthy interviews with Malcolm, and talked to him numerous times over the phone, and each time he had been impressed with Malcolm's probing intellect, playful humor, and bracing bluntness about the condition of race relations in America. Dudar had accompanied

Goldman on several of the long interviews, and Helen's respect for Malcolm—and his for her—had only strengthened Peter's esteem for the man.

With his diminutive build, frizzy blond hair, and narrow bow ties, Goldman looked more like a young college professor than a hardened journalist. His father, Walter Goldman, was a Jewish native of St. Louis who had studied engineering and dreamed of writing novels, but had turned to selling shoes for a living during the Depression. Walter met Peter's mother, a Presbyterian named Dorothy Semple, on a trip to Philadelphia. After marrying, they moved to Greenwich Village, where Goldman and his older sister Patricia started school until Walter took a managerial job with a shoe chain back in St. Louis. Peter finished high school there, then enrolled at Williams College, the then all-male institution in remote western Massachusetts. He had never visited Williams before he enrolled, and he quickly discovered that with his Jewish surname he would never be accepted into the Waspy fraternity scene that dominated campus life. So he spent a largely solitary four years majoring in English and contributing articles to the small weekly student newspaper.

By the time Goldman graduated from Williams, he knew he wanted to be a writer, and he figured the best way to make a living at it was to become a reporter. So he applied to the Columbia School of Journalism in New York City to learn the basics of the trade, then went back to his hometown to look for a job. Nationally, St. Louis was known mostly as the home of the *Post-Dispatch*, the paper that had been founded by the legendary Hungarian immigrant publisher Joseph Pulitzer and that boasted a huge bureau in Washington, D.C., and one of the country's best-known political cartoonists, Bill Mauldin. But Goldman calculated that a rookie like him would find opportunity more quickly at the *Post-Dispatch*'s scruffier, more conservative morning rival, the *Globe-Democrat*. So he applied for a position there and quickly became a jack-of-all-trades for the city desk, covering local crime and political stories and regularly performing "rewrite" duty, pulling strands of other people's reporting together on deadline.

Of all the wordsmiths in the newspaper trade in that day, Goldman particularly admired Murray Kempton, the pipe-smoking liberal columnist for the *New York Post*. So Peter chipped in with several other Kempton fans in the *Globe-Democrat* newsroom to purchase a subscription to the *Post*. Studying that paper's coverage, its tabloid ink invariably coming off on his hands, Goldman began to notice a rare woman's byline attached to features stories with a distinctively descriptive voice. He committed the name to memory: Helen Dudar.

In the winter of 1960, the *Globe-Democrat* sent Goldman to Boston to cover a scandalous murder trial with a St. Louis angle. Lynn Kauffman was a lively, attractive twenty-three-year-old who had taken a job as an assistant to a Far Eastern Studies professor at Washington University in St. Louis. After living with the professor and his family in Singapore, Kauffman was on her way back to the United States aboard a Dutch freighter when she fell into an affair with the ship's radio operator. He was a handsome Dutchman named Willem Van Rie, whose father was a Catholic school headmaster and whose unsuspecting wife was the daughter of a wealthy leather manufacturer. By the time the ship reached port in Boston, however, the romance had fizzled, and shortly after it set sail again for New York City, Kauffman's half-naked body was found washed up off Boston Bay. Under police questioning, Van Rie admitted that the couple had quarreled one night after he found Kauffman sobbing in her cabin. He had asked if she was pregnant and "beat her unmercifully" when she lunged at him, he said. Although Van Rie insisted that his former lover was still alive when he last saw her, a grand jury saw enough circumstantial evidence to issue a murder indictment.

When Goldman arrived in Boston in February, he joined a scrum of out-of-town journalists that included reporters from *The New York Times*, *Time* magazine—and Helen Dudar of the *New York Post*. On the first day of testimony at the Suffolk County Courthouse, someone introduced them, and Goldman immediately recognized the name he had seen in the pages of the *Post*. But several days later, Dudar had already forgotten Goldman's name when she was looking to fill the gaps of some courtroom testimony she had missed. "Hey, St. Louis," she called out, flashing a wide smile before she asked if she could see Peter's notes. Dudar stood barely taller than five feet, and spoke with an accent that betrayed her upbringing on suburban Long Island, but at that moment Goldman thought she was as captivating as any Hollywood leading lady. "Her words hit me like a '30s movie line," he recalled, "the kind of thing Rosalind Russell might have said in the pressroom classic *His Girl Friday*, which permitted me the fleeting illusion I was Cary Grant. I was smitten."

A month later, Willem Van Rie was acquitted by an all-male jury after sixteen hours of deliberation. By then, Goldman and Dudar were dating, and Peter sensed that he had found his soul mate. Nine years older than him, Dudar was the more seasoned reporter and a versatile writer. Unlike Goldman, she hadn't had the advantage of an undergraduate English degree or a stint in journalism school. Growing up in Island Park, a middle-class community on the South Shore of Long Island, Dudar had been bitten by the journalism bug in high school, becoming the editor of her high school paper and learning to type well enough to win a speed and accuracy prize. She enrolled at the University of Wisconsin but didn't have enough money to finish her degree, so at nineteen years old she went to work at the Long Island newspaper *Newsday*.

Dudar's first job, paying $25 a week, was to answer reader questions about cooking recipes and household repairs in the voice of a man in a column called "Let Prof. Do It." Then she graduated to reporting on local government, courts, and police, helping *Newsday* win a Pulitzer Prize for exposés that sent a local racketeer to prison. But she had always dreamed of living in New York City, so in her early thirties she applied for and landed a job at the *New York Post*, then owned by the most powerful woman in the newspaper business, publisher Dorothy Schiff.

Quiet and self-effacing by nature, Goldman was delighted to find someone who shared so many of his journalistic and cultural interests but was so open, effusive, and perceptive in talking about them. Later, *Webster's* dictionary would illustrate how to use the word "sinewy" by quoting a line from one of Dudar's stories—"a demanding, sinewy intelligence"—and Peter would think that description fit Helen herself to a T. Unlike so many men in that misogynistic era, he had no problem accepting Dudar as his equal, and in many areas his better. Never a good driver, for example, Peter was happy to have Helen take the wheel when they started taking car trips together—a skill that she had honed when, for a 1946 *Newsday* feature story, she had submitted to a rigorous Army Air Force driving test. Goldman was also not at all surprised when among all the journalists who covered the sensational Boston murder trial, it was Dudar who won a major prize for her work, becoming one of the first recipients of a human-interest reporting award named after legendary *New York Times* feature writer Meyer Berger.

After seven years in St. Louis, Goldman had already been hankering to get back to New York City, the site of his happy childhood memories of Greenwich Village and invigorating graduate school year at Columbia. Professionally, that move represented graduating from "Double-A ball to the big leagues," as he thought of it. But Goldman also wanted to shift from local reporting to writing about national politics and race relations, and he felt he needed a better academic grounding in those areas. So he decided to apply for a Nieman Fellowship—the prestigious journalistic award that paid for mid-career journalists to take a year off to live and attend classes at Harvard University.

Now, that plan took on a more personal urgency. Spending a year at Harvard would also put Peter only a four-hour train and subway ride away from Manhattan, where Helen lived. Goldman applied for the Nieman, and was accepted.

When Goldman arrived on the Harvard campus the next fall, he was assigned a room in the oldest and most historic student residence on campus. Adams House consists of a complex of former mansions that dated back to the eighteenth century. Luminaries from President Franklin Delano Roosevelt to the novelist William Burroughs had spent their undergraduate years there, and its extravagances included a public room whose walls were clad in gold leaf and a swimming pool in the basement. But Goldman didn't care much about his lodgings. He was too focused on his quest to round out his education in American history and politics. With Dudar still working full-time at the *New York Post*, the two agreed to limit their romantic visits to weekends, either in New York or Boston, leaving Peter free to lose himself in his studies during the week.

In the entire 343-page Harvard course catalog, however, Goldman couldn't find a single course devoted to the subject he most wanted to explore during his sabbatical year: the history and sociology of Black America. As a boy in grade school, he had first become fascinated by the subject when he read *Native Son*, novelist Richard Wright's complex portrait of a young Black Chicago youth named Bigger Thomas who is doomed by the forces of discrimination and racist expectations to act out white society's worst stereotypes and become a rapist and murderer. As an adult, Goldman had marveled at the more inspiring spectacle of the Montgomery Bus Boycott, as the entire Black population of the Alabama capital united to stage a year-long boycott demanding desegregation of the city's bus system. In the process, Goldman became what he described as a "conventional white civil rights liberal," admiring of the boycott's leader, the Reverend Martin Luther King Jr., and his gospel of racial integration and nonviolent protest.

Yet as it happened, Goldman was at the right place at the right time to be among the early readers of a major new academic study of the small Black religious sect that was openly challenging King's integrationist vision. In January 1961, just as Goldman was about to begin his spring semester at Harvard, a thirty-six-year-old Black sociologist at nearby Boston University named C. Eric Lincoln published a book version of his doctoral thesis on the Nation of Islam, also known as the NOI.

With the title of his book, *The Black Muslims in America*, Lincoln gave the group a label that the NOI disliked but that would stick to it in press coverage and in the public imagination from then on. While expressing his own disapproval of separatism, Lincoln explained why the NOI's focus on Black self-determination, self-love, and self-discipline had a deep appeal for inner city Blacks struggling to escape extreme poverty, addiction, and the toll of incarceration. He highlighted the influence of one NOI leader in particular: Malcolm X, the minister of Mosque No. 7 in Harlem, whose following had grown so strong that local politicians such as U.S. congressman Adam Clayton Powell Jr. relied on his support to get elected.

Just as Lincoln was completing his research in early 1960, Malcolm X had come to speak at Boston University. Throughout the book, Lincoln quoted from that address to capture Malcolm's uncanny ability to make the NOI's message of separatism and self-defense sound entirely reasonable from the Black point of view. Crediting the success that the NOI and its leader, Elijah Muhammad, had achieved in turning around the lives of Black criminals, Malcolm pointed out: "He has taken men who were thieves, who broke the law—men who were in prison—and reformed them so that no more do they steal, no more do they commit crimes against the government. I should like to think that this government would thank Mr. Muhammad for doing what it has failed to do toward rehabilitating men who have been classified as hardened criminals."

Conjuring up what Dr. King's counsel of nonviolence might look like to a proud Black military veteran, Malcolm told the Boston crowd: "The Negro is a fighting man all right. He fought in Korea; he fought in Germany; he fought in the jungles of Iwo Jima. But that same Negro will come back here, and the white man will hang his mother on a tree, and he will take the Bible and say, 'Forgive them Lord, for they knew not what they do.' This Negro preacher makes them that way. . . . Where there is a slave like that, why you have a slave-making religion."

In the spring semester, Goldman picked up a copy of Lincoln's just-published book and was midway through reading it when he learned that Malcolm X would soon be making an appearance at Harvard. Malcolm had accepted an invitation from students at Harvard Law School to engage in a debate on integration with Walter Carrington, a Black graduate of Harvard's college and law school who was then in private practice in Boston and would later serve as America's ambassador to Senegal and Nigeria. So it was that on the evening of Friday, March 24, 1961, Goldman left his Adams House dorm room just south of Harvard Yard and made his way in a chilly drizzle to Sanders Theatre, the amphitheater housed in Memorial Hall, the massive Gothic structure on the north side of campus.

As Goldman neared Memorial Hall, he caught his first glimpse of the Fruit of Islam paramilitary guards who accompanied Malcolm wherever he went. Some were posted outside the hall, while others watched from under trees in the distance. Goldman recalled how striking they looked, with their conservative suits, bow ties, and buzz haircuts, standing at ramrod attention and with impassive looks on their faces. Once inside Sanders Theatre, Goldman saw that a section of the auditorium was filled with other NOI members, who had been bused in from Harlem. He took a seat among the white students in another section and looked down at the stage to see Malcolm for the first time, as tall and fit as his bodyguards but with a look on his light-colored, bespectacled face that radiated warmth and a kind of serene spirituality.

The debate with Walter Carrington began with opening statements, and Malcolm went first. He started with a long defense of the NOI as an authentic branch of Islam, full of obsequious praise for the Honorable Elijah Muhammad. Goldman found this part forgettable except for the forceful sound of Malcolm's voice echoing through the wood-paneled hall. But when Malcolm turned from theology to politics—launching a barbed attack on the mainstream civil rights movement and its focus on integration and nonviolence—Goldman was suddenly transfixed. Malcolm seemed to be talking directly to him as he dismissed civil rights battles that Goldman had cheered on over the previous decade as hollow exercises designed to make white liberals feel better while lulling Black people into a false sense of racial progress.

Taking a jab at the lunch counter sit-in student movement that was just then sweeping the South, Malcolm scoffed: "A cup of tea in a white restaurant is not sufficient compensation for three hundred ten years of free labor." On the vaunted *Brown v. Board of Education* decision, he pointed out: "NAACP Attorney Thurgood Marshall has admitted publicly that six years since the Supreme Court decision on desegregation of the schools, only six percent desegregation has taken place. This is an example of integration! . . . Four black children in a New Orleans white school is token integration. A handful of black students in the white schools in Little Rock is token integration. None of this is real integration. It is only a pacifier to keep those awakening black babies from crying too hard."

When Malcolm concluded by demanding that Blacks be given land to create their own separate homeland, though, Goldman couldn't agree. Surely that was as unnecessary as it was impractical, he thought. Still, Malcolm's description of what the civil rights landscape looked like to millions of proud and weary Blacks had made a powerful impression. For the first time, Malcolm had shaken two tenets of what Goldman described as his "white liberal views on the world of race"— that the South was the "locus of the tragedy" and that "Jim Crow was the central struggle." In an indictment of conditions for Blacks in the North as much for those in the South, Malcolm told the Harvard crowd: "This is the core of America's troubles today: and there will be no peace for America as long as twenty million so-called Negroes are here begging for the rights which America knows she will never grant us. . . . If we receive equal education, how long do you expect us to remain your passive servants, or second-class citizens? There is no such thing as a second-class citizen. We are full citizens or we are not citizens at all."

When Malcolm finished, Carrington took the stage to argue in favor of integration. Then the back-and-forth began, and Goldman got a taste of the intellectual jousting skills that Malcolm had honed as a member of a prison debate team while he was serving time in his early twenties. Carrington made light of the NOI's calls for a separate Black homeland by mocking its predictions of a race war in the year 1984 if it didn't happen. "I don't know whether they influenced George Orwell or he influenced them," Carrington quipped. The line drew loud applause from the white audience—but Malcolm was ready with his own clever retort in support of separatism. "You people wouldn't be here at Harvard if your forefathers hadn't said 'Liberty or Death,'" he noted, gesturing to the benches full of white students.

When Malcolm asserted that "there is no more apartheid in South Africa than in America," the crowd hissed, and again he shot back with a witty zinger. "That is what the serpent did to Eve in the garden," he joked about the heckling sound, turning to smile at the Harvard officials who had warned him in advance about the student tradition of hissing at speakers in Sanders Theatre. As one of them recalled it, Malcolm's grin seemed to say: "See, I told you about this. It's o.k."

Goldman left Memorial Hall that evening impressed and intrigued, thinking that Malcolm was nothing like the scary figure portrayed in the media. And although he didn't know it, Goldman wasn't the only conventional white civil rights liberal to come away with that reaction. Roger Fisher was a Harvard Law professor who had been asked to introduce the two speakers that night and to host a dinner for them beforehand at the Harvard Faculty Club. Fisher was surprised by Malcolm's ease in that clubby setting, and by his artful way of disarming his faculty dinner companions. Worried about how to introduce Malcolm to the crowd, Fisher had consulted one of his aides. "Don't you dare call Malcolm a Negro," the aide warned. "That word reminds us of 'nigger.'" But when Malcolm got wind of the query, he smiled and told Fisher that he sometimes found it "useful" to be called a Negro.

Thirty years later, Fisher and his wife would search for words to describe the impression of the man they came to know that night over dinner and on the walk from the Faculty Club to Sanders Theatre. The words that came to mind were "'handsome, attractive, forceful, caring, committed, generous, energetic, absolutely no sham or pretense, nothing superficial, open human, totally sincere," Fisher recalled. "Although we had disagreed with his ideas and much of what he said, both of us had admired him as a human being and liked him enormously."

The Nieman Fellowship was well-known as a stepping stone for ambitious regional reporters looking to move up in the profession. For precisely that reason, there was an unwritten rule that local newspapers would give their blessing to reporters to apply for the sabbatical with the understanding that they would return to their old jobs for at least one year. By the end of his time at Harvard, Goldman already knew that he wanted to ask Dudar to marry him, but now this looming obligation gave his decision more urgency. So Peter popped the question, and Helen accepted, and they were married in a small ceremony in mid-July. They agreed that after one year, they would move together to New York City, but in the meantime Dudar would take a leave from the *New York Post* and accompany Goldman back to St. Louis, where she planned to look for freelance assignments.

But there were no supportive female publishers like Dorothy Schiff in St. Louis, and Dudar struggled to find work. When she did, it was with a magazine start-up called *FOCUS/Midwest*, funded by a Jewish Holocaust survivor named Charles Klotzer, who had come to St. Louis as a refugee after World War II. In the debut issue, Dudar sent shock waves through St. Louis high society with a satirical piece on a local tradition known as the "Veiled Prophet Ball." In this annual rite, a secret all-male society of St. Louis power brokers elected one of their own to preside over an ostentatious parade, during which young women competed for the title of "Queen of Love & Beauty." After the article appeared—archly subtitled "Virgin Cult in St. Louis"—the *Post-Dispatch* predicted that "it will cause comment both indignant and approving, which is one of the things a new magazine needs." A local gossip columnist sniffed: "We doubt very much, after reading the article, that the author ever was tapped as the Veiled Prophet's Queen of Love & Beauty."

Meanwhile, Goldman decided to make the most of his last year at the *Globe-Democrat* by delving deeper into the world that had been opened up to him at Harvard by C. Eric Lincoln's book and Malcolm X's speech. He pitched the paper's city editor on a story about the small Nation of Islam presence in St. Louis, headquartered in a former dry-goods store known as Mosque No. 28 on the predominantly Black North Side of the city. The editor agreed, and by the time Goldman was finished reporting, he had enough material for four separate stories. They ran on the front page of the *Globe-Democrat* on consecutive days in the first week of 1962, and constituted one of the most in-depth looks at the Black Muslim phenomenon to appear in the white press anywhere in America up to that point.

In the series, Goldman introduced the paper's readers to the local NOI leader, Minister Clyde X, a thirty-one-year-old Mississippi native whom he described as a "glowering, moon-faced giant" on "the fleshy side of 200 pounds." Born Clyde Jones, the minister had first heard talk of the Nation of Islam outside a pool hall in Detroit, where he worked as an air-hammer operator in a car factory after serving in the Army in Korea. Changing his name to Clyde X, Jones joined the NOI in Detroit and quickly proved such a zealous convert that Elijah

Muhammad tapped him to take over the sect's tiny, struggling operation in St. Louis.

With epigrammatic verve, Goldman characterized the NOI's teachings to his white Midwestern readers. They consisted, he wrote, of a stew of "orthodox Islamic doctrine, reinterpreted Biblical parables, historical fact and fancy, Puritanical morality, 'buy-black' economics, doomsday prophecy, racism, nationalism and lesser ingredients." The Black Muslims believed that they were descended from a highly developed African civilization that existed for 666 trillion years before it was destroyed by a white race created in a laboratory experiment by a disaffected Black scientist named "Yacub." Using armed force and "tricknology," these white "devils" had overwhelmed the Black race, forced them into bondage, and brought them to America as slaves. But then in the 1930s, the Islamic God Allah had appeared in Detroit in the human form of a man named Wallace Fard Muhammad. Before mysteriously disappearing, Fard took a young Black migrant from Georgia named Elijah Poole under his wing, and anointed Poole as the apostle who would lead Black Americans to their salvation under the title of the Honorable Elijah Muhammad.

As outlandish as that origin story might have sounded, Goldman explained, the Nation of Islam had attracted tens of thousands of Black followers across urban America for some very concrete reasons. Impoverished and imprisoned Blacks found an explanation for their suffering in the belief that white people were inherently evil creatures engineered to do them harm. The sect's strict code of behavior also helped to battle addictions and impose discipline on lives that had spiraled out of control. As Goldman described it, that code included prohibitions against "drinking, smoking, swearing, taking narcotics, promiscuity, eating pork and other forbidden foods, wearing flashy or immodest clothes, using cosmetics, going to night clubs and movies, overeating, owning big cars and, if possible, buying anything on credit." Young urban Blacks, meanwhile, were drawn by the cool image of the "Fruit of Islam"—those sleek young men in dark suits and bow ties who served as bodyguards and enforcers for the NOI mosques.

Yet in St. Louis, Goldman assured his readers, the Nation of Islam had failed to catch on to the degree that it had in other cities such as New York and Chicago. Although Clyde X boasted of having recruited more than a thousand local members, Goldman found evidence of no more than two hundred. The major cause of this lackluster showing, he concluded, was the minister himself. Although Clyde X came off as mild-mannered and polite with white reporters, behind the closed doors of the mosque he struck fellow believers as excessively loud and angry. He was seen as a hypocrite who lived on the integrated West Side of town, rather than among his people on the North Side, and drove a showy two-tone 1960 Mercury sedan. Local members also questioned why Clyde X was sending more than a thousand dollars a month of their donations to Chicago to help fund a lavish $20 million mosque complex there. So great had the internal grumbling grown, Goldman reported, that Elijah Muhammad had sent emissaries from Chicago to stave off a brewing rebellion against Clyde X's leadership.

To further illustrate Clyde X's shortcomings, Goldman compared him unfavorably to his impressive counterpart at Mosque No. 7 in New York City. "The most effective Muslim leaders, like Malcolm X, are men with quick and agile minds and a facility at dealing with either friendly or hostile audiences," Goldman wrote. "They have the per-sonality ingredient that social scientists call 'charisma'—the seemingly magic ability to attract an unquestioning following. Observers of the Muslim movement here feel that Clyde X lacks this magic, that his main asset on the Muslim balance sheet is his unflinching personal loy-alty to Elijah Muhammad."

In including that flattering passage about Malcolm X in his series on the Black Muslims of St. Louis, Goldman would later insist, he had no intention of sending a hidden message to the fascinating speaker he had heard at Harvard. But several weeks after his four stories ran, he received a phone call at the *Globe-Democrat* newsroom. He picked up and heard the voice of Malcolm X himself on the line. Malcolm told Goldman that he had read his stories about the St. Louis mosque, was impressed with them, and wanted to know if he would like to meet the next time Malcolm came to town.

Goldman didn't have to think twice. Of course he would like to meet, he responded. That night, Peter shared the news with Helen and asked if she would like to join him for the interview. Undeterred by everything she knew about the Nation of Islam's views on the subservience of women, she readily agreed, and they would both be impressed to see how easily Malcolm accepted Dudar as Goldman's journalistic and intellectual equal.

———

When Malcolm X arrived in St. Louis in that early spring of 1962, Goldman and Dudar received instructions to meet him at a luncheonette on the North Side called the Shabazz Frosti Kreem. It was a hangout for members of Mosque No. 28 that served food that complied with the NOI's dietary restrictions, and Goldman had come to know the establishment well from his months of reporting his *Globe-Democrat* series. On an otherwise run-down block, the modest luncheonette stood out for its cleanliness, with scrubbed floors and vinyl tables visible though clean, unscarred windows.

When the two reporters arrived, the place seemed empty. They waited outside on the street until a car drove up, with the beefy figure of Minister Clyde X at the wheel, and Malcolm X climbed out. Although Goldman had observed Malcolm from afar at Harvard, it was the first time he had taken the measure of the man up close. He was struck yet again by how good-looking Malcolm was, and by how he carried himself. "He was a tall, coppery man," Goldman recalled, "six-feet-three and long muscled, with close-cut hair, cool gray-green eyes and the straight-up bearing of a soldier, or a priest."

Malcolm led his visitors inside and motioned for them to a table. Then he walked to a jukebox on the wall and deposited a coin. The strum of a guitar and a soft, plaintive voice filled the room. "Why are we called Negroes?" it asked. "Why are we deaf, dumb and blind?"

Goldman recognized the voice of Louis X, the leader of Mosque No. 11 in Boston, who before joining the Black Muslims had been a calypso singer born Louis Eugene Walcott and known as the "Charmer." At the time, he was seen as a protégé of Malcolm's, although that perception would later change once Malcolm broke with the NOI, and even more so in the decades following Malcolm's assassination, when Louis X became better known as Louis Farrakhan. But in the early 1960s, after Harry Belafonte topped the white billboard charts with calypso ballads such as the "Banana Boat Song," Louis X had scored a minor hit in Black America with the song now playing on the jukebox. Called "A White Man's Heaven Is a Black Man's Hell," it was a damning recitation of white pillage, enslavement, and exploitation of Black and Native American people through history set to a deceptively soothing bongo beat.

Sitting down at the table with Goldman, Dudar, and Clyde X, Malcolm motioned to a waiter behind the counter to bring four cups of coffee. "Coffee is the only thing I like integrated," he said with a playful smile, trotting out what Goldman would come to recognize as one of his stock icebreakers with white reporters.

Over the ranging, nearly three-hour conversation that followed, Goldman and Dudar probed to see if Malcolm actually believed the Nation of Islam's teachings about Black superiority and white degeneracy. Didn't science show that the makeup of people of both races was overwhelmingly the same? they asked.

In response, Malcolm launched into a quicksilver lecture that mixed genetics with linguistics. "A person can have a teaspoon of black blood in him, and that makes him black," he said. "Black can't come from white, but white can come from black. That means black was first. If black is first, black is supreme, and white is dependent on black. Genetically, white is recessive. 'Recessive' has the same Latin root as 'recess'; it means 'retreat,' or 'minus.' If you were in France, for 'white,' you'd say *blanc*. In Spanish, *blanco*. The English equivalent of black or *blanco* is not 'white' but 'blank.' The white people constitute a race that is blank—that has lost its pigmentation."

Malcolm pointed at his coffee cup. "To withdraw pigmentation changes the chemical composition," he said with another broad smile. "It has a weakening effect. Like the cream in this coffee."

Elaborating on his case for Black superiority, Malcolm startled Goldman and Dudar by offering evidence that would have offended most of their Black acquaintances. "An example: music," he said. "Music involves vibration, or life itself. It has a different effect on whites than on blacks—as much a difference as night and day—because the so-called Negro has this vibration."

Goldman thought to himself: Is he saying that Blacks have natural rhythm?

"We don't hate," Malcolm continued. "The white man has a guilt complex—he knows he's done wrong. He knows that if he had undergone at our hands what we have undergone at his, he would hate us. But it's easier for a white man to hate than a black man. The black man is naturally happy-go-lucky."

Dudar broke in. Wasn't that a white stereotype about Blacks? she asked.

Malcolm shrugged off the question. Those descriptions only bothered Blacks who were desperate to impress white people. "The Negro intellectual you come into contact with doesn't want to be identified with stereotypes," he said. "He doesn't want to be identified with something different from what America represents, because he wants to open the door and get in. So he'll dispute that. But it's true."

Whenever Goldman and Dudar asked what Malcolm thought of something a moderate civil rights leader had said—a Dr. King, or a Roy Wilkins of the NAACP—Malcolm scoffed. He dismissed their playbook of nonviolent social protest as "this mealy-mouth, beg-in, wait-in, plead-in kind of movement." He argued that the racial integration they advocated could only be brought about by government force, and wasn't to be desired in any event.

What about criticism from other Black leaders of Malcolm's militant tone?

"That's etiquette," Malcolm replied dismissively. "Etiquette means to blend in with society. They're being polite. The average Negro doesn't even let another Negro know what he thinks, he's so mistrusting. He's an acrobat. He had to be to survive in this civilization." By contrast, Malcolm argued, he didn't have to hold his tongue because he didn't care what white people thought of him. "By my being a Muslim," he said, "I'm not interested in being American, because America has never been interested in me."

Only once in the three-hour interview did the two reporters manage to throw Malcolm off-guard—and to elicit a shared laugh. Dudar asked what would happen if businesses run by NOI members, like the luncheonette where they were sitting, became more profitable. Wouldn't the owners grow more bourgeois-minded and want to join the NAACP?

Malcolm began to give a serious answer when Dudar interrupted and said she was only kidding.

Malcolm "chuckled," Goldman recalled, then "said it couldn't happen."

After the interview was over and Malcolm said his goodbyes outside the Shabazz Frosti Kreem, one more moment stuck in Goldman's memory. It was one of the few times he stopped asking questions and offered Malcolm a personal opinion. "I remember saying at one point that our best hope lay not in the separation of the races as he and the Muslims proposed," he recalled, "but in a single society in which color no longer made a critical difference."

In a sharp tone, Malcolm chided Goldman for being naive. "You're dealing in fantasy," he snapped. "You've got to deal in facts."

As soon as Goldman's obligatory year back in St. Louis was up in the summer of 1962, he applied for reporting jobs in New York City. He was waiting to hear back about an interview with *The New York Times* when he was offered a writing tryout at *Newsweek* magazine. The trial went so well that Goldman was offered a position on the spot—as a junior writer in the National Affairs department. As it turned it, it was a fortuitous time for a journalist interested in racial issues to be joining that publication. The previous year, the twenty-eight-year-old weekly had been purchased by Philip Graham, the publisher of *The Washington Post* and husband of Katharine Meyer Graham, the daughter of that paper's owner, Eugene Meyer.

An outspoken liberal and adviser to then Vice President Lyndon Johnson, Phil Graham promoted a social friend named Osborn Elliott, then the magazine's business editor, to the top editorial job. The new editor's nickname—"Oz"—hinted at his blue-blood social status, as did his predilection for bow ties and three-martini lunches. But Elliott's preppy veneer and jovial manner masked a deep sense of noblesse oblige, as well as a fierce competitiveness with *Newsweek*'s longtime rival, *Time* magazine, where Oz had worked for more than a decade.

By the time Goldman showed up for work in the National Affairs department in a crowded corner of the *Newsweek* offices on Madison Avenue, Elliott had begun to see a journalistic and commercial opportunity in the civil rights story, which was being covered slowly and awkwardly in *Time*. Sensing his own opening, Goldman announced his interest in writing about Black America to the National Affairs editor. When a roundup of civil rights stories was scheduled for an issue in late August, Goldman suggested a story on the Nation of Islam—and let it be known that he had already met Malcolm X and might be able to secure an interview.

With his new *Newsweek* press badge as a calling card, Goldman arranged to meet Malcolm at the Black-owned Hotel Theresa in Harlem. Once again, their conversation stretched for several hours, with Goldman asking earnest, probing questions and Malcolm parrying back with quick, blunt answers often tinged with playful irony. When Goldman challenged Malcolm about how many "signed-up" members the Nation of Islam actually had—*Newsweek*'s reporting suggested that it might have been no more than ten thousand nationwide—Malcolm responded that many more followers had "signed up mentally." As evidence, he cited the number of Black New Yorkers who could recognize the Muslim greeting.

"If you drive out of the Lincoln Tunnel into New York and say '*As-salaam-alaikum*' to the first Negro you'll see, he'll say, '*Wa-alaikam-salaam*,'" Malcolm insisted. "A majority of the Negroes in New York are pro-Muslim to the degree where we know they would become active in an emergency."

When sort of emergency? Goldman pressed.

Malcolm smiled, recognizing the attempt to get him to suggest a racial crisis scenario that might make news. "Let's just say an emergency," he responded.

Goldman went on to write a story for *Newsweek* that assumed its readers had little knowledge about the Nation of Islam and was openly skeptical of Elijah Muhammad's separatist teachings and god-like claims. "The Muslim Message: All White Men Devils, All Negroes Divine," read the headline. But for a mainstream white publication at the time, the account was unusually perceptive about how Muhammad ran his operation—and how central Malcolm X was to its success. "To deliver the message," Goldman wrote, "Muhammad, 64, has set up some 30 'mosques' (ranging from the second floor of a rundown Atlanta furniture store to a made-over synagogue in Chicago) and staffed them with ministers of mixed talent but undivided loyalty. He has a ward heeler's penchant for awarding jobs to relatives, and his son Wallace is regarded as his heir apparent. But his key man is his willowy, whip-smart New York minister and national representative, Malcolm X."

A month later, *Newsweek* assigned Goldman to report on the bid by James Meredith, a twenty-nine-year-old Air Force veteran, to become the first Black student to enroll at the University of Mississippi. Attorney General Robert F. Kennedy had dispatched U.S. Marshals to escort Meredith onto the campus, and Goldman arrived with reporter Karl Fleming just as more than three thousand white students and local segregationists stormed the quad to attack the federal lawmen with stones, bottles, and bricks. The next day, the two watched as a small army of U.S. soldiers and state National Guardsmen rolled onto the campus in tanks to restore order. Goldman's gripping seven-page account of the siege would win a prestigious Sigma Delta Chi award for excellence in magazine journalism—and it instantly cemented his place as the writer *Newsweek* turned to on big civil rights stories.

A year later, in August 1963, Goldman went to report on the March on Washington for another *Newsweek* cover. As he was milling around the Capitol Hilton on the eve of the march, he was approached by the Black journalist Louis Lomax, his frequent source of news and gossip from Harlem. Talking in a hushed voice, Lomax led Goldman up an elevator and down a long hallway to a room full of some fifty cocktail-sipping Black VIPs. In the middle of the gathering sat Malcolm X, holding forth as he nursed a cup of coffee. He wasn't supposed to be there, since Elijah Muhammad had told NOI ministers to steer clear of the march, and Malcolm later would publicly mock it as "the Farce on Washington." Yet that evening, Malcolm seemed eager to engage Goldman about news from the civil rights front, particularly the so-called Children's Crusade in Birmingham and how its leaders could justify allowing the city's Black youth to be attacked by police dogs in the name of nonviolence.

When Goldman returned home to New York, he told Dudar about his latest encounter with Malcolm, and how much he seemed to be chafing at the NOI's policy of "noninvolvement." As Peter would later put it, Malcolm appeared desperate for "a place in the Negro leadership, at least coequal with [Roy] Wilkins and [Whitney] Young and [Martin Luther] King; he may even have imagined himself speaking from the steps of the Lincoln Memorial, pitting his religion and his gifts of oratory against King's, and trooping with the march leaders to the White House to confront John Kennedy. [But] he saw no way to achieve any of this without making the Muslims relevant, which was to say involving them visibly in the struggle."

====

Neither Goldman nor Dudar was entirely surprised, therefore, when four months later Malcolm and Elijah Muhammad began to part ways. Most of the press coverage about the split would focus on two causes: first, Malcolm's comments about the Kennedy assassination; and later, his revelations about Muhammad's infidelity. But Peter and Helen had long sensed a third point of tension building between the two men— over Malcolm's hunger to be a constructive player in the civil rights struggle and not just a caustic critic.

In early December, as soon as Goldman heard about Malcolm's suspension from the NOI, he called him at the office of *Muhammad Speaks* in Harlem.

"Mr. Peter Goldman!" Malcolm exclaimed when he picked up the phone. "I haven't heard your voice in a good while!"

Goldman said that *Newsweek* was doing a brief story and that he was looking for comment.

Malcolm acknowledged that his crack about Kennedy had been unwise and didn't protest his punishment. "I'm in complete submission to any judgment Mr. Muhammad makes," he said. "I should have kept my big mouth shut."

Then Malcolm asked what Goldman thought of the turn of events. "I was surprised," Peter recalled. "Our periodic interviews had become almost conversations, but he had never asked my opinion before. It made him seem, for that fleeting moment, almost vulnerable. I told him I was sorry he had been set down—that he had a lot to tell us and that white people needed his voice even more than blacks did."

Four months later, Goldman and Dudar attended the press conference at the Park Sheraton Hotel in downtown Manhattan where Malcolm announced that he was leaving the NOI and forming the new organization he called Muslim Mosque Inc. Dressed less severely than usual in a pin-checked suit and blue tie, Malcolm arrived at the room he had booked to find it overflowing with print and television reporters. Perspiring under the hot TV lights, he made official what Peter and Helen had been speculating: that he intended not only to lead a separate religious flock but also to begin engaging with the civil rights struggles of the day. He was open to working with more mainstream Black leaders, Malcolm announced, and he would even accept white financial support.

After the press conference, Malcolm invited Goldman and Dudar to accompany him uptown to Lewis Michaux's bookstore in Harlem. During another long private interview, Malcolm went beyond what he said at the Sheraton about his break with the NOI, making news that Goldman would include in a *Newsweek* story titled "Malcolm's Brand X." Despite the fact that Muhammad had personally ordered the suspension over the Kennedy assassination remarks, Goldman reported, Malcolm blamed the rupture on advisers who had turned the Messenger against him. "If you put the wrong information into a computer, it can only come back the way you put it," he said.

At the press conference, Malcolm had also unveiled plans to form a "political apparatus," separate from Muslim Mosque Inc., that he would later name the Organization of Afro-American Unity. In addition, he floated the idea of forming Black "rifle clubs" in states where carrying firearms was legal. At the bookstore, Goldman got Malcolm to elaborate on that provocative proposal. "Whites will never correct the problem on moral, legal or ethical reasons," Malcolm said. "But they're realists enough to know that they don't want Negroes running around with guns." Then Goldman described the "sardonic smile" that crossed Malcolm's face when he predicted what would happen if those gun clubs were ever formed. "I bet they pass a bill to outlaw the sale of rifles," Malcolm joked, "and it won't be filibustered, either."

Several weeks later, Dudar published her own five-part series in the *New York Post*, under the overall title "The Muslims and Black Nationalism." Helen, too, broke news by reporting that Malcolm was studying the telegenic Christian evangelist Billy Graham as a model for how to expand his post-NOI crusade. She described the disorganized scene at the new makeshift headquarters of Muslim Mosque Inc. at the Hotel Theresa. It was a small room on the mezzanine floor with glass doors painted black and a green-tinted chalk board, once used by a Black brokerage firm, scribbled with a plea for real estate tips. "Please report all possible Mosque sites to Minister Benjamin 2X," read the note. "WE MUST OBTAIN A MOSQUE."

Dudar also shared an unsettling anecdote that suggested Malcolm's spiritual growth was still very much a work in progress. At a Sunday night meeting at the Theresa, he made a clumsy comparison between Jewish victims of the Nazis and enslaved Black Americans, then pointed at a *Post* reporter named Al Ellenberg. "Now there's a reporter who hasn't taken a note in half an hour," Malcolm taunted. "But as soon as I start talking about the Jews, he's busy taking notes to prove that I'm an anti-Semite." But Dudar also noted that Malcolm phoned Ellenberg to apologize several days later, and she pointed to that gesture as evidence of the private man she and Goldman had come to know in their encounters. "As a matter of fact, on the telephone is almost the only time that the outsider hears the non-public Malcolm," Dudar wrote. "Then the faceless listener, no longer an audience of a symbol, becomes a person. Malcolm's speech tunes down from oratory to conversation and he is relaxed, humorous, beguiling and at his most straightforward."

Malcolm himself reached out to compliment both Dudar and Goldman on these articles—but only through intermediaries, lest anyone discover how friendly he had become with two white envoys from the establishment press. In his epilogue to *The Autobiography of Malcolm X*, Alex Haley would recall that Malcolm once asked him to telephone Dudar to "tell her he thought very highly of her recent series—he did not want to commend her directly." Similarly, after *Newsweek*'s "Brand X" story was published, Goldman received a phone call from "one of his people," as Peter put it, reporting that Malcolm considered the piece "fair."

Less than a year later, Malcolm was dead, and Goldman and Dudar were left to explain his violent end and complex legacy to the readers of *Newsweek* and the *New York Post*. Dudar was blunt in describing how much Malcolm had done to put the Nation of Islam on the map, and how quickly its membership and fundraising had foundered after he left. "One thinks of the Black Muslims in terms of Malcolm X, not Elijah Muhammad," she concluded.

In a story for *Newsweek*, "Death of a Desperado," Goldman was even more pointed in spelling out the reasons Elijah Muhammad and those around him might have wanted Malcolm out of the way permanently. Goldman had interviewed Malcolm one last time after his first trip abroad in 1964, and found him now fully engaged in the political role he had long shown signs of coveting. But more than ever, Goldman noted, Malcolm's high political and global profile threatened the old NOI guard in Chicago, and gave them a pretext to demonize him for associating with white and foreign devils.

Then came the increasingly personal attacks that Malcolm had made on Elijah Muhammad in his final months. "Back in the U.S., he attacked his old guru," Goldman wrote. "He accused the Chicago command of financial irregularities. He said the Muslims were flirting with the Ku Klux Klan. And he charged Muhammad with personal immorality; in one errand on a trip to Los Angeles last month, he conferred with two former Muslim secretaries who have filed paternity suits against Muhammad. The Muslims wanted him killed, Malcolm said, 'because I know too much.'"

Once Malcolm was buried, Peter Goldman would turn back to his growing workload as the rising star of *Newsweek*'s National Affairs staff. But he had come to know Malcolm X too well, and learned too much about the people who wanted him dead, to leave the murder story alone for long.

THREE

The Trial

From the beginning, the police investigation into Malcolm's murder was a working theory is search of actual suspects. Within hours of the assassination, a probe was launched by the Manhattan North Homicide Squad, which operated out of the Georgian-style brick station house of the 34th police precinct a little less than a mile north of the Audubon Ballroom. Because the case was so high-profile, Joseph L. Boyle, Manhattan North's assistant chief inspector, took charge. He was joined by an Irish veteran homicide detective named John Keeley, who had been on duty at the station house when the first reports of the shooting came in. Also on the team were two long-serving Italian detectives from the 34th Precinct, Ferdinand "Rocky" Cavallaro and Tom Cusmano; two Black detectives, Jimmy Rushin and Warren Taylor; and as many as fifty other detectives and patrolmen who worked the case at one point or another in the early weeks.

For all their experience investigating murders, however, none of these lawmen knew much about the complicated internal politics of the Nation of Islam, or much at all about the Black Muslim movement outside New York City. As far as they were concerned, the case looked like the kind of old-fashioned turf war they were used to seeing among street gangs and Mafia families, with one local gang looking to get rid of a defector who had formed another gang and was threatening to siphon off recruits and money.

In interviewing witnesses to the chaotic scene at the Audubon

Ballroom that day, the detectives heard dozens of conflicting accounts of how many plotters had taken part. "You got everything," Keeley recalled. "You get it was four guys with beards, or it was a green man with long hair. We got stories that up to ten were involved. You have to weed out what's incredible and come up with a basic description of what happened." So it was ballistics, more than eyeballs, that led police to the conclusion that they were looking for three killers. The chief medical examiner at Bellevue Hospital, who had performed the autopsy on Malcolm, retrieved nine shotgun slugs from his body, three of them wedged deep in his spine. Three handgun bullets and twenty-one bullet wounds were found running from Malcolm's chin down to both of his hands and legs. Tests revealed that all the bullets as well as others retrieved from the bloody ballroom scene came from three firearms: a shotgun, a .45 caliber pistol, and a 9mm semiautomatic believed to be a Luger.

That ballistics evidence matched up with the one suspect the police already had in custody. Talmadge Hayer, the gunman who had been attacked and badly wounded by Malcolm's followers as he tried to escape from the Audubon Ballroom, was found with a clip of .45 caliber bullets in his pants pocket. When a forensics team later examined the makeshift smoke bomb that had created a diversion during Malcolm's speech—a sock stuffed with scraps of photographic film and safety matches wrapped in handkerchiefs—they found Hayer's fingerprints on the film.

But nothing else about Hayer appeared to support the local gang war hypothesis. He was twenty-three years old and lived in Paterson, New Jersey, the gritty industrial city on the other side of the Hudson River. His rap sheet showed an arrest for disorderly conduct in his teens, and another when eighteen guns stolen from a Paterson gun shop turned up in the basement of the house where Hayer lived with his mother and younger sisters. At first, the Manhattan detectives found no immediate clues linking Hayer to the Nation of Islam, let alone to the Harlem mosque.

Yet rather than expanding their investigation to New Jersey, the police detectives kept their focus on Harlem. They became even more wedded to the turf war scenario when Mosque No. 7 was firebombed the day after the assassination. To avoid a police patrol that had been stationed in the street outside, four men in a station wagon pulled up around the corner of the mosque, which was located on the fourth floor of a building on the corner of 116th Street and Lenox Avenue. Carrying a shopping bag full of bottles and rags and a five-gallon can of gasoline, two of the men snuck up to the roof of an adjoining building, then climbed down the fire escape to the fourth floor. Breaking the windows, the two men lit up several Molotov cocktails and hurled them inside. Then they scurried back to the roof, dumped the gas can and the shopping bag, and fled. Firemen fought the blaze for two hours but were unable to prevent the interior from being gutted and the roof and an entire outside wall from collapsing. In the winter chill, water from the fire hoses formed icicles on the burned-out shell, making it look like a gruesome ice sculpture.

The day after the assassination, chief detective Boyle also received a phone tip that helped attach new names to the gang war thesis. The call came from an inspector in the Bronx who had been reminded by one of his men, a detective named Jack Kilroy, of a shooting arrest he had made in early January. The victim was a prison guard named Benjamin Brown who had joined the NOI mosque in Harlem, then quit it to establish his own fledgling storefront operation called the Universal Peace mosque in the Bronx. One day, Brown was hanging a picture of Elijah Muhammad in the window when three members of the Fruit of Islam from Harlem drove by to harass him. Later that day, Brown was headed toward his car after locking up when a .22 caliber bullet exploded into his back and into his right lung.

Brown survived the attack and gave testimony that led police to arrest two members of the Fruit of Islam. He described the two men as members of an enforcement squad practiced in firearms and karate that was dispatched to punish anyone who displeased the Harlem leadership. One was a thirty-year-old out-of-work house painter with a round, light-brown face and pencil mustache named Thomas Johnson. Known inside the Harlem mosque as Thomas 15X, Johnson had been found in possession of a .22 caliber Winchester rifle when the cops searched his home. The other was a tall, muscular, lean-faced twenty-six-year-old lieutenant in the Fruit of Islam named Norman Butler, or

Norman 3X. Out of work and taking vocational classes to become an appliance repairman, Butler was a Navy veteran and former Pinkerton guard who once tried to apply to the police academy but was rejected because he had already fathered two children out of wedlock with an older woman he met in his late teens. He was also such a feared karate master that Detective Kilroy and his men wore steel-reinforced face masks when they went to arrest him at his Bronx apartment. Even then, according to Keeley, Butler managed to dent a protective metal mask that the detective was wearing with a karate chop before he was subdued.

━━

With speculation about more tit-for-tat violence running rampant, Boyle and his detectives zeroed in on the suspects in the Benjamin Brown case. Never mind that the two men were each out on $10,000 bond awaiting trial in that case, and might have been reluctant to participate in an attack on one of the most visible public figures in New York City while they were already on the NYPD's radar screen. After discovering that Thomas 15X Johnson had gone out of town for a few days, the detectives moved first on Norman 3X Butler. Around midnight on the Thursday after the assassination, police in two cars arrived outside Butler's apartment in a Bronx housing project. Detective Kilroy called his phone number to confirm he was there, and then he and the other policemen went up and knocked on the door.

Butler was lying on the living room sofa in his pajamas, watching television and resting his legs, which had been bruised by blows from police blackjacks when he was taken into custody over the Benjamin Brown shooting. "What's it all about?" he asked coolly. Not wanting to invite another karate attack, the detectives pretended to want Butler's help in the Malcolm case. They asked him to come with them to the 34th Precinct, and they watched as he got dressed in a blue suit and tweed overcoat to make sure he didn't arm himself. At the station house, Butler was placed in a room behind one-way glass. On the other side, a parade of witnesses from the Audubon Ballroom murder scene looked him over until two said they recognized him as one of the gunmen.

When the detectives finally informed Butler of the charges against him, he firmly denied them. He said he was at home on the afternoon of Malcolm's killing, resting his injured legs. During more than three hours of questioning, he never wavered from this account, and did nothing to hide his contempt for the white cops and their attempts to rattle him.

At one point, one of the Italian detectives, Rocky Cavallaro, took Butler into a separate room and tried to appeal to him with man-to-man straight talk. "Look—you're being arrested for murdering Malcolm X," Cavallaro said. "You've been identified. You want to tell us about it?"

"That's ridiculous," Butler repeated. "I didn't kill him."

Around four in the morning, without any confession, Butler was booked for murder and transferred to the dingy city jail known as the Tombs to await trial without bail. The next morning, the police released a perp walk photo—of Butler looking clear-eyed and defiant in his tweed overcoat and porkpie hat—in time to make the afternoon papers on the eve of Malcolm's funeral. Also scheduled that Saturday was the opening of a three-day Nation of Islam convention in Chicago. Surrounded by a small army of Fruit of Islam security, Elijah Muhammad delivered a stemwinding keynote speech in which he simultaneously denied the NOI's involvement in the murder and suggested that Malcolm had it coming. Malcolm "got what he preached," Muhammad said to loud applause and cries of "yes, yes" and "that's right!" from the crowd of 7,500 in the Chicago Coliseum.

Briefing reporters from the *New York Post*, a law enforcement source all but admitted that the police had felt pressure to make the Butler arrest before those weekend events. "The Muslims are afraid of Malcolm's people and Malcolm's people are afraid of the Muslims," the source said. "The city is afraid and Harlem is afraid. Everyone asks what the police have been doing, and this is what we are doing. This is something we can show."

By the following week, the police found another witness who helped assemble the fragile pieces of their gang war theory. Stocky and balding, Cary 2X Thomas was a former heroin addict, high school dropout, and Korean War vet who had been discharged for attacking an officer. Now thirty-five, he had left his wife and three kids and joined the Nation of Islam just in time to fall under Malcolm's spell and then side with him in his split from Elijah Muhammad. On the day of the assassination, Thomas had been among Malcolm's armed body-guards, stationed in a booth on the side of the ballroom, although he admitted to the police that he froze up when the mayhem started and never unholstered his .357 Magnum.

When Thomas was first questioned, he had appeared too fright-ened to talk. Then after a week of questioning, he suddenly opened up. He told the detectives that he had seen all three suspects—Hayer, Butler, and Johnson—at the murder scene, and painted a picture of the role each had played. According to Thomas's initial account, it was Hayer who stood up and drew the attention of Malcolm's guards by shouting about someone going through his pockets. Then it was But-ler and Johnson who rushed the stage and fired on Malcolm.

Although Thomas seemed hazy on other details, his testimony gave police the evidence they needed to move on Thomas 15X John-son. They waited for Johnson to show up at his next court appearance in the Benjamin Brown case, then arrested him after Cary 2X Thomas identified him from a distance. In his perp walk photo, a stony-faced Johnson was still dressed for what he thought would be his court date, in a tan suit and dark tie, with his pencil mustache neatly trimmed.

Even after the men of Manhattan North Homicide had three sus-pects to match the number of guns used in the murder, they were still nervous about their star witness. Given his shaky personal and finan-cial history, they worried, Cary 2X Thomas might change his story or simply disappear. So they didn't take any chances once Thomas testi-fied to the grand jury that handed down three murder indictments in mid-March 1965. Thomas was ordered held in custody until the trial started, and Rocky Cavallaro and the two Black detectives were as-signed to baby-sit him. For the next eight months, Cary 2X was paid $3 a day as a "material witness," and released from confinement only on special occasions to go to the movies with his minders.

In the year between the arrests and the trial, the original New York County assistant district attorney assigned to the case—Herbert J. Stern—also stepped aside. A bright and ambitious hard worker just four years out of University of Chicago Law School, Stern had signed off on the initial indictments based on the evidence that the NYPD already had on Butler and Johnson in the Benjamin Brown case, and because he found them "arrogant" for insisting on their innocence while refusing to give up any information about the Nation of Islam. Stern was also dismissive of the conspiracy theories floating around Harlem, scoffing privately that he didn't believe that a Central Intelligence Agency hit squad would have included someone as inexperienced as Talmadge Hayer or been so sloppy as to leave the shotgun behind in the ballroom. Stern found it persuasive, too, that the witnesses who put Butler and Thomas at the scene of the crime included several of Malcolm's own bodyguards. Yet as those witnesses started to give conflicting testimony before a grand jury—and later to change their testimony at trial—someone as shrewd and conscientious as Stern might have sensed a problem and slowed the rush to judgment. But just as the trial was about to get underway, the U.S. Justice Department offered Stern a new position fighting organized crime in New Jersey. There, he would do a more thorough job of prosecuting a string of cases against corrupt politicians, union leaders, and mob bosses before serving for a decade and a half as a judge on the U.S. District Court for New Jersey.

In mid-January 1966, the Malcolm X murder case finally went to trial before Judge Charles Marks, an imperious seventy-two-year-old who was responsible for sentencing a quarter of all the convicts on death row in New York State at that time. Jury selection took a long first week, finally producing a nine-member panel of six men and three women, among them three Black jurors, including a mild-mannered, bespectacled Manhattan chemist who was selected foreman. The other jurors included a motorman and a signal man for the subway, a Linotype operator, a department store worker, a garbageman, a draftsman, a retired jeweler, and a housewife.

With Stern gone, the job of prosecuting the case went to a veteran assistant district attorney named Vincent Dermody, a cop's son who had grown up in the Bronx and was considered one of the wiliest courtroom lawyers in the D.A.'s office. In his opening statement, Dermody promised to prove that the three suspects had carried out the entire assassination plot by themselves. He charged that Hayer and Butler created the diversion in the crowd, while Johnson opened fire on Malcolm with a shotgun. Then, as Johnson dropped the shotgun and ran away, Hayer and Butler approached Malcolm's prone body and riddled it with handgun bullets before fleeing toward the exits themselves.

Butler and Johnson were both represented by Black public defenders who had been assigned by the court and were paid meager flat fees of $2,000 each. With financial assistance from his family, only Hayer had retained his own attorney, a seventy-four-year-old denizen of Little Italy named Peter Sabbatino, who had represented more than three hundred murder suspects in his career. Sabbatino was also the only defense attorney to make an opening statement. He claimed that Hayer came to hear Malcolm X speak out of curiosity, serendipitously found a clip of .45 bullets in a bathroom and put it in his pocket, and was the victim of mistaken "mob identification" after the shooting. Now, Sabbatino charged, the state was targeting Hayer to protect the man who had shot him in the thigh outside the Audubon Ballroom: Malcolm's security guard Reuben Francis.

Cary 2X Thomas, the bodyguard who had been kept under wraps since the grand jury indictment, was called as the prosecution's first witness. From his position in a booth on the side of the ballroom, Thomas testified, he noticed Talmadge Hayer and Norman 3X Butler sitting together in the crowd, then saw Hayer stand up and shout: "Man, what are you doing with your hands in my pocket." Thomas said he heard the sound of gunfire and saw a man standing over Malcolm on the stage; when the man turned around, it was Thomas 15X Johnson, holding a sawed-off shotgun. Later, Cary 2X said, he saw Hayer and Butler from behind as they appeared to shoot up Malcolm's fallen body. "I didn't see the guns, but I saw the pumping motion," Thomas recalled, lifting his arm and pointing a finger simulating a firing motion.

Once cross-examination began, however, it became clear what a wobbly witness Cary 2X Thomas was, even after having a year to prepare for his testimony. He couldn't recall when he had joined the Nation of Islam or first met Malcolm X. Along with his history as an addict and pusher, Thomas had to admit that he had violated the NOI's strict moral code by abandoning his family and once getting so drunk that he was taken to Bellevue Hospital. At Bellevue, he had also undergone psychiatric examination after shouting "I did not kill Jesus Christ!" While in police custody after the indictment, Thomas had been charged with arson after setting fire to a mattress. Most damning, from a legal point of view, Thomas conceded that he had changed his story since appearing before the grand jury. There, he had testified that Hayer alone caused the distraction and that Butler and Johnson stormed the stage firing handguns.

Over the next two weeks, the prosecution presented nine other witnesses who described having seen at least one of the three defendants at the Audubon Ballroom. One of them was Charles X Blackwell, the bodyguard who offered Malcolm a ride to the event and was later stationed on the stage during his speech. Blackwell described climbing down from the stage after he saw Hayer and Butler argue in the middle of the audience. Then he heard gunfire, and turned around to see the same two men fleeing with their guns. As he chased Hayer and Butler, Blackwell recalled, he noticed Johnson, unarmed and looking "startled" and "scared," at the back of the ballroom. But that account differed from what Blackwell had told the grand jury, where he testified that Hayer and Butler were sitting in the front of the room and that someone else created the distraction farther back. Meanwhile, the only other witness who described spotting Thomas 15X Johnson with a shotgun was Blackwell's friend Fred Williams, but Williams couldn't recall seeing the shotgun fired or many other specifics about which he was questioned on the witness stand.

The prosecutors also produced a surprise witness to bolster their case. He was a thirty-one-year-old subway worker named Ronald Timberlake, who had joined Mosque No. 7 when Malcolm was the minister, then become an early member of the OAAU. Timberlake was among the Malcolm followers who chased Talmadge Hayer out of the Audubon Ballroom after the shooting, and he picked up the .45-caliber pistol after Hayer dropped it. Rather than turn the gun over to the police, Timberlake took it home and alerted the FBI, for whom he was an informant. His FBI handlers arranged for Timberlake to hand the gun over to the NYPD and helped persuade him to testify. At the last minute, Timberlake insisted on appearing in closed session, and the judge agreed to clear the courtroom before calling the jury in. All the drama may have made the jury pay special attention when Timberlake proceeded to insist that he saw Butler attacked outside the ballroom along with Hayer—a detail that wasn't supported by any other evidence or testimony.

For the defendants, however, the most damaging moment in the prosecution phase of the trial didn't take place on the witness stand. When Betty Shabazz was called to testify, looking solemn in a black dress and black velvet hat, she described hearing the sounds of gunfire and of her husband gasping for air as she scrambled to shield her four young daughters. Dermody made no effort to get Betty to identify the killers, and the defense didn't bother to cross-examine her. But as Betty was leaving the stand, she stopped close to the table where the defendants and their lawyers sat. "They killed him," she cried out, starting to turn toward the defendants before two court attendants clutched her arms and hustled her toward the doorway. "They had no right to kill my husband."

Judge Marks immediately instructed the jury to disregard what they had just seen. Nonetheless, observers would pinpoint Betty's outburst as the moment when the outcome of the trial became a foregone conclusion, despite the dramatic turn of events that was about to unfold during the defense presentation.

———

Talmadge Hayer's lawyer, Peter Sabbatino, thought it would be a slow workday for him, so he was late getting to court on the first Monday after the defense phase began. Several days had passed since his client finished testifying. Sabbatino had walked Hayer through the story the lawyer foreshadowed in his opening statement—about Hayer's spontaneous decision to attend Malcolm's speech, his accidental discovery of a .45 bullet cartridge in the men's room, and his surprise at being attacked outside the Audubon Ballroom. Now twenty-four years old, Hayer had kept calm on the stand and held his own under cross-examination, during which he denied having any idea how his fingerprints ended up on the smoke bomb hurled during the attack.

Since then, Norman 3X Butler's court-appointed attorneys had taken over. That Monday, they were scheduled to question Butler's relatives about his alibi: that Norman was home in the Bronx nursing his sore legs on the afternoon of Malcolm's assassination. So Sabbatino was taken by surprise when he arrived at the courthouse and heard what everyone was buzzing about: unbeknownst to him, Hayer had decided to confess that he had taken part in the killing. In the holding pen outside the courtroom that morning, Hayer had also promised his two fellow defendants to tell the jury that they had nothing to do with the plot.

When Hayer confirmed that he wanted to testify again, Sabbatino tried to force a recess.

As soon as the jury returned from lunch, Judge Marks invited Butler's court-appointed lawyer, William Chance, to call his next witness.

"Talmadge Hayer," Chance announced.

Sabbatino leapt to his feet and asked to approach the bench. Chance joined him there, and motioned for a stenographer to take notes of the hushed sidebar.

"If your Honor please, I represent the defendant Butler," Chance said. "After a conversation with the defendant Butler as it relates to a conversation he had with Talmadge Hayer, he has asked me to call Talmadge Hayer as a witness in his defense—demanded that I call Talmadge Hayer."

Marks turned to Sabbatino. "Do you want to say anything?" he asked.

"Well, I should think, your Honor, as his attorney," Sabbatino sputtered, "I should have an opportunity to speak with Hayer privately."

Several more delays ensued, as Hayer left the courtroom to confer with Sabbatino, and then the judge ordered all the lawyers into his robing room for another conference. Eventually, it became clear that Hayer was determined to go forward with his confession and Sabbatino withdrew his objections.

As Hayer took the stand, the judge addressed him.

"Mr. Hayer, has anyone forced you to be willing to testify here this afternoon?" Marks asked.

"No, sir," Hayer responded. "I just want to tell the truth, that's all."

Chance took over the questioning, and asked Hayer to repeat what he had told Norman 3X Butler and Thomas 15X Johnson in the holding pen that morning.

"Now, will you tell us what the conversation was?" Chance asked.

"Well," Hayer said, "I told Mr. Butler and Mr. Johnson that I knew—that I know they didn't have anything to do with the crime that was committed at the Audubon Ballroom February 21st, that I did take part in it, and that I know for a fact that they weren't there, and I wanted this to be known to the jury and the Court, the judge. I want to tell the truth."

"Now, were you alone in this involvement at the Audubon?" Chance asked.

"No, sir," Hayer replied.

"Will you now name for the Court who the other people were?" Chance asked.

"No, sir, I can't reveal that," Hayer answered.

"Do you know those names?" Chance asked.

"I do," Hayer responded.

When the judge explained that he could order Hayer to answer the question about the other accomplices, the witness still refused to do so. Once it became clear that Hayer wasn't going to give up other names, Chance asked one final question.

"Prior to February 21st, 1965, did you know Butler or Johnson?" Chance asked.

"No, sir," Hayer responded.

"Had you ever seen them before?" Chance asked.

"No, sir," Hayer answered, "never saw them."

═══

Approaching the witness stand, prosecutor Vincent Dermody began an aggressive cross-examination. First he expressed disbelief that Hayer had only just announced his plan to confess to his fellow defendants that morning in the holding pen.

"And what, if anything, did either Butler or Johnson say when you told them that?" Dermody asked.

"Well, they said 'About time,' or 'It's about time, I'm glad it's this way,'" Hayer responded. "You know. That 'we was wondering when you was going to do this, tell the truth.'"

Under more questioning from Dermody, Hayer revealed that he had wielded the .45 pistol identified in the shooting and had fired on Malcolm X's body "maybe four times." He denied that he was the one who shouted "Get your hands out of my pocket," but said he knew who did. Yet once again, Hayer refused to reveal other names. He also denied knowing who planned the assassination or receiving "direct orders," and said he only took part in the plot because he "was offered some money for doing it."

Even when the judge informed Hayer that he could be held in contempt of court for refusing to divulge the identity of the other culprits, he didn't budge.

"Besides yourself, how many other people were involved in the killing of Malcolm X, to your knowledge?" Dermody asked.

"Four," Hayer replied.

"Do you know the names of these four people?" Dermody asked.

"I do," Hayer answered.

"Give us the names of these four people you were involved with," Dermody demanded.

"I will not," Hayer persisted.

Asked how he had arrived at the Audubon Ballroom, Hayer said that he had met one of the other plotters at a bus terminal in Washington Heights shortly before two o'clock in the afternoon.

"Will you tell us, Mr. Hayer, was there any plan laid out among you and these other four people as to [how] the assassination would take place?" Dermody asked.

"Yes," Hayer said.

"When was this plan made?" Dermody asked.

"I won't say," Hayer said.

"I didn't hear you," Dermody said.

"I will not say," Hayer repeated.

Hayer did offer more details about how the plot unfolded, however. He confirmed that he had stationed himself in the front row of the audience with the .45 automatic pistol, alongside another plotter armed

with a German 9mm Luger. Then he offered a physical description of
the third man, who fired at Malcolm X with the sawed-off shotgun.

"Do you know the man who had the shotgun?" Dermody asked.

"I do," Hayer replied.

"How long had you known this man by name as of February 21st,
1965?" Dermody asked.

"About a year," Hayer answered.

"Would you describe this man for us?" Dermody said.

"Dark skin, husky, had a beard," Hayer said.

As it happened, this wasn't the first time the jury had heard a
description of the man with the shotgun that didn't fit Thomas 15X
Johnson, who was light-skinned and had a mustache. Earlier, a defense
witness named Ernest Greene, a twenty-year-old Black student who
was in the audience during the speech, had recalled seeing a dark-
skinned, bearded man fire the shotgun. Dermody tried to suggest that
Hayer was simply borrowing that description from Greene, but Hayer
held his ground.

"I know, I know the person," Hayer insisted of the unnamed dark-
skinned man.

Led by Dermody's questions, Hayer described how he and the four
other men had carried out the murder. To distract Malcolm's bodyguards, one man shouted the "pocket" line, while another hurled the
smoke bomb. In the confusion, the dark-skinned man with the shotgun
moved in and blasted Malcolm in the chest. Then Hayer and the other
man with a handgun got up from the front row and approached Malcolm's fallen body to finish the job.

"And, according to the plan, was it after the blast went off, was that
when you and the man next to you went into action?" Dermody asked.

"It was," Hayer answered.

"How far from Malcolm were you when you fired the .45 a few
times?" Dermody asked.

"Ten feet," Hayer responded.

"And at the time you fired at Malcolm was he standing or in a
prone position?" Hayer asked.

"A prone position," Hayer answered.

"And did you fire right into his body?" Dermody asked.

"I did," Hayer confirmed.

"Mr. Hayer, let me ask you this question," Dermody continued. "Did you have any reason, personal reason, to shoot Malcolm X?"

"Not personal," Hayer responded.

"Were you hired to do so?" Dermody asked.

"I was," Hayer answered.

"For money?" Dermody asked.

"Yes, sir," Hayer said.

When Dermody confronted the witness with his earlier testimony claiming innocence, Hayer made no attempt to deny that he had committed perjury under oath. It was "all lies," Hayer confirmed, and "a story I made up." But beyond describing what his fellow shooters were wearing—not tweed coats, as other witnesses had described, but a black overcoat, and two brown three-quarter town coats—he refused to say any more about who the others were or where they came from.

"Were any of these men you say were involved with you, were any of them from New York City?" Dermody asked.

"I will not say," Hayer responded.

For all Hayer's insistence on wanting to tell the truth, however, some of his answers to Dermody's questions still sounded suspiciously evasive. When asked if his fellow plotters were Black Muslims, he first replied "No, they weren't"—but then quickly he added, "To my knowledge."

Calling Hayer back to the witness stand the next morning, Dermody confronted him with two photographs. Taken three years earlier, they showed a karate exhibition that had taken place at the Nation of Islam mosque in Newark, New Jersey. One of the young people in the photos looked a lot like Hayer.

In his first trip to the witness stand, Hayer had denied that the youth in the photographs was him. But this time, he refused to say whether he had taken part in the karate competition, or ever set foot in the Newark mosque. At least five times, Hayer repeated a version of the answer: "I have nothing to say about that."

And so the cross-examination went for the rest of that Tuesday morning, with Hayer refusing to give more specifics, and the defense

attorneys raising increasingly loud objections to the prosecutor's bul-
lying tone.

Finally, in closing, Dermody asked again how much Hayer was paid
to participate in Malcolm's assassination. "Was it for twelve pieces of
silver?" he asked. "Was it, Mr. Hayer?"

Yet even this sarcastic reference to the betrayal of Jesus of Naza-
reth by Judas Iscariot didn't end the squabbling between the lawyers.

"My recollection is, your honor, is that the Bible refers to twenty
pieces of silver, or am I wrong?" said Sabbatino.

"Thirty pieces is my recollection," said Chance.

"I think both of you are wrong," said Judge Marks, insisting on
having the last word on Holy Book references. "If you read the Roman
trial and the Hebrew trial, probably your education in that respect will
be better. Because I have read both."

———

The next day, Norman 3X Butler took the stand—and walked straight
into a trap set by Dermody, the veteran prosecutor with twenty-three
years of grilling trial witnesses under his belt. Sensing that he needed
to create some new drama to blunt the impact of Hayer's surprise confession, Dermody prodded at Butler's racial pride and contempt for
non-Muslims. The result was a series of combative exchanges that were
bound to sit poorly with a jury of middle-class white and Black professionals conditioned to disapprove of any behavior that smacked of the
"uppity Negro."

The day began with his lawyer, William Chance, leading Butler through an account of his whereabouts on the day of Malcolm's
assassination. In the morning, Butler said, he went to see a doctor
at a hospital near his home in the Bronx to get his inflamed legs examined. From there, he briefly stopped by a Muslim diner near the
mosque in Harlem. But by one o'clock, Butler insisted, he was back
at home in his pajamas resting his legs, and he didn't go out again for
the rest of the day.

When Chance started asking if Butler had gone anywhere near
the Audubon Ballroom, Dermody repeatedly interrupted to object
to the wording of the answers. Each time Butler gave an insistent

denial—"Emphatically no," "Positively no," or "Absolutely no"—the prosecutor asked the judge to demand one-word answers.

Having thus gotten under the witness's skin, Dermody began his cross-examination with a meandering line of questioning about Butler's checkered employment history. By the time he got to the point, Butler had already figured out what the prosecutor was insinuating.

"As a matter of fact, Mr. Butler, weren't you being supported—" Dermody asked.

"Negative," Butler interrupted.

"You haven't heard a question," Dermody said.

"I know what you're going to ask," Butler said. "No."

"What was I going to ask?" Dermody said.

"You were going to ask if I was supported by the mosque," Butler said.

"Isn't that a fact?" Dermody followed.

"Well, I answered that question," Butler shot back.

"As a matter of fact, didn't you tell one of the detectives—" Dermody continued.

"I never did," Butler interrupted again.

"Would you let me finish my question?" Dermody said.

"I know what you're going to say," Butler said.

"Let him finish," the judge instructed Butler.

"What was I going to ask you?" Dermody said, preparing his hook.

"Did I ever tell a detective that?" Butler said.

"You knew I was going to ask you that?" Dermody said, floating the hook closer.

"Certainly," Butler said, taking the bait. "I know what you're going to say before you say it."

At this point, Chance knew things were going badly enough for his client that he requested a two-minute recess for "personal reasons."

By the end of the cross-examination, Butler had managed to get on the judge's bad side, too. Dermody asked Butler another long set of questions about the hierarchy within the Fruit of Islam and whether, as a lieutenant, he would have had to take orders from anyone else. Butler was so combative that Judge Marks finally intervened. When Butler and his lawyer suggested that the judge had "misunderstood" one of

Butler's answers, Marks replied indignantly: "I am not confused, I told you that, at any point in this trial."

Finally, on the last two days of testimony, Thomas 15X Johnson had his turn on the stand. Under direct questioning, he quietly described spending the day of Malcolm's murder at home with his pregnant wife and young children. He arose at dawn to say the Islamic prayers, Johnson said, then read the Koran for an hour. After that, he spent the day cooking for his family and cleaning their Bronx apartment until another couple came by to inform them of Malcolm's death at about four o'clock.

Seeing how self-composed Johnson appeared, Dermody took a different tack on cross-examination than he had with Butler. Rather than trying to rattle the witness, he reminded the jury of Johnson's troubled history before he joined the Nation of Islam. He forced Johnson to admit that he had once been a heroin addict who supported a $15-a-day habit as a numbers runner and lookout man for gamblers, and that he had racked up five criminal convictions by the age of twenty-five. Butler's lawyer rose to object that the questioning was "prejudicial" and then went through the motions of demanding a retrial. Haughty as ever, Judge Marks denied the petition and instructed the lawyers to be ready with their summations the following Monday.

Peter Sabbatino faced a quandary, since he was now representing a client who had confessed to murder and admitted to perjury in the process. So in his closing arguments, Sabbatino tried to get jurors to believe that Hayer had lied the second time, and only acted to save his two fellow defendants. "There was no reason for this lad to do what he did except a high sense of Christian charity," the lawyer argued, throwing in an extra suggestion of proof that Hayer wasn't a Muslim. In the two-and-a-half-hour summation, Sabbatino floated the idea that the assassination plot had been hatched from within Malcolm's inner circle. The "arch-boss of this conspiracy," the lawyer bellowed to the jury, was Reuben Francis, Malcolm's trusted security guard and the man who shot Hayer in the thigh as he was fleeing the Audubon Ballroom.

Taking an hour and forty minutes for his summation, William Chance argued that his client was a victim of religious persecution.

The only reason Norman 3X Butler and Thomas 15X Johnson were on trial, Chance contended, was that they were members of the Nation of Islam, and law enforcement was determined to prove that Malcolm was shot for being a defector, like Benjamin Brown. But that explanation didn't make sense, Chance contended, because it was the NOI that had suspended Malcolm and then made clear he wasn't welcome back. "The theory of the people's case that the motive for killing Malcolm X was because he left the Black Muslim movement is totally absurd," Chance boomed in his resonant baritone, his suit jacket and vest left unbuttoned as he paced in front of the jury box.

Yet when Vincent Dermody made his closing argument for the prosecution the next day, he doubled down on the local turf war theory, going so far as to let NOI headquarters in Chicago off the hook. "We never said we'd prove that Elijah Muhammad ordered this death," Dermody said. "I have been accused of putting the Black Muslims on trial. I submit this is not fact." Instead, Dermody argued that the enforcers from the Harlem mosque staged a hit in broad daylight as a warning to other potential defectors in their ranks. "Is it abusing your common sense," he flattered the jury, "to say that it was an object lesson to Malcolm's followers, telling them that this is what can happen and will happen?"

Addressing the testimony that Butler and Johnson were both at home on the day of the murder, Dermody asked the jury to choose between those alibis and the ten witnesses who claimed to have seen one or both men at the Audubon Ballroom. "Somebody is lying," he pointed out. In his four-hour-and-twenty-minute summation, Dermody saved his strongest condemnation for Talmadge Hayer. Hayer's last-minute confession was the "futile, desperate gesture," he said, of a man caught red-handed and trying to spare his fellow defendants. "Hayer knew he was going down, buried under a mountain of evidence, and he tried at the last moment to do the noble thing," Dermody said in a sarcastic tone. "Somewhere along the line, it was decided, by whom I cannot say, that he was a dead duck and he should take the fall."

In the end, however, the confession made no difference. After receiving their charge from the judge the next day, the nine jurors deliberated for twenty hours before finding all three men guilty of murder in the first degree. While *The New York Times* and other mainstream newspapers described the tense scene in the courtroom as the verdict was read, reporters from the radical press focused on all the questions the trial had left unanswered. "Who ordered the assassination?" asked Herman Porter, a reporter for *The Militant* who had covered the trial from the beginning. Did the police or the FBI have advance knowledge of the attack? Were some of the killers deliberately allowed to get away, or never pursued at all?

For the next five and a half decades, those questions would consume conspiracy theorists and serious reporters and historians alike, starting with the quietly obsessive Peter Goldman of *Newsweek*. At a final hearing the next month, Charles Marks listened to the defense lawyers' last pleas for leniency, then icily called the three defendants before him and confirmed a mandatory sentence of life in prison. As the session ended, Peter Sabbatino, the street-smart defense attorney, had a last comment for the self-satisfied judge. "I don't think you have a solution here," Sabbatino predicted, "that history will support."

PART TWO

INSPIRATION

1966–1972

FOUR

The Autobiography

For Barney Rosset, it was Malcolm X's death that made the chance to publish the story of his life so enticing. Born and raised in Chicago, the son of a bank president, Rosset had dropped out of two colleges and served as an Army officer in the Pacific during World War II before purchasing the small Grove Press publishing house with a loan from his father. Rail-thin and restlessly energetic, Barney displayed a disdain for convention and a talent for provocative marketing from a young age: at twelve, he started a school newspaper called *Anti-Everything*. At Grove Press, he deployed those personal traits as a business strategy. Defying censors and prudes, and sometimes ending up in court, he published previously banned erotic fiction including *Lady Chatterley's Lover* and the novels of Henry Miller, and used the proceeds to champion Beat poets and translations of playwright Samuel Beckett and revolutionary Che Guevara. Before Rosset knew anything about Malcolm X's personal backstory, he confessed, he viewed Malcolm as a bit of "a fringe person"—until murder was added to the picture. When asked what made him suddenly see the potential for a successful book, Rosset replied bluntly: "Malcolm got assassinated, that's number one."

On the Monday morning after Malcolm's death, Rosset arrived at the Grove Press headquarters on lower Broadway and read the front-page story about the murder in *The New York Times* and listened to other accounts on the radio. At nine o'clock, his lieutenants came into Rosset's office for their morning staff meeting, and Malcolm was the first topic of conversation. "It had to be Elijah Muhammad's people," said Richard "Dick" Seaver, the top editorial deputy. Another Army vet who lived in France after World War II and translated French authors on the side, Seaver had become friendly with Malcolm's confidant, Benjamin 2X Goodman, and heard details from him about Malcolm's bitter split from the NOI. Rosset himself wondered aloud about the involvement of the FBI and the CIA. Meanwhile, others zeroed in on the implications for the memoir Malcolm was said to be writing for Grove's larger and more commercial competitor, Doubleday. "To me, what makes it worse, we'll never get to read his autobiography," said Harry Braverman, Grove's in-house expert on radical economics.

Decades later, memories would differ about what happened next. According to Dick Seaver, Rosset called another nine a.m. staff meeting just three days later. When his colleagues walked into his office, Seaver recalled, Rosset had "a slight smile of triumph on his face."

"I have some interesting news," Rosset reported. "Doubleday have renounced their rights to publish Malcolm's autobiography. It seems they're concerned for the safety of their employees. What would keep whoever killed Malcolm, they're saying, from using violence against his publishers? The book apparently attacks the Nation of Islam pretty viciously."

"Then we should publish the book," Seaver recalled saying, to a chorus of agreement in the room.

When Rosset warned about "the risk of retaliation," Seaver recalled, the response from the controversy-hardened Grove editors was "a collective shrug."

According to this account, Rosset immediately contacted the agent for the book, identified as Malcolm Reiss at the Paul R. Reynolds literary agency. Reiss then set up a meeting with Malcolm's collaborator, Alex Haley, described by Seaver as "an amiable, intelligent, slightly overweight black man who had served in the U.S. Navy for twenty years . . . and retired with the goal of becoming a writer and with the luxury of a government pension that allowed him to live frugally and indulge his fantasy." Haley told the Grove editors that the book was almost finished, and that until days before the assassination Malcolm had been scheduled to visit him in upstate New York to go over it one last time. Rosset agreed to buy the rights on the spot, Seaver recalled, and only afterward did Reiss send them two carbon copies of the manuscript. "We read it immediately and we were overwhelmed," Seaver recalled. "Remarkable. Deeply intelligent. Shorn of any self-indulgence. True, it would need work, but the essential was there."

Correspondence and testimony from Doubleday and the agents involved in the deal told a different story. Alex Haley was indeed a client of the Paul R. Reynolds firm, the oldest literary agency in the country, founded in 1893 by Paul Revere Reynolds Sr., a descendant of the Revolutionary War hero. Reynolds's son, Paul R. Reynolds Jr., had taken over the firm and gone on to represent an impressive roster of authors who ranged from the bestselling potboiler writer Irving Wallace to Richard Wright. Initially, when the editor of Doubleday had raised the prospect of getting a book out of Malcolm X after Haley had interviewed him for *Playboy*, the patrician Reynolds was horrified and advised Haley against it. Reynolds changed his mind, however, after learning from his daughter, a student at the University of Pennsylvania, what an enthusiastic response Malcolm received from students when he spoke at that campus.

Haley's correspondence confirms that Paul Reynolds was his key point of contact in developing the autobiography project and negotiating the publishing deal with Doubleday. Although Malcolm Reiss may have played some role in getting the manuscript to Grove Press, he was still preoccupied with his own fiction agency in 1965 and didn't join the Reynolds agency full-time until a year later. The future head of the Reynolds agency, John Hawkins, recalled that after Doubleday pulled out of their deal, the agents went to Grove Press, not the other way around, and later in the winter of 1965 after getting turned down by several other publishing houses. That timeline is supported by a letter that Doubleday's editor in chief, Ken McCormick, wrote to Haley on March 16—three weeks after the assassination—informing him for the first time that Doubleday was pulling out of the deal and that he had authorized Paul Reynolds to show it to other publishers. "In a policy decision at Doubleday, where I was a minor contrary vote,"

McCormick informed Haley, "it was decided that we could not pub-lish the Malcolm X book. I want you to know how much I respect the enormous energy and inspiration you poured into that book."

All the accounts agree that Grove paid $20,000 for the rights to the book and planned a first hardcover printing of ten thousand cop-ies, a modest number even by its niche standards. Seaver recalled concerns about whether white readers would buy the book, and how many white-owned bookstores would agree to sell it, particularly in the segregationist South and conservative West and Midwest. Rosset himself was unmoved by the part of the story involving the Nation of Islam, but impressed with Malcolm's "strong attitude on behalf of black people—his call to self-reliance and equality." So for the cover of the hardcover edition, Rosset chose a photograph of Malcolm that made him look like a disheveled professor, in a light suit with his tie askew and an intent look on his face behind the horn-rimmed glasses. In what amounted to a crash timetable in the publishing world, Seaver went to work with Haley to meet a publishing deadline of October 1965. The hope at the time, Seaver recalled, wasn't to rack up sales but to get a few respectful reviews, the kind that would mark *The Autobiography of Malcolm X* as a serious book and an important contribution to the national conversation on racial issues.

Alex Haley inherited his sense of ambition from his father and his gift for dramatic storytelling from his grandmother and great-aunts. As Alex liked to put it, his father, Simon Haley, "bootstrapped" his way out of the sharecropping fields of North Carolina, working as a railway porter and doing other odd jobs to pay for an education that led him to positions as dean of agricultural studies at several historically Black colleges. Meanwhile, Alex's grandmother Cynthia and her sisters raised him and his two younger brothers after their mother, Bertha, passed away when the boys were still children. Sitting on their front porches, dipping snuff, the elderly women regaled Alex with stories of his an-cestors, beginning with a slave named Kunta Kinte, who was brought to America from Africa in the Middle Passage and would later serve as the inspiration for Haley's bestselling novel, *Roots*.

A wayward student, Haley dropped out of college at the age of eighteen and enrolled in the Coast Guard (not the U.S. Navy, as Dick Seaver would later recall). He was assigned to kitchen mess hall duty and relieved the boredom of long days at sea in the Pacific during World War II by helping shipmates write love letters to their sweethearts at home. When the war was over, he applied for transfer to the Coast Guard's public relations department, and began to sell freelance articles to various publications. By the time he had put in his twenty years and was eligible to retire with a small pension, Haley had been recognized for his writing talent with a title created especially for him: "Chief Journalist" of the Coast Guard.

The year was 1959, and Haley began his new career as a full-time writer by moving with his wife and two children to New York City and getting a job at *Reader's Digest*, the monthly collection of short articles about American life that at the time was the bestselling publication in the country. Before retiring from the Coast Guard, Haley had heard from a friend about a "black man's religion" that was winning converts in Detroit. He started gathering information about the Nation of Islam, which had come to wider public attention that year with the airing of the sensationalist five-part television series *The Hate That Hate Produced*, hosted by Mike Wallace. A liberal Republican himself, Haley pitched the story to the rock-rib conservative editors of *Reader's Digest*. The editors sent him back a letter saying they would be interested in a story that conveyed, as he later put it, both "what is said against this organization" but also "what they say of themselves."

Haley began his reporting by going to Harlem in search of Malcolm X. Walking into the Muslim restaurant down the street from Mosque No. 7, he found Malcolm making a call from a phone booth. When Malcolm emerged, Haley approached and conveyed his intention to write a story about the Nation of Islam.

Malcolm eyed him suspiciously. "You're another one of the white man's tools sent to spy!" he said.

Haley explained that he was on assignment for *Reader's Digest* and produced the letter from his editors.

"Well, you should certainly know that nothing the white man writes and signs is worth the paper it is written on," Malcolm shot back.

Malcolm said he would need time to consider the request, but in the meantime invited Haley to attend open meetings at the mosque. Several days later, Malcolm summoned Haley back to the restaurant and informed him that he would have to seek permission directly from Elijah Muhammad. After clearing the expense of a plane ticket with *Reader's Digest*, Haley flew to Chicago and was invited to dine with Elijah Muhammad at his home. Muhammad never mentioned the *Reader's Digest* piece, and instead complained in a soft voice about being persecuted by the FBI and the IRS. But afterward he communicated his approval to Malcolm, and as soon as Haley returned to New York he started to get more cooperation.

Published in the March 1960 edition of *Reader's Digest*, Haley's article made good on the promise to present both sides of the Nation of Islam story. Titled "Mr. Muhammad Speaks," it focused on the NOI leader, portraying him as both dangerous and highly influential. "As head of a fast-growing, anti-white, anti-Christian cult," Haley began, "this mild-looking man is considered 'the most powerful black man in America.'" While quoting critics who used terms like "black fascism," Haley gave a respectful account of the NOI's reach, estimating that it had attracted seventy thousand followers to fifty "Temples of Islam" in twenty-seven states. Haley ended the piece by describing the NOI's growth as a wake-up call to right-thinking Americans of both races. "It is important for Christianity and democracy to help remove the Negroes' honest grievances," he wrote, "and thus eliminate the appeal of such a potent racist cult." After the story appeared, Haley received a letter from Muhammad thanking him for upholding his promise to be even-handed in presenting the NOI story. On the heels of the letter, Haley also received a complimentary phone call from Malcolm X, who was grateful to have been mentioned only briefly as Muhammad's "whip-smart assistant."

Two and a half years later, Haley approached the NOI leaders again for an article to appear in *The Saturday Evening Post*. This time, he was one of two reporters on the story, along with a white contributor to the *Post* named Alfred Balk who, it would later be revealed, relied on the FBI for much of his information about the Black Muslim movement. Published in the January 26, 1963, issue, the resulting piece was far more critical of Elijah Muhammad and of the NOI as a whole than the *Reader's Digest* story, while paying far more positive attention to Malcolm X. Titled "Black Merchants of Hate," it described Muhammad as a "short, rather unimpressive-looking man" who preached an "insidious" doctrine of Black supremacy and presided over "hate-filled rallies" while commanding a paltry "hard core of 5,500 to 6,000" full-fledged NOI members. By contrast, Malcolm was depicted as a "lanky, energetic, good-looking man" with a devoted congregation in Harlem who, with a flick of his hand, had called off a brewing riot after one of his followers was clubbed by police.

Based on these new interviews, Haley also touched on Malcolm's personal life for the first time, evoking his "bitter memories" of childhood. Malcolm described his father as a Baptist preacher who had moved his wife and eight children from Omaha, Nebraska, to Lansing, Michigan, where he was targeted for being "too aggressive on racial matters." When Malcolm was six, his father was found dead on the streetcar tracks with his "head bashed in and his body mangled," Malcolm told Haley. "We almost starved to death." Haley described how Malcolm had left Michigan after the eighth grade and moved to Boston and then to Harlem, where he was known as "Big Red" and fell into a life of drug use, hustling, and petty crime. Convicted of larceny at the age of twenty-one, Malcolm embraced the Nation of Islam in prison both as a means of putting his life in order and of assigning blame for his father's death and his teenage descent. "When I heard the white man was a devil," he told Haley, "it clicked."

In the next paragraph, Haley and Balk drew a line from Malcolm's youthful struggles and prison epiphany to his new life of faith and militancy. "Articulate, single-minded, the fire of bitterness still burning in his soul, Malcolm X travels the country—organizing, encouraging, trouble-shooting in local Muslim organizations," they wrote. "He appears on radio-TV interviews and speaks and debates on street corners, in Muslim temples and on college campuses. Malcolm X and his wife, a former nurse, are so dedicated to militant accomplishment of Muslim goals that they named one daughter Attila [*sic*] (for the leader of the Huns) and another Qubillah [*sic*] (after Kublai Khan). While Muhammad appears to be training his son Wallace to succeed him when he retires or dies, many Muslims feel that Malcolm is too powerful to be denied the leadership if he wants it."

For the FBI, *The Saturday Evening Post* piece served the destabilizing purpose its agents had intended when they leaked their intelligence on the NOI to Alfred Balk. The story hinted at growing tension between Malcolm and Elijah Muhammad, and behind the scenes that rift grew even wider with suspicions that Malcolm had deliberately spun Haley to elevate himself and diminish the Messenger. For Haley, meanwhile, the interviews for the *Saturday Evening Post* suggested that there was a good deal more to be mined in Malcolm's compelling life story. And as it happened, he had just begun to cultivate a relationship with another publication that would allow him to take his connection to the complex Black militant leader to the next level: Hugh Hefner's *Playboy* magazine.

In 1962, almost a decade after founding *Playboy*, publisher Hugh Hefner was looking for new ways to add more intellectual substance to the magazine's mix of naked pinups, risqué cartoons and jokes, and short stories and features about the life of the dating single man. The previous year, Hefner had launched another magazine, called *Show Business Illustrated*, only to fold it when it failed to make a profit. But that business flop gave Hefner an idea for a new feature to incorporate into *Playboy*: in-depth interviews with high-profile celebrities. At his Chicago headquarters Hefner summoned a young associate editor named Murray Fisher and told him to look through the defunct spinoff for unpublished stories that might be converted to the question-and-answer format.

As it happened, Alex Haley had submitted a profile to *Show Business Illustrated* of Miles Davis, the jazz trumpeter, in which Davis spoke in unvarnished terms about the racism he experienced despite his worldwide fame. Fisher contacted Haley and encouraged him to seek more time with the irascible jazz superstar. Reluctant at first, Davis consented only after Haley tracked him down at a boxing gym and accepted his invitation to spar in the ring. Condensed and shaped by Fisher, Davis's provocative exchanges with Haley were published in the

September 1962 issue as the first ever *"Playboy* Interview"—the offering that would go on to gain renown as "the No. 2 feature" that made that magazine's reputation.

Having pioneered the format, Haley and Fisher began to discuss inviting Malcolm X to be their next interview subject. They knew it wouldn't be an easy sell, not only because *Playboy* was a white publication but also because its libertine values were so at odds with the ascetic teachings of the Nation of Islam. But they calculated correctly that Malcolm would find it hard to resist the chance to reach the magazine's nationwide audience, and to shore up his relationship with NOI headquarters by taking the opportunity to heap praise on Elijah Muhammad. Malcolm warily accepted Haley's offer and agreed to meet over several days at a corner table of the Muslim diner in Harlem—a multistage process that would become standard practice for the *Playboy* interview. Conjuring up the scene, *Playboy's* editors described Malcolm calmly sipping "African coffee" and whispering asides to hovering aides, while speaking not with the scary zeal of a separatist fanatic but "the impersonal tone of a self-assured executive."

Published over nine pages in the May 1963 issue, Haley's interview defied the prevailing stereotypes of Malcolm and the Nation of Islam in several other telling ways. On the one hand, Malcolm went out of his way to pay deference to Elijah Muhammad, describing him as the "one leader who has the qualifications necessary to unite all elements of black people in America" and swatting away Haley's attempt to suggest that Malcolm was poised to replace him. "I personally don't think I or anyone else am worthy to succeed Mr. Muhammad," Malcolm insisted. He also dutifully echoed Muhammad's calls for physical separation of the races and theories of Black genetic superiority, claiming that Christ, Beethoven, and Columbus all had Black blood.

Yet at the same time, Malcolm challenged the perception of the Nation of Islam as a narrow cult. He argued that millions of middle-class Blacks who worshipped as Christians and publicly aligned themselves with Martin Luther King Jr. silently supported the Black Muslims and their gospel of racial pride and self-reliance. "Now you'll hear the bourgeois Negro pretending to be alienated [from the NOI]," Malcolm said, "but they're just making the white man think they don't go for what

Mr. Muhammad is saying. This Negro will say he's so against us, he's just protecting the crumbs he gets from the white man's table."

Far from ranting about the evils of white people, Malcolm projected a cool indifference to white support—even from the sort of well-intentioned liberals who were likely to read *Playboy*. He accused white backers of the civil rights movement of giving Blacks a false sense of racial progress, and declared that he preferred the "candor of the Southern segregationist to the hypocrisy of the Northern integrationist." Commenting on Jewish support for the civil rights movement, Malcolm gave an answer that contained both crass stereotypes—ones that he would later repudiate, if never entirely shed—and a grudging admiration for the way American Jews had dealt with their own marginalized status. "The Jew is always anxious to advise the black man," Malcolm said. "But they never advise him how to solve the problem the way Jews solved their problem. The Jew never went sitting-in and crawling-in and sliding-in and freedom riding, like he teaches and helps Negroes to do. The Jews stood up, and stood together, and they used their ultimate power, the economic weapon."

Most memorably, Malcolm added provocative new details to the personal story that Haley had started to outline in *The Saturday Evening Post*—and in his own voice. He revealed that his father was not only a Baptist preacher but also "a militant follower of Marcus Garvey," the early-twentieth-century Black nationalist who exhorted American Blacks to seek a separate homeland in Africa or the Caribbean. Recounting his father's death on the trolley tracks in Lansing, Michigan, Malcolm charged that local white supremacists had targeted his father for "preaching Garvey's message." He explained that he had inherited his light skin from his mulatto mother, who was the daughter of a woman who had been raped by a white man. "I hate every drop of white blood in me," Malcolm declared. He described how after his father's death, he became a "public ward" and was sent to an all-white school, where he excelled at class and sports before quitting after the eighth grade. He also dramatized the descent into a life of crime that had preceded his imprisonment and discovery of the Nation of Islam. "I was in numbers, bootleg liquor, 'hot' goods, women," Malcolm told Haley. "I sold the bodies of black women to white men, and white women to black men. I was in dope. I was in everything evil you could name."

To illustrate the dramatic arc of his odyssey, Malcolm harked back to the Harvard event at which Peter Goldman had first encountered him two years earlier. "I often think, sir," Malcolm told Haley, "that in 1946, I was sentenced to 8 to 10 years in Cambridge, Massachusetts as a common thief who had never passed the eighth grade. And the next time I went back to Cambridge was in March 1961, as a guest speaker at the Harvard Law School forum. This is the best example of Mr. Muhammad's ability to take nothing and make somebody."

Throughout his series of meetings with Haley, Malcolm expressed skepticism that the white editors of *Playboy* would actually go through with publishing many of the things he said in the interview. "You know that devil's not going to print that!" he blurted several times. When the issue with the interview came out in late April 1963, Malcolm was astonished to see it on newsstands. "[Malcolm] was very much taken aback when *Playboy* kept its word," Haley recalled, and he "began to warm up to me somewhat." For the first time, Malcolm started to call Haley unprompted, alerting him to speeches and television appearances and inviting him to functions at the Harlem mosque.

One *Playboy* reader who was intrigued by the Malcolm interview was Ken McCormick of Doubleday, then the largest book publisher in America. A modest but keenly perceptive man with a track record of editing writers as varied as Somerset Maugham and Dwight Eisenhower, McCormick saw the potential for a memoir about Malcolm's life, and he reached out to Haley's agent, Paul Reynolds, to set up a lunch meeting. When McCormick asked what more Haley knew about Malcolm beyond what had appeared in *Playboy*, he mentioned Malcolm's obsession with punctuality and spartan, caffeine-fueled diet. But otherwise, Haley recalled, "I realized how little I knew about the man personally, despite all my interviews."

Haley agreed to present the book proposal idea to Malcolm. They met at the Muslim restaurant, and Malcolm responded with a startled expression. "It was one of the few times I have ever seen him uncertain," Haley recalled.

"I will have to give the book a lot of thought," Malcolm answered warily.

Two days later, Malcolm summoned Haley back to the restaurant. "I'll agree," he said. "I think my life story may help people to appreciate better how Mr. Muhammad salvages black people." But Malcolm had two conditions: that any of his earnings from the book go to the Nation of Islam, and that Elijah Muhammad himself approve the project.

Now seventy years old and suffering from severe bronchitis, Muhammad had relocated from Chicago to a vacation home in Phoenix, Arizona, that had been purchased with NOI funds. Haley flew to Phoenix and was granted a one-on-one audience. If Muhammad felt any personal resentment that Malcolm was being offered a book deal, he hid it behind hoarse ramblings about the Nation of Islam's success in saving lost souls and a vague offer to Haley to come to work as an in-house writer for the NOI. Then a coughing fit came on, and Muhammad hurriedly granted his consent before scurrying out of the room.

"Allah approves," Muhammad gasped. "Malcolm is one of my most outstanding ministers."

Back in New York, Haley and Malcolm signed a "Memorandum of Agreement" with Doubleday on May 27, 1963, to produce "an untitled non-fiction book" of 80,000 to 100,000 words. They agreed to an advance of $20,000 to be split evenly between them, with a payment of $2,500 each up front. The initial deadline for turning in the manuscript was set for October 1963, and Malcolm stipulated that his share of any future royalties after publication go to the Nation of Islam. In June, Doubleday distributed internal guidance to its staff estimating that between hardcover and paperback editions, the book would sell fifteen thousand copies in its first year of publication, and as many as twenty thousand copies over time.

Haley then drafted a separate letter to Malcolm outlining the terms of their collaboration. Haley promised that "not a sentence, a paragraph, or a chapter" would appear in the book without Malcolm's approval, and that anything Malcolm wanted to see in the book would be included. In exchange, Malcolm agreed to submit to a series of extended interviews on a regular timetable. Later, Haley would extract an additional promise that he could write a commentary at the end of the book without showing it to Malcolm. Over the summer of 1963, Malcolm began visiting Haley's studio apartment in Greenwich Village two or three times a week, usually arriving around nine in the evening and staying for around three hours before driving his blue Oldsmobile home to Queens.

For Haley, the process was extremely slow and frustrating at first. Malcolm would arrive at each session making only half-joking suggestions that the apartment was bugged. "Testing, testing, one, two, three . . ." he said as he entered Haley's studio, carrying a businessman's hard leather briefcase. Rebuffing invitations to talk about his personal life, Malcolm kept repeating jargon from his public speeches, full of obsequious praise for "the Honorable Elijah Muhammad." A devout Christian and proud veteran, Haley had to tolerate Malcolm's mocking of the Black church and the U.S. military. After several months, Haley was on the verge of giving up the project and returning his advance when he stumbled upon a way to break through Malcolm's defenses.

Haley noticed that Malcolm kept looking for pieces of paper to make notes, so he began placing napkins by his side when he served coffee. After the sessions, Haley gathered up the napkin scraps and tried to detect clues as to what Malcolm was really thinking. He found one note that conveyed a strong suspicion of women, so at the next session Haley pressed Malcolm on the subject. "You can never trust any woman," Malcolm replied, adding that he had told even his wife, Betty, that he only trusted her 75 percent. "I don't completely trust anyone," Malcolm told Haley, adding, "You, I trust about twenty-five percent."

A few days later, Malcolm arrived in Greenwich Village in a particularly nasty and distracted mood. As he paced back and forth ranting about the events of his day, Haley asked: "I wonder if you'd tell me something about your mother." Suddenly Malcolm stood still. He looked at Haley for a long time, then began pacing again, but more slowly and in a narrow circle. He said he could picture his mother, Louise Little, bent over a stove, in a worn gray dress, trying to make a full meal for her large family out of whatever food was in the house. That mental image seemed to unlock something inside him, and from then on Malcolm started to talk in a stream-of-consciousness fashion about his early childhood.

The memories started with a story his mother had told Malcolm about a life-changing event that occurred when he was still in the womb. The Ku Klux Klan raided the family's house in Omaha, Nebraska, while Malcolm's father, Earl Little, was out of town preaching, smashing windows and terrifying his wife and their young children. As soon as Louise gave birth to Malcolm, Earl moved the family to Wisconsin and then to Lansing. But in Lansing, too, Earl was targeted, by a local white supremacist organization called the Black Legion. When Malcolm was three, the Little house burned to ground, and his parents told their children that the Black Legion had done it to punish Earl for being an "uppity nigger."

An imposing man of six foot four who had been raised in rural Georgia and dropped out of school after the fourth grade, Earl Little dressed the part of a man of learning, favoring bow ties and round rimmed glasses. Raised on the West Indies island of Grenada, Louise Little was more educated than her husband and spoke with an elegant Caribbean lilt. Malcolm recalled that his mother would often correct his father, sometimes enraging him so much that he beat her. Louise also had delicate features and very light skin, a genetic inheritance from the older white man in Grenada who had gotten her Black mother pregnant. Louise viewed her own conception as an act of rape, Malcolm told Haley, and she projected that shame onto him, treating him more harshly than his brothers and sisters because of his tawny complexion.

Earl favored Malcolm, meanwhile, for his good looks and prized birth order as the seventh of his eleven children, three with a former wife. Malcolm shared warm recollections of his father taking him on the road, where the young boy would sit rapt as the strapping preacher stirred crowds with sermons on the Bible and lectures on the nationalist message of Marcus Garvey. Yet it was images of his mother that Malcolm associated with his father's demise on the streetcar tracks of Lansing. One evening, Earl abruptly announced that he was going into town, and Louise called after him, possessed by a vision that he was in danger. In the wee hours, Malcolm heard her screaming when police arrived at the house. The next morning, Malcolm learned that his father was dead, but not from his mother, who was shut up in her bedroom in a state of delirium that continued through Earl's funeral days later.

Cheated out of an insurance payout by a company that insisted Earl had committed suicide, Louise struggled to support her children on her own and slowly sank into dementia. When Malcolm was thirteen, she was sent to a state mental institution in Kalamazoo, Michigan, where she would spend the next twenty-six years and reach the point where she no longer recognized Malcolm when he visited. "I can't describe how I felt," he told Haley. "The woman who had brought me into the world, and nursed me, and advised me, and chastised me, and loved me, didn't know me. It was as if I was trying to walk up the side of a hill of feathers. I looked at her. I listened to her 'talk.' But there was nothing that I could do."

After starting to talk to Haley about his mother, Malcolm worked up the courage to visit her in Kalamazoo for the first time in decades—a trip that opened the floodgates of memory even wider. In mid-November 1963, Haley wrote to Paul Reynolds and his editors at Doubleday to describe a letter he had received from Malcolm. "It may shock you to learn that two weeks ago I had dinner with my mother for the first time in 25 years and she is now home and residing with my brother in Lansing, Michigan," Malcolm reported. "It was only after opening up and speaking quite freely about her to you during the interview that the subconscious block I had erected was removed, enabling me to remember many things that I had blocked out of my mind."

After listening to Malcolm's vivid recollections of his early childhood for several months, Haley felt he had enough material to start the book. But having never written anything of that length before, he was at a loss as to how to organize the rest. Then he reminded himself that he knew how to write for periodicals, and decided to think of each chapter as its own magazine story, with a theme and a catchy beginning and end. From that epiphany flowed the ultimate shape of the book, with each leg in Malcolm's journey marked by a vivid chapter title.

In chapters titled "Nightmare," "Mascot," and "Homeboy," Malcolm would tell of losing both his parents and of being shunted from reform school to foster parents before he ran away to live with his sister in Boston. In "Laura," "Harlemite," "Detroit Red," and "Hustler," he would chronicle his move to New York City and brief descent into the world of hustling and drug dealing, before he escaped a vengeful Black mob boss in a chapter called "Trapped" and was arrested and sent to prison in a chapter called "Caught." The crime was breaking and entering to snatch back a stolen watch that he had pawned, but Malcolm attributed the harsh ten-year sentence handed down by the court to the judge's disdain when he found out that he had a white girlfriend who served as a lookout.

In "Satan" and "Saved," Malcolm described his violent behavior when first sent to a Massachusetts prison in Charlestown, followed by his transfer to the state's Norfolk Prison Colony, where he met a fellow convict who convinced him that the path to liberation for the Black man began with seeking knowledge. At the age of twenty-two, Malcolm honed his reading and writing skills by copying a dictionary, joined the prison debate team, and went to sleep each night reading books from the prison library on subjects ranging from Greek and Roman philosophy to the history of slavery and European colonialism.

"I have often reflected on the new vistas that reading opened to me," Malcolm would recall. "I knew right there in prison that reading had changed forever the course of my life. As I see it today, the ability to read awoke inside me some long dormant craving to be mentally alive. I certainly wasn't seeking any degree, the way a college confers status upon its students. My homemade education gave me, with every additional book that I read, a little bit more sensitivity to the deafness, dumbness, and blindness that was afflicting the black race in America. Not long ago, an English writer telephoned me from London, asking questions. One was, 'What's your alma mater?' I told him, 'Books.' You will never catch me with a free fifteen minutes in which I'm not studying something I feel might be able to help the black man."

While Malcolm was behind bars, he was introduced to the Black Muslim movement in letters from his older brothers and sisters, who had become converts. He gradually embraced the faith and began writing what would become scores of letters to Elijah Muhammad. In a chapter titled "Savior," he would tell of being released from prison after six years and traveling to Chicago to offer up his life in service to the Messenger. By the thirteenth chapter in the book, he would be "Minister Malcolm X," the head of the Harlem mosque and Muhammad's most visible and fervent national apostle, spreading the word of the Nation of Islam in subsequent chapters called "Black Muslims" and "Icarus" that charted his rise to national prominence as a sought-after speaker and media lightning rod.

As the end of 1963 neared, Haley was confident he had the makings of a powerful sin-to-salvation story reminiscent of *The Confessions of St. Augustine*. Over the previous months, he had also discovered another way of disarming his wary subject. Haley introduced Malcolm to a childhood friend from Tennessee named George Sims, who was a fellow avid reader. Haley would invite Sims to his apartment on evenings when Malcolm was there, and the two men would fall into long conversations about Shakespeare and other favorite authors that he had started reading in the Norfolk Prison Colony. Those exchanges helped make Malcolm forget about the troubles of the day and put him in a positive mood to field questions for the book.

One night during this period, Haley was awoken by phone call at four in the morning. It was Malcolm, calling from Los Angeles, where he was on a speaking trip.

"Alex Haley?" Malcolm said without identifying himself.

"Yes?" Haley answered sleepily, recognizing the voice. "Oh, hey, Malcolm."

"I trust you seventy percent," Malcolm said.

———

Until it became public, Haley had detected only slight hints of the strain between Malcolm and Elijah Muhammad. After a white admirer called out to Malcolm from a car window, he joked that he would like to form a "white chapter" of his followers, then immediately forbade Haley ever to write about the comment. "Mr. Muhammad would have a fit," Malcolm said. But it wasn't until a day after it happened, in December 1963, that Haley learned about Muhammad's suspension of Malcolm for his comments about the Kennedy assassination.

As they were wrapping up a long night's work on the book, Malcolm told Haley to call him in the morning, when he alerted him to the first news stories coming out about the suspension. Sounding shaken, Malcolm instructed Haley to meet him at the offices of *Muhammad Speaks* in Harlem. There, Malcolm fielded a stream of concerned phone calls from supporters and reporters such as Peter Goldman of *Newsweek*. Although Malcolm told the callers that he accepted the decision, Haley noticed that his voice was full of hurt and his neck had turned bright red.

Despite that turn of events, Haley believed that he already had enough of Malcolm's personal story to write the redemption tale he originally envisioned. He started to present Malcolm with a few draft chapters, on which Malcolm scribbled editing notes with a red-ink pen. ("Kids are goats!" Malcolm objected when he saw the word used as a synonym for children.) In February 1964, Malcolm flew to Miami to watch Muhammad Ali, then still known as Cassius Clay, fight Sonny Liston for the heavyweight boxing title. Malcolm had befriended Clay several years earlier when the boxer first started showing interest in the Nation of Islam, and after Clay's upset victory over Liston, Malcolm stood by his side when he confirmed the rumors of his ties to the NOI to the media.

But a sign of how damaged Malcolm's own relationship with the NOI had grown came when Haley asked for help in getting the new champ to sit for a *Playboy* interview. "I think you had better ask somebody else to do that," Malcolm replied. Soon afterward, Haley received an anxious letter from Malcolm at the house in upstate New York that he had rented to work on the book. Malcolm asked if the book contract could be amended to direct his proceeds not to the NOI but to his new organization, Muslim Mosque Inc., or to Betty if he should die. Then he added a P.S.: "How is it possible to write one's autobiography in a world so fast-changing as this?"

That narrative dilemma became inescapable a month later, when Malcolm announced that he was severing all ties with the NOI. Now both he and Haley realized that their initial story line and timetable for the autobiography had been completely overtaken. For the first time, Haley also heard Malcolm voice direct criticism of Elijah Muhammad. Malcolm insisted that he, not Muhammad, deserved credit for expanding the NOI's hard-core membership exponentially, to some 400,000, over the previous decade. He also disputed the NOI's explanation for his suspension. The swipe at President Kennedy "wasn't the real reason at all," Malcolm said. "I made stronger statements before. . . . [It was] jealousy in Chicago, and I had objected to the immorality of the man who professed to be more moral than anyone."

Listening to these new attacks, Haley grew worried that Malcolm might want to revise the chapters that had already been written, to eliminate praise for Elijah Muhammad or minimize his influence on Malcolm's prison conversion and rise within the NOI. Coming back from upstate to meet Malcolm in person, Haley argued that the story would be more dramatic if the early chapters reflected how he felt about Muhammad at the time, and didn't telegraph to readers how those feelings would later change. Malcolm responded that he had also been pondering that question and had reached the same conclusion. "I'm going to let it stand the way I've told it," Malcolm promised. "I want the book to be the way it was."

With Haley writing at his upstate house and Malcolm scrambling to launch a new movement, evening-long interviews were no longer possible. So in fleeting phone calls and brief road trips, Haley gathered material for a new chapter, called "Out," that detailed Malcolm's exit from the Nation of Islam. Then in late March 1964, Malcolm informed Haley that he would be making his first pilgrimage to the Islamic holy cities of Mecca and Medina. During the trip, Malcolm wrote Haley excited postcards and letters describing the wider world of Islam he was discovering, all signed with the new name he had taken: "El-Hajj Malik El-Shabazz." Sporting a new reddish goatee, Malcolm returned to give a press conference at the Hotel Theresa, where he described to reporters how the trip had transformed his outlook on the racial struggle at home and abroad. "My trip to Mecca has opened my eyes," he confessed. "I no longer subscribe to racism. I have adjusted my thinking to the point where I believe that whites are human beings . . . as long as this is borne out by their humane attitude toward Negroes."

Haley would describe the profound impact of Malcolm's 1964 travels on his spiritual and political thinking in new book chapters titled "Mecca" and "El-Hajj Malik El-Shabazz." Returning from a second Africa trip that fall, Malcolm asked Haley to drive down from his upstate house to meet him at JFK Airport in Queens. Pulling out a diary he had kept during his travels, Malcolm sketched out his thoughts about the global ties he was forging that he asked Haley to incorporate into the book. "What I want to stress is that I was trying to internationalize our problem, to make the Africans feel their kinship with us as Afro-Americans," Malcolm said as Haley took notes. "I made them think about it, that they are our blood brothers, and we all came from the same forefathers. That's why the Africans loved me, the same way the Asians [Malcolm met at Mecca] loved me because I was religious."

In a final chapter, "1965," Haley would convey, in Malcolm's voice, the pan-Africanist and other alliance-building ideas he was developing in the first two months of that year. But Haley would save for his own "Epilogue"—the first-person commentary that Malcolm had agreed could be added to the book without his review—what he saw of the messy reality of Malcolm's life in those last weeks. Six months after announcing the formation of his new political movement, the Organization of Afro-American Unity, Malcolm was struggling to counter the growing perception around Harlem that the new group wasn't accomplishing anything, and that its purpose and message weren't clear. Attendance at the OAAU's sporadic rallies at the Audubon Ballroom was dwindling, making it harder to raise funds. To ease the financial strain, Haley persuaded his book agent, Paul Reynolds, to advance Malcolm a payment against future profits from the book, but weeks later the money was gone. "It's evaporated," Malcolm said sheepishly. "I don't know where."

Much would later be written about how haunted Malcolm appeared in these last weeks, as death threats against him mounted. But in Haley's telling, Malcolm was just as upset about the prospect of losing his house in Queens as the NOI took legal action to evict him and his family. "A home is really the only thing I've provided Betty since we've been married, and they want to take that away," he lamented to Haley. The symbolic importance that Malcolm attached to the house as a refuge for his family was reflected in his decision to allow a young Black photographer named Don Hogan Charles, then on assignment for *Ebony* magazine, to take a picture of him standing in front of a window in his living room peeking through the curtains as he hoisted an

M1 carbine rifle in the air. In his epilogue, Haley would surmise that it was anger over the eviction order that caused Malcolm to ramp up his public feud with Elijah Muhammad in early 1965, accusing him of "religious fakery" and traveling to Los Angeles to encourage two former secretaries who had filed paternity suits against Muhammad to persist with their case in the face of NOI intimidation.

On Saturday, February 20, the day before the assassination, Haley received a phone call from Malcolm at 3:30 in the afternoon. At first, he didn't recognize the voice, which he described as sounding "as if he had a heavy, deep cold." Malcolm was calling to talk once again about real estate—and book advances. He described to Haley how, after being firebombed out of his home, he had returned with moving men to haul away the family's smoke-filled furniture and other belongings before the court ordered them thrown out on the street. He also reported that he had taken Betty shopping for a new house, and they had found a modest property in a predominantly Jewish section of Long Island that she liked and where they thought their daughters would be safe. But a $3,000 down payment was required, and all he had in the bank was $150. Malcolm asked Haley if he could request another advance from Doubleday against his royalties for the still unpublished autobiography, and Haley promised to make the call to Paul Reynolds on Monday.

Abruptly changing the subject, Malcolm made a comment that for decades afterward would feed the conspiracy theories about what happened at the Audubon Ballroom the following day. He was referring to the failed attempts on his life that had already taken place, and the sudden way French authorities had blocked him from entering their country less than two weeks earlier. "The more I keep thinking about this thing, the things that have been happening lately, I'm not sure that it's the Muslims," Malcolm said. "I know what they can do, and what they can't, and they can't do some of the stuff recently going on. Now, I'm going to tell you, the more I keep thinking about what happened to me in France, I think I'm going to stop saying it's the Muslims."

Then Malcolm pivoted again, and ended the last conversation he would ever have with Haley on an upbeat note. "You know," he said, "I'm glad I've been the first to establish official ties between Afro-Americans and our blood brothers in Africa," and then he hung up.

Alex Haley never hid his desire to turn *The Autobiography of Malcolm X* into a bestseller. That ambition was clear in letters that he wrote to his agent Paul Reynolds and Doubleday's Ken McCormick, before Doubleday dropped the book and it was acquired by Grove Press. "For this man is so hot, so HOT, a subject, I know you agree . . . this man is so pregnant with millions or more sale potential," Haley wrote to the two men with a keen sense of commercial foresight as early as the spring of 1964. Within hours of hearing the news of Malcolm's murder the day after their last phone conversation, Haley fired off another letter to Reynolds that was both mournful and opportunistic. Although "none of us would have it this way," Haley wrote, interest in the book was now at a "peak." Haley pointed to the consolation for Betty Shabazz of hardcover, paperback, and international royalties that could provide a "financial legacy to [Malcolm's] widow and four little daughters."

Haley was now freed from his written promise to get Malcolm's approval for any subsequent decisions made to enhance the salability of the book. Among those choices was to commission an "Introduction" from journalist M. S. Handler of *The New York Times*—one of the few white reporters, along with Peter Goldman and Helen Dudar, whom Malcolm had come to like and trust, and who could reassure white readers uncertain about what to expect from such a controversial Black figure and his still unknown ghostwriter.

For decades afterward, other biographers would identify ways that Haley shaped Malcolm's story to make it more commercial, and to steer the book toward a conclusion that comported with Haley's own more conservative views on racial politics. Reporting would suggest that Haley, perhaps with Malcolm's encouragement, exaggerated the degree of Malcolm's sinfulness in his late teens, in order to make his salvation in his early twenties all the more dramatic. Characters given only first names or nicknames in the book, such as Malcolm's friend "Shorty," were judged to be composites to whom were attributed traits and actions based on more than one person.

Yet if Haley's aim in taking liberties with Malcolm's story was to gain the widest possible readership for the book, he succeeded beyond even his own dreams. When the hardcover edition appeared in October 1965, the first run of ten thousand copies ordered by Grove Press sold briskly, and Barney Rosset ordered fourteen more printings within the year. Just as gratifying to Rosset and Grove editor Dick Seaver, the hardcover received the kind of positive, high-profile reviews for which they had positioned it. "*The Autobiography of Malcolm X* is a brilliant, painful, important book," wrote *New York Times* book critic Eliot Fremont-Smith. "The book raises many difficult questions, and it is a testament parts of which many readers will not approve. But as a document for our time, its insights may be crucial; its relevance cannot be doubted." Shortly after publication, in the influential *New York Review of Books*, a glowing review by the legendary left-wing investigative reporter I. F. Stone was accompanied by a haunting illustration of a gravesite cross toppled over to resemble an "X." "From tape recorded conversations, a Negro writer, Alex Haley, put together the *Autobiography*; he did his job with sensitivity and devotion," Stone wrote. "Here one may read, in the agony of this brilliant Negro's self-creation, the agony of an entire people in search of their identity."

Based on the better-than-expected sales of the $7.50 hardcover edition, Grove Press went all out for the paperback edition, released in the summer of 1966. Rosset ordered a much larger first printing and picked a more arresting image for the book jacket, a close-up photograph of Malcolm clenching his teeth and thrusting his right finger defiantly in the air. Rosset also took a piece of advertising copy that he had written for the hardcover and put it on the cover of the paperback, making the book sound like a thriller as much as a memoir. "He rose from hoodlum, thief, dope peddler, pimp . . . to become the most dynamic leader of the Black Revolution," the paperback cover read. "He said he would be murdered before this book appeared."

Later, Dick Seaver maintained that he and Rosset always thought the book would have its greatest sales potential when it became affordable to a wide audience of Black readers and young people. Sure enough, Grove's pocket-size mass market edition, initially priced at $1.25, proved such a sensation that, according to one report, the book had sold six million copies worldwide by 1977. In the 1980s, after Grove

Press fell on hard times, publication rights were acquired by Ballantine Books. In the following decades, Ballantine would issue scores of new paperback, hardcover, digital, and audio editions, as the *Autobiography* became a fixture of book clubs and of high school and college curricula across America.

But for generations of readers, *The Autobiography of Malcolm X* would have an impact that went beyond the classroom. Whatever its value as a manifesto of political ideas, or a reliable artifact of Black history, the book would strike deep personal chords, particularly for young people struggling with issues of identity, family, community, and the meaning of life. Reading the book would be described as life-changing by impressionable readers from Kareem Abdul-Jabbar, for whom it spurred the decision to embrace the Muslim faith, to the teenage Barack Obama.

As a young man in prison, Malcolm had discovered the unique power of books to communicate across time and space, to allow a Black eighth-grade dropout and convicted thief to commune with the likes of Herodotus, Pliny, and Shakespeare. And so Malcolm's *Autobiography* would allow him to speak to millions in his wake, not in the fiery tone of the man himself but in the intimate, confessional voice on the printed page. That voice spoke of the loss of fathers and mothers; of the quest for identity through changes in name, dress, and location; and of an ever-looming awareness of death. As the literary scholar Albert E. Stone has written, the book took readers on "an actual yet symbolic journey: from west to east, from sin to salvation, from blindness to sight and insight, from distrust to the beginnings of trust, from false social selves to a more authentic identity." The dramatic license taken by Alex Haley to incorporate all these universal themes in Malcolm's testament left much ground for future biographers to dispute. But it also produced a work that has remained timeless in its power to make readers of all backgrounds see themselves in Malcolm's story.

FIVE

Black Power!

In 1952, the same year that Malcolm X was released from prison, an eleven-year-old immigrant named Stokely Carmichael arrived in New York City from Trinidad. Carmichael had been raised on that Caribbean island by a grandmother and three aunts after his parents, a carpenter named Adolphus Carmichael and his wife, May, left for America when Stokely was a baby. But now the grandmother had passed away, and Adolphus and May had sent for Stokely and his sister to join them in the small apartment where they and two younger siblings lived in the Bronx.

Beginning to sprout up into the tall, lanky figure he would have as an adult, Stokely also possessed a winning smile, an absorbent mind, and a fast tongue. After the Carmichaels moved into their own house in the North Bronx, a fixer-upper that Adolphus all but rebuilt, Stokely was admitted to the Bronx High School of Science, a magnet school then housed in a large Gothic building on 184th Street that drew talented students from across New York City. On weekends, the curious teenager also began venturing out to Harlem, where he first encountered Malcolm X, now running the nearby Nation of Islam mosque, among the "step-ladder" speakers who held forth on 125th Street every Saturday.

Carmichael was enthralled with how Malcolm and the other step-ladder speakers conjured up the glories of Black history and the rapid spread of Black anticolonial uprisings around the world. Even more, he was captivated by the way they spoke. "The effect of the speakers on me was more than political, it was rhetorical," Carmichael would recall in a memoir, looking back at his path to becoming the man who later popularized the "Black Power!" cry. "Beyond the message, there was the influence of style," Carmichael observed. "Important elements of my adult speaking style—the techniques of public speaking in the dramatic African tradition of the spoken word, can be traced to those street-corner orators of Harlem. To them and the Baptist preachers of the rural South. To be successful, both had to be highly skilled in poetic and rhetorical terms, and flawless in crowd psychology. To hold, inspire, and work their audience, they had to be powerfully persuasive and quick-witted and sure-footed."

With friends from Bronx Science, Carmichael also began to frequent two of Malcolm's favorite haunts in Harlem: Lewis Michaux's National Memorial African Book Store on 125th Street, and the Schomburg Collection of books on Black history and culture on 135th Street. Hanging around the Schomburg, Stokely heard a story about Malcolm X that left a deep impression. The minister was driving by the center one day when he saw a group of young Black men playing craps on the sidewalk outside. He got out of the car, walked over to them, and put his foot on the dice.

"My young brothers, you know what this building is?" Malcolm asked.

The young men gave Malcolm a blank look.

"Yeah, I thought so," Malcolm said. "This is the Schomburg Collection. It's got damn near everything ever written by or about black people. And what are you doing? Instead of being inside learning about yourself, your people, and your history, you're out here in darkness shooting dice. That's what's wrong with us, why Mr. Muhammad says, 'If you want to hide something from the black man, put it in a library.'"

For college, Carmichael set his sights on Howard University, the renowned historically Black institution in Washington, D.C., after meeting a group of Black activists from the school while attending a student protest in the nation's capital. As soon as he enrolled, Stokely joined their organization, called the Nonviolent Action Group (NAG). During his freshman year, NAG invited Malcolm X to the school to

debate Bayard Rustin, the Black civil rights leader and committed pac-
ifist who would go on to organize the March on Washington. Held in
Cramton Auditorium, the largest indoor gathering place on campus,
the event was billed with the provocative title "Integration or Separation?"

Until that evening, Carmichael and the other NAG members viewed
themselves as followers of Rustin, whom they had invited to the campus
several times before. To most of them, Malcolm was still an intriguing
"novelty," as Stokely would put it, given the way he had been "demon-
ized all over the white press." But at a dinner hosted by NAG before
the debate, the students got to meet Malcolm in person, and to experience his magnetism up close. He arrived late, after being interviewed
for the campus newspapers by a NAG member named Michael Thelwell. "Upon his appearance in the small dining room the atmosphere
completely changed," Carmichael recalled. "Suddenly the room became
totally silent but strangely charged. . . . There he stood, smiling almost
diffidently in the doorway. Tall, slender, his horn-rimmed glasses glis-
tening, the expression of his lean face alert, carrying himself erect, with
a formality, a quiet dignity, in his posture, yet beneath it an unmistakable
warmth."

"*Salaam aleikum*, brothers and sisters," Malcolm said with a bow
and a wide smile. "Sorry if I'm a little late, but your young editors
turned me every which way but loose."

During the dinner, Malcolm even managed to charm the only faculty member present, a dean named Patricia Roberts, who would later
serve as a cabinet secretary under President Jimmy Carter. Roberts
asked a pointed question, Carmichael recalled, and Malcolm gave her
"a long challenging look accompanied by his slightly ironic grin. Their
eyes locked for an instant. Then Dean Roberts, before she looked
away, actually seemed to blush and emit something that sounded suspiciously like a soft giggle."

When the dinner group arrived at Cramton Auditorium, the hall
was packed, with fellow activists but also hundreds of more typical
Howard students readying themselves for conventional careers in the
Black middle class. Rustin went first, and was cogent but rushed in making his appeal for "Integration." Then Malcolm rose and mesmerized

the crowd with a detailed case for "Separation." He drew repeated applause with his rapid-fire indictment of "the American white man" as "the world's greatest racist," "killer," and "liar," citing the ugly history of slavery and Jim Crow but also the genocide of Native Americans, the internment of Japanese Americans during World War II, and the violations of foreign treaties and agreements throughout U.S. history. But Malcolm got his loudest and most emotional response with his appeal to racial pride and solidarity.

"Before you were American, you were black," Malcolm declared, as the crowd roared.

"Before you were a Republican, you were black," he continued, as the response grew louder.

"Before you were a Democrat, you were black," he concluded, to the loudest cheers yet.

For Stokely, it was a moment of personal and communal epiphany. "What Malcolm demonstrated that night in Cramton Auditorium on the Howard campus," he recalled, "was the raw power, the visceral potency, of the grip our unarticulated collective blackness held over us."

Three years later, Carmichael had graduated from Howard and joined the Student Nonviolent Coordinating Committee (SNCC), the civil rights organization formed several years earlier by Black students from NAG and other campus activist groups who had been at the forefront of the brave lunch counter sit-in protests and Freedom Rides designed to test court decisions banning racial restrictions on interstate travel. Stokely was driving with fellow SNCC organizers from Mississippi to Alabama when a bulletin came across the car radio: "Former Black Muslim leader Malcolm X has been shot and killed." For all his usual chattiness, Carmichael sat in "dead silence," he recalled, as he absorbed the awful news from New York City. "Who had killed the brother?" he asked himself. "The report said the shooters were black. That one had been captured. Yeah, sure, I thought. How convenient. I didn't for a moment believe that. It was not the whole or the true story. I knew that. Instinctively."

As fate would have it, Carmichael was traveling to Alabama at that moment to test a political proposition that Malcolm himself had begun to lay out ten months before he was killed. In April 1964, shortly after announcing his split with the Nation of Islam, Malcolm had given a groundbreaking speech he called "The Ballot or the Bullet." Delivered on two separate occasions, in churches in Cleveland and Detroit, the speech rejected the NOI's long-standing policy of boycotting the evil white political system and implicitly answered critics who accused Malcolm of advocating violence. In the speech, Malcolm argued that ballots could be just as effective as bullets. But he also counseled Blacks to be "politically mature" in the use of their electoral clout—to seek the vote not merely as a legal right but also as an instrument of raw political power. "What does this mean?" Malcolm asked. "It means that when white people are evenly divided, and Black people have a bloc of votes of their own, it is left to them to determine who's going to sit in the White House and who's going to sit in the dog house."

Over the previous few years, Carmichael had reached a similar conclusion as a SNCC organizer in rural Mississippi. Working under the famously brave and self-effacing SNCC organizer Bob Moses, he had helped register hundreds of new Black voters in parts of the state where Blacks had been kept out of the political process for generations. Carmichael had worked with Moses to organize "Freedom Summer"—bringing a thousand Black and white college students to organize across Mississippi during their summer vacations in 1964—and to mount a bid by a newly formed Black faction of the state Democratic Party to unseat the avowedly segregationist white state delegation at the presidential convention in Atlantic City that August. But Carmichael had been badly disillusioned by two heartbreaking setbacks that summer. On the eve of Freedom Summer, an interracial trio of SNCC organizers went missing in rural Mississippi and were later found to have been brutally murdered and buried by the local Ku Klux Klan. And in Atlantic City, the Democratic Party establishment conspired to block the bid to unseat the white Mississippi segregationists, insulting the Black delegates with a token offer of two nonvoting seats on the convention floor.

Now, in the winter of 1965, Carmichael was headed to Alabama with a goal more in keeping with Malcolm's muscular conception of Black political participation. He intended to focus on a county where Blacks represented a large enough share of the population that they could form their own political party and elect their own Black candidates to county offices. By the spring, Carmichael had zeroed in on Lowndes County, an impoverished Cotton Belt backwater where onerous poll taxes and literacy tests had kept Blacks from voting for sixty years. Over the next year, partnering with a local activist group that had already started registering a handful of Blacks in the area, the SNCC organizers succeeded in registering more than two thousand Blacks across Lowndes County.

With the help of SNCC's white, Atlanta-based research director, Jack Minnis, Carmichael discovered an obscure state law that laid out procedures for establishing a new state party from scratch. One requirement was to hold a nominating convention, which the new party—officially named the Lowndes County Freedom Organization—managed to do on a sunny morning in early May 1966. Seven Black candidates were selected to run in the fall election for offices that included county sheriff and school superintendent. The other requirement was that the new party adopt a symbol that would be recognizable to voters who couldn't read. With more help from SNCC's Atlanta headquarters, the new party leaders settled on a symbol that would quickly take on a historic life of its own: a black panther.

In rapid succession, two more surprise events then thrust Carmichael into a national spotlight that no rival to Dr. King had enjoyed since Malcolm's murder. Later in May, SNCC held its annual retreat outside Nashville at which the group's chairman, the moderate future congressman John Lewis, was expected to be reelected. But in a heated all-night meeting, an initial vote in favor of Lewis was challenged by SNCC militants, and in a revote Carmichael was elected the new chairman. Several weeks later, James Meredith, the Black Mississippi native who had become a national figure when he enrolled at the University of Mississippi, which set off a bloody riot, embarked on a solo march across the state to champion the cause of voter registration. On the second day of his trek, Meredith was ambushed by a white supremacist firing a gun loaded with birdshot, leaving him with scores of flesh wounds that put him in the hospital for two weeks.

Vowing to carry on Meredith's crusade, the leaders of the nation's leading civil rights group—now including Stokely Carmichael of SNCC—convened for a planning meeting in Memphis. But after another heated all-night strategy meeting, Roy Wilkins of the National Association for the Advancement of Colored People (NAACP) and Whitney Young of the Urban League withdrew from the effort. That left Carmichael and Dr. King as the two most visible faces of a new march across Mississippi that would be covered by national media as though it was a sequel to the historic voting march from Selma to Montgomery, Alabama, the year before.

In *The New York Times*, Gene Roberts, the paper's top "race beat" reporter, made the comparison to Malcolm explicit in his analysis of how the Meredith March stood to elevate Stokely Carmichael and his militant new message. "Reporters and cameramen drawn to a demonstration of the magic of Dr. King's name stay to write about and photograph Mr. Carmichael as he demonstrates and talks alongside the older civil rights leader," Roberts wrote. "This is an advantage that Malcolm X never had as he exalted the Negro and attacked the 'duplicity' and 'hypocrisy' of the white man."

A week later, the Meredith Marchers arrived in the town of Greenwood, deep in the Mississippi Cotton Belt. Carmichael had arranged for sleeping tents to be put up on the grounds of a segregated Black school, but as they were being erected the local white police showed up and arrested Stokely and two other organizers for trespassing. Carmichael spent the rest of the day in the town jail and was released just in time to address a rally of marchers and local Black supporters who had assembled in a sandlot ball field in the Black neighborhood known as Baptist Town. As darkness fell, he climbed onto the back of a truck lit with generator power and vented his fury to the crowd of five hundred below.

"This is the twenty-seventh time that I have been arrested, and I ain't going to jail no more!" Carmichael cried out. "The only way we're going to stop them white men from whupping us is to take over. We've been saying freedom for six years and we ain't got nothing. What we're gonna start saying now is: 'Black Power'!"

In unison, the crowd shouted back Carmichael's words: "Black Power!"

"We want Black Power!" Stokely repeated, five times in a row, and each time the crowd echoed: "Black Power!"

"That's right," Carmichael picked up. "That's what we want. Black Power! We don't have to be ashamed of it. We have stayed here. We have begged the president. We've begged the federal government—that's all we've been doing, begging and begging. It's time we stand up and take over. Every courthouse in Mississippi ought to be burned down tomorrow to get rid of the dirt and the mess. From now on, when they ask you what you want, you know what you tell them? What do we want?"

"Black Power!" the crowd cried.

The next day, a brief Associated Press account of the Greenwood rally and the call-and-response chants of "Black Power!" was picked up by more than two hundred newspapers across America. CBS News producers reached out to Carmichael and invited him to Washington, D.C., to appear on that Sunday's episode of *Face the Nation*. On the show, he defended the Black Power slogan to a panel of skeptical white journalists inquiring if the expression meant seizing power by force. From the national newsmagazines *Time* and *Newsweek*, to the Black periodicals *Jet* and *Ebony*, and to the editorial pages of *The New York Times* and scores of other white- and Black-owned newspapers, coverage of the "Black Power!" cry suddenly became the biggest race story of the summer. What exactly did it mean? the stories asked. And how much of a threat did it pose to the playbook of nonviolent protest, interracial coalition-building, and focus on legislation and the courts that had guided the civil rights movement for a decade, since the Montgomery Bus Boycott of 1955 and 1956?

Titled "The Architect of Black Power," the *Ebony* profile traced the origins of Carmichael's focus on Black Power back to Trinidad—where as a boy he had seen Black people in positions of political influence even under British colonial rule—and to Malcolm X. *Ebony*'s editor-in-chief, Lerone Bennett, also an eminent historian, wrote the story, and he suggested to Carmichael that they visit Lewis Michaux's National Memorial African Book Store in Harlem. "Malcolm is still living," Michaux exclaimed as Stokely entered the store. "When you walked in, Malcolm smiled." Answering Bennett's queries about the meaning of Black Power, Carmichael delivered a pointed critique of the limits of middle-class racial integration that was very reminiscent of Malcolm. "Integration never speaks to the problem of what happens to the black school or the black community after two or three people move out 'to integrate,'" Carmichael observed. "That's the problem we must force America to speak to; that's the problem Black Power speaks to."

Elsewhere in the story, however, Bennett indicated how unlike Malcolm Carmichael could be in his lack of rhetorical and behavioral discipline. Inside SNCC, Bennett revealed, Stokely was known as "Stokely Starmichael" for his love of media attention, and as "the Magnificent Barbarian" for his tendency toward outrageousness. In the months after the Greenwood speech, Carmichael repeatedly squandered opportunities to tell the Lowndes County Freedom Organization story, or to give any other clear explanation of Black Power. At an October retreat of SNCC's central committee, he was confronted by Ruby Doris Smith Robinson, the tough-minded young Spelman College graduate who had been elected to the number two position of executive secretary at the spring SNCC retreat, in charge of running the day-to-day operations out of the Atlanta headquarters. Carmichael's public speeches had become full of attention-grabbing "clichés," she wrote in a memo circulated during the meeting, that were hurting fundraising and doing little to help SNCC's mission of voter registration in the South.

Chastened by the internal criticism, Carmichael promised his colleagues that he would assume a lower profile. But he couldn't resist when white campus activists at the University of California at Berkeley invited him to give a speech at a conference on Black Power in late October. That appearance at Berkeley's open-air Greek Theatre drew an overflow crowd of mostly white students—and had two side effects with historic consequences. In the home stretch of California's governor's race, Republican actor-turned-politician Ronald Reagan made opposition to Carmichael's visit to Berkeley a major campaign issue, helping to turn out a white "backlash vote" that propelled him to his first victory on the road to becoming America's fortieth president. And to help stir up interest in Stokely's appearance around the Bay Area, event organizers imported flyers from Lowndes County featuring the black panther logo—an image that would capture the imagination of two Black community college students from Oakland who were thinking of forming their own political movement and who had also been deeply influenced by Malcolm X.

Huey Newton and Bobby Seale were both children of the Great Migration, the exodus that brought more than six million Blacks from the rural South to the urban North and West in the decades between World War I and the 1960s. Born in Louisiana and Texas, respectively, Newton and Seale moved to the Oakland area at the end of World War II with parents who hoped to find jobs in the booming defense economy. Yet no sooner had their families arrived than Oakland was hit with a perfect storm that would devastate dozens of Black communities in the decades after the war. Manufacturing jobs dried up and white city residents fled to the suburbs, leaving the population of the inner city predominantly Black. Large swaths of those Black neighborhoods were torn down in the name of urban renewal, or cut off from the rest of the city by new highway construction. As Black crime rates rose in the absence of other economic opportunities, neighborhood policing became a thing of the past. The white police officers who patrolled Black Oakland lived elsewhere, and to the local residents they began to look and behave more and more like an occupying army.

Slight of build, with a sweet light-brown face that belied his hot temper, Newton struggled with learning disabilities as a child, and only taught himself to read properly in his late teens. Hoping to attend college like his older brother, Marvin, he borrowed Marvin's copy of Plato's *Republic* and looked up words in the dictionary until he could comprehend entire sentences and paragraphs. Huey became literate enough to follow Marvin to Merritt College, a community college in Oakland. While there, Huey began to attend meetings of a group called the Afro-American Association (AAA), led by a Black graduate of the Berkeley law school named Donald Warden. Joining AAA study groups that met at a Chinese restaurant on Telegraph Avenue, New-ton was introduced to the works of Booker T. Washington, W. E. B. DuBois, Ralph Ellison, and James Baldwin. But soon Huey became disillusioned with Warden, concluding that the middle-class activist looked down on less well-educated Oakland Blacks and was using the AAA to drum up private legal business.

After parting ways with the AAA, Newton was still intrigued enough to attend a day-long conference titled "The Mind of the Ghetto" that Warden staged at Oakland's McClymonds High School in the summer of 1963. The participants included Cassius Clay, the brash, lightning-quick Black boxer from Louisville, Kentucky, who had won a gold medal at the 1960 Olympics and turned professional later that year. Accompanying Clay was Malcolm X, who unbeknownst to the wider public had become Clay's friend and spiritual adviser as the boxer began the process of conversion that would lead to his joining the Nation of Islam and taking the name Muhammad Ali. As Malcolm spoke to the crowded high school auditorium, he deeply impressed Newton.

"Here was a man who combined the world of the streets and the world of the scholar," Huey recalled thinking of Malcolm, "a man so widely read he could give better lectures and cite more evidence than many college professors. He was also practical. Dressed in the loose-fitting style of a strong prison man, he knew what the street brothers were like, and he knew what could be done to reach them. Malcolm had a program: armed defense when attacked, and reaching the people with ideas and programs that speak to their condition. At the same time, he identified with the causes of their conditions instead of blam-ing the people."

Before breaking with the AAA, Newton was also introduced at one of their meetings to Seale, an older Air Force veteran who had returned to Oakland to live with his parents after being court-martialed for ar-guing with a colonel. The two briefly lost touch when Newton was sentenced to prison for two years for attacking an acquaintance with a steak knife after getting into an argument at a party. When Newton got out, he and Seale met again at Merritt College, and they joined a campus activist group called the Soul Students Advisory Council (SSAC). This time, Newton clashed with the middle-class leader of the SSAC, Kenny Freeman, whom Huey sized up as an armchair radical who was all talk and no action.

Freeman and the other SSAC leaders fashioned themselves followers of an underground movement called the Revolutionary Action Movement (RAM), which advocated armed overthrow of the American government. They carried around copies of a book titled *Negroes with Guns*, written by RAM's spiritual leader, Robert F. Williams. A former member of the NAACP in North Carolina, Williams had abandoned nonviolence and called for Blacks to take up arms after watching a local white man accused of raping a Black woman go free. When the FBI put out a warrant for his arrest on a trumped-up kidnapping charge, Williams fled to Cuba, where several SSAC members had visited him.

To put the pro-gun posturing of the SSAC radicals to the test, Newton proposed an idea inspired by Malcolm X. To commemorate the first anniversary of Malcolm's assassination in February 1966, Huey suggested that the SSAC stage a protest outside the college demanding more courses and better conditions for Black students—and do so while marching carrying pistols and rifles. To dramatize his point, Newton showed up at an SSAC meeting with dozens of armed Black supporters he had recruited from the Oakland streets. But the meeting quickly erupted into name-calling, and Newton and Seale stormed out. "So Huey and I jumped up, and we said, 'Well, fuck it. We resign,'" Seale recalled in his autobiography. As the two were leaving, they vowed: "We're going to the black community and . . . [create] an organization to lead the black liberation struggle."

Eight months later, Newton and Seale made good on that promise, drafting a "Ten Point Program" that would serve as the founding document for a new organization they called the Black Panther Party for Self-Defense. They chose the Black Panther name after seeing the image of the prowling animal on one of the Lowndes County Freedom Organization campaign flyers that were circulating around the Bay Area in advance of Stokely Carmichael's speech at Berkeley. In conceiving the Ten Point Program, they borrowed from a variety of thinkers, including the Francophone revolutionary philosopher Frantz

Fanon, Che Guevara, and Mao Tse-tung. But by Newton's account, their greatest influence was Malcolm X.

"Bobby had collected all of Malcolm X's speeches and ideas from papers like *The Militant* and *Muhammad Speaks*," Newton recalled. "These we studied carefully. Although Malcolm's program for the Organization of Afro-American Unity was never put into operation, he made it clear that Blacks ought to arm. Malcolm's influence was ever-present . . . the words on this page cannot convey the effect that Malcolm has had on the Black Panther Party, although, as far as I am concerned, the Party is a living testament to his life work. I do not claim that the Party has done what Malcolm would have done. Many others say that their programs are Malcolm's programs. We do not say this, but Malcolm's spirit is in us."

Indeed, the structure and language of Newton and Seale's Ten Point Program bore a remarkable resemblance to the speech that Malcolm had delivered at the Audubon Ballroom in June 1964 launching his Organization of Afro-American Unity. Malcolm's manifesto presented a five-point agenda, which he unveiled in this order: "1. Establishment," "2. Self-Defense," "3. Education," "4. Politics and Economics," and "5. Social." In each of these areas, Malcolm articulated both a broad statement of principle and a specific plan of action. He also began with a mission statement reminiscent of the Declaration of Independence: "Convinced that it is the inalienable right of all our people to control our own destiny . . ." Although Newton and Seale may not have known it, Malcolm had also written an outline for a chapter that was later excluded from the *Autobiography* that included a section called "What We Muslims Want . . . What We Believe."

In their plan, Newton and Seale offered ten points, each similarly divided into a statement of action ("What We Want") and a statement of principle ("What We Believe"). Instead of invoking the Declaration of Independence, they lifted its preamble word for word, ending their manifesto with Thomas Jefferson's famous words: "When, in the course of human events, it becomes necessary for one people to dissolve the political bands which have connected them with another . . ."

Of Newton and Seale's ten points, some were ahead of their time, such as a demand for financial reparations for slavery. Others were wildly unrealistic, such as a demand for the immediate release of all

Black prisoners from American jails. But the agenda item on which they intended to take immediate action was the one Malcolm had listed second in his OAAU speech, and that Newton and Seale put front and center in the name of their new organization: the Black Panther Party for Self-Defense.

"We want an immediate end to POLICE BRUTALITY and MURDER of black people," the two declared in the seventh of their ten points. "We believe we can end police brutality in our black community by organizing black self-defense groups that are dedicated to defending our black community from racist police oppression and brutality. The Second Amendment to the Constitution of the United States gives a right to bear arms. We therefore believe that all black people should arms themselves for self-defense."

By the end of 1966, Newton and Seale had acquired an M1 rifle and a 9mm pistol from a Japanese American activist at Merritt College who later turned out to be an informant for the FBI. They had also acquired copies of California legal manuals specifying the "open carry" gun laws that gave state residents the right to carry firearms in public as long as they were visible. Driving around Oakland, the two looked for incidents of white police officers questioning Black residents. Getting out of their car, Newton and Seale would stand at a distance, brandishing their weapons and law books to let the policemen know that they were keeping an eye on them. "Shock-a-buku," Newton called the surprise patrols, and for a few months they worked, as the police gave the two men nasty looks but went away without making any arrests.

=====

The influx of Southern Blacks to the West Coast during and after World War II—followed so rapidly by the drying up of economic opportunity and more militaristic policing of Black neighborhoods—also brought about a transformation in California's prison population. By the early 1960s, almost a fifth of the 24,000 inmates in the state's penal system were Black, and they had become increasingly vocal about mistreatment at the hands of white prisoners, guards, and prison officials. At the forefront of the protests were Black prisoners who had joined the Nation of Islam—a number that corrections officials counted at 219 in 1962, but was likely higher when private sympathizers were taken into account. And it was the confrontational posture of the Black Muslim converts, more than their religious beliefs, that first attracted a tall, outspoken convict named Eldridge Cleaver to their ranks after he was sent to San Quentin Prison for attacking a white couple in a parked car, tying up the man and attempting to rape the woman.

Born in Arkansas, Cleaver was named after his father, Leroy Eldridge Cleaver Sr., a violent and unfaithful man who abandoned his wife and children shortly after he moved them to Los Angeles when Leroy Jr. was three years old. While his mother supported the family by working as a high school janitor, Eldridge, as he was called by the time he was a teen, drifted into a life of drugs and petty theft that took him in and out of reform school and to jail for marijuana possession. At twenty-three, he was sentenced to hard time for "assault with intent to kill" in the rape case, and assigned to San Quentin. After a brief flirtation with Marxism, Cleaver embraced the Nation of Islam and became a leader in letter-writing campaigns and hunger and work strikes to protest prisoner mistreatment. In early 1963, he was tapped by the head of the NOI mosque in Los Angeles to lead the San Quentin flock after the previous prison minister was killed in a clash with guards, and the warden responded by getting Cleaver transferred to Folsom Prison.

When Malcolm X broke with the Nation of Islam in 1964, Cleaver became the first Muslim at Folsom to side with him. At a secret meeting, he informed his fellow converts that he was also renouncing Elijah Muhammad, and he began making copies of Malcolm's speeches and circulating them around the prison. In his own jail cell, he took a portrait of Elijah Muhammad out of a frame on the wall and replaced it with an image he clipped out of *The Saturday Evening Post*, of Malcolm kneeling in prayer inside a Cairo mosque. "Soon I had the ear of the Muslims, and it was not long before Malcolm had other ardent defenders in Folsom," Cleaver recalled. "In a very short time Malcolm became the hero of the vast majority of Negro inmates. Elijah Muhammad was quickly becoming irrelevant, passé."

On the day of Malcolm's murder, Cleaver was in the prison mess hall watching the movie screened for prisoners on Sundays when a fellow prisoner appeared in the dark and whispered the news in his ear. Over the next four months, Cleaver poured his emotions and reflections into an essay, "Initial Reactions on the Assassination of Malcolm X," that was later included in his book *Soul on Ice*. Malcolm meant so much to Black prisoners, Cleaver wrote, because he had served time himself and saw American "penology" the way they did: not as an instrument of justice but as a "vicious PPP cycle: prison-parole-prison" that turned Blacks into "victims of a dog-eat-dog social system."

Beyond the prison walls, he proclaimed, Malcolm stood for a call to Black empowerment that transcended his affiliation with Elijah Muhammad and the Nation of Islam. "It was the awakening into self-consciousness of twenty million Negroes which was so compelling," Cleaver wrote. "Malcolm X articulated their aspirations better than any other man of our time. . . . If he had become a Quaker, a Catholic, or Seventh-Day Adventist, or a Sammy Davis–style Jew, and if he continued to give voice to the mute ambitions of the black man's soul, his message would still have been triumphant; because what was great was not Malcolm X but the truth he uttered."

Driven by a determination to carry on Malcolm's work, Cleaver set out to win early release from prison. In a community paper, the *Sun Reporter*, he found a classified ad for a white lawyer named Beverly Axelrod, who defended Black clients. When the petite, dark-haired attorney started visiting Cleaver in Folsom Prison, they devised an ambitious and novel strategy to secure his freedom. Beginning in the summer of 1965, Cleaver wrote a series of provocative essays about his spiritual and political transformation behind bars, including one in which he renounced his past as a rapist and characterized it as "an insurrectionary act." Axelrod smuggled the essays out of Folsom and passed them on to Edward Keating, the white publisher of the San Francisco–based journal *Ramparts*. A convert to Catholicism who had turned *Ramparts* into a voice of the pro–civil rights, antiwar left, Keating began publishing the essays and urging influential writers such as Norman Mailer and Thomas Merton to write to prison authorities on Cleaver's behalf. With the help of those letters—and a job offer from Keating—Cleaver was granted parole and walked out of Folsom Prison on December 12, 1966.

Cleaver went to work as a staff writer for *Ramparts,* and in his spare time he launched two ventures devoted to studying and spreading Malcolm X's ideas: a local radio show, and a gathering space in San Francisco called the Black House. In February 1967, he had the idea of commemorating the anniversary of Malcolm's assassination by inviting his widow, Betty Shabazz, to appear in San Francisco. Still in a fragile state two years after the murder, Betty agreed to the trip on condition that security be provided. At a planning meeting at Black House, Huey Newton and Bobby Seale showed up and offered the services of the Black Panthers.

On the day of Shabazz's arrival, a group of Panthers met Betty at the airport and accompanied her to the *Ramparts* offices in San Francisco, where Cleaver was waiting to conduct an interview. For the first time, Cleaver saw the Panthers fully armed and in the attire they had adopted, featuring leather jackets and stylish dark berets. He was even more impressed when, after the interview was concluded, Huey Newton faced down one of the police officers who had gathered in the street outside.

As Newton passed by, holding his M1 rifle aloft, one of the officers snapped: "Don't point that gun at me!"

Newton stopped and nodded toward the policeman's pistol. "What's the matter, you got an itchy trigger finger?" he taunted. "You want to draw the gun?"

When the officer didn't respond, Newton loaded a shell into his rifle. "Okay, you big, fat racist pig, draw your gun," he said. "We're waiting."

After a tense stare-down, the policeman stepped aside and let the Panthers and Shabazz pass.

"You're the baddest motherfucker I've ever seen," Cleaver recalled thinking as he watched Newton's show of bravado. Soon after, he contacted Newton and Seale and offered his help. Within a matter of months, Cleaver had resigned from *Ramparts* and joined the Panthers full-time as "Minister of Information."

Two weeks after Eldridge Cleaver was released from prison in 1966, a Black home in the Jefferson Park neighborhood of Los Angeles became the site of a new holiday called Kwanzaa. Dressed in African tunics and headdresses, the celebrants greeted each other with the Swahili words for "What's new?": "*Hahari gani?*" They lit a large wooden candelabra called a kinara, then sat down on the floor amid wicker baskets filled with fruit to hold hands, sing songs, and tell folk stories. Every day for the next week, they repeated the ritual, each time celebrating a different theme with a Swahili name: *Umoja* (Unity), *Kujichagulia* (Self-Determination), *Ujima* (Collective Responsibility), *Ujamaa* (Cooperative Economics), *Nia* (Purpose), *Kuumba* (Creativity), and *Imani* (Faith). On the last night, there was a holiday meal called Karamu, or "Feast of Faith," featuring platters of spicy food that everyone passed around and ate with their hands, emulating the simplicity of their African ancestors. Beginning on the day after Christmas and lasting a week, the holiday also allowed the participants to avoid being exploited by white merchants and shop for gifts at post-holiday discounts.

The inventor of the Kwanzaa holiday was a twenty-five-year-old Black cultural nationalist named Ron Karenga, who also took his inspiration from Malcolm X. Born Ronald Everett, he had grown up on a Maryland chicken farm and dropped out of high school to follow an older brother to Los Angeles. There, Ron began attending African history and language classes at Los Angeles City College, a community college with open enrollment, and changed his last name to the Swahili word for "Keeper of Tradition."

In the fall of 1962, Karenga transferred to UCLA just in time to hear Malcolm speak there. Although Malcolm spent much of the address praising Elijah Muhammad and trumpeting his message of political separatism, it was his call for Blacks to develop and celebrate their own unique culture that made the biggest impression on Karenga. "The American Negro is a Frankenstein, a monster who has been stripped of his culture and doesn't even know his name," Malcolm proclaimed to an auditorium full of students. Afterward, Karenga approached the stage to ask questions, and Malcolm was impressed enough to invite him to "eat bean pie and talk abstract," as Ron later put it, at a Muslim restaurant near the NOI's Los Angeles mosque.

After the assassination at the Audubon Ballroom sixteen months later, Karenga met a cousin of Malcolm's named Hakim Jamal, who had moved to Los Angeles. Together, they began hosting a weekly study group at the Aquarian Bookstore in the South Central neighborhood to carry on the legacy of the Organization of Afro-American Unity. Those conversations took on a new urgency after the Watts Rebellion in August 1965. Less than a month later, Karenga and Jamal announced the founding of a new Black cultural nationalist movement they called "US." Suggested by Malcolm's cousin, the name was intended to give new meaning to the national initials: Instead of "United States," it stood for "United Slaves." Although Karenga and Jamal had joined Malcolm in breaking with the Nation of Islam, US also emulated the NOI in demanding "complete acceptance of an alternative lifestyle," as historian Scot Brown put it. Followers were expected to take new Swahili names, dress in African garb, and adhere to strict dietary and behavioral rules. The US movement also had a paramilitary arm modeled after the Fruit of Islam, called the Simba Wachanga, or "Young Lions," with weekly drill sessions to train children in the martial arts.

When Karenga was profiled by *Newsweek* magazine in August 1966, he posed with a shaved head, thick dark sunglasses, a handlebar mustache—and a picture of Malcolm X hanging on the wall behind him. But by then, Karenga had begun to turn US into his own "cult of personality," as Scot Brown put it. He had split with Jamal, assumed the Swahili title of Maulana—or "Master Teacher"—and published a book of sayings called *The Quotable Karenga*, akin to the *Quotations from Chairman Mao Tse-Tung*, also known as "The Little Red Book." Karenga issued commandments about how and when members of the organization could speak, counseled female followers to remain "submissive," advocated polygamy to increase the sect's numbers, and made ominous predictions of a seven-year countdown to a race war.

Karenga's increasing militancy and visibility also put US on a collision course with the new Black Panther Party for Self-Defense. After the Betty Shabazz visit to San Francisco that united Eldridge Cleaver with Huey Newton and Bobby Seale, a sequence of dramatic events put the Panthers on the national map. Once armed Panthers began monitoring police, a Republican state senator named Don Mulford proposed a bill to repeal California's open carry laws. In May 1967, twenty-six armed Panthers traveled to Sacramento to protest the bill, which would go on to pass easily, and the resulting photos of the brawny armed Black men wearing berets and carrying pistols and rifles made front-page news across the country.

That October, Huey Newton was involved in a confrontation with police that left an officer dead. Although Newton had passed out during the clash and denied pulling the trigger, he was sent to jail to await trial for murder. With Newton behind bars, Cleaver took control of the Panther messaging. He orchestrated a nationwide "Free Huey!" campaign and distributed a popular poster he had staged of Newton sitting on a wicker throne holding a rifle in one hand and a spear in the other. In a video produced by Cleaver, members rallied outside the courthouse where Huey was jailed, chanting "Off the Pigs" and "The revolution has come! Time to pick up the gun!"

As the Panthers and Karenga's US movement both grew in size and attention, FBI director J. Edgar Hoover stepped up his targeting of all the Black activist groups. Under a program called COINTELPRO—for "Counterintelligence Program"—the FBI had long spied on Dr. King and Malcolm X, looking for evidence of personal misconduct or ties to foreign powers that could be used to compromise them. Launching an expanded version of the campaign in March 1968 called COINTELPRO-BLACK HATE, Hoover wrote a memo to the bureau's forty-one field offices instructing them to do everything possible to prevent the emergence of a "messiah" who could "unify and electrify" Black America. A month later, Dr. King was assassinated in Memphis—timing that conspiracy theories would insist wasn't accidental, despite the ultimate legal verdict that the gunman, James Earl Ray, acted alone.

As Black neighborhoods across the country erupted in violence after King's murder, Eldridge Cleaver led an armed raid on an Oakland police station that resulted in the wounding of several officers and the death of an early Panther recruit, party treasurer Bobby Hutton. Still on parole for his rape conviction, Cleaver fled the country rather than face another long prison term, escaping first to Cuba and then to Algeria. Meanwhile, Bobby Seale became mired in a series of legal battles that would preoccupy him for several years—first as the eighth defendant in the Chicago Seven trial charging activists with inciting unrest during the 1968 Democratic convention, then as an accused accomplice in the murder of a suspected Panther informant in New Haven, Connecticut.

In the FBI's 1969 annual report, Hoover described the Panthers as "the greatest threat to internal security of the United States," and the bureau increased the pace of what would eventually total 233 covert actions against them. Playing on the isolation of the jailed Newton and exiled Cleaver, FBI agents faked letters to each man purporting to come from party members complaining about the other. In Los Angeles, the local FBI bureau manufactured derogatory cartoons about the Panthers that they attributed to Karenga's US. In January 1969, that feud came to a head with a shoot-out between Panthers and US followers on the UCLA campus that left two popular Panthers dead. In Chicago, the FBI set out to undermine a charismatic twenty-one-year-old Black leader named Fred Hampton, who had emerged as head of the local Panther chapter and exhibited a talent for reaching out to Black gang leaders and white activists. In December 1969, using information supplied by a Black FBI informant, police raided Hampton's home, provoking a gun battle during which Hampton was shot to death in front of his pregnant girlfriend.

If Fred Hampton would decades later be portrayed as the embodiment of Hoover's vision of a leader who could unite various Black groups in the 2021 film *Judas and the Black Messiah*, it was because by the time of his murder, all the other Black Power pioneers had lost the capacity or credibility to fill that role. After being released from jail in 1970, Huey Newton became enmeshed in party infighting and drug and alcohol addiction, and in 1989 died in a gun battle on the streets of Oakland at the age of forty-seven. By the time Eldridge Cleaver returned to America, he had become a born-again Christian, and would later veer into crack cocaine use and far-right politics before dying at sixty-two. Bobby Seale survived into his eighties but became increasingly eccentric, hawking barbecue sauce and rewriting history to claim credit for everything people recalled as appealing about the Panthers. Driven paranoid by the feud with the Panthers, Ron Karenga went to prison for trying to torture a confession out of two female followers he thought were trying to kill him with poison crystals. After serving time, he became a respected professor of African American studies, but his days as an effective street organizer were done.

In May 1967, Stokely Carmichael stepped down as SNCC's chairman after only one year. The position went to a previously little-known SNCC staffer named H. Rap Brown, who soon proved be even more extreme in his rhetoric than Stokely, without any of the humor and charm. Meanwhile, Carmichael continued to travel and give speeches conjuring up the improbable prospect that the Black minority in the United States would rise up to emulate the anticolonial uprisings of Black majorities in countries across Africa. Changing his name to Kwame Ture, Carmichael moved to a life of exile in Guinea, enjoying the hospitality of autocratic left-wing leader Ahmed Sékou Touré and answering phone calls with an increasingly quixotic greeting: "Ready for Revolution!"

Before Carmichael died of prostate cancer at the age of fifty-seven, he wrote an autobiography with the help of his former Howard University classmate Michael Thelwell. In the memoir, he speculated wistfully that, had Malcolm X lived, he might have sought a merger between the Organization of Afro-American Unity and the Student Nonviolent Coordinating Committee. "Malcolm had always, always, been respectful and supportive of us in SNCC," Stokely maintained. "Of all the civil rights groups, I knew he felt closest to us, in spirit." Carmichael noted that just weeks before his assassination, SNCC's field officers in Selma, Alabama, Silas Norman and Fay Bellamy, had invited Malcolm to give a speech at that city's historic Brown Chapel AME Church. The speech was a hit with all the young Black activists in attendance, despite press accounts that focused on Malcolm's provocative jabs at civil rights moderates. "Sure his presence there had upset some people," Carmichael wrote, "but grassroots Africans in Selma had been really responsive."

Buying into unproven speculation that police or intelligence agencies had something to do with Malcolm's murder, Carmichael argued that his death had in fact been white America's loss. Malcolm was the sole Black leader of his age and experience, Stokely insisted, who could have harnessed the violent forces that were being unleashed as the civil rights movement moved from the South to the North and from the church to the inner city streets. "See," Carmichael wrote, "Malcolm was the only figure of that generation, the only one, who had the natural authority, the style, language, and charisma to discipline rank-and-file urban youth. The only one who commanded that kind of respect. Over and over you saw it. Time and again. Many times you saw a crowd of angry Africans fixing to tear the place up, and the only person who could reason with them, cool them out, was Malcolm. That was because the masses knew him and trusted him. Now they'd killed him. Bad mistake."

SIX

The Athletes

L ong before Malcolm X befriended the greatest boxer of his generation, he experienced the unique power of a Black champion to capture the imagination of his people. Malcolm was a twelve-year-old in
Lansing, Michigan, when Joe Louis won the heavyweight crown from
the white boxer James J. Braddock in 1937. Suddenly, Malcolm recalled
in the *Autobiography*, "every Negro boy old enough to walk wanted to
be the next Brown Bomber." Malcolm's older brother Philbert threw
himself into a successful amateur boxing career, and Malcolm tagged
along to the gym to watch him train. At thirteen, Malcolm began to
box himself, as a bantamweight, taking advantage of his tall, lean frame
to pretend that he was sixteen. In his first fight, with members of his
family looking on, he was knocked silly by an older white boy named
Bill Peterson. Humiliated, Malcolm went back to training even harder,
but in a rematch he was floored by Peterson's first punch. "That white
boy was the beginning and the end of my fight career," Malcolm recalled with wry self-deprecation. "A lot of times in these later years
since I became a Muslim, I've thought back to that fight and reflected
that it was Allah's work to stop me: I might have wound up punchy."

After joining the Nation of Islam, Malcolm had stopped playing
or following sports, in keeping with Elijah Muhammad's instruction
that "sport and play" were "filthy temptations" that detracted from a
life of spirituality. So Malcolm didn't recognize the boxer who would
become known as Muhammad Ali when the two men first met in 1962.

By then, Cassius Clay, as he was still known, was well into a meteoric rise from a youth boxing program in his hometown of Louisville, Kentucky, where he learned the sport from a policeman and part-time boxing coach Cassius first met while reporting the theft of a bicycle. Clay had won dozens of amateur fights and, at the age of nineteen, brought home a gold medal in the light heavyweight category from the 1960 Rome Olympics. Now, Clay was being talked about as a contender for the heavyweight crown—and, with the grandiose professional wrestler known as Gorgeous George as his model, drawing the attention of the national press as much for his outrageously boastful pronouncements as for his graceful dancing-and-ducking boxing style.

Unbeknownst to those reporters, Clay had also discovered the Nation of Islam. While he inherited his mocha-skinned good looks from his mother, Odessa, Clay had absorbed a prickly sense of racial pride and suspicion of white people from his father, Cassius Clay Sr., a hard-drinking sign painter who blamed racism for his limited professional opportunities. In his travels for boxing competitions, Cassius Jr. had become intrigued by the sight of NOI members, with their formal garb and talk of racial separatism. He had committed to memory the sect's best-known anthem, "A White Man's Heaven Is a Black Man's Hell," by the Boston minister Louis X. After moving to Miami to train after the Olympics, Clay befriended Sam Saxon, an NOI follower who began taking him to services at Mosque No. 29, located in a former storefront in the city's Black Overtown neighborhood. In the summer of 1962, Saxon invited Cassius and his younger brother Rudy to accompany him to Detroit to attend an NOI rally that would feature speeches by the faith's leader, Elijah Muhammad, as well as his most famous lieutenant, the New York minister Malcolm X.

Before the rally, Saxon escorted Cassius and Rudy to the Student Luncheonette, a Muslim diner next to Mosque No. 1. Seeing Malcolm seated at the back of the restaurant, the three men approached to introduce themselves.

"I'm Cassius Clay," the boxer said, holding out his hand.

Malcolm didn't know the name, but he didn't let on. He politely shook the hands of the visitors, exchanged a few words, then went back to preparing his remarks for the rally.

For Clay, seeing the 3,500 Nation of Islam members assembled at Detroit's Olympia Stadium and watching the pageantry surrounding Elijah Muhammad's address was powerful proof of the NOI's reach and appeal. Most memorable of all was the electrifying stage presence of the man he had just met at the diner. Malcolm X had organized the rally after a deadly April 1962 shoot-out with police in Los Angeles. He invited Detroit's white police chief, who came and sat at the front of the audience. But that didn't keep Malcolm, in his warm-up speech for Elijah Muhammad, from launching into a fiery denunciation of racist police practices. Clay was astonished. "My first impression of Malcolm X was how could a black man talk about the government and white people and act so bold, and not be shot at?" he recalled. "How could he say these things? Only God must be protecting him."

Over the next few months, Clay looked for more opportunities to hear Malcolm in person. In September, his picture appeared in *Muhammad Speaks* at an NOI rally in St. Louis. Clay recalled being struck by the courage Malcolm showed in traveling without a huge security entourage—and by his blunt description of the way white America dehumanized Black people, starting with the names by which they were called. "He was so radical at that time, and yet he walked with no bodyguard, fearless," Clay recalled. "What also attracted me [was when Malcolm said] 'Why we called Negroes? Chinese are named after China. Cubans are named after Cuba, Russians after Russia, Germans after Germany. All people are named for their country. What country is called Negro?'" When Malcolm talked about the indignity of "slave names" that Blacks had inherited from white enslavers, Clay thought to himself: "Man, so true."

Despite Elijah Muhammad's warnings about sports and athletes and Clay's flamboyant public persona, Malcolm was won over by the earnest demeanor the boxer displayed in private. The two began to meet regularly, and Malcolm started referring to Clay as his little brother. Malcolm introduced Cassius to his family, and offered him advice on the pitfalls of being in the public eye. "I liked him," Malcolm recalled. "Some contagious quality about him made him one of the very few people I invited to my home. Betty liked him. Our children were crazy about him. Cassius was simply a likable, friendly, clean-cut, down-to-earth youngster. I noticed how alert he was even in little details. . . . Not only was Cassius receptive to advice, he solicited it. Primarily, I impressed upon him to what a great extent a public figure's success depends upon how alert and knowledgeable he is to the true natures and to the true motives of all of the people who flock around him."

Increasingly, Malcolm also began to envision the public relations boost that Clay could provide to the Nation of Islam, if he were able to openly proclaim his budding affiliation. Given the controversy surrounding the NOI, however, Malcolm understood that Clay could only afford to go public if and when he won the heavyweight crown held by a bruising ex-con, Sonny Liston. In order to have a shot at Liston, Clay would first have to defeat the third-ranked heavyweight contender, a compact but tough journeyman named Doug Jones. So, without informing Elijah Muhammad or anyone else in the NOI hierarchy, Malcolm made plans to attend the Jones fight, held at Madison Square Garden in March 1963.

Fueled by all the publicity generated by Clay's trash talk and predictions of a fourth-round knockout, the Jones fight drew the largest turnout for any boxing match since the Joe Louis era. So many celebrities gathered at ringside that the press barely noticed Malcolm X among them. In the end, the grueling fight went the full ten rounds, and Clay barely won a decision that many in the booing crowd thought should have gone against him. The way was now paved for a title match against Sonny Liston—although Malcolm was one of the few people outside Clay's inner circle who believed that the brash contender had any prayer of beating the fearsome champion.

When the Liston fight was finally scheduled to take place at the Miami Beach Convention Hall in late February 1964, Malcolm had other reasons to root for Clay's victory. By then, Malcolm had privately confronted Elijah Muhammad with his knowledge of the Messenger's adultery, and Muhammad had announced Malcolm's ninety-day suspension. Believing with most of the rest of the world that Clay would lose to Liston, the NOI leadership in Chicago showed little interest in backing the fighter or advertising his growing ties to the faith. But Malcolm calculated that, if Clay were to win, Chicago would suddenly see the value of bringing him into the fold, and Malcolm could win his way back into the Messenger's good graces by helping to make that happen.

Not yet recognizing the full extent of the rift between Malcolm and Elijah Muhammad, Clay invited Malcolm and his family to Miami to watch him train. Clay paid all the expenses as a wedding anniversary gift to Betty, and installed the family at the Hampton House motor hotel in Overtown, the nicest of the city's Green Book hotels, so named because they appeared in the travel guide of that color identifying Southern hotels and eating establishments that welcomed traveling Blacks. Clay came to the hotel to play games with Malcolm's daughters, and Malcolm visited Clay's training camp and countered all the press talk about Liston's invincibility by reminding Cassius of the tale of David and Goliath. "He told me that I was young, strong and skillful," Clay recalled. "He told me that he knew that I would win because time was on my side. Malcolm helped me focus on my strengths and he strengthened my belief in myself." After Betty and the girls returned to New York, however, the press started writing stories about Malcolm's presence in Miami and Clay's growing ties to the Nation of Islam. When one of the white promoters threatened to cancel the bout over the adverse publicity, Malcolm agreed to go back to New York and to return only for the fight itself.

When Malcolm arrived back in Miami on the eve of the bout, he checked into the Hampton House and gave interviews to two prominent white journalists, predicting a Clay upset despite the eight-to-one odds against him. "To be a Muslim is to know no fear," Malcolm told Murray Kempton, then writing for the *New York World Telegram*, and later made the same point to the freelance magazine writer George Plimpton. Backstage before the fight, Malcolm joined Clay in Islamic prayer, kneeling and facing Mecca. He showed Clay photos of Liston and the former heavyweight champion Floyd Patterson posing with their own Christian "spiritual advisers."

"This fight is for the truth," Malcolm told Clay, according to Haley's account in the *Autobiography*. "It's the Cross and the Crescent fighting in a prize ring—for the first time. It's a modern Crusades—a Christian and a Muslim facing each other with television to beam it off Telstar for the whole world to see what happens! Do you think Allah has brought about all this intending for you to leave the ring as anything but the champion?"

Taking his place in the seventh row away from the ring, Malcolm watched with the rest of a crowd of more than eight thousand as Clay seized early command of the fight. He danced away from Liston's heavy punches, then began to land his own blows and opened a cut under Liston's left eye. But as Clay went to his corner after the fourth round, he felt an intense burning sensation in his own eyes—caused, it would later be widely speculated, by liniment with which Liston had laced his gloves. Fighting all but blind through the fifth round, Clay absorbed Liston's punches, tiring the defender out and giving his vision time to clear. In the sixth round, he unloaded on the exhausted champion, inflicting so much punishment that when Liston went to his corner he spit out his mouth guard and refused to come out for round seven. As the referee declared Clay the winner by a technical knockout, the new champion pranced around the ring and taunted his doubters. "Eat your words!" he shouted toward the dozens of sports reporters at ringside, all but three of whom had predicted a Liston victory. "I'm king of the world!"

After the fight, Clay accompanied Malcolm back to the Hampton House for a celebration with dozens of supporters in the motel's small ground-floor luncheonette. Dressed in NOI fashion in a dark suit and thin black bow tie, Clay wolfed down a bowl of ice cream and playfully sparred with members of his entourage. Malcolm telephoned Alex Haley, his autobiographical collaborator, and put Clay on the line, boasting in the background that "his little brother had done marvelously well." Then Clay and Malcolm retreated to Malcolm's bedroom for a quieter and more serious conversation with Jim Brown, the Cleveland Browns running back who himself was contemplating an early retirement from pro football to focus on a budding movie acting career. Both friends impressed on Clay the freedom that he now had to speak his mind—and the opportunity to do more good for the Black race. Yet according to Brown's account, when Malcolm briefly left the conversation, Clay suggested that he was now aware of the irreparable split between Malcolm and Elijah Muhammad, and that he believed he had no choice but to side with the Messenger. Clay "loved Malcolm," Brown would write in his own memoir, "but from that day on, he would never again be his friend."

In fact, the rupture between Malcolm and Clay was more drawn out and personally painful than Jim Brown suggested. The next day, the new champion was peppered with questions about his ties to the NOI when he gave his first post-fight press conference in the Miami Beach Convention Hall's Veterans Room. More subdued than most sports reporters had ever seen him, he expressed admiration for the sect's sober behavior code and metaphorically endorsed its gospel of racial separatism. "In the jungle, lions are with lions and tigers with tigers, and redbirds stay with redbirds and bluebirds with bluebirds," Clay said. "That's human nature, too, to be with your own kind. I don't want to go where I'm not wanted." Channeling the advice that Malcolm had given him at the Hampton House the night before, Clay sent a new message of independence to reporters, boxing fans, and his white financial backers in Louisville. "I don't have to be what you want me to be," he declared. "I'm free to be who I want."

Yet if Malcolm had hoped to use this turning point in Clay's life to win his own way back into the Nation of Islam, the wily Elijah Muhammad was one step ahead of him. After showing no interest in the fight, Muhammad now told a group of followers in Chicago that Clay's religious faith had helped him win and described the new champion as "a follower." The next day, reporters approached Clay at the Hampton House as he was having breakfast with Malcolm and asked about Elijah Muhammad's statement. "That is true, and I'm proud of it," Clay said. Then he repeated one of Malcolm's own favorite lines in describing his conversion experience. "A rooster crows only when it sees the light. Put him in the dark and he'll never crow. I have seen the light and I'm crowing."

Three days later, Clay traveled to New York City for a victory tour orchestrated by Malcolm. He checked into the Theresa, Malcolm's temporary headquarters, where the two men met for an hour in Malcolm's room. They joined a crowd of five hundred to view a film of the Liston fight at a movie theater in midtown Manhattan, after which an Associated Press photographer snapped a picture of Clay signing autographs as a beaming Malcolm looked on. The next day, Malcolm took Clay to an interview with the *New York Amsterdam News*, during which the new champ announced that he was renouncing the name of the "Kentucky slave master" he was given at birth. From then on, Clay declared, "I will be known as Cassius X." On the third and fourth day of the visit, Malcolm escorted Clay and his brother Rudy through the halls of the United Nations, introducing them to envoys from Africa and Asia, and Cassius tantalized the press with hints that he might tour Africa with Malcolm.

At this point, Malcolm was just days away from announcing his split from the Nation of Islam, and he was clearly hoping the New York visit would persuade Clay to join him. But in the jockeying for Clay's allegiance, Elijah Muhammad had one move that Malcolm couldn't match. After days of seeing the news stories and photographs of Clay and Malcolm together, the NOI leader went on a Chicago radio broadcast to make an offer he knew the new champ couldn't refuse. "I hope he will accept being called by a better name," the NOI leader declared, referring to Clay's birth name and his new choice of Cassius X. "Muhammad Ali is what I will give to him as long as he believes in Allah and follows me." Hearing that announcement in his blue Oldsmobile, Malcolm immediately grasped the power of Elijah Muhammad's gesture to Clay. "That's political!" Malcolm shouted to an aide with him in the car. "That's a political move. He did it to prevent him from coming with me."

Once Clay accepted his indelible new name, and Malcolm announced his plans to leave the NOI to *The New York Times*, both men knew that they could no longer be seen together in public. When Clay—now Muhammad Ali—made his first trip to the NOI headquarters in Chicago since the Liston fight in mid-March, he answered press questions about his relationship with Malcolm with a quip clearly intended to please Elijah Muhammad. "Muhammad taught Malcolm X everything he knows," Ali said. "So I couldn't go with the child, I go with the daddy." Yet Ali still felt close enough to Malcolm to meet privately with him on another visit to New York in late March. In an interview with a reporter who had learned of that encounter, Malcolm gallantly defended Ali against attacks in the press, and touted the new champion's potential to be a transformative racial figure across the globe. "We are brothers, and we have much in common," Malcolm said. "I frankly believe that Cassius is in a better position than anyone else to restore a sense of racial pride not just to our people in this country but all over the world."

After that, the two men would come face-to-face again only one more time before Malcolm's assassination eleven months later. Once Malcolm embarked on his pilgrimage to Mecca and tour of Africa in April 1964, the Nation of Islam sent Ali on his own tour of the continent. On the eve of Ali's departure, Malcolm sent his friend a telegram with the advice that he could no longer give him in person. "Because a billion of our people in Africa, Arabia and Asia love you blindly," he counseled Ali, "you must now be forever aware of your tremendous responsibilities to them. You must never say or do anything that will permit your enemies to distort the beautiful image you have here among our people."

The next morning, Ali arrived at the Ambassador Hotel in Accra, Ghana, just as Malcolm was leaving with his packed bags. As Ali got out of his car, Malcolm tried to greet him. "Brother Muhammad!" he called out. "Brother Muhammad!"

Ali ignored the overture, walking past Malcolm with an entourage that included Elijah Muhammad's son Herbert, who had been assigned by the NOI to be the champion's new manager.

Malcolm chased after them. "Brother Muhammad!" he repeated. "Brother Muhammad!"

This time, Ali wheeled around and glared at Malcolm. "You left the Honorable Elijah Muhammad," he snapped. "That was the wrong thing to do."

The poet Maya Angelou, who was traveling with Malcolm, recalled "the heavy mood" that hung over Malcolm as he retreated from the encounter and got into her Fiat sedan for the ride to the airport. "I've lost a lot," Malcolm muttered. "A lot. Maybe too much."

Meanwhile, Ali proceeded to ridicule Malcolm to journalists covering his trip. "Man, did you get a look at him?" Ali said mockingly at the Ambassador Hotel later that day, describing the new look that Malcolm had adopted during his travels. "Dressed in that funny white robe and wearing a beard and walking with that cane that looked like a prophet's stick? Man, he's gone. He's gone so far he's out completely." Ignoring Malcolm's advice about comporting himself with dignity during the trip abroad, Ali bragged that when he got to the United Arab Emirates, with its tradition of polygamy, he was going to build "a castle" with "a throne room" and take three wives who would feed him grapes, rub olive oil on his muscles, and shine his shoes. A fourth wife, named "Peaches," Ali joked, would "sing or play music, maybe."

That night, reporter Lloyd Garrison filed a story to *The New York Times* describing Ali's tense run-in with Malcolm at the Ambassador Hotel. "Clay Makes Malcolm Ex-Friend," read the blunt headline. "Champion Ridicules Former Muslim in Ghana Talkathon." Whether Malcolm ever read the story isn't known, but he was embarrassed enough by the encounter that he later pretended that it never happened in the *Autobiography*. Instead, Malcolm suggested that he did Ali a favor by steering clear of him in Africa, and imagined that instead of mocking him, Ali still appreciated his loyalty. "The next morning, a Saturday, I heard that Cassius Clay and his entourage had arrived" in Ghana, reads the *Autobiography*'s version. "There was a huge reception for him at the airport. I thought that if Cassius and I happened to meet, it would likely prove embarrassing for Cassius, since he had elected to remain with Elijah Muhammad's version of Islam. . . . I knew that Cassius knew I had been with him, and for him, and believed in him, when those who later embraced him felt that he had no chance. I decided to avoid Cassius so as not to put him on the spot."

═══

On the night of Malcolm's assassination ten months later, a fire broke out in the Chicago building where Muhammad Ali had an apartment. Rushing home from dinner with his wife, Sonja, Ali found reporters waiting to ask him for comment about Malcolm. He was "surprised and saddened" by the murder, Ali responded perfunctorily. Meanwhile, police concluded that the fire had been set by a drunk neighbor who fell asleep on his couch smoking a lit cigarette. Yet according to Sonja, that didn't stop Ali from speculating privately that "someone started it [the fire] on purpose"—implying that he suspected Malcolm allies of targeting him for retribution. A few days later, at a Savior's Day rally in Chicago—the annual birthday celebration of NOI founder Wallace Fard Muhammad—Elijah Muhammad denied involvement in the assassination but denounced Malcolm as a "hypocrite." At the same event, Malcolm's brothers Philbert and Wilfred faulted him for taking "a dangerous course" by breaking with the NOI. Seated as a guest of honor on the dais, Ali could be heard murmuring "Amen!" and "Yes, sir!" to the attacks on his slain former friend.

Speculation about a retaliatory attack by Malcolm followers continued to hang over Ali's rematch with Sonny Liston in Lewiston, Maine, that May. Meeting with reporters beforehand, Ali was asked about a rumor that a carload of assassins was heading to Maine from New York. "I fear no living man, only Allah!" Ali shouted, pounding his fist on a table. "The hell with Malcolm's boys! Who are they?" After winning that second fight with a shocking knockout just minutes into the first round, Ali wrapped himself even more tightly in the NOI's embrace. He severed ties with his white financial backers in Louisville, made Herbert Muhammad his exclusive manager, and divorced Sonja after Herbert suggested that she was insufficiently devout.

For most of the next five years—in what should have been his athletic prime—Ali was banned from boxing for his refusal to serve in the Vietnam War. Yet while defending that stance in language reminiscent of Malcolm—famously declaring that "no Viet Cong never called me a nigger"— Ali continued to jab at his former mentor. Appearing on the televised interview show *Firing Line*, Ali chafed at host William F. Buckley Jr.'s queries about the estrangement between the two men. Malcolm, Ali told Buckley, "was nothing until the Honorable Elijah Muhammad made him great. Now you seem to try to make it look like he was a leader and he was powerful." When Buckley persisted, Ali erupted. "Whites destroyed Malcolm X!" Ali argued, by making him believe that he was bigger than Elijah Muhammad. Visibly exasperated, he tried to cut off any more questions about Malcolm. "He's dead now," Ali snapped, "and we don't talk about dead people."

Yet unbeknownst to Ali, he would have Malcolm partly to thank for his eventual victory in a four-year battle to keep from going to prison for resisting the draft. In April 1967, Ali reported to a Houston induction center but refused twice to step forward when his birth name of Cassius Clay was called. Two months later, a House jury convicted him of violating the Universal Military Training and Service Act, and a district judge sentenced him to five years behind bars. Ali's lawyers filed an appeal while simultaneously seeking reinstatement of his boxing license. The latter came through in 1970, and Ali tried to get his title back from the new heavyweight champion, Joe Frazier, losing a grueling fifteen-round fight by decision. But even then, Ali still risked jail time if he lost his final appeal to the Supreme Court in 1971.

When the justices first voted on Ali's case in secret session, they came down five-to-three against him, with Thurgood Marshall recusing himself because he had been solicitor general charged with enforcing the draft laws when the verdict was initially issued. Chief Justice Warren Burger assigned Justice John Harlan to write the majority opinion. But a Harlan clerk who had read *The Autobiography of Malcolm X* urged his boss to reconsider. The book's descriptions of Malcolm's religious conversion and the Nation of Islam's stance against war had convinced the clerk that Ali was sincere in his insistence that he was a "conscientious objector" to the draft. Doubtful at first, Harlan studied the matter in greater depth and came to agree with the clerk. Harlan then circulated a memo to the other justices arguing that the Justice Department had erred in dismissing Ali's religious defense. The justices decided to vote again, and this time they agreed unanimously to overturn Ali's draft-dodging conviction.

During his years of exile from the ring, Ali also got a taste of the kind of imperious treatment from Elijah Muhammad that had driven Malcolm out of the Nation of Islam. Two years into his boxing ban, Ali gave an interview to broadcast sports journalist Howard Cosell in which he lamented his loss of income and declared his interest in fighting again if the money involved was sufficient. Viewing that admission as a sign of weakness and signal that Allah and the Nation of Islam couldn't provide adequately for him, Elijah Muhammad announced that he was suspending Ali from the NOI and stripping him of his new name. "We will call him Cassius Clay," the NOI leader wrote in an editorial published in *Muhammad Speaks*. Ali promptly apologized and the suspension was lifted, although some observers suggested that Ali was now acting more out of self-preservation than continued conviction. Once Ali fought his way back to the heavyweight title, he quietly confided his disillusionment with the NOI during an interview with the white sports journalist David Kindred. "I would have gotten out of this a long time ago," Kindred reported Ali as whispering to him. "But you saw what they did to Malcolm X. I ain't gonna end up like Malcolm X."

In the decade after Ali began to box again, he staged a riveting comeback that reshaped his bad boy image and cemented his place in the pantheon of sports. He beat Frazier in two epic rematches, the second of which, widely known as "the Thrilla in Manila," took place in the Philippines. He won the heavyweight title fight in 1974 against a heavily favored George Foreman, who had dethroned Frazier, in a fight that took place in Zaire and was immortalized as "the Rumble in the Jungle." Ali lost the crown to Leon Spinks after not taking the young upstart seriously, then willed himself back into fighting shape at the age of thirty-six to win a rematch and claim the title for an unprecedented third time. As he began to show signs of the Parkinson's disease that would still his once dazzling speech and movement, he retired and then unwisely un-retired to fight a series of embarrassing final bouts that likely accelerated his physical and mental decline. Even so, his last three decades of disability were marked by deeply moving public appearances—most memorably when a visibly shaking Ali lit the torch at the opening ceremony of the 1996 Summer Olympics in Atlanta, and when President George W. Bush placed the Presidential Medal of Freedom around his neck at the White House in 2005.

By the time Ali died in 2016, he was honored as much for the stands that had once made him so controversial as for his prowess in the ring. His opposition to the disastrous war in Vietnam looked brave and prophetic in retrospect, and his boastful verse was celebrated as a precursor to the cultural revolution of hip hop. After Elijah Muhammad died

in 1975 and Ali converted to orthodox Islam, the furor over his religious faith faded away. Like Malcolm, Ali came to renounce the NOI's
doctrine of racial separation and insistence that whites were devils.
"I don't hate whites," Ali declared after Elijah Muhammad was gone.
"That was history, but it's coming to an end. We're in a new phase, a
resurrection."

Of all the public actions he had taken in his past, Ali expressed a
sense of remorse for just one: his repudiation of Malcolm X. In *The
Soul of a Butterfly: Reflections on Life's Journey*, a meditative memoir he
cowrote with his daughter Hana and published in 2003, Ali retold the
story of how he had walked away from Malcolm in Ghana forty years
earlier. "Turning my back on Malcolm was one of the mistakes that I
regret most in my life," he wrote. "I wish I'd been able to tell Malcolm I
was sorry, that he was right about so many things. But he was killed before I got the chance. He was a visionary—ahead of us all. . . . Malcolm
was the first to discover the truth, that color doesn't make a man a
devil. It is the heart, soul, and mind that define a person. Malcolm X
was a great thinker and an even greater friend. I might never have become a Muslim if it hadn't been for Malcolm. If I could go back and do
it all over again, I would never have turned my back on him."

In the fall of 1965, the future basketball legend Kareem Abdul-Jabbar
arrived at the University of California, Los Angeles as the most touted
college recruit in a generation. Still known by his birth name—Lew
Alcindor, short for Ferdinand Lewis Alcindor Jr.—he had grown by age
eighteen to seven feet two inches tall, making him the most dominant
high school center in the country despite his bony build. At Power
Memorial Academy, an all-boys Catholic School in New York, Alcindor
had led his team to fifty-nine consecutive victories and several Catholic league titles. *Sports Illustrated* had singled him out for mention after
he averaged 26 points a game in his junior year. Of all the colleges that
scouted him, Alcindor chose UCLA because of its renowned basketball program led by John Wooden, the quietly rigorous coach who had
guided the Bruins to the last two consecutive NCAA championships.
But Alcindor was also an A student with an avid interest in current

events, and he saw UCLA as a place where, with Coach Wooden's blessing, he could continue to expand his mind while further honing his formidable athletic skills.

For a young Black man of his generation, Alcindor had in some ways led a relatively sheltered life. His father, Ferdinand Alcindor Sr., was a taciturn transit policeman and amateur jazz musician who had moved his family uptown from Harlem to the quieter neighborhood of Inwood when Lew was three years old. His mother, Cora, was a more sociable department store clerk who prized education above all else for her only child. Lew had attended Catholic schools throughout his youth, and was shy and studious by nature. But he had also had experiences that gave him a keen personal awareness of racism and interest in the national struggle for equal rights. As a young teen, Lew was sent by his parents to visit family in North Carolina, where he witnessed the humiliations of Jim Crow up close. In a misguided attempt to motivate Alcindor during a sluggish game, his white high school coach had used a racial slur in accusing him of not hustling. "You're acting just like a *nigger*!" the coach told him. During summer vacations, Lew had worked as an intern at the Schomburg Center for Black history in Harlem, and on a student newspaper for which he covered the 1964 riot that broke out after a white policeman shot and killed a fifteen-year-old Black boy.

So during the summer break after his freshman year at UCLA, Alcindor was eager to read the recently published memoir by Malcolm X, the slain Black leader whom Lew had seen speak on the streets of Harlem in his high school years. From the start, *The Autobiography of Malcolm X* electrified him. "I started the book with intellectual curiosity," he recalled decades later, "but soon began seeing the parallels between his life and mine. Our families were both from the Caribbean: His mother had come from Grenada, while my people came from nearby Trinidad. His father had been a follower of the black nationalist Marcus Garvey; my grandparents had been sympathetic to his ideas. His description of racism in his hometown of Lansing, Michigan, matched my experiences in New York and North Carolina. He pointed out that schoolroom textbooks ignored the role of black people, despite the fact that the first martyr of the American revolution was a black man named

Crispus Attucks. My research at the Schomburg had revealed the same truths. Within a few pages, I was passionately engrossed, reading frantically yet not wanting the book to end."

One scene from the book in particular stuck with Alcindor. To illustrate the power of the Nation of Islam to transform lives, Elijah Muhammad put two glasses next to one another on a counter, one filled with dirty water and the other with clean water. "You want to spread my teachings?" Muhammad told Malcolm. "Don't condemn if you see a person has a dirty glass of water, just show them the clean glass of water that you have. When they inspect it, you won't have to say that yours is better." Alcindor, who had recently celebrated another birthday, thought to himself: "I was only nineteen years old, but I knew I'd been drinking from that dirty glass most of my life." In his reading of the story, the dirty water wasn't a metaphor for an unclean lifestyle, as it had been for the young Malcolm and many other prison converts, but for having accepted an identity imposed on him by society rather than one he chose himself. "I was riveted by Malcolm's intimate story of how he came to realize he'd been the victim of institutional racism, which had imprisoned him long before he'd landed in an actual prison," he recalled. "That's how I felt: imprisoned by an image of who I was supposed to be."

Shaken to question his Catholic upbringing, Alcindor spent the next two years investigating a variety of other religions, from Hinduism and Buddhism to various Protestant faiths. But the more he read about Islam, the more he felt its pull both as a belief system and as a link to an ancestral past in Africa and to a community of people of color around the world. While back in New York in the summer before his senior year, Alcindor started to attend a Sunni mosque in Harlem, to perform Islamic prayers and to memorize passages from the Koran. He also fell under the influence of a cleric named Hamaas Abdul Khaalis, who, like Malcolm, had split from the Nation of Islam. Born Ernest McGhee, Abdul Khaalis started his own Islamic sect that became known as the Hanafi Muslim movement. Early that summer, another teacher at the New York mosque had suggested that Alcindor affirm his faith by changing his name to "Abdul Kareem," or "Generous

Servant." Abdul Khaalis urged Kareem to add one more name to reflect another side of his personality —"Jabbar," or "powerful."

That winter, Alcindor confided his conversion to Coach Wooden and his basketball teammates during a late-night bull session aboard a bus taking the team to away games across the Midwest. But it wasn't until two and a half years later—once he had led the Milwaukee Bucks to an NBA Championship in his second season as a professional—that Alcindor legally changed his name to Kareem Abdul-Jabbar. Just as Malcolm X had stressed the need for Blacks to free themselves mentally as well as legally, Abdul-Jabbar would later describe the wait as a test of his own psychological independence. "All my life, I had allowed others to name me," he wrote, "and even when they had done so with my permission and encouragement, I still had the feeling I was letting others decide who I was. This time, though, I had fought my way past all those who doubted me, and while I appreciated all my coaches and teachers, I had fought beyond them, too, to stand on my own and say, 'I named myself. This is the man I choose to be, not the man the world expects me to be.'"

During his sophomore year at UCLA, Lew Alcindor received another life-changing invitation that could be traced back to Malcolm X. In 1964, at the Hampton House motel in Miami, Malcolm had talked long into the night with Cassius Clay and quarterback Jim Brown after Clay won the heavyweight title. Malcolm's message: both athletes had an opportunity and a duty to also fight in the social arena. Three years later, in April 1967, Muhammad Ali had done just that by refusing to be drafted to serve in Vietnam. However, that decision didn't sit well with Herbert Muhammad, the son of Elijah Muhammad who had been assigned by the Nation of Islam to act as Ali's manager. Herbert claimed to be worried about Ali's loss of income but he also stood to lose a tidy sum himself if Ali didn't continue fighting. So Herbert reached out to Jim Brown to ask if he could get Ali to reconsider, calculating that Brown would also want Ali to keep boxing because he had a financial stake in a company that promoted Ali's fights.

Instead of trying to dissuade Ali, Brown convened what came to be known as "the Cleveland summit." He asked Ali to meet privately with a group of prominent Blacks to explain his thinking. That group included Boston Celtics basketball great Bill Russell and ten other well-known athletes as well as Carl Stokes, the Cleveland attorney who was about to run for mayor. Knowing that Alcindor had become friendly with Ali, Brown invited the UCLA basketball star to participate. Alcindor readily accepted, even though he had to pay his own way to Cleveland. "I was excited to finally be part of the political movement in a more direct and active way," he recalled. "I also wanted to help Ali if I could because he made me feel proud to be African American."

On June 4, Brown's delegation met with Ali at the Negro Industrial and Economic Union on the East Side of Cleveland. A number of the participants were military veterans— including Stokes and Brown himself—and several arrived determined to talk Ali out of resisting the draft. But during an intense grilling that lasted several hours, Ali held his ground, explaining his religious objections to war and his specific opposition to Vietnam as a conflict that was being waged by a disproportionately Black fighting force while tens of thousands of draft-age white men avoided the draft by staying in school. "Ali argued that it was a war against people of color fought by people of color for a country that denied them their basic civil rights," Abdul-Jabbar later recalled in a memoir. "In the end, he convinced us and we decided to support him."

Describing the impact of that experience on his own sense of social responsibility, Abdul-Jabbar invoked Malcolm X. "The Cleveland Summit had catapulted me from grumbling college sophomore to a national spokesperson for political and social issues involving African Americans," he wrote. "It was what I wanted, but the pressure was even greater than it was playing basketball because the stakes were so much higher. Winning a basketball game wasn't the same as trying to secure voting rights, educational opportunities, and jobs for the disenfranchised. Failing to score on a hook shot meant missing a few points. Failing to articulate a position clearly and convincingly could affect people's lives. It was scary, but I felt ready. As Malcolm X had said, 'If you want something, you had better make some noise.'"

A year later, Alcindor was invited to another meeting of elite Black athletes, this time to decide whether to boycott the 1968 Summer

Olympics in Mexico City. The gathering was hosted by Harry Edwards, the San Jose State College sociologist who had first proposed a boycott as a way to protest the crisis in Black America months after the assassination of Martin Luther King Jr. and the week of national protests that followed. Alcindor was the top pick for America's Olympic basketball team, after leading UCLA to two straight national championships. Yet "I was torn," he recalled. "Joining the team would signal that I supported the way people of color were being treated in America—which I didn't. Not joining the team would look like I didn't love America—which I did."

Finally, after listening to the debate among the athletes, Alcindor opted to stay away from the games, which earned him hate mail calling him "an ungrateful nigger." But his stand only made fleeting news. The protest everyone would remember from that Olympics was staged by two Black sprinters who chose to go to Mexico City: a twenty-four-year-old Texan named Tommie Smith and a twenty-three-year-old Harlem native named John Carlos, who as a teen had been one of Malcolm X's most devoted young followers.

By the time John Carlos was fourteen, he had become aware of Malcolm X by listening to his appearances on local radio in New York City. "I was intrigued with what he had to say and more so how he was saying it," he wrote in his 2011 memoir, *The John Carlos Story*. "He said it with so much dignity and strength." Then the teenager began hearing the name on the lips of older men in the Harlem barber shop where he got his hair cut. "It was Malcolm this and Malcolm that," Carlos recalled, "and I wanted to see and hear it for myself, on his home turf and in his mosque." So he asked permission from his father to attend an event where Malcolm would be speaking at the Nation of Islam mosque on 116th Street and Lenox Avenue. "Son, you can go down there," John's father replied, "but don't go down there and get in any trouble."

When Carlos arrived at the mosque, he took a seat at the back of a room that was packed not only with NOI members but also with scores of other Harlem residents. He didn't know what Malcolm looked like, so he asked a man seated nearby to point him out.

"Man, that can't be Malcolm X," Carlos said when the man gestured toward a tall, slender figure in the front of the room.

"That's him," the other man assured Carlos.

"Can't be," Carlos said.

"Why?" the man asked.

"Man, 'cause he's too light-skinned," Carlos said. "Malcolm X is a black guy. This guy is like the Black Jew, right?"

Yet as soon as Malcolm went to the podium and opened his mouth, Carlos recognized the powerful voice and message he had heard on the radio. "Standing as straight as a sentry and with the confidence of a CEO, Malcolm spoke about trying to build character and confidence among our people," Carlos recalled. "He said that he looked out onto Harlem and saw no self-esteem or pride in who we were as people. Malcolm wasn't speaking to the best angels of our nature. He was speaking to the distance that we had to travel if we are going to be seen and respected as human beings, not animals, servants or slaves."

Even at that young age, Carlos had begun to feel the pull of the kind of destructive forces Malcolm was describing. Unlike many of his Harlem peers, John came from a stable, supportive family. His father, Earl Vanderbilt Carlos, known as "Big Earl," had made his way from the sharecropping fields of South Carolina to fight in World War II and then opened his own shoe repair business in Harlem. His Jamaican-born mother, Vioris, had been raised in Cuba and worked as a nurse's aide at New York's Bellevue Hospital. But by his early teens, John was struggling at school as a result of undiagnosed dyslexia, and had fallen in with a gang that heisted goods off freight trains that stopped in Harlem. So, sitting at the back of the Harlem mosque that day, he felt that Malcolm was talking directly to him, voicing thoughts he didn't yet have the words to express.

"I remember being blown away," Carlos recalled. "Malcolm didn't speak like Dr. King or Representative Adam Clayton Powell or any of the church-trained speakers I'd ever seen. It was like he was blowing out my eardrums without raising his voice. He didn't perform any kind of theatrics with either his pitch or his tone. There was no showmanship in the man. His power, and the response of the audience, grew out of the fact that he was articulating ideas we were thinking about all the time but didn't really have a language or vocabulary to express. For me, it was like he grabbed on to my frustrations and turned them into logic."

Carlos kept returning to the mosque to hear Malcolm speak, and started following him around afterward. "Like a scampering puppy dog," Carlos recalled, he would chase after Malcolm as he walked with brisk strides through the streets of Harlem. Bemused by the attention from the young fan, Malcolm would make Carlos catch up before he generously answered his questions.

"Why do you believe what you believe?" Carlos asked. "And why aren't there more individuals out there doing what you are doing?"

Malcolm replied that the spread of the Nation of Islam and the size of his crowds showed how many Blacks shared his views. But more didn't speak out themselves, he said, because Blacks were "so fragmented as a people." In answering the teen's eager questions, Malcolm "was remarkably without ego," Carlos recalled. "He never said that maybe people came to hear him speaking because they wanted to hear him speak!"

Inspired by his new hero, Carlos took his first steps as a social activist. At his Harlem high school, he organized a protest against substandard cafeteria food. Ordered by the school principal to leave his office, "I just stood there," he recalled, "ramrod straight like Malcolm and stared into his eyes." For two weeks, students brought lunches to school in paper bags, and the principal finally agreed to their demands after Carlos threatened to contact reporters from *The New York Times* and the *Daily News*. At the housing project where his family lived, Carlos went on a crusade against a caterpillar infestation that was keeping his mother from using the courtyard. When the building manager brushed him off, Carlos began dousing trees in the courtyard with gasoline and setting them on fire to kill the insects. Police were called, and Carlos was hauled into court, where he accused the manager of pocketing city funds earmarked for pest removal. Under questioning from the judge, the manager confessed, and Carlos was set free.

At nineteen, Carlos was still following Malcolm around, by now with the long legs and loping gait of a budding track star. But on the fateful Sunday in February 1965, he was in a rural area outside New

York City with a friend who was helping him practice for his driver's license test. On the car radio on the way back into the city, the two heard the news that Malcolm had been shot in the Audubon Ballroom. The friend drove straight to the hospital where Malcolm's body had been taken, and they joined the anxious crowd outside just as word started to spread that Malcolm was dead. For Carlos, immediate grief was followed by lingering guilt, a kind of magical thinking that he could have prevented the murder. "I felt like if I was in that ballroom that night, maybe I could have seen something or noticed something and maybe he wouldn't have been shot," Carlos recalled. "I know that doesn't sound too logical and I can't explain it in a way that makes sense. It just took a lot out of me for a long time because I had a feeling that in some way, shape, or form, I would have been able to do something to intervene. I was just in love with the man. Maybe it was because he made time for me on the streets. Maybe it was because he made me raise my head up high. But it definitely always seems like he was always two steps ahead of us."

Just eight days after the murder, Carlos married his girlfriend, Kim, and nine months later she gave birth to a baby girl, named Kimmie. "No coincidence, but it was a week after Malcolm was assassinated," Carlos later explained. "I felt this urge to move forward, to grow up, to be my own man. My head was twisted with emotion at the time." By then, Carlos had emerged as one of the best high school sprinters in the Northeast—dominating races in distances from 60 to 220 meters—and he was getting feelers from major track programs across the country. But because his grades were so poor, most schools demanded that he first attend two years of community college. At an open track meet in New Jersey, Carlos befriended a white sprinter from East Texas State University who encouraged him to visit that school. The white track coach there was so eager to recruit Carlos that he offered him full tuition and agreed to bend NCAA rules to waive academic requirements and to arrange for a job in the area for Kim.

Shortly after he arrived in East Texas, the welcome mat was rolled up. Carlos had to get used to being called "boy," "son," and "that Nigra fella." He and Kim were instructed to use segregated public bathrooms and to refrain from socializing with whites. "Don't you ever play with this little nigger girl again!" a white father shouted at his daughter after she befriended Kimmie. At the track, the white coach flaunted his authority over Carlos, leading to a series of angry confrontations. During one, the coach pulled out a hammer and swung it at Carlos, after which Carlos had to be talked out of quitting the team on the spot.

Not long afterward, news arrived from the outside world that would put an end to the ugly chapter in East Texas and open a life-changing new one for Carlos. In the mail, he received an issue of *Track & Field* magazine with a story about a Black scholar at San Jose State College, Harry Edwards, who along with two of the school's top sprinters was proposing to organize a boycott of the upcoming 1968 Summer Olympics. Edwards and the two Black track stars—Tommie Smith and Lee Evans—cited a list of grievances, from the overall racist treatment of Blacks in America to the stripping of Muhammad Ali's boxing title and the refusal of International Olympic Commission (IOC) president Avery Brundage to ban the apartheid states of South Africa and Rhodesia from the games. As news of the proposed boycott spread, Carlos was approached for an interview by a reporter for the East Texas State student newspaper. Carlos agreed to talk on condition that the reporter publish his remarks in full, with no editing.

"To his credit," Carlos recalled, "he agreed and we dropped a piece that set our little campus on its ear. The article quoted me saying that even though the Olympics had been my dream since I was a little boy, I would be proud to give it up for the greater good. I spoke about all my experiences and my family's experience with racism in East Texas and asked how I could represent a country that had treated me and mine so terribly. I spoke in harsh and unflinching terms about the school, the community, the state of Texas and the country and made it clear that if I was fortunate enough to be chosen for the US Olympic team, I would support the boycott."

As Carlos put it, "the flames from this story shot up faster than those trees I threw gasoline on all those many years ago to kill the caterpillars." The school's athletic director called all the Black athletes at the school together and lectured them to "love it or leave it" when it came to associating East Texas State with any talk of an Olympic boycott. Two other Black members of the track team were stripped of their athletic scholarships for failing a science test, a move that Carlos interpreted as a warning shot at him and a prelude to recruiting other Black athletes who would be asked to spy on him. Not wanting to stick around to find out, he abruptly quit the team and left East Texas with Kim and Kimmie, not knowing what lay ahead.

The young family moved back to Harlem, and several weeks later Carlos was at his mother's house, helping her with some painting chores, when the phone rang. It was Harry Edwards on the line, asking Vioris if he could speak with her son. When John got on the phone, Edwards told him that he had heard about his troubles in East Texas and his interview with the student newspaper. Now Edwards and the other boycott organizers were in New York City for a planning meeting, and he wanted to know if Carlos could attend.

Standing an imposing six feet eight inches tall, Harry Edwards had himself been a champion discus thrower as an undergraduate at San Jose College. He was also a serious student fascinated by the nexus between race and sports, and he earned a degree with honors in sociology. In 1962, Edwards became friendly with the Harlem journalist Louis Lomax when Lomax spoke at San Jose State and Edwards was assigned to act as a guide. After receiving a graduate school fellowship from Cornell, Edwards decided to write his doctoral thesis on the Black Muslim family and he asked Lomax for an introduction to Malcolm X. Lomax vouched for Edwards, telling Malcolm that the young graduate student was "bright." A meeting in Harlem was arranged to which Edward brought a sheet full of questions and during which a photo was snapped of the two men together, Edwards sporting a goatee modeled after Malcolm's.

In 1967, two years after Malcolm's assassination, Edwards returned to San Jose State as an assistant professor and chaired a conference on Black youth at which he announced the launch of the Olympic Project for Human Rights (OPHR). The aim was to use the spotlight of the approaching 1968 Olympic Games to dramatize the plight of Blacks from the United States to apartheid South Africa—and the use of the term "human rights" was a conscious homage to Malcolm's use of that term during his global travels in the last year of his life.

When John Carlos arrived at the planning meeting held at an elegant hotel in downtown Manhattan, he found that Edwards had assembled not only well-known athletes but also leading civil rights leaders, among them Martin Luther King Jr. and his aides Ralph Abernathy and Andrew Young. Introduced to King, Carlos peppered the great man with questions, including one about the sanitation workers' strike King was supporting in Memphis. What kept King going back to the city despite ugly violence and threats of worse to come? Carlos asked. "John, I have to go back and stand for those that can't stand for themselves," King replied.

Carlos left the hotel meeting inspired to give his "heart and soul," as he put it, to the OPHR. But just weeks later, Dr. King was gunned down in Memphis, and the campaign lost the prospect of the worldwide publicity it might have gained if King had joined Black boycotters outside the gates of the Mexico Olympics. Around the same time, the IOC announced that it would ban South Africa and Rhodesia from the games. The move made it look like the IOC was responding to the OPHR's demands, and complicated the bid to throw a harsh spotlight on Brundage, the longtime IOC president whose history of controversy dated back to his support for holding the 1936 Olympics in Nazi Germany. In their private meetings, Black athletes who had supported the boycott began to voice second thoughts, arguing that they deserved the chance to compete after years of hard work and sacrifice. "Our pressure, at least on that front, had worked," Carlos recalled of the South Africa news. "But it also served to make a lot of our allies say, 'Well, we accomplished that. So let's line up and go for the gold!'"

By this time, Carlos had forged a personal alliance with protest leaders Tommie Smith and Lee Evans, the two Black sprinters from San Jose State against whom he competed while at East Texas State. Disheartened, the three conceded that they no longer had support for a mass boycott and that staying away from the Olympics by themselves wouldn't get much attention. So they grudgingly completed the process of qualifying for the U.S. track team and arrived at the games in a state of uncertainty, which only increased after the Mexican government staged a bloody crackdown on protesting students on the eve of the Games and Edwards decided it wasn't safe for him to travel to Mexico City.

But as the finals grew closer for the 200 meters—the event in which Smith was favored and Carlos was also considered a strong contender—John had a new idea. After both men made it through their quarterfinal heats, Carlos approached Smith on the track and outlined the plan: if both won medals, they could stage a protest during the awards ceremony while the eyes of the entire Olympic stadium and the international media were on them. "Tommie nodded his head with a dead-serious look on his face," Carlos recalled, "and then we started talking about the symbols we would use. We had no guide, no blueprint. No one had ever turned the medal stand into a festival of visual symbols to express our feelings. We decided we wanted to wear black gloves to represent strength and unity. We would have beads hanging from our necks, which would represent the history of lynching. We wouldn't wear shoes to symbolize the poverty that still plagued so much of black America. On the medal stand, all we would wear on our feet would be black socks."

The two sprinters had already been racing in black socks for some time, and their wives, who had accompanied them to Mexico City, supplied the black gloves and beads. Both men qualified for the finals, and Carlos resolved to run for second place and allow Smith to finish first. But as the race started, Carlos pulled into the lead, then looked behind him for signs that Smith would close the gap with the "Tommie Legs" kick for which his friend was famous. Sure enough, Smith pulled ahead in the home stretch and Carlos eased up, not sensing that a white Australian sprinter named Peter Norman was gaining on him. As he crossed the finish line, Carlos saw Norman out of the corner of his eye and realized that the Australian had edged ahead, leaving John with the bronze medal while Tommie took gold.

Carlos and Smith had come to like Peter Norman, and knew in advance that he was also a threat in the 200. So they shared their protest plan before the race, and Norman offered to wear an OPHR button as a sign of support if all three made it onto the medal stand. As it turned out, Norman's second-place finish only served to enhance the visual power of the scene that unfolded as the three men mounted the medal stand in the middle of the vast University Olympic Stadium.

As the silver medalist, Norman took first position at the front of the three-tiered platform. Smith climbed onto the higher riser behind him, and Carlos stood behind Tommie on another lower level. Sticking to their plan, both Americans had taken off their shoes and stood with black socks visible beneath their official USA track suits. Each wore a single black glove, Smith on his right hand and Carlos on his left. Around Carlos's neck was a string of beads that his wife, Kim, had loaned him. As "The Star-Spangled Banner" began to play, the American flag was raised, and Smith and Carlos turned in its direction as a sign of respect. Then Tommie put his head down and thrust his black-gloved hand high above his head. Behind him, Carlos echoed the gesture, but with a slightly more bent arm in case anyone tried to disrupt the protest. "I wanted to make sure in case someone rushed us, I could throw down a hammer punch to protect us," Carlos recalled.

Loud boos quickly filled the stadium, and that was only the beginning of the fierce backlash that greeted all three men. Smith and Carlos were abruptly ordered to leave the Olympic Village with their wives. They returned to America to vicious media attacks, which included being described as looking like "black-skinned storm troopers" by television sports broadcaster Brent Musburger. The strain of the Olympic controversy continued to hang over both men as they tried to establish professional careers as football players and then as educators, and contributed to the breakup of both of their marriages. Nine years later, Kim Carlos took her own life. In Australia, Norman was hounded for decades and denied opportunities and honors that should have come his way.

Yet with time, the Mexico City protests came to be seen very differently—as a brave and unforgettable image of racial solidarity and the fight for equal justice in the United States and around the world. Tommie Smith, John Carlos, and Harry Edwards all lived to be celebrated as visionary champions of human rights, while the internal Olympic movement spent decades trying to shed the legacy of bigotry and arrogance that marked the long Avery Brundage era. In 2005, Smith and Carlos were reunited at the unveiling of life-size statues in their honor at San Jose State College, now University, where John transferred to finish college in late 1968. A decade later, President Obama invited the two as honorary guests to a celebration of the 2016 U.S. Olympic team at the White House.

The ultimate lesson of his life story, Carlos would conclude, was one he first learned in his teens from Malcolm X. "Malcolm gave me the verbal justification and the political confidence to do what I felt in my gut: to act," he recalled. Looking back, he saw that willingness to stand for things larger than sports as his greatest accomplishment and source of pride. "Forty-four years later, Tommie and I are the ones without regrets," Carlos wrote in his memoir. "The people who have regrets are those who could have taken a stand, but chose to remain silent. They are the ones asked at public events—by students and teachers, by athletes and couch potatoes—if they were among those who stood up in 1968. My emancipation has become their burden. I take no pleasure in this. There is no 'I told you so' escaping from my lips or crossing my mind. But it is a lesson for all the young people rising up today, from Spain to the South Side of Chicago. Seize your moment in time. The only true regrets in life come from inaction."

SEVEN

The Black Arts Movement

In the early 1960s, the provocative Black poet and playwright later known as Amiri Baraka was living in lower Manhattan and had become a fixture in the Beat Generation arts scene under his original pen name, LeRoi Jones. He had married a white poet and editor, Hettie Cohen, and they had two young daughters together. But political change in the world outside had started to shake Jones's sense of racial identity and artistic purpose. In 1961, he was asked to join a delegation of Black American authors to an international writers' conference hosted by Fidel Castro, the new communist leader of Cuba. During the trip, Jones became friendly with the left-wing Black intellectuals Harold Cruse and John Henrik Clarke, and bonded with Robert F. Williams, the former NAACP official from North Carolina who had fled to Cuba and published the Black armed self-defense manifesto *Negroes with Guns*.

In 1963, Jones was jolted by events in the United States. Thousands of Blacks marched on Washington, and a bloody civil rights confrontation in Birmingham was punctuated by a gruesome church firebombing that left four Black schoolgirls dead. When President Kennedy was assassinated in November, Jones channeled his mixed emotions into a work he called "Exaugural Poem: For Jacqueline Bouvier Kennedy who has had to eat too much shit," published in *Kulchur*, a downtown literary journal.

Shortly afterward, Jones learned of Malcolm X's suspension from the Nation of Islam. Puzzled and angered by the news, Jones thought back to the times he had seen Malcolm on local TV shows in New York, fearlessly speaking truths about American race relations that he never heard anyone else express publicly. In one appearance, Malcolm challenged the effectiveness of nonviolence and racial integration in a debate with Kenneth Clark, the renowned Black psychologist whose studies of Black schoolchildren had been cited in the Supreme Court's *Brown v. Board of Education* ruling in 1954. "One night I saw Malcolm lay waste completely to Kenneth Clark," Baraka recalled in his 1984 book titled, in homage to his hero, *The Autobiography of LeRoi Jones*. "This kind of thing would thrill me so completely because what Malcolm said were things that had gone through my mind but he was giving voice to. Or he'd say things and instantly it'd make sense or confirm something I'd not even thought but felt."

The example of Malcolm's outspokenness set Jones on a new path toward writing plays and social essays—the art forms that would bring him his greatest fame. "Malcolm's works had me turning tricks whether I knew it or not," Baraka wrote in his memoir. "What it meant to my life immediately was words in my head coming out of my mouth." First, Jones began to work characters and dialogue into his poems. Then he began to experiment directly with drama. At the Poets Theatre on St. Marks Place in Greenwich Village, he staged a short play called *The Eighth Ditch*, about a homosexual rape, that was shut down by police after several performances. "I can see now that the dramatic form began to interest me because I wanted to go 'beyond' poetry," Baraka recalled. "I wanted some kind of action literature . . . to put characters on a stage and pretend to actual life. I read a few years ago in some analysis of poetry that drama is a form that proliferates during periods of social upsurge, for those very same reasons. It is an action form, plus it is a much more popular form than poetry. It reaches more people and its most mass form today is of course television and, secondarily, film."

Born and raised in Newark, New Jersey, Everett Leroy Jones was the son of Coyette Leroy Jones, a postal worker, and Anna Russ, a social worker. Within the class structure of Newark's Black population at the time, he described his family as lower-working-class "Browns," as compared with more disadvantaged and less well-educated "Blacks," and more well-to-do "Yellows." Jones attended racially mixed public schools in Newark and began college at the local campus of Rutgers University before transferring to Howard University, the historically Black college in Washington, D.C.

Jones quickly found himself alienated from the status-conscious "Yellow," or light-skinned, students who dominated student life at Howard and what Jones saw as their vain dreams of making it in a white society that would never fully welcome them no matter what the tone of their skin. As Jones put it with his characteristic mixture of profane insight and hyperbole: "All we were being readied for was to get in, to be part of the big ugly which was that ugly because it would never admit us in the first motherfucking place! We were being taught integration and nothing of the kind existed. If so, why were we there in the second motherfucking place? We were readied for a life as a lie. We were readied for yellow and the best of us were black and brown. We were readying for utopia and that is bullshit in the third motherfucking place. Only craziness could be the result."

Jones dropped out of Howard and joined the Air Force, where he ended up feeling even more out of place. He was assigned to a virtually all-white weatherman unit in rural Illinois, then to a flying squadron in Puerto Rico where he was also one of the only Black faces. To ease his loneliness and channel his turbulent thoughts, Jones started writing poems and submitting them to publications back on the mainland. One day, he was summoned by the first sergeant, who informed him that an anonymous letter writer had accused him of being a communist after seeing him reading a copy of the literary journal *Partisan Review*. Jones was removed from the flying squadron, stripped of his security clearance, and assigned first to gardening duty and then to a clerical job in the officers' quarters. Finally, he was officially given an "undesirable discharge" after rejection letters were found in his desk drawer on letterhead from the Congress for Cultural Freedom, the shadowy group that funded the *Partisan Review* at the time and was later revealed to be a CIA front.

On Christmas leave while still in the Air Force, Jones had visited an old friend from the Howard University track team, Steve Korret, who had moved to Greenwich Village with hopes of becoming a writer. Looking to follow in Korret's footsteps, Jones answered newspaper ads that led him to a job stocking shelves at the Gotham Book Mart on West 47th Street and to a cold-water walk-up rental apartment on East 3rd Street. A jazz fan, Jones eventually found another job, as a shipping clerk at a record magazine, where he met Hettie Cohen, the white Jewish native of suburban Long Island who worked as the editor's assistant and also aspired to write poetry.

Jones and Cohen became romantically involved, and Hettie had an abortion upon learning she was pregnant. When she became pregnant again, Jones proposed marriage, and in 1959 the first of their two daughters was born. Living together first in Hettie's apartment in the Village, then farther uptown on West 20th Street, the couple worked together to launch their own literary journal, *Yugen*. The publication became a vehicle for Hettie and Jones—who was now writing poetry under the stylized version of his middle name, LeRoi—to become friends with some of the leading lights of the downtown arts scene. Boozy and sexually incestuous, this mostly white social circle included Allen Ginsberg, Jack Kerouac, the novelist Hubert Selby, and Diane di Prima, a poet who would later become Jones's mistress and the mother of Jones's third mixed-race daughter.

By 1964, *Yugen* had run its course, and Jones had turned his energies from poetry to drama and social criticism. He wrote a full two-act play called *Dutchman and the Slave*, about a subway encounter between an inquisitive young white woman who strikes up a conversation with and then kills an angrily repressed young Black man, that won the 1964 Obie Award for best off-Broadway play. That year, Jones also published *Blues People*, a widely hailed collection of essays about jazz and other Black musical traditions. With the success of both works came invitations to speak and teach around the country—as well as the attention of admiring young women, more and more of them Black, with whom he had a series of affairs. Back in New York, Jones also became the center of a group of Black male artists and intellectuals to whom he proposed forming a new organization that would mix cultural and political advocacy. His suggested name for the still amorphous group: "the Black Arts."

In February 1965, news of Malcolm X's death upended LeRoi Jones's life yet again. On the third Sunday of the month, Jones and his family were attending a party to celebrate the 8th Street Bookshop, a popular Greenwich Village hangout known for its distinctive cast-iron facade that had moved across the street from its old location at the corner of West 8th Street and MacDougal Street. Liberal Republican mayor John Lindsay mingled with the crowd of poets and artists, and almost a hundred bottles of champagne were consumed. Dressed in the donnish clothes he favored at the time—a hunting jacket, tweed cap, and round dark glasses—Jones was in the middle of a conversation when the Black photographer Leroy McLucas burst into the bookstore, sobbing. "Malcolm is dead!" McLucas cried out. "Malcolm is dead! Malcolm has been killed!"

Stunned, Jones clustered with McLucas and the other Blacks in the bookstore, leaving his wife and two young daughters to the side. "I felt stupid, ugly useless," he recalled. "Downtown in my mix-matched family and my maximum leader/teacher shot while we bullshitted and pretended." The next day, Jones held a press conference to announce that he was opening a new cultural center that he planned to call the Black Arts Repertory Theatre/School (BARTS) in an empty four-story brownstone he had found on West 130th Street in Harlem. Jones went home to the family apartment in Cooper Square and started packing, and several days later he abandoned Hettie and his girls and moved uptown. His five-year-old daughter Kellie pleaded with him not to leave, Jones recalled, but "in a minute or so, I was gone. A bunch of us, really, had gone, up to Harlem. Seeking revolution!"

In the end, Jones's stay in Harlem was heady but brief. He and his fellow founders spruced up the run-down brownstone on 130th Street and raised money with a benefit concert at the Village Gate jazz club that featured a musical who's who that included John Coltrane, Betty Carter, Elvin Jones, McCoy Tyner, Archie Shepp, and Afrofuturist Sun Ra and his Arkestra. In late April, Jones led a festive opening day parade in the streets of Harlem, waving a huge black and gold flag with the name of the school emblazoned over the images of an African spear and the masks symbolizing tragedy and comedy. Over that weekend and throughout the summer, BARTS members took to the streets of Harlem to stage poetry readings, performances of plays by Jones and others, and concerts featuring Albert Ayler, Sun Ra, and others.

Inside the brownstone, the BARTS founders taught classes for the local youth and other members of the Black community in playwriting, poetry, painting, music, and martial arts. Pitching that education mission, Jones and his comrades applied for and received a $40,000 summer grant from a program called HARYOU—for Harlem Youth Opportunities Unlimited—that doled out money to worthy programs benefiting young people in the neighborhood and was in turn funded by the Office of Economic Opportunity in Washington, D.C., under President Johnson's War on Poverty program.

Often, however, Jones and other BARTS founders seemed to go out of their way to portray the Black Arts enterprise as less about promoting Black culture and more about condemning white people. Before making the Village Gate available for the BARTS fundraiser, its white owner, Art D'Lugoff, asked Jones to participate in a panel discussion about art and politics at the jazz club that was covered by reporters for the *New York Post* and *The Village Voice*. During the heated discussion, Jones declared that "white America represents the most repressive force on earth" and accused D'Lugoff of paying Black musicians less than white stars. Denying the charge, an angry D'Lugoff shot back: "LeRoi, you're a racist and a bigot."

When the floor was opened for questions, Jones insulted two flustered white women who rose to quiz him about his vision for social change. He called one woman "rotten fruit" and the other "a rotten cancer" who was "disqualified from humanity for your acts." After describing the tense scene in *The Village Voice*, reporter Jack Newfield noted: "On the way out all the 'rotten fruits' and 'rotten cancers' were handed leaflets written by Jones asking for contributions for his Black Arts Repertory Theatre."

At the end of the summer, HARYOU cut off funding for the BARTS program, and its supporters responded by picketing the program's headquarters and denouncing its Black administrators as Uncle Toms. The Associated Press sent a Black reporter named Hollie West to do a story on the controversy, and the resulting piece focused not on BARTS's service to the community but on its anti-white message. "Each night in a makeshift Harlem theater a group of young Negroes give vent to their hatred of white people," the article began. West went on to describe a satirical play written by Jones called *Jello*, based loosely on the *Jack Benny Show*, that ended with a character modeled after the Black butler Rochester killing all the white cast members. He quoted Jones as saying, with his usual flair for outrageous exaggeration: "I don't see anything wrong with hating white people. . . . The force we want is of 20,000 spooks [Blacks] storming America with furious cries and unstoppable weapons. We want actual explosions and actual brutality."

Latching on to the AP story, the influential ABC radio commentator Paul Harvey wrote a piece for his nationally syndicated newspaper column, "Your Tax Dollar Used to Encourage Rioting." From then on, any hope of receiving additional government support was lost, and the BARTS program fell apart due to lack of funds and feuding among the founders over just how far to go in backing up their bluster about violent revolution. Two of them—brothers from Hackensack, New Jersey, named Charles and Raymond Patterson—squatted in the 130th Street headquarters and talked obsessively about taking up arms. At the end of the year, exhausted by the infighting, Jones abruptly moved to his hometown of Newark with his new Black live-in girlfriend. Shortly thereafter, a police raid on the 130th Street brownstone uncovered a makeshift shooting range and a cache of guns that Charles Patterson had assembled in the basement.

In his autobiography, Jones acknowledged that a combination of "confused" politics and "juvenile" behavior toward potential Black allies like Harry Belafonte had played a role in the demise of BARTS. He also conceded that his "Hate Whitey" talk made him an inviting target for accusations of reverse racism and hypocrisy, particularly in light of his interracial marriage. Yet for all the controversy, news of the Black Arts Repertory Theatre/School spread quickly throughout Black America and served as an inspiration for similar initiatives in cities across the country. In San Francisco, there was Black Arts West. In Chicago, there were the Afro-Arts Theater and the Organization of Black American Culture; in New Orleans, the Free Southern Theater. In Detroit, a Black Arts Convention held at the Central United Church in June 1966 drew some three hundred people, and was followed by a second convention the next summer.

Awareness of the growing movement was also enhanced by an array of existing and new publications that included *Negro Digest, Liberator, Umbra, Freedomways*, and the short-lived *The Cricket: Black Music in Evolution* and *Soulbook: The Quarterly Journal of Revolutionary Afroamerica*. As Jones described the impact of the yearlong BARTS experiment: "The idea of the Black Arts, the concept of the black revolutionary artist organizing arts institutions, particularly theaters, in the black community, caught on. . . . Word of the concept of Black Arts far exceeded what we had actually done, but the concept itself was important."

Once back in Newark, Jones founded another Black arts hub, called Spirit House, and published *Home*, a book of essays that charted his intellectual odyssey from Greenwich Village bohemian to Harlem nationalist. The book ended with a piece titled "the legacy of Malcolm X and the coming of the black nation," which laid out Jones's analysis of the connection between Malcolm's vision and the Black Arts Movement. Malcolm had redefined the Black nationalism of Marcus Garvey, Jones argued, to focus not on seeking a new homeland abroad but on developing a new way of being Black in America. "The point is that Malcolm had begun to call for Black National Consciousness," Jones wrote. "We do not want a Nation, we are Nation." In cultivating that new consciousness, Jones contended, Black artists and thinkers had an essential role to play. "The Black artist, in this context, is desperately needed to change the images his people identify with, by asserting Black feeling, Black mind, Black judgment," Jones wrote. "The Black intellectual, in this same context, is needed to change the interpretation of facts toward the Black Man's best interests, instead of merely tagging along reciting white judgments of the world."

Jones also set another example that would be followed by scores of Black artists of his generation: he took a new Islamic name. Not long after the Newark Rebellion of 1967, two men identifying themselves as

Sunni Muslims paid Jones a visit and urged him to convert to their orthodox branch of the faith, just as Malcolm X had done after his break
with the Nation of Islam. The men told Jones that he should have a
name befitting his new leadership role in the Black community, and referred him to an Islamic priest named Hajj Heesham Jaaber who had
helped bury Malcolm. The priest bestowed on Jones the Arabic hon-
orific "Ameer Barakat," or "Blessed Prince." At the encouragement of
Ron Karenga, the Black cultural nationalist who founded Kwanzaa, Jones
then adopted a Swahili translation of that title: Amiri Baraka. "The name
change seemed fitting to me," Baraka recalled. "Not just the flattery of
being approached by these people, especially Heesham, and not just the
meaning of the Blessed Prince, but that idea that I was literally being
changed into a blacker being. I was discarding my 'slave name' and embracing blackness."

If Amiri Baraka was the flamboyant driving force behind the Black Arts
Movement, poet Larry Neal was its most devoted interpreter. Known
as an adult for his oversized eyeglasses and handlebar mustache, Neal
was born in Atlanta and raised in Philadelphia. His father, Woodie
Neal, was a railway porter who loved to read, while his mother, Mag-
gie, did everything she could to provide her children with the best
education available to Blacks of their generation and class. Larry attended Roman Catholic High School in Philadelphia and then enrolled
in nearby Lincoln University, one of America's oldest historically Black
colleges. Shortly before he graduated with a dual degree in history and
English in 1961, Neal became involved in radical politics after learning
of the Bay of Pigs, the failed U.S. coup against Fidel Castro in Cuba.
While pursuing a master's degree in folklore from the University of
Pennsylvania, he got a job in a Marxist bookstore, where he started to
read *Revolution: Africa, Asia and Latin America*, a left-wing quarterly.

At the invitation of a white left-wing activist named Bill Davis, Neal
traveled to New York and paid a visit to Lewis Michaux's bookstore.
For the impressionable young student of African American history, it
was like a religious experience. "The square in front of the bookstore

was a mind-blower," Neal recalled. "From here, one could feel emanating all of the necessary but conflicting strands of African-American nationalism. For more than thirty years, this corner had been the area for a community discussion on the Nature and Destiny of the Colored Peoples of the World." After listening to the Saturday soapbox speeches outside, Neal and Davis entered the bookstore, and Michaux ushered them into a back room whose walls were covered with photographs of icons of Black history such as Harriet Tubman, Sojourner Truth, and Marcus Garvey. "There was a heaviness about the room," Neal recalled, "as if it were crowded with ghosts. The spirit that drew the people to Harlem Square every day was being manifested in the room; ghosts emanated out of old books, photos, and the sounds and rhythms of Mr. Michaux's voice."

Around this time, Neal also became aware of Malcolm X, who was still the minister of the Nation of Islam mosque in Harlem. Describing the visceral impact that listening to Malcolm had on him and his friends, Neal wrote: "Then we began to hear Malcolm, the black voice skating and bebopping like a righteous saxophone—mellow truths inspired by the Honorable Elijah Muhammad, but shaped out of Malcolm's own style, a style rooted in black folk memory, and the memory of his Garveyite father. We could dig Malcolm because the essential vectors of his style were more closely related to our urban experiences. He was the first black leader, in our generation, to resurrect all of the strains of black nationalism lurking within us. In the precise sense of the word, his stance was radical, rooted in a long strand of flesh-filled nights, and sea deaths, and cotton deaths, and revolutionary deaths; Malcolm was the Opener, the Son of the Word made flesh, and for the first time in our lives, we had a voice to offset the weaknesses and the temptations that we saw around us."

In 1964, Neal moved to New York for a job as s a copywriter for the publisher Wiley and Company. He started submitting poetry to *Liberator*, the progressive literary journal, and soon after was named its arts editor. In his spare time, he attended meetings of the Revolutionary Action Movement, the pro–armed self-defense movement started by Robert F. Williams, and became part of the group around LeRoi Jones

that was laying the groundwork for the Black Arts Repertory Theatre/
School.

Unlike Jones, Neal was present at the Audubon Ballroom on the
day of Malcolm's assassination. He arrived late and took a seat at the
back of the ballroom facing the left side of the stage. Neal recalled
the light flooding through the windows on that sunny February day,
and the striking diversity of the crowd, from militant-looking young
Black men to matronly women dressed in their Sunday finest. His description of what happened next tracked with the other eyewitness
accounts that were presented at the murder trial: the sudden commotion in the crowd; the loud burst of shotgun fire; the sight of Malcolm
reeling backward from the speaker's podium; and the sounds of wailing
and crying that suddenly filled the room.

In the aftermath, Neal recalled, black nationalists wrestled with
a sense of guilt "that they had not done enough to support Malcolm
when he was alive," and bickered over who was to blame for the murder.
"We considered the CIA, the right wing, the Zionists, and the mafia,"
he recalled. "Lacking facts and a clear orientation, we found these con-
siderations merely led to interminable days of agonizing arguments,
and charges, and countercharges." Nonetheless, a rising generation of
young militants was united in their conclusions about what Malcolm's
sacrifice meant for them. "But even though Malcolm's death—and the
manner of it—emotionally fractured black radicals, there were two central facts that all factions of the movement came to understand," Neal
wrote. "And they were: that the struggle for black self-determination
had entered a serious, more profound state; and that for most of us,
non-violence as a viable technique of social change had died with Malcolm on the stage of the Audubon. . . . After Malcolm's death, thousands of heretofore unorganized black students and activists became
more radically politicized."

Like Baraka, Neal paid tribute to Malcolm by throwing himself into
the launch of the Black Arts Repertory Theatre/School. "Larry Neal
was one of those who was always in and out," Baraka recalled, "helping
with programs and giving us some rational counsel." He participated
in poetry readings and taught classes at the government-supported

summer school for local children. But Neal's involvement with BARTS was soured by conflicts with Charles Patterson, the radical from Hackensack who talked tough about armed revolution and stashed guns in the brownstone's basement. By the summer, those insurrectionist rumblings had caught the attention of the FBI, whose agents began compiling reports and collecting newspaper articles about BARTS's activities and finances and cultivating sources who infiltrated the summer school. In September, "Deke" DeLoach, the number three official at the agency, sent a memo to John Mohr, the assistant to Director J. Edgar Hoover, relaying suspicions about BARTS's ties to violent "hoodlums" passed on from Chuck Stone, the well-known journalist who at the time was an aide to Harlem congressman Adam Clayton Powell.

After Neal's wife temporarily became involved with another man, Neal took up with a woman who was also being pursued by Charles Patterson. In March 1966, Neal was making his way from the subway toward 130th Street and Seventh Avenue, steps from the BARTS brownstone, when Patterson appeared with a pistol and pumped a bullet into his leg. "The shooting of Larry Neal shocked me," recalled Baraka, who by that point had relocated to Newark and responded to the news by procuring a sawed-off shotgun that would later cause him his own problems when he was arrested for illegal possession of a firearm during the 1967 Newark Rebellion. In retrospect, the attack on Neal would be remembered as an example of the ugliness that was involved in the yearlong BARTS experiment, which included not just the anti-white posturing but disturbing instances of misogyny, homophobia, and anti-Semitism. In the following years, Neal would briefly accept a symbolic position as the "education director" of the Black Panther Party, but for the most part he would confine himself to the life of critic and scholar, writing and revising some of the Black Arts Movement's most memorable mission statements.

In "The Black Arts Movement," a defining essay published in the summer 1968 edition of *The Drama Review*, the influential arts quarterly,

Neal laid out three fundamental tenets of the movement. The first was that its creative product was by and for Black people, and wasn't aimed at appealing to white audiences or searching for universal meanings. "The Black Arts Movement is radically opposed to any concept of the artist that alienates him from his community," Neal began, echoing Malcolm X's contention that Blacks had been brainwashed and divided by white culture. In the next sentence, Neal associated himself with the cry that Stokely Carmichael had unleashed two years earlier. "The movement is the aesthetic and spiritual sister of the Black Power concept," Neal wrote. "As such, it envisions an art that speaks directly to the needs and aspirations of black America."

Neal's second tenet was that the Black Arts Movement was based on a fundamentally different aesthetic than white culture, rooted in completely different sources. "It is the opinion of many Black writers, I among them," he wrote, "that the Western aesthetic has run its course: it is impossible to construct anything meaningful within its decaying structure." Drawing on his love of avant-garde jazz and his master's degree in Black folklore, Neal argued that Black artists should construct their worlds out of music, rhythms, language, myths, and symbols derived from Africa and its diaspora and from the era before racial integration in America. He cited Ron Karenga's contention that "the struggle for self-determination" begins with culture, and laid out the seven most important criteria for constructing a distinct one for Black America. "Mythology" was number one, followed by "History." After that came "Social Organization," "Political Organization," "Economic Organization," "Creative Motif," and "Ethos." Nowhere mentioned was the value celebrated in most contemporary white Western culture: the search for individual fulfillment and happiness outside a communal context.

Neal's third tenet was that Black art should have a social purpose, not just to entertain but to unite and mobilize. This was different from the "protest art" of the civil rights era, he argued, which addressed itself to white society and asked for its treatment of Black people to change. Instead, Black arts should give Black people cultural and psychological weapons to assert their own identity and fight for their own interests. "Poetry is a concrete function, an action," Neal wrote. "No more abstractions. Poems are physical entities: fists, daggers, airplane poems, and poems that shoot guns." Even more useful to the racial up-lift project than poetry was theater. "For theatre is potentially the most social of all the arts," Neal wrote. "It is an integral part of the social-izing process. It exists in direct relationship to the audience it claims to serve." Singling out the play *Who's Afraid of Virginia Woolf?* and the musical *Hello, Dolly!* as examples of self-absorbed and escapist white theater, Neal offered sympathetic readings of four politically charged plays by Baraka—*Dutchman, Slave Ship, Jello,* and *Black Mass*—and also praised works by Black playwrights Ron Milner, Jimmy Garrett, and Ben Caldwell.

Concluding the essay, Neal turned again to Malcolm X, as a sub-ject for Black artists looking to reimagine the future by mining the past. "Afro-American life and history is full of creative possibilities," he wrote, "and the movement is just beginning to perceive them. Just be-ginning to understand that the most meaningful statements about the nature of Western society must come from the Third World of which Black America is a part. The thematic material is broad, ranging from folk heroes like Shine and Stagolee to historical figures like Marcus Garvey and Malcolm X."

In its early years, dozens of other pioneers of the Black Arts Move-ment joined Neal in pointing to Malcolm's words and life story as guiding lights for the race. In 1968, Neal and Baraka coedited an al-most seven-hundred-page collection of poems, essays, and plays titled *Black Fire,* published by William Morrow, that represented the most extensive anthology of the movement to that date. The collection in-cluded three poems that paid direct homage to Malcolm: Neal's own "Malcolm X—An Autobiography," Marvin E. Jackmon's "That Old Time Religion," and Welton Smith's "Malcolm." Also included was an essay called "African Responses to Malcolm X," by Leslie Alexander Lacy.

To the male poets of the Black Arts school, Malcolm was an exam-ple of fearless masculinity, as reflected in "A Poem for Black Hearts" by LeRoi Jones, and "Portrait of Malcolm X" by Etheridge Knight, whose first published poems were written while Knight was in prison for robbery. After meeting Malcolm personally in 1962, poet and play-wright Ishmael Reed wrote a poem, "Fanfare for an Avenging Angel," that was never published but that Reed presented to Malcolm before he was killed. Malcolm was also revered by the leading female writers of the movement, as witnessed by the poems "Malcolm X" by Gwendolyn Brooks, "Malcolm" by Sonia Sanchez, and "For Malcolm X" by Margaret Walker.

Like Malcolm, Neal would come to regret the antagonistic edge of his earlier views before he, too, died at a young age—of a heart attack at forty-three in 1981. Contributing to a collection of essays, *The Black 70's*, published in 1970, Neal eloquently captured and then critiqued the racially chauvinistic and anti-white tone of the 1965 BARTS project in Harlem. "Where we were going, we did not know," he wrote. "But one thing was certain, we knew that, as James Brown says, we were a 'New Breed.' At first we were smug and self-righteous in this new-found knowledge of ourselves. We were often arrogant and pushy. . . . The more we probed our history and history of the Third World, the more angry we became, the more nourished our hate for the white world. . . . This was a necessary reversal. But it led to some contradictions, the most important of which was that our nationalism could not exist primarily in contra-distinction to white nationalism. We could never hope to develop a viable concept of self, if that concept were purely based on hating 'crackers.'"

In the last decade of his life, Neal took back his criticism of the novelist Ralph Ellison, whom he had once dismissed as having nothing to offer the New Breed. In a passionate essay, "Ellison's Zoot Suit," he praised the author of *Invisible Man* for setting a nonideological bar for Black artistic excellence. Neal also embarked on an admiring study of Zora Neale Hurston, the contrarian Black author and anthropologist. In a posthumous collection of Neal's work, another iconoclastic Black intellectual, the critic Stanley Crouch, remembered him as much for this later questioning as for his youthful certainty. "Larry Neal is important," Crouch wrote, "because he was one of the first who had been taken in by the self-separation of black nationalist thinking to realize how little it had to offer and how easily it prepared the way for demagogues."

As for Amiri Baraka, he would go through several more phases of morphing creatively and repudiating his earlier incarnations, just as he had done in moving from Greenwich Village to Harlem in the

THE BLACK ARTS MOVEMENT

mid-1960s. By the time he wrote his autobiography in 1984, he had become a Marxist, and he dismissed much of the Black nationalist posturing of the BARTS year in Harlem as performative and politically incoherent. Yet most literary critics judged Baraka's creative output during this Marxist period to be markedly inferior to anything he had done in his Beatnik or nationalist phases. Baraka has "sacrificed artistic vitality on the altar of his political faith," wrote the critic Darryl Pinckney in *The New York Times*. "The change in Baraka's work is bewildering: it is almost a parody of revolutionary art. Frankly, it is tiresome."

By the end of the 1990s, Baraka's reputation had recovered, and he was widely sought after as a teacher and lecturer and named New Jersey's poet laureate. Then Baraka wrote a poem about 9/11 that suggested the Israelis had known about the 2001 terrorist attack in advance, and the state legislature tried to strip him of the honor and then eliminated the position altogether. The controversy called renewed attention to a persistent strain of anti-Semitism that ran through decades of Baraka's work, and contributed to the decidedly mixed assessments of his legacy that were published when he died in 2014 at the age of seventy-nine.

Of all the young Black artists who were inspired by Malcolm X in the early days of the Black Arts Movement, perhaps the most widely recognized today are poet Maya Angelou, renowned for her bestselling memoir *I Know Why the Caged Bird Sings*, and playwright August Wilson. In 1964, Angelou was living in Ghana with her teenage son when Malcolm visited the country after his trip to Mecca. The two became friends, and Angelou resolved to move back to America to help launch the Organization of Afro-American Unity, a plan upended by Malcolm's murder. Asked later what young people should know about Malcolm, Angelou would single out his "incredible sense of humor," his deep "love" of Black people, and the "courage" he showed that year in publicly admitting he had been wrong to demonize white people.

In the mid-1960s, August Wilson was a little-known poet from Pittsburgh who had joined that city's version of BART, the Centre Avenue Poets Theater Workshop. Wilson contributed to *Signals*, a local literary journal, and wrote a heartfelt but unpolished poem called "For Malcolm X and Others." In February 1968, Wilson, then twenty-three, was among the speakers at a three-day symposium held at the

Afro-American Institute of Pittsburgh to commemorate the anniversary of Malcolm's assassination, an event that included art exhibits, jazz workshops, and a keynote address by Amiri Baraka. "When you see a revolution going on—and it's your revolution—you don't get out of the way," Wilson told the crowd when it was his turn to speak. "You join in."

Yet when Wilson turned to writing for the theater full-time a decade later, he largely steered clear of politics. In his play *Two Trains Running*, a character briefly mentions a local march taking place on Malcolm X's birthday, but Wilson made no effort to make political statements in his masterpieces *Fences* and *The Piano Lesson*, or seven other plays he set mainly in Pittsburgh's Black Hill District neighborhood in different decades of the twentieth century. By avoiding easily dated polemics, Wilson succeeded as much as any American artist of his generation in fulfilling the ambition of the Black Arts pioneers to create distinctively Black worlds—constructed out of Black language, Black history, and Black symbolism—that would show just how powerful and enduring a "Black aesthetic" could be.

When Jimmy Garrett first met Malcolm X in 1962, he was a brash, idealistic nineteen-year-old who had discovered a passion for civil rights work. Born in Texas, Garrett had moved to Los Angeles with his family at the age of twelve, joined the local branch of the Congress of Racial Equality while still in high school, and gone south to participate in one of the last Freedom Rides. Returning to Los Angeles, he was tapped as a youth representative to a steering committee of a local activist coalition called the United Civil Rights Committee (UCRC). In May 1962, a group from the UCRC went to hear Malcolm speak at a church when he visited the city in the wake of a bloody clash between police and members of the Nation of Islam. When the speech was over, the gangly Garrett stood up in the front row to ask a question, and a bemused Malcolm invited him onto the stage. "That little young brother down there," Malcolm said, "come on up here on this platform and ask your question in front of all the people."

Garrett bounded onto the stage and challenged Malcolm's remarks, which at the time were still full of the NOI gospel on racial separatism and white evil. "I said I thought his hateful behavior was nonsense, that everybody loves everybody," Garrett recalled. But then Malcolm deftly turned the tables on him, explaining to the audience why Garrett's brotherly love talk was a naive delusion. "He took my question as an example and he beat me up with it," Garrett recalled. Afterward, Malcolm had one of his bodyguards ask the UCRC group permission to take Garrett to dinner. The two had a long conversation during which Malcolm shared memories of his late teens, when he was still living the life of a petty criminal, and they stayed in periodic touch until Malcolm's death in 1965.

By then, Garrett was running the Los Angeles office of the Student Nonviolent Coordinating Committee and raising money from Hollywood liberals such as Marlon Brando and Jane Fonda. In August 1965, Garrett was expected at a fundraiser at the home of movie stars Elizabeth Taylor and Richard Burton when the Watts Rebellion broke out. Garrett joined the protests in the streets and never made it to the fundraiser, and his fellow organizers and SNCC officials in Atlanta were so furious that Jimmy thought it best to quit the organization and apply to college. He had been observing the growth of white campus activist groups such as the Students for a Democratic Society (SDS), and he made a bet with a fellow SNCC organizer that he could form a similar Black activist group on a predominantly white campus. Of the schools that admitted Garrett, he decided that San Francisco State College (later University) offered the most fertile ground for such an experiment, so he enrolled there as a second-semester freshman in the winter of 1966.

At the time, there were a mere 150 Blacks amid San Francisco State's student population of eighteen thousand, and they were scattered among Black fraternity and sorority types, athletes, and bookworms. Working with a fellow freshman named Jerry Varnado, Garrett founded a Black Student Union that welcomed students from all those factions, as well as any Black staff who wanted to join. "If they were Black, then they were members of the BSU," Garrett recalled. Next, Garrett set out to instill within the BSU a greater sense of "Black Consciousness," the buzzword for a sense of Black identity and pride that was spreading among young Blacks in 1966. As a way to get the Black students think-ing more deeply about their shared history and culture, Garrett wrote and circulated a document he titled "Justification for Black Studies."

Around the same time, a group of white students had persuaded San Francisco State's young liberal-minded white president, John Sum-merskill, to allow them to start an informal program of classes taught by students called the "Experimental College." When the Black Student Union tried to create a program of study within that larger initiative, they clashed with the white founders over philosophy and control. So in the fall of 1967, the Black students launched their own, independent "Black Studies Curriculum." The following year, in 1968, they began a protest calling for the creation of an official Black Studies depart-ment. That demonstration grew into a strike that all but shut down the college for five months until a new president, the Japanese Ameri-can semantics professor and future U.S. senator S. I. Hayakawa, finally relented and agreed to form a full-fledged academic department called the College of Ethnic Studies.

The push for what history would remember as the birth of Black Studies on white campuses was also led by a young anthropology pro-fessor at San Francisco State named Mary Lewis. A resident of the "Flatlands" neighborhood bordering Berkeley and Oakland, Lewis was the godmother of Kamala Harris, who would go on to become Ameri-ca's first female and Black vice president and the Democratic nominee for president when Joe Biden abandoned his reelection bid in 2024. Kamala's mother, Shyamala Gopalan, had immigrated from India and was studying endocrinology at the University of California at Berkeley when she and Lewis became friends during the campus protests of the mid-1960s. Gopalan met and married another immigrant student, from Jamaica—Kamala's father, Donald Harris—but the union didn't last long. After the divorce, Shyamala's closest friends remained the young Black intellectuals at the center of the Malcolm-inspired "Black Conscious-ness" movement in the Bay Area—including "Aunt Mary," as Kamala and her younger sister, Maya, knew Lewis; Lewis's brother, "Uncle Freddy"; and "Uncle Aubrey," as the girls knew Aubrey LaBrie, a leader of the Black Student Union at SFS and teacher of a course on Black Nationalism in the Experimental College.

Some of the earliest Black Studies courses at San Francisco State were also taught by outside professors invited by the Black Students Union. Among the visitors were Amiri Baraka and the poet Sonia Sanchez, who herself had been deeply influenced by a meeting with Malcolm X in the early 1960s. A native of Birmingham, Alabama, Sanchez had gone to college in New York City and was teaching high school English when she went to hear Malcolm give one of his street corner speeches on a drizzly day in Harlem. Skeptical at first, Sanchez found herself nodding in agreement with Malcolm's appeals to Black pride and indictments of white racism. "Yeah, that's right," Sonia thought to herself. "That makes sense. That's logical."

When the speech was over, Sonia approached Malcolm. Fighting through the lingering trace of a childhood stutter, she told him that she liked some of what he said but didn't agree with all of it.

Malcolm smiled and responded in a gentle voice. "One day you will, sister," he said. "One day, you will."

By the time Sanchez arrived at San Francisco State in 1968, the Black student population had grown to nine hundred, largely thanks to a special recruitment program run by the Black Student Union with the blessing of President Summerskill. So many students—most of them Black, a few Hispanic—showed up for Sanchez's first class on African American literature that every seat was taken, and more students sat on file cabinets and spilled out into the hallway. Sanchez began by filling a blackboard at the front of the class with the names of great figures in Black history, from Martin Luther King Jr. and Malcolm X to W. E. B. Du Bois, Frederick Douglass, and Harriet Tubman. The students recognized only two names: King's and Malcolm's. "I said that's alright," Sanchez recalled, "because by the end of the semester you will not only recognize those people, but you'll realize just how we got a Malcolm and a Martin in a place called America." In addition to works from the Black Arts Movement, Sanchez also introduced the students to great Black authors of the Harlem Renaissance such as Langston Hughes, Zora Neale Hurston, and Claude McKay.

A half century later, when the history of people of color was routinely taught in colleges and high schools across the United States, critics complained about the negative psychological impact on white students. Criticizing a proposed new Advanced Placement course in Black Studies in Florida in 2023, Governor Ron DeSantis charged that the curriculum was designed to demonstrate the legacy of "white supremacy" and to make white students feel guilty about their privilege. Yet in the beginning, Jimmy Garrett, Sonia Sanchez, Amiri Baraka, and the other pioneers of Black Studies were focused not on educating whites but getting Blacks to understand their own history—a call they had all first heard from Malcolm X.

In 1962, another future Black Arts luminary— poet and playwright Ishmael Reed—was a budding journalist hosting a local radio program in his hometown, Buffalo. When Malcolm came to town, Reed's producer invited him on the show and suggested that the topic be Black history. Introducing his guest to the audience, Reed used the word "distorted" to describe Malcolm's view of that history. "No," Malcolm snapped. "I'd say that it was cotton patch history." As Reed recalled it, "That remark sat me down. In those days, the textbooks, if they covered Black History at all, showed Blacks alternatively picking cotton and partying. . . . For the history of Reconstruction, we were informed not by W. E. B. Du Bois's *Black Reconstruction* but by *Gone With the Wind*. We were educated to fit into 'the Anglo mainstream' and told that we were without a history."

By inspiring the demands that more than "cotton patch history" be taught in that American educational mainstream, Reed declared a half century later, Malcolm X deserved to be hailed as "the father" of modern Black Studies.

═══

In January 1965, just weeks before Malcolm X's assassination, tenor saxophonist John Coltrane released his breakthrough album, *A Love Supreme*. Recorded with his jazz quartet in just one session, the album explored new territory in both sound and message. Rather than using Western chords as the basis for improvisation, as he and a generation of bebop jazz musicians had for more than a decade, Coltrane riffed over subtly shifting "modes" more common to African and Asian music. He also presented the work not as a collection of musical stories, rooted in the blues or borrowed from Broadway musicals, but as an extended four-part hymn that sounded at times like furious preaching, and at others like meditative chanting. Over the next few years, *A Love Supreme* became one of the best-selling jazz albums of the era and served as a kind of soundtrack to the Black Arts and Black Power movements, playing in the background as a generation of young Blacks contemplated, discussed, and debated their embrace of a new Black consciousness.

Close observers credited both the direct and indirect influence of Malcolm X on *A Love Supreme* and the rest of the searchingly spiritual music that Coltrane produced between 1965 and his death two years later at the age of forty. After moving to Huntington, Long Island, with his wife, Alice, in 1963, Coltrane would make trips into New York City just to hear Malcolm speak. "Once he came back," Alice recalled, "and I asked him how was the lecture, and he said he thought it was superb." While touring Japan in 1966, Coltrane was asked what he thought of Malcolm. "I admired him, I admired him," Coltrane replied with emphatic repetition. Meanwhile, it hardly seemed a coincidence that Coltrane became preoccupied with themes of Islamic and Eastern religion and universal brotherhood at precisely the time Malcolm was making his trip to Mecca and embracing the politics of pan-Africanism. As Black religion and music scholar Richard Brent Turner explains it, "they were both jazz brothers in spirit who became known for their 'openness to self-transformation' on an international level." With his usual flair for a clever phrase, Amiri Baraka described Coltrane as "Malcolm in the New Super Bop Fire."

The more accepted name for this post-bebop sound was "Free Jazz," and many of its other prominent figures were also obsessed with Malcolm. In December 1966, Nat Hentoff, the noted jazz critic, wrote a story for The *New York Times Magazine* assessing the new musical movement. In "The New Jazz—Black, Angry, and Hard to Understand," Hentoff traced the trend's rise from Ornette Coleman, a shy Texas native who produced shrieking blues with a plastic alto, to even more atonal and outspokenly political practitioners such as tenor players Albert Ayler and Archie Shepp. Much as Larry Neal had enumerated the criteria for Black Arts, Shepp defended "Free Jazz" against complaints from flummoxed white jazz fans by declaring that he was now focused on playing for Black audiences using African rhythmic and shouting traditions. Shepp acknowledged his own debt to Malcolm X with a composition he titled "Malcolm—Semper Malcolm." As Shepp put it to Hentoff, "Malcolm knew what it was to be faceless in America and to be sick and tired of that feeling. And he knew the pride of black, that negritude that was bigger than Malcolm himself."

Also in late 1966, Julius Lester, a SNCC organizer who also served as an editor of *Sing Out!*, a folk music magazine, wrote a widely discussed essay in that publication called "The Singing Is Over: The Angry Children of Malcolm X." In it, Lester explained to the magazine's mostly white liberal readers why he and other young Blacks were turning away from the folk songs and gospel music associated with the nonviolent civil rights movement. With biting run-on humor, Lester described the kind of marches that featured Black and white demonstrators singing "We Shall Overcome" and "This Little Light of Mine" as a "cop's billy club went upside your head shine shine shining as you fell to the pavement with someone's knee crashing into your stomach and someone's foot into your back until a cop dragged you away, threw you into the paddy wagon and off to the jail you and the others went, singing 'I Ain't Scared of Your Jail 'Cause I Want My Freedom. Freedom! Freedom!'"

As Lester explained it, even young Blacks who had sung such songs and taken part in such protests had soured on nonviolence in the face of ugly resistance to the gains of the civil rights era in the South—and outright hostility toward demands for jobs and fair housing in the North. Instead, they were turning toward the slain martyr who had predicted both backlashes. "As Malcolm X once said," Lester recalled, "everything south of the Canadian border was the South. There was only up South and down South now, and you found 'crackers' in both places." Like so many others, Lester noted how Malcolm's influence on the young Black generation had only grown in the wake of his assassination, as they realized how powerfully his words and example still spoke to them.

"More than any other person Malcolm X was responsible for the new militancy that entered The Movement in 1965," Lester wrote. "Malcolm X said aloud those things Negroes had been afraid to say to each other. His clear, uncomplicated words cut through the chains on black minds like a giant blowtorch. His words were not spoken for the benefit of the press. He was not concerned with stirring the moral conscience of America, because he knew—America had no moral conscience. He spoke directly and eloquently to black men, analyzing their situation, their predicament, events as they happened, explaining what it all meant for a black man in America."

In describing the kind of music that he and his generation coveted now, Lester insisted that it had to start with a language and beat that were distinctly Black. "Negroes do have a language of their own," Lester argued.

The words may be English, but the way a Negro puts them together and the meaning that he gives them creates a new language. He has another language, too, and that language is rhythm. It is obvious in music, but it is also expressed in the way he walks and the way he talks. There is a music and rhythm to the way he dresses and the way he cooks. This has been recognized by Negroes for some time now. "Soul" is how these things peculiarly black are recognized by black men in America. In Africa they speak Negritude. It is the same. The recognition of those things uniquely theirs which separate them from the white man. "Soul" and Negritude become even more precious when it is remembered that the white man in America systematically tried to destroy every vestige of racial identity through slavery and slavery's little brother, segregation. It is a testament to the power of "Soul" that it not only survived, but thrived.

So powerful, in fact, was the "Soul" music described by Lester that over the coming decades it would be thoroughly appropriated by mainstream corporations and cultural institutions. In response, a new generation of young Blacks would innovate another completely new form of music, rooted in Lester's ingredients of Black language, rhythm, and themes of pride and survival. That new music would come to be known as hip hop, and many of its most important pioneers would also draw inspiration from Malcolm X.

PART THREE

OBSESSION

1969-1979

EIGHT

A Letter from Prison

S till a man of few words in person, with his diffident smile and book-
ish bow ties, Peter Goldman by the late 1960s had become one of
the most prolific writers at *Newsweek*. He was now the star of the National Affairs staff, whose stories ran at the front of the magazine and
who chronicled the rough-and-tumble world of presidential campaigns
and Washington politics in addition to pressing social issues like civil
rights. Every week, via teletype machines, *Newsweek* reporters from
around the country sent Goldman reams of raw but detail-rich files,
and he retreated into his small office at the magazine's Madison Avenue headquarters and produced polished cover stories and lengthy
features, working past midnight and into the weekend as the Sunday
morning printing deadline approached.

Yet in spite of his heavy workload, Goldman was intrigued when
he was approached in 1969 with an offer to write a short biography of
Malcolm X. It came from Penguin Books, the British-owned publisher
that specialized in compact but high-quality paperbacks. The proposal
appealed to Goldman because of his lingering personal respect and
affection for Malcolm, but also because Malcolm's unsparing view of
American race relations had come to look all the more relevant in the
four years since his assassination. When they were alive, Goldman had
thought of Martin Luther King Jr. and Malcolm X as dueling prophets—
one of a hopeful dream of eventual racial harmony, the other of the

harsh reality of ongoing racial strife. Now that they were both gone, Malcolm's forecast was proving to be the more prescient of the two.

For four straight summers, the anger and frustration in urban Black neighborhoods that Malcolm so powerfully channeled had boiled over into violent riots. His doubts about Dr. King's strategy of nonviolent protest were now shared by a generation of young Blacks who embraced a militant cry of "Black Power!" Malcolm's distrust of white goodwill had been borne out by a "backlash vote" that helped put Richard Nixon in the White House and make segregationist George Wallace a hero to millions outside Alabama. Meanwhile, Blacks across America were responding to Malcolm's psychological message, rejecting the label "Negro" and manifesting a new sense of racial pride. Afros, dashikis, and a "Right on, Brothers and Sisters" lingo of racial solidarity were bringing to vivid life Malcolm's vision of a cultural nation-within-a-nation.

Once Goldman began reporting and reflecting, however, he realized that he had more to say about Malcolm than could be contained in the 180 pages that Penguin was looking for. He also happened to have a friend and former colleague who had become the head of another major publishing house, Harper & Row. A descendant of Founding Fathers John Jay and Benjamin Franklin, John "Jay" Iselin was a blue blood with a patrician commitment to civil rights, much like his longtime friend Osborn Elliott, *Newsweek*'s top editor. Elliott had hired Iselin and promoted him to National Affairs editor, making him Goldman's boss, before Iselin quit in 1969 to become the publisher of Harper & Row. When the two had lunch and Goldman shared his desire to do a "deeper dive" into the Malcolm story than Penguin would allow, Iselin replied: "Bring that book over here."

Goldman spent the next three years working on the project, devoting his weekends of Sunday and Monday, putting in extra hours after work, and taking a seven-month leave to write the final manuscript. He decided early on not to attempt a conventional cradle-to-grave biography, figuring that he couldn't compete with the dramatic account of Malcolm's youth and religious conversion in the by now widely read *Autobiography*. "I short-handed the deep past," he conceded. Instead, he zeroed in on the parts of Malcolm's story that interested him most, and which he understood best from their personal interactions: the tense period leading up to the split with the Nation of Islam; the frenetic last year before the assassination; and the hurried investigation and trial that ended with three Black men being sentenced to life in prison.

In all, Goldman conducted most of nearly a hundred interviews for the book he titled *The Death and Life of Malcolm X*, relying for the rest on *Newsweek* reporters and stringers in foreign countries which Malcolm had visited. For the two thirds of the book devoted to Malcolm's life, Goldman set out, as he put it, to speak to "everyone I could find who actually knew him, and was willing to talk to a white journalist with a Jewish surname." Betty Shabazz spoke with him twice but declined to give an official interview. Malcolm's half sister, Ella Collins, who had taken over what was left of the Organization of Afro-American Unity, backed out of a scheduled sit-down. So did Earl Grant, the Malcolm adviser who took a picture of his bullet-ridden body in the Audubon Ballroom that ran in *Life* magazine. But Goldman had better luck with the longtime Malcolm associates who had helped establish Muslim Mosque Inc., including his close aides Benjamin 2X Goodman and Charles 37X Kenyatta. He also swapped insights with Malcolm confidants among the Harlem intelligentsia, such as the writer John Oliver Killens and Goldman's longtime source, the gossipy author and filmmaker Louis Lomax.

By the time Goldman turned in his manuscript in the spring of 1972, he had assembled the most thorough portrait of Malcolm in his final years yet to appear in print. It was far more detailed than accounts in the press, and more psychologically and politically nuanced than the last chapters of the *Autobiography*. In Goldman's telling, Malcolm in that period seemed by turns exuberant and anxious, liberated and adrift. "To encounter him in those days," he wrote, "was like meeting a man coming out of a lightless cellar and blinking at the day." Goldman attributed the air of vulnerability not just to death threats and eviction worries but also to the loss of institutional and ideological structure that the NOI had provided. "Silence was not Malcolm's gift; speech was," Goldman observed. "He was most engaging personally, I thought, after he left the Nation, not because he suddenly got brotherly toward white folks—he didn't—but because he accepted his own complexities as a man. But he reached the height of his powers as a public speaker in his later Muslim years, when he could still fit his own widening knowledge of the world to the certainties and mythologies of Black Islam; doubt is unbecoming in evangelists and revolutionaries."

With the skeptical eye of a former city desk reporter, Goldman described Malcolm's lack of success in achieving the concrete goals he set after splitting with the Nation of Islam: the messy, hand-to-mouth state of the Organization of Afro-American Unity; and the failure to get African leaders dependent on U.S. government aid to pay more than lip service to his plan to bring the cause of American racism before the United Nations. But with the evocative voice of the literature major he had been in college, Goldman captured why Malcolm had emerged as a folk hero to Black Americans nonetheless. For white readers, meanwhile, he explained why Malcolm sounded a clarion call to them, too—and why his message could no longer be denied in the wake of the Watts Rebellion, Dr. King's assassination in Memphis, and the damning conclusions of the Kerner Commission, which blamed the urban unrest sweeping America on the country's long history of "pervasive discrimination and segregation." As Goldman put it:

> What interested Malcolm first was the decolonization of the black mind—the wakening of a proud, bold, impolite new consciousness of color and everything color means in white America. In his lifetime, he was called irresponsible, which pleased him; an extremist, which didn't bother him, given the justice of his cause; an apostle of hate and violence, which injured his pride and mistook his purpose. . . . He was a man of human vices as well as human strengths; he could be demagogic on a platform and ruthless in a fight; he was profligate with his time and his rhetoric, at the expense of other requirements of leadership. He was not a saint, really; neither was he a strategist or a seminal thinker or even a major leader, if one defines leadership in the narrow sense of having a large and organized following under one's proximate control. Malcolm X was something more important than any of those things. He was a prophet. . . .

What was prophetic in Malcolm's ministry was a way of seeing. Marcus Garvey anticipated some of it, and Elijah Muhammad
taught him a lot of it. But Malcolm transmuted it and combined
it with an intuitive genius for modern communications—he was
the first of the media revolutionaries—and it was he in catalytic
chemistry with his times who really began the difficult passage
from Negro to black consciousness. . . .

He brought the case for the prosecution; he said the things
that black people had been afraid to say, even to think, for all
those years; he got it all out in the open, the secrets and the
guilts and hypocrisies that underlay the public mythology of
the melting pot. A lot of it got lost in his scare image, in which
he was not wholly blameless, and a lot more in the ad hominem
attacks against him; we have progressed as a civilization from
murdering the bearers of bad news to describing them in our
wire-service dispatches and six o'clock newscasts as "controversial." But he forced us to respond to him even then—forced
white people to examine their consciences and black people to
confront their color—and to that extent he won. It was hereti-
cal when Malcolm called America a racist society; but a mostly
white, entirely middle-class Presidential commission affirmed
it a scant three years after his death, and now it has become
a commonplace. The keepers of America's public conscience
are its city editors, and their threshold of boredom is low; you
can't make the papers calling America racist anymore.

Goldman devoted the last third of the four hundred pages of *The Death
and Life of Malcolm X* to the murder investigation and the trial. He
interviewed all the detectives and trial lawyers involved in the case,
and mined the more than four thousand pages in the trial transcript,
compiled in five thick volumes at the New York City Department of
Records. Goldman also tried without success to secure prison interviews with the three defendants— Talmadge Hayer, Norman 3X Butler,
and Thomas 15X Johnson. He was blocked by none other than Edward Bennett Williams, the criminal defense attorney renowned for

representing controversial clients from Joseph McCarthy and Jimmy Hoffa to Adam Clayton Powell Jr. (Williams also did legal work for *The Washington Post*, the sister publication of *Newsweek*.) After the convictions, Williams had agreed to file an appeal at the behest of "friends" of the defendants, as he vaguely described them. Given that Williams didn't come cheap, the funding almost certainly came from the Nation of Islam, which would have wanted to support Hayer but not raise eyebrows by excluding Butler and Johnson from the appeal. In his filing, Williams argued that the closed testimony of Ronald Timberlake, the FBI informant who found Hayer's gun, had deprived the defendants of a fair trial. The appeal was unsuccessful, but at that point Williams was unwilling to run the risk that his clients might say something to a reporter that could complicate potential future appeals.

Various conspiracy theories had swirled around the murder from the beginning, and Goldman focused much of his reporting on assessing their plausibility. One had come to be known as the "Second Man" theory. The day after the murder, early editions of several New York City newspapers reported that police apprehended two gunmen outside the Audubon Ballroom, one as he was fleeing the building and the other as he was being attacked by a mob. Later editions described the arrest of only one suspect. "In this theory," as Goldman put it, "the second suspect was a secret agent who participated in the murder; the fact that he was arrested and got into the papers at all was seen as a blunder of the White Power Structure—and the fact that he disappeared from print between editions was evidence of its sinister control of the press." Interviewing the policemen at the scene, however, and reviewing the reports they filed immediately afterward, Goldman concluded that two separate cops had simply described the arrest of the same suspect: Talmadge Hayer.

Another theory held that the CIA plotted the assassination, to stop Malcolm from going any further in rallying African countries and the United Nations to his cause. According to this argument, the agency had previously tried to poison Malcolm during a visit to Egypt in 1964, and the French government had turned him away in early 1965 when they got wind that the CIA planned to target him there. But when Goldman consulted with longtime *Newsweek* stringers in both countries, and reviewed news reports filed at the time, he found more prosaic explanations. In Cairo, Malcolm had likely suffered a bout of food poisoning. And in Paris, the expulsion may have actually come at the behest of France's allies in Africa. "A more credible version," Goldman wrote, "was that the French acted on the representation of two of their lately liberated colonies, Senegal and the Ivory Coast, that Malcolm—aided and abetted by [Egyptian president Gamal Abdel] Nasser and [Ghanaian president Kwame] Nkrumah—might try to incite African students to overthrow moderate, pro-Western governments like their own."

As for the trial, Goldman found ample fault with both the defense and prosecution cases. Paid a meager flat fee of $2,000 apiece, the court-appointed attorneys representing Butler and Johnson never had the resources to mount a strong defense in a case that featured little physical evidence and hinged almost entirely on identifying and interviewing eyewitnesses. Neither those attorneys nor Peter Sabbatino, Hayer's lawyer, seemed very knowledgeable about the internal politics of the Nation of Islam. In their haste to get convictions, meanwhile, prosecutors had ignored the almost universal view among the detectives that more than three plotters were present in the Audubon Ballroom. But in the end, Goldman didn't himself uncover any new evidence to suggest that Butler and Johnson weren't involved in the murder. Nor did he follow up on the mystery of how Hayer—coming from Paterson, New Jersey—found himself in Harlem, and who the other plotters Hayer alluded to but refused to name during the trial might have been.

Ever since the assassination, questions had also been raised about whether the police or the FBI had an informant inside Malcolm's camp. By the time Goldman finished his book, such a plant had been identified. He was Gene Roberts, a Malcolm bodyguard who was working undercover for the Bureau of Special Services and Investigations (BOSSI), a secretive intelligence unit within the NYPD. That fact came to light in 1970, when Roberts testified in a separate court case involving the Black Panthers. Goldman wasn't able to interview Roberts for the book, but he learned from other sources that Roberts had first joined Malcolm's breakaway mosque pretending to be a clothing salesman, and he came to be trusted enough to be called "Brother Gene."

During the trial, several allusions were made to Roberts's presence in the Audubon Ballroom. One witness recalled turning over the Luger pistol found at the scene to "Brother Gene." Others described Roberts throwing a chair that slowed the escape of Talmadge Hayer. Prosecutors also knew it was Roberts who tried to administer mouth-to-mouth resuscitation to Malcolm from a photo that appeared in *Life* magazine. In the book, Goldman rightly explained why Roberts was never asked to testify himself: prosecutors didn't want to blow his cover. But he didn't question whether awareness of Roberts's double role—or any evidence he might have provided on the stand—could have sowed doubts in the minds of the jurors and altered their verdict.

Goldman did put his finger, however, on the most glaring hole in the prosecution's case: it never explained who might have ordered the assassination. Far from participating in a cover-up, he reported, the detectives and the assistant district attorney assigned to the case, Herbert Stern, had pursued numerous leads that pointed to "higher-ups"— some to the Harlem mosque, others directly to NOI headquarters in Chicago. But the code of silence among followers of both Elijah Muhammad and Malcolm prevented them from nailing down conclusive evidence. "The investigators heard a lot of names and ran down a lot of tips during the long inquiry," Goldman concluded, "and none of them led to anything you could come into court with." As Stern explained to Goldman: "We were dealing with paid assassins, and they weren't giving anybody above them up. You can believe, feel, know, but that isn't legal proof. And that really drove you crazy; it meant to the investigators that they were closing the Malcolm X murder case without being able to say who had Malcolm X murdered."

The first edition of *The Death and Life of Malcolm X* appeared in early 1973 to admiring reviews. In *The New York Times*, the Black author and book editor Orde Coombs called it "shiningly eloquent" and argued that Goldman had refuted the idea that white authors couldn't write convincingly about Black subjects. Malcolm "would have, I think, approved of Goldman's biography, and this is no faint praise," Coombs concluded. Meanwhile, Goldman went back to his day job at *Newsweek*, writing many of the magazine's cover stories about the Watergate scandal, the rise of Jimmy Carter, and other big news of the day.

Four years later, in late 1977, Goldman was in his office at *Newsweek* when he received a package of mail forwarded from Harper & Row. Inside was a neatly typed single-spaced letter, sent from an address in Ossining, New York. Only as he started reading the letter did Goldman realize that the address was for Sing Sing, the famous prison in that town in the suburbs north of Manhattan. The sender was Norman 3X Butler, one of the three men jailed for Malcolm's murder. Butler had taken a new Islamic name—Muhammad Abdul Aziz—and seemed to have come across Goldman's book in the prison library. The letter read as follows:

IN THE NAME OF GOD, THE BENEFICENT,
MOST MERCIFUL

Muhammad Abdul Aziz (Norman Butler),
Prisoner # 137416 354
Hunter Street, Ossining, New York
October 14, 1977

Dear Mr. Goldman,

I have just read your book, *The Death and Life of Malcolm X*. I wish in your research for the book you had attempted to speak to me. On the other hand, the way you have me depicted in the book—on the assumption that you believe that—I can see why you didn't.

Of course, I have spent nearly thirteen years in prison now, so in a way this whole thing seems axiomatic. But, as you indicate in the book, the real murderers are yet to be caught. When I say this, I do not refer to the higher ups, as you call them, although as you say, they have not been brought to book yet either. My reference was to myself and Mr. Johnson.

Time seems to have left the kind of mark which says the case is over, and finished. But that is not true. It cannot be true because I am not guilty of the crime which has taken thirteen years of my life so far.

Over the years, I have considered the nature of people and

things, and one thing is clear to me: Anytime that we find in one people, culture, or group, or what have you, disagreement with one another because of politics, or religion, which in many cases is considered a life and death struggle, and one falls into the hand of the other, "the captive" is viewed and judged by the standards of "the captor," which is not justice in the objective sense. However, that is a long story and I didn't write to you to have a historical or a philosophical discussion. I did write to tell you myself—for whatever it may be worth—that I did not kill Minister Malcolm X.

On second thought, I will say this, the mentality that prosecuted and convicted me was not a mind looking to defend or bring about justice, but a mind looking for ways to defend itself against its fears and its guilt.

That mind, as expressed through the press, created monsters and naturally, you can so easily do anything to monsters, since "they are not like us."

Mr. Goldman, if you are really sensitive and have a mind that has arisen from the framework developed before that manifested in the sixties, a mind that inquires to know the truth, I suggest that you dig deeper. Your reward may be a satisfied mind—one that has finally found truth and is therefore at rest. There are very few minds which find that in our times.

Thank you for allowing me a few moments of your time.

Sincerely, M. A. Aziz

For Muhammad Aziz, the decade since his conviction in the Malcolm X murder trial had been a time of both emotional anguish and intellectual growth. After receiving life sentences in the spring of 1966, he and his two fellow defendants had been sent to the Clinton Correctional Facility, the notorious maximum security prison in New York's Adirondack Mountains better known by the name of the town in which it is located: Dannemora. For the next year and a half, all three men were kept in a solitary confinement wing known as "the Box." Placed at first on an otherwise empty tier, in cells far enough away from one another that they couldn't communicate, the three were eventually moved to adjoining cells before being separated again and sent to separate prisons. During that time, Aziz's wife had divorced him, and he had lost virtually all contact with his six children, who were between the ages of ten and one when he went to jail.

With decades behind bars stretching before him, however, Aziz resolved not to waste any more of his life. His next stop was the Attica Correctional Facility, the vast maximum security prison surrounded by fortress-like walls and turrets in western New York. Attica offered classes for prisoners who wanted to continue their education, and Aziz began a course of study that would eventually allow him to get a college diploma and earn a master's degree in religious studies. He also became a spiritual leader within the prison's Black Muslim population, recognized with the informal title of "resident imam."

In the summer of 1971, Aziz was working to control what he saw as a brewing revolt over living conditions at Attica when authorities abruptly transferred him to Sing Sing. A month later, more than a thousand Attica prisoners broke out of their cells, occupied the prison yard, and took forty-three guards and other prison staff hostage. Four days of tense negotiations followed before police and guards in riot gear stormed the yard under cover of deafening helicopters and launched a siege that left thirty-three prisoners and prison employees dead. Reflecting back on what the media labeled the "Attica prison riot," Aziz would later insist: "I had the influence to keep that riot from happening."

Shortly after Aziz was moved out of Attica, Talmadge Hayer, his codefendant in the Malcolm X murder trial, was transferred into the prison. Hayer had also taken a new Islamic name since the 1966 conviction—Mujahid Abdul Halim—and become a prison imam. When the revolt took place, Halim was put in charge of guarding the hostages—a task he performed successfully until the bloody raid, but for which he was later slapped with a kidnapping charge. During the siege, Halim was also among the striking prisoners who met with a group of sympathetic "observers" whose presence they had requested during the failed negotiations—a contingent that included well-known figures such as Tom Wicker, the *New York Times* columnist, and William Kunstler, the defense attorney in the Chicago Seven case.

As it happened, Kunstler already knew all about Halim's connection to Malcolm X's assassination. Kunstler had become friendly with Malcolm in the early 1960s, after inviting him onto a radio program that he hosted. He liked Malcolm immediately, and was struck by how humorous and generous he could be in person, so different from his scary image in the press. The two stayed in regular touch, and Kunstler had even picked Malcolm up at the airport when he returned from his last trip abroad, just a week before the assassination. Kunstler recalled how uncharacteristically tired and disheveled Malcolm looked, and how fatalistic he sounded. "I'm going to be dead," Malcolm said. "I know what I'm talking about."

After Halim—then Talmadge Hayer—was arrested, his family had tried to hire Kunstler to represent him. Still torn up after attending Malcolm's funeral, Kunstler refused to defend a man charged with killing his friend. But a year later, Kunstler came to regret that decision when he saw Hayer mishandle his attempt to establish the innocence of Norman 3X Butler and Thomas 15X Johnson. When they met at Attica, Kunstler took Halim aside and quizzed him about why he had undercut that testimony by refusing to name his real accomplices. "I'm between a rock and a hard place," Halim protested.

A few years after that encounter, however, Halim's predicament began to ease. In 1975, Elijah Muhammad died at the age of seventy-seven, after years of battling respiratory illness, heart disease, and encroaching senility. Muhammad's son Wallace, who had fallen out with his father a decade earlier, took control of the Nation of Islam and renamed it the World Community of Islam in the West (WCIW). Adopting his own new name of Warith, the son publicly repudiated the father's most extreme views and acknowledged his history of adultery, even announcing that nine illegitimate children would share in Elijah Muhammad's inheritance. Warith Muhammad also committed the WCIW to adhering to the orthodox version of Islam practiced around the world, a directive that was followed by Halim, Aziz, and most of the other Black prisoners across the United States who had been members of the NOI.

For Halim, the new beginning was also accompanied by a crisis of conscience. In discussions with the New York State prison system's official Islamic chaplain, an imam named Nuriddin Faiz, Halim confessed his lingering sense of guilt over the two other men who had gone to prison for Malcolm X's murder. Faiz persuaded Halim that he needed to make another attempt to correct the injustice, and together the two decided to seek the help of the lawyer Halim had met during the Attica revolt: William Kunstler.

═══

With his bushy gray sideburns and gravelly voice, Kunstler was then one of the most recognized defense lawyers in America, although he hadn't started out on that path. After graduating with honors from Columbia Law School, he practiced routine estate and divorce law for a decade before boredom led him to accept an invitation to try civil rights cases in the South. Electrified by the experience, Kunstler became a "battler, not a barrister," as he put it, and he went on to represent a wide array of prominent clients he viewed as having been wronged by the government. Kunstler reached the height of his fame during the tumultuous Chicago Seven trial, during which he and his clients, accused of planning a riot during the 1968 Democratic convention, were slapped with 181 contempt citations by a hard-nosed judge. But by the late 1970s, Kunstler hadn't tried a high-profile case in some time, so he gladly accepted the opportunity he regretted having passed up a decade earlier: to take a case that might uncover the truth about who killed his friend Malcolm X.

On the last day of November 1977, Kunstler and Nuriddin Faiz visited Mujahid Halim at the prison where he had been transferred after Attica: the Eastern Correctional Facility in New York's Ulster County, also known by the town in which it is located: Napanoch. Entering the castlelike brick prison with its pointed green metal roof, Kunstler brought Halim a pad of lined note paper to write out an affidavit that could be submitted as new evidence. In his sprawling handwriting,

Halim did what he refused to do at the 1966 murder trial: begin to identify the other accomplices who helped him carry out the assassination.

Contrary to his original trial testimony, Halim wrote that he had in fact been a follower of the Nation of Islam, that he had not been paid, and that he acted out of disgust at Malcolm for turning against Elijah Muhammad. "I thought I was fighting for truth & right," he wrote. Without specifying where, Halim revealed that he had been approached in the summer of 1964 by two fellow NOI members he identified as "Brother Lee" and "Bro. Ben." After posing questions designed to confirm their new recruit's negative opinion of Malcolm, the two men introduced Halim to two additional conspirators he identified as "Willie X" and "Wilbour or a name like it." In the course of several more meetings, the five men settled on the Sunday afternoon meeting at the Audubon Ballroom as offering the best opportunity to carry out their plot. "Therefore the plan was to kill this person there," Halim wrote.

In an account that was vivid in some areas but still vague in others, Halim described how the plotters piled into Wilbour's car and "drove to N.Y.C."—his only hint that the men came from outside the city. They parked the car several blocks away and "two at a time drifted into the Ballroom early." Halim and Lee took seats in the front, with Willie and Ben directly behind them. Meanwhile, Wilbour seated himself in the back of the room, poised to distract the audience by pretending that someone had picked his pocket, then by throwing a smoke bomb. Halim was armed with a .45 handgun, Lee with a Luger, and Willie X with the shotgun that ballistic tests would show dealt the fatal blows. "The plan was that when the shooting started people would be running all over the place & with this we would get out of the Ballroom," Halim wrote. Sure enough, the plot almost went off without a hitch until Halim got shot in the leg as he fled, slowing him down enough that he was apprehended by police officers outside the building.

Halim signed the affidavit "Thomas Hagan," the name under which he was mistakenly booked on the day of the shooting and that followed him in court documents ever since. Below his name was that of his witness: "William M. Kunstler." Halim ended the statement by reaffirming the innocence of his two codefendants. "This affidavit is factual to the best of my knowledge," he wrote. "Thomas 15X Johnson and Norman 3X Butler had nothing to do with this crime whatsoever."

Imprisoned seventy miles away in Sing Sing, Muhammad Aziz had no way of knowing that Mujahid Halim would sign that affidavit in late November when Aziz wrote his letter to Peter Goldman in mid-October. However, Goldman didn't receive the letter until the beginning of December—likely because it was slowed down by Sing Sing authorities or by the mail room at Harper & Row, or both. By the time Goldman wrote a letter back to Aziz, on December 8, he had read news reports of Halim's new confession. Goldman explained that he had tried and failed to get permission to interview the three defendants for the book, and had been obliged to rely on accounts from their lawyers as well as "antagonistic sources" among the police, prosecutors, and Malcolm's followers. "But my mind has always remained open," Goldman wrote, "and now that I have not only your letter, but a news account of Hayer's affidavit, in support of you and Mr. Johnson, I will of course be watching developments in court with great interest." Goldman then asked if Aziz would be willing to continue their correspondence, and concluded that "if further inquiry satisfies my mind that the verdict in your trial was wrong, I would be happy to say so."

Three weeks later, on December 22, Aziz wrote back to take Goldman up on his offer. They began a "pen pal-ship," as Goldman put it, that continued for several months, usually with weeks passing between their letters, likely due to mail surveillance at Sing Sing. Eventually Goldman gave Aziz his home phone number and signed papers to get on the list of people he was permitted to call collect. Goldman grew accustomed to receiving phone calls from Sing Sing at all hours at home—and so did his wife, Helen, who would often have to inform Aziz that her husband was at the *Newsweek* office. Aziz became comfortable calling Goldman "Peter" instead of "Mr. Goldman," and sometimes they would go entire calls without any discussion of the murder case. Aziz provided updates on a budding courtship with a woman who came to visit him in prison. In turn, Goldman mentioned that he was battling a kidney stone, and Aziz offered tips for herbal remedies.

Meanwhile, Mujahid Halim's efforts to get the murder case reopened were going nowhere. Offering Halim's affidavit as "newly discovered evidence," William Kunstler filed a petition to vacate the convictions of Aziz and Khalil Islam with the office of Robert Morgenthau, the scion of the Morgenthau financial and political dynasty who was in his third year of what would eventually stretch into a thirty-four-year term as Manhattan's district attorney. Kunstler also seized on the belated revelation that Gene Roberts, the Malcolm bodyguard, was an undercover cop, arguing that the defendants had a right to know that at trial. But Roberts filed his own affidavit, claiming that he had no evidence to exculpate Butler or Thomas, and Morgenthau issued a lengthy response denying Kunstler's petition.

Seeking to strengthen his case, Kunstler sent Nuriddin Faiz, the Islamic chaplain, back to Napanoch in February 1978 to coax more details out of Halim. In a second affidavit written out in front of Faiz, Halim revealed that Ben and "Leon," as he now called "Brother Lee," first approached him on the street in Paterson. Halim indicated that he "knew these men well"—suggesting that they were all members of the NOI mosque in Paterson. "I learned from them that word was out that Malcolm X should be killed," he reported. Halim disclosed that the other two conspirators, whom he now identified as "William X" and "Wilbur, or Kinly," came from Newark. He also confirmed that he had purchased the murder weapons and manufactured the smoke bomb, and he reiterated yet again that Butler and Johnson were innocent.

After Morgenthau opposed Kunstler's motions several more times, the case finally made its way to Judge Harold Rothwax of New York State Supreme Court. A slightly built man with a brusque manner and easily triggered temper, Rothwax had begun his career as a civil rights attorney defending indigent clients and activists such as Abbie Hoffman, but he had grown increasingly conservative and supportive of prosecutors once he ascended to the bench. On the first of November, Rothwax handed down a decision rejecting Kunstler's appeal, on the grounds that Halim's new account amounted to no more than a "somewhat more specific" version of testimony that had failed to persuade a jury a decade earlier. "No criminal case," Rothwax concluded haughtily, "is ever proved beyond all doubt."

For Peter Goldman, however, Halim's affidavits—combined with his yearlong communications with Aziz—were more than enough to settle his own doubts. Goldman now "smelled a rat in the whole original prosecution," as he put it, and he was determined to do everything in his own power to bring the injustice to light. He resolved to write a new ending for a second edition of *The Death and Life of Malcolm X*, and to use his position at *Newsweek* to spread the word about the new evidence in the murder case. But first, the reporter in Goldman wanted to meet with Aziz and the other defendants face-to-face, and by the spring of 1979, Muhammad Abdul Aziz had gained enough trust to extend that invitation. "He sent me a letter," Goldman recalled, "suggesting that I come to Sing Sing with a tape recorder."

NINE

Three "Pawn Sacrifices"

Always a reluctant driver, Goldman took the hour-long train ride from Manhattan to Ossining. At the station, he hailed a taxi to Sing Sing, where he expected to be taken to the visitors' area to meet Aziz. Instead, a guard picked Goldman up in a prison jeep, drove him across a huge courtyard, and led him to an office that Aziz had been assigned as the prison's resident imam. It was "about the size of an ample bedroom," Goldman recalled, and contained two desks. As Aziz rose to greet his visitors, Goldman noted how strong he looked after more than a decade in prison—with broad shoulders and a torso kept lean by karate and other daily exercise. He also observed that Aziz had been allowed to grow his hair into an Afro with long sideburns, and was wearing his own sweater over prison-issued green pants—another sign of the special status he had attained at Sing Sing. "That doesn't happen for ninety-nine-point-nine percent of prisoners," Goldman thought.

The guard asked if Goldman wanted him to stay, and Goldman declined, after which the guard left the room without placing any time limit on the visit. According to Islamic custom, Aziz offered his visitor something to eat: a slice of carrot cake. Goldman accepted, then sat opposite Aziz at one of the desks, unpacked his tape recorder, and began the interview. When Goldman asked what life had been like in prison, Aziz harked back to his eighteen months in solitary confinement and how he had learned to fight the tedium with reading and exercise. That led to study toward a college degree once he arrived in Attica. "I'm taking more credits over here now," Aziz said, referring to Sing Sing. "I want to take business. Not that I want business, but that's the only way to make money." Aziz expressed pride in his role as prison imam, offering spiritual guidance to his fellow prisoners and helping to keep peace with the Sing Sing guards. "I've saved them a lot of problems," Aziz said. "Not because I was trying to save them problems. I don't mean it that way. But just being me. Just doing the work that Islam assigns for a person to do, so to speak, saves them a lot of problems."

The loss of his marriage and the separation from his children were clearly a source of pain, but Aziz spoke about them philosophically. "I think I gained something from being here," Aziz told Goldman. "I mean, I lost a lot. From a family perspective, there's no doubt about that. But I think that I gained something. Spiritually. Intellectually. I think that I've proven . . . the kind of development that can come in a place like this when a person is positively motivated. So I think that there are benefits from having done this or gone through it. Whether they outweigh the bad things that have happened remains to be seen."

Despite the ease the two had developed over the phone, Goldman was prepared to see Aziz become testy once the interview turned to the circumstances of his arrest and conviction. Yet while showing occasional flashes of anger, Aziz remained composed and coolly analytical for the rest of their long exchange. To Goldman, his demeanor reflected Aziz's growth as a person, but also his understanding that the combativeness he had shown in court a decade earlier wouldn't do him any good now that he was trying to appeal to the judicial system and to the press to get his sentence overturned. "We had a very civilized conversation," Goldman recalled. "He didn't project anger at me. I sensed that he knew he was playing his last card."

Goldman took Aziz back to his role at the Harlem mosque before the assassination, as a top Fruit of Islam enforcer. While Malcolm was still in charge, Aziz had sometimes been assigned to his security detail, but the two had never known each other well. After the split, Aziz admitted, he had shared the NOI's view of Malcolm as a traitorous publicity seeker. "The Caucasians made him," Aziz scoffed. "The media made him." When Goldman asked if he would have participated in a hit against Malcolm if he had been asked, Aziz was honest enough not to dismiss the question. "I really don't know, to tell you the truth," he said after a long pause. But Aziz was less candid about the assault on Benjamin Brown, the FOI defector who had tried to set up his own storefront mosque in the Bronx.

Aziz maintained that he hadn't been involved in the attack on Brown, and that he was so badly beaten during the arrest that he couldn't have participated in the Audubon Ballroom attack. "New York's finest made sure I didn't kill Malcolm," Aziz said with a short, sardonic laugh. "They busted in my door. Put a pistol in my mouth, handcuffed me behind my back, threw me on the floor by the door. One had his knee in my chest. Was beating me in the face with a pistol. Asking me who shot Brown, and I didn't know, because I didn't even know he got shot. . . . My children and my wife screaming, and they're tearing the place apart, asking my children, 'Where's the gun? Where's the gun?'"

Goldman pressed Aziz on conflicting accounts in the Benjamin Brown case that had damaged his credibility during the Malcolm trial. Goldman recalled that police involved in the first arrest testified that as they entered Aziz's apartment, he attacked an officer with a karate chop so violent that it dented the metal mask the officer wore for protection. Aziz shook his head. "There were too many guns," he said. "I would have been dead." Why had Aziz told the grand jury and the trial jury two different stories about which of his legs was injured? Goldman asked. Aziz responded by hitching up his green prison trousers to show gray scar tissue on both shins. "So I was in no condition to do anything," Aziz said. "I couldn't even walk."

Aziz was just as adamant about another reason he couldn't have been involved in the Audubon Ballroom hit. "Everyone who was what we call soldiering at that time knew me," he told Goldman. "Was no doubt in anybody's mind who I was. I couldn't even have gotten in the door [of the ballroom]." In another new development supporting that argument, William Kunstler had obtained an affidavit from Benjamin 2X Goodman, Malcolm's former top aide. Now calling himself Benjamin Karim and living in Richmond, Virginia, he confirmed that Malcolm's bodyguards were under orders to report suspicious-looking individuals directly to him, which would have included anyone still working for the Harlem mosque. Karim was also scanning the audience for unfriendly faces when he spoke for almost an hour ahead of Malcolm. Karim insisted that he had given all that information to the authorities at the time, but they declined to call him as a trial witness. Before updating his book, Goldman would also conduct another interview with Karim, who agreed that if Mohammad Aziz (then Norman 3X Butler) or Khalil Islam (then Thomas 15X Johnson) had been at the ballroom, he would have noticed them.

Echoing his trial testimony, Aziz said he had never met Mujahid Halim (then Talmadge Hayer) before the trial, nor any of the accomplices whom Halim was now naming. But for the first time, he shared a story that might have explained how the New Jersey hit men came to believe they were acting at the direction of Elijah Muhammad. In the summer of 1964, Muhammad's second son, Elijah Jr., traveled to New York and met with ministers and Fruit of Islam commanders from up and down the East Coast. E-2, as the son was known, angrily listed Malcolm's offenses—from the poaching of NOI members, to public statements about Elijah Muhammad's infidelity, to the fight to stay in the house in Queens. Then Muhammad Jr. made clear just how upset NOI headquarters in Chicago was with the Harlem mosque for allowing Malcolm to get away with it all.

"So the people in New York, in a sense of speaking, got sat down, and security people rolled in from everywhere—captains from all over the country," Aziz said, describing the E-2 summit. "There were about five hundred guys, some number like that. And New York was made to look bad because they wasn't doing anything about this that happened in their own back yard. 'What we got to do—bring in people from all over to take care of your business?' . . . And he says, 'That house is ours, and the nigger don't want to give it up. Well, all you have to do is go out there and clap on the walls until the walls come tumbling down, and then cut the nigger's tongue out and put it in an envelope and send it to me, and I'll stamp it approved and give it to the Messenger.' That's what he said, and that, at that time, was death. Back then, that was an order."

Shortly after Goldman visited Aziz in prison, at the end of April 1979, William Kunstler launched one more long-shot bid to get his new evidence about Malcolm X's murder before the American public. Having reached a dead end with the New York courts, Kunstler appealed to the Congressional Black Caucus in Washington, D.C., to call for a House investigation into the assassination. In a formal petition that he shared with the media, Kunstler went a step beyond Mujahid Halim's two affidavits and identified the names and addresses of three of his accomplices. "Ben" and "Leon" were Benjamin Thomas and Leon Davis, both living on Hamilton Avenue in Paterson, New Jersey. "Willie X"— the man Halim said had wielded the double-barreled shotgun—was William Bradley, a resident of South Orange Avenue in Newark who by then was serving his own prison sentence in the Essex County Correctional Facility. The fifth accomplice, along with Talmadge Hayer, was identified as Wilbur Kinley—his last name would later turn out to be "McKinley"—and described as living in Newark but with no street address. Kunstler also contended that FBI files, which were becoming public as a result of the 1975 Senate hearings into the agency's abuses, would support Halim's assertions—a suggestion that the FBI might have had its own information about the New Jersey hit squad.

Seizing on Kunstler's appeal as a news peg, Goldman wrote a full-page story in the next issue of *Newsweek*, titled "Who Killed Malcolm X?" Without repeating the names and addresses in the petition, the story summarized Halim's account of a five-man murder plot hatched in New Jersey, and offered more damning information that had surfaced in FBI files. Several years after the assassination, FBI agents in Chicago had boasted in a memo to Washington headquarters about having "developed" the feud between the Nation of Islam and Malcolm that led to the assassination. From his prison interview, Goldman also shared Aziz's story about the "cut the . . . tongue out" directive to NOI commanders, including the incendiary "n-word" and revealing that the exhortation had come from "a member of [Elijah] Muhammad's family."

Shortly after that story appeared, Goldman made his next reporting trip, to meet face-to-face with Khalil Islam, the former Thomas 15X Johnson. The weather was stormy on the day that Goldman flew to the Clinton Correctional Facility, the prison known as Dannemora, where Johnson was now incarcerated. After flying to Burlington, Vermont, Goldman boarded a tiny puddle jumper that took him on a harrowing ride over a turbulent Hudson River to the prison's location in the northeast corner of New York State. Although Islam had also become a prison imam and was taking college courses, he didn't have the privileged status that Aziz enjoyed at Sing Sing. Instead of an office, guards brought Goldman to the main visitors' area, where Islam sat waiting behind a plain Formica-covered table.

With his broad, handsome face and caramel-colored skin, Islam looked like he might have hailed from the Black middle class, Goldman thought. But Islam's hoarse, tough-guy voice was more in keeping with his past as a onetime heroin addict who had dropped out of high school and lived on the streets for a decade before being introduced to the Nation of Islam while serving time for drug possession on Hart Island in the Bronx. When Goldman asked about the family Islam had started after getting out of jail and joining the Harlem mosque, he sounded more stoic than sentimental. In the thirteen years since his conviction, he had been shuffled back and forth between a half-dozen prisons, making it difficult to maintain contact with his wife and children. When they did talk, his wife shared accounts of harassment from Malcolm supporters, who had vandalized her house and slashed the tires on her car. Islam encouraged her to divorce him and start a new life, but she resisted. Now, he found it hard to pick up the phone, even when he had permission. "I'm a very proud person," he told Goldman. "So I stopped calling for long periods of time. Wouldn't call. And any time I do call, I get all tensed up because I know what I'm going to hear."

As the conversation turned to the murder trial, Islam maintained his hardened, streetwise tone. At the time of the assassination, he had been a member of the Harlem mosque for five years, having first joined because he was attracted by Malcolm's speeches. Before Malcolm's exit, Islam frequently served in his bodyguard detail, and he even did errands that brought him to the family home in Queens. So the prosecution's argument that he could have entered the Audubon Ballroom without being recognized was nonsense, Islam stated flatly. He also scoffed at Talmadge Hayer's change of heart during the trial, saying that he had immediately told Hayer and all the defense lawyers that it wouldn't make a difference as long as no other accomplices were named. "I knew the only way his statement would help us was if it replaced us with somebody else," Islam told Goldman. "So when we went up to the defense table, the lawyers asked me what I thought, and I said no. I said, 'I know I'm finished. You know I'm innocent . . . but I don't see how this thing is going to help us.' My lawyer says, 'Are you crazy? Don't you want to go home?' I said, 'How am I going to go home? Do you have the people who did it? Is he going to give that up? No. So what good is his statement?'"

Even now, a decade later, Islam conveyed the air of someone who felt his fate was sealed and there was little he could do about it. When Goldman asked the same provocative question he had posed to Aziz— would Islam have taken part in a plot against Malcolm if asked—the answer came quickly. "Murder? Naw," Islam said. "I can't think of any circumstances where a person would walk up to me and say, 'Listen, so and so and so and so,' and I would just jump off on his say-so and go and kill somebody. I was upset, yeah, but I'm the type of person, man, that I don't get that emotional. I like to reason things out." Yet unlike Aziz, Islam refused to engage in speculation about where the accomplices whom Halim was now naming might have received their orders. As Goldman rose from the table after a long but frustrating exchange, he sensed that he had "drained the well dry," as he put it, and that he wasn't going to get any further in puncturing Islam's code of omertà. "I'm aware of the fact that I was used," Islam concluded vaguely. "I'm aware of the fact that there's some inside involvement. But I just can't put my hands on it."

When Goldman first set out to interview the third inmate, Mujahid Halim, he didn't expect to feel much sympathy for the man. By the time he had met face-to-face with Muhammad Aziz and Khalil Islam, Goldman was all but sure both men were innocent. But he knew that Halim was guilty, by his own admission, and he pictured having to steel himself to talk for several hours to a man who had pumped bullets into Malcolm X's body. Goldman had quite a different reaction, however, when he arrived at Napanoch prison, a hundred miles north of New

York City, and was escorted into a visiting room to meet Halim. Still only thirty-eight after a decade in prison, Halim had a small build, baby face, and wide-set eyes that made him look much younger. He also radiated a sense of sincerity about his new identity as a prison imam, and his belated attempt to make amends for all the harm he had done, to Malcolm and to his two fellow defendants. "To my astonishment, I liked him," Goldman recalled. "There was something sweet about him."

Like Malcolm himself, Goldman discovered, Halim had reached a turning point when he lost faith in Elijah Muhammad. Even after facing trial and prison with no support from the NOI's leadership, Halim had continued to believe in the Messenger. But then Elijah Muhammad died, and his son Wallace confirmed everything Malcolm had said about the great man's failings. Wallace "began to explain to us that his father was only a man like any other man," Halim said. "This was heavy. I was like a ball of clay that was rolled up—had to be put back together again. Just broke down my whole concept of things." All of a sudden, it dawned on Halim that the man he worshipped had deceived him, and that the man he had condemned and helped kill might have been right. "I remember some of the ministers used to say that time reveals all things, and for the longest time, I always thought that time would tell that what that man was saying was wrong," Halim said, referring to Malcolm. "Well, time has told. Time has told us a lot of things he said was true."

Trying to understand what had motivated Halim, Goldman asked about his upbringing in Paterson, in the days when he was still known as Talmadge Hayer. Halim was one of seven children in a family in the poorest neighborhood of that once-thriving New Jersey city, which had fallen into steep decline after World War II as factories shut down and white residents fled to the suburbs. As a boy, Halim said, he dreamed of becoming someone important, like a doctor or a lawyer. But when a grade school teacher asked him to tell the class what he wanted to be when he grew up, he could only bring himself to say "truck driver"— like his father. Halim dropped out of high school in the tenth grade, and took a series of entry-level jobs in Paterson's machine shops and textile mills. He first became aware of the Nation of Islam when he saw Fruit of Islam foot soldiers, with their shaved heads and karate-honed bodies, selling copies of *Muhammad Speaks* on street corners. In his teenage imagination, he envisioned them doing battle with the Ku Klux Klan, the evil white vigilantes he had heard his parents describe from their childhood in the Carolinas, before they came north in the Great Migration. "Had their own army, man," Halim said, recalling his initial fascination with the NOI. "I thought we were going to fight this white, blue-eye devil."

Halim began going to services at a Paterson dance hall that served as a satellite mosque to the larger one in Newark. He also started studying karate and participating in local competitions— including the one held at the Newark mosque that he had denied entering during the murder trial, despite photographic evidence. At the age of twenty-one, Halim applied for the "X" that marked his formal entry into the NOI. But he struggled with maintaining the discipline required of new converts, and was suspended several times. Once, he was found with stolen guns; another time, he roughed up a wayward NOI member without permission from higher-ups. In early 1964, Halim returned to the Paterson mosque after one of those exiles just as Malcolm X was quitting the Nation of Islam. Suddenly all the ministers in Paterson and Newark were full of condemnation for Malcolm and his public disclosures about Elijah Muhammad's extramarital affairs. Halim was also struck, he told Goldman, by the cartoon in *Muhammad Speaks* that showed Malcolm's severed head bouncing toward a graveyard to join other traitors from history.

It was around this time that two older "brothers" from the local Fruit of Islam—the men he had now identified as Benjamin Thomas and Leon Davis—drove up to Halim as he was walking down the street in Paterson. They invited him to take a ride and started peppering him with leading questions about Malcolm. Eager to prove his loyalty to Elijah Muhammad, Halim gave them the kind of answers they were looking for. "I felt, from what was being said by Malcolm and what was being said by the ministers, that it was really putting the FOI to a test," he told Goldman. "I had a lot of love and admiration for the Honorable Elijah Muhammad, and I just felt that this is something I had to stand up for. . . . Maybe I was manipulated . . . I don't know. I didn't see it that way at the time. I just believed, man, and I was the type of person that if I had to stand up for what I believed, I would do it. I would go all the way."

By the end of the spring of 1964, Ben and Leon had recruited two more plotters—the men Halim identified as William X Bradley and Wilbur "Kinley"—but they still didn't have a plan for how to attack Malcolm. Through the summer and fall, the five men met at Ben's house, or on car rides around northern New Jersey, debating various scenarios. After driving to Queens to see Malcolm's house, they decided it was too heavily guarded. Finding a place to target Malcolm on the streets of Harlem seemed like too much effort. "I was working," Halim told Goldman. "Far as I know, we all were. We couldn't just run over to New York and ride around." So as winter set in, the five men zeroed in on the Audubon Ballroom, where Malcolm was holding regular meetings of his new organization, the OAAU.

The five went to a rally at the Audubon Ballroom and discovered that, although Malcolm had bodyguards, no one searched people at the door. The police presence also seemed light. Still, they didn't make the final decision to attack on February 21, 1965, until the night before, after they paid to get into a Saturday night dance at the ballroom and searched the building for escape routes. "It was just a chance," Halim told Goldman. "A long shot, I guess. But we just felt we would have to move on it, in the ballroom, and that's what we did. Why there? I don't know. It was the only place we knew he would be there."

The next morning, the five drove from New Jersey to Harlem in Wilbur's Cadillac and parked on a street near the ballroom that would take them quickly back to the George Washington Bridge. They entered the building with guns under their winter coats, and no one stopped or questioned them. Halim and Leon Davis took their places on folding chairs in the front row to the left of the stage, with William Bradley and Ben Thomas behind them, while Wilbur McKinley positioned himself farther back to create the disturbances that would distract Malcolm's bodyguards. But once the hall filled up and Benjamin 2X Goodman appeared to give his warm-up speech, Halim got cold feet. He started to wish that he wasn't there, he told Goldman, and he had to fight off his fear by telling himself that he was doing the will of Allah.

When Goldman asked him to describe what happened once Malcolm came onstage, Halim suddenly had trouble getting his words out. He looked up at the ceiling and spoke in an anguished whisper, as though he was reliving the chaos all over again. "Somebody sitting maybe in the middle," Halim said, describing the distraction created by McKinley. "Pretend somebody pickpocketing him. Threw the bomb and go through some changes. Willie fired the shotgun. We fired our guns and ran. A lot of commotion and stuff. There was quite a few guns in that place being fired. I got shot in the left leg and didn't even know it because there was this guy shooting on my right side. . . . I fired off a couple of shots, but for the most part I was just trying to get out. Just hopped, man, hopping on one leg, and there was one person, he was running in front of me, I think it was Leon—the other people I couldn't see. . . . And I slid down the banister. Fell on the ground. And don't ask me how or why—there was an officer out there, and it was fortunate, because my life was spared."

Turning to the trial, Goldman asked why Halim had changed his testimony at the last minute. At first, Halim explained, he thought he could get away with pretending that he had come to the Audubon Ballroom only to hear Malcolm speak, because the prosecution didn't seem to have any hard evidence to the contrary. Then he learned that his fingerprints had been found on remnants of the smoke bomb he had made by stuffing a roll of flammable camera film into a sock. "I thought the film burned up, man!" Hakim said when he first confessed his guilt to his two codefendants. By that time, he realized that Butler and Johnson might be headed for conviction, too, as he listened to all the trial witnesses who claimed to have seen them at the scene. "So I decided to do something," Halim told Goldman. "I had to try to exonerate the brothers. But I didn't name any names. At the time, I just couldn't." Now that Halim was finally naming those names, Goldman asked, did he have any sense of where—or whether—the men who recruited him on the streets of Paterson got their orders?

Halim said he had a hunch. Of the five, he said, Thomas was the one who had some kind of position within the local NOI hierarchy, so he always assumed that "Brother Ben" might have been in communication with someone else. But Halim never brought up the subject. "I didn't ask a whole lot of questions as to who's giving us instructions and who's telling us what," he said. "I thought that somebody was giving instructions: 'Brothers, you got to move on this situation.' But I felt we was in accord. We just knew what had to be done." Like Aziz and Islam, Halim gave the impression of believing that he had taken a fall for the larger Nation of Islam, and of accepting that it was his duty as a loyal Muslim to do so. As Goldman spoke with the three men a decade later, the image that came to his mind was prisoners of war "who had fallen into enemy hands." But before the interview at Napanoch was over, Halim would offer a metaphor that the *Newsweek* wordsmith thought was even more apt. All three men, Halim said, had been "wasted like pawn sacrifices in somebody's wild chess game."

Once Goldman had recorded Halim's detailed firsthand account of how Malcolm's murder was planned and carried out, he was determined to get it to the widest possible audience. The one-page story that he had written for *Newsweek* in May, before interviewing Halim, hadn't gotten as much attention as he hoped. So in the summer of 1979, Goldman reached out to Ed Klein, another former *Newsweek* colleague, who had become the editor of the widely read Sunday magazine of *The New York Times*. The result was a five-thousand-word feature story that appeared in the August 19 issue of that publication titled "Malcolm X: An Unfinished Story?"

In the piece, Goldman gave *Times* readers a detailed account of Halim's version of the assassination, complete with the first names of his four New Jersey accomplices. Two of the plotters "were still active Muslims in New Jersey," Goldman reported. A third "was doing time in state prison for another, unrelated felony." Although Goldman didn't specify, the man who fit that description was the shotgun wielder whom Goldman identified as "Willie X" and whom Kunstler also identified by his last name—Bradley—in his petition to the Congressional Black Caucus. Goldman also reported that "a Muslim imam"—likely Nuriddin Faiz—had located this plotter in prison and tried to persuade him to come forward to help Aziz and Islam. First denying any involvement in the murder, Goldman wrote, the prisoner had snarled at the imam that "he was not going to jeopardize himself for anyone."

For the *Times* magazine piece, Goldman also flew to Chicago to interview Wallace Muhammad, the leader of the new, more mainstream version of the Nation of Islam. When asked if he thought his father had given a direct order to kill Malcolm, Wallace said he "doubted it," Goldman wrote, after how close the two men had been for so many years. Still, Wallace accused jealous courtiers in Chicago of turning his father against Malcolm and creating a "fiery" and "volatile climate" that made an act of vengeance all but inevitable. "The talk of retaliation," he told Goldman, "or stopping hypocrites who were trying to tear down our Nation of Islam—I think they just got drunk on that and said, 'Well, we'll stamp out all of them who disagree with us.'" In his father's last decade, Wallace admitted, the Fruit of Islam had become "nothing but just a hooligan outfit, a hoodlum outfit."

Ever the dry-eyed journalist, however, Goldman ended the *Times* piece on a weary note of realism about the probable fates of Aziz and Islam. "The reasonable doubts that now cloud the verdict against them may never be settled or even addressed by Congress or the courts," he predicted. "Talmadge Hayer may have waited too long to speak, so long that the agencies of our justice resist even contemplating the likelihood that he is at last telling the truth." And sure enough, at that moment in time it had become too late—for Hayer, and also for Goldman, in his noble attempt to use his skills as a reporter and writer to help free two wrongfully convicted men.

The *New York Times* piece did get some notice, and was picked up by the *Chicago Tribune* and several other major regional newspapers. Goldman also helped Halim edit and distribute a first-person account of the murder plot, through a newspaper syndicate run by a friend of his wife Helen's. But by the fall, the Congressional Black Caucus had passed on William Kunstler's petition for a new investigation—in part, Kunstler heard from his sources, because Betty Shabazz made it known that she didn't want to relive Malcolm's murder. And when Goldman made one last call to District Attorney Morgenthau's office, he received a curt call back from a woman in the press office. "I've been instructed to tell you," the woman said, "that we consider this case closed."

For Goldman, all that was left now was to fulfill a promise, the one he had made to Aziz in his first letter to Sing Sing. "If further inquiry satisfies my mind that the verdict in your trial was wrong," he had written, "I would be happy to say so." Goldman went to work to write a new ending to his book, laying out all his new evidence and how it had changed his own mind. His friend Jay Iselin had left Harper & Row, and the new top editor didn't see much commercial value in reissuing the book. So Goldman found an academic publisher—the University of Chicago Press—which had launched a book series called "Blacks in the New World," edited by August Meier, a respected white scholar of Black history.

In the fall of 1979, a second paperback edition of *The Death and Life of Malcolm X* appeared with a new thirty-nine-page last chapter that Goldman titled "Afterthoughts." The epilogue ended with a wistful meditation on how awareness of Malcolm's life seemed to be fading, along with society's interest in getting to the bottom of his death. "Those two were locked away and forgotten," Goldman wrote, referring to Aziz and Islam, "and now the memories of Malcolm too have begun to dim a little, even in the streets he walked only fourteen years ago. A black psychologist mentioned Malcolm's name recently to a class of teenaged kids in Harlem, and got only the dimmest show of recognition; he displayed Malcolm's photograph, narrow tied and Ivy tailored, and was asked 'Why the dude dress so funny?' But the young blacks in that classroom, who were in diapers when Malcolm died, were raised by parents who knew who Malcolm was and were touched by him. It is not the memory of his face that is his legacy to them, but the force of his bearing, his example—and his witness to the world of the possibilities of blackness in white America."

Goldman's summation was eloquent—but also premature. As it turned out, the last chapter on proving the innocence of Muhammad Aziz and Khalil Islam had yet to be written, and those Harlem parents were not the last generation to discover in Malcolm a shining prince.

PART FOUR

REDISCOVERY

1983–2020

TEN

The Rappers

B y the early 1980s, Betty Shabazz could feel the world's interest in her husband slipping away. She herself was focused on building her own career, after several years following the assassination when she was too fearful to leave her new house in the suburbs north of New York City. While raising six daughters, Betty had resumed her education, earning her bachelor's degree and then a doctorate in educational administration. She took a position running a health sciences program at Medgar Evers College, a predominantly Black branch of the City University of New York. To supplement her income from the royalties of the *Autobiography*, she occasionally accepted invitations to speak or to appear at commemorative rallies, but the number of those events was dwindling and attendance was sparse compared to the earliest Malcolm X Days. When Betty visited Malcolm's grave at Ferncliff Cemetery, not far from her home in the town of Mount Vernon, she found no signs of visitors, just a plot spotted with weeds.

Then, in 1983, a skinny, intense young white man showed up at Betty's office at Medgar Evers College carrying a music tape. He introduced himself as Keith LeBlanc, and explained that he was a drummer and producer for record companies that specialized in the new urban music genre then known as rap. On the tape, LeBlanc had taken fragments of Malcolm X's speeches and set them to a beat produced on a drum machine, a recording device that allowed musicians to create background tracks with digitally created or previously recorded sound clips. For the song's recurring refrain, LeBlanc had spliced together Malcolm's voice saying his name, "Malcolm X . . . ," and the words "No Sell Out," from a speech he had delivered in 1963. In between, he had sprinkled a dozen more of Malcolm's most memorable lines, such as "The only thing power respects is power" and "If you're afraid to tell the truth, then you don't deserve freedom."

LeBlanc hoped to play the tape for Betty and ask her permission to release it as a commercial record. But as he talked excitedly about how hard he had worked on the project, she cut him off.

"Look, stop talking," Betty said. "This is my life. I will listen to the tape and call you after I have heard it."

So LeBlanc gave Betty the only phone number at which he could be reliably reached at the time—at his mother's house—and left the office to await her response.

At that point, it had been a decade since the music that came to be called hip hop was born in the beleaguered New York City neighborhood known as the South Bronx. Once farmland owned by wealthy colonial leaders, and later heavily populated by striving Jewish immigrants, the area had become predominantly Black and Puerto Rican by the 1970s. The construction of two major highways—the Cross Bronx Expressway and the Major Deegan Expressway—had destroyed much of the middle-class housing stock and cut remaining residents off from the rest of the city. As white residents fled to the suburbs, city services and local schools went into steep decline.

Landlords abandoned or largely ceased upkeep of scores of apartment buildings, and the neighborhood became infamous for its waves of arson. Throughout the decade, the image of the South Bronx as an "enduring symbol of America's urban catastrophe," as one reporter put it, was further enhanced by visits from politicians who made a show of touring its burned-out streets, and by the attention the neighborhood's plight received during media coverage of World Series games played at Yankee Stadium in the Bronx and of rampant looting during the 1977 New York City blackout.

Amid all the devastation, however, a new cultural movement took root at the block parties that the youth of the South Bronx threw to distract them from their troubles. At first the music played was mostly disco and funk, and it was provided by local disc jockeys, or DJs, who played their albums on two separate turntables so they could mix songs and keep the music flowing. Then in 1973, a Jamaican immigrant named Clive Campbell, who went by the nickname DJ Kool Herc, figured out a way to keep the beat flowing, too. He would put copies of the same record on his two turntables and play only short instrumental and percussion "breaks," switching back and forth to extend the groove. Campbell had also amassed an extensive collection of funk and disco records with particularly addictive breaks, and had access to huge speakers loud enough to power dance parties indoors or out. After a party he threw to help his sister buy new school clothes in August of that year, dance parties hosted by Kool Herc became the talk of the neighborhood.

Other South Bronx DJs quickly adopted and built upon Campbell's innovations. Cuts in school budgets had eliminated the introduction to musical instruments that launched many of the pioneers of jazz, so this new generation innovated with records instead. Lance Taylor, known as DJ Afrika Bambaataa, expanded the repertoire of sounds, incorporating reggae and salsa and European electronic music. Theodore Livingston, who went by Grand Wizzard Theodore, perfected "scratching," or creating a break within the breakbeat by sliding a record back and forth underneath a turntable needle. Joseph Saddler, nicknamed Grandmaster Flash, figured out how to repeat longer breaks by calculating the amount of record rotation it took to play them, then "back spinning" to the same spot over and over again.

Meanwhile, three other pillars of what would become the foundation of hip hop culture took hold. Visual graffiti artists embraced the new music, showcasing their kaleidoscopic calligraphy on flyers for the block parties and on building walls, subway cars, and buses across the city. Dancers at the block parties waited for the extended instrumental runs to display their most athletic and inventive moves, which came to be known as "break dancing." Showmen and women began taking on the role of "masters of ceremony" at the neighborhood parties. Calling themselves MCs for short, they warmed up the crowd before the music started, and added another level of entertainment by "freestyling," or making up, raps that matched the rhythm of the long breakbeats. In a new version of the age-old Black cultural tradition of verbal exaggeration and sparring known as "playing the dozens," MCs engaged in live rap battles, and made competitive boasts a mainstay of increasingly inventive lyrics they composed on paper before performing them.

═══

By the late 1970s, the first rap records began to appear. Introduced to the new music by their son, a veteran record producer named Joe Robinson and his wife, former R&B singer Sylvia Robinson, formed a rap-focused record company called Sugar Hill Records, named after the Sugar Hill neighborhood in Harlem. Sylvia Robinson went scouting for up-and-coming rappers and found three performing at a pizzeria and other venues in Englewood, New Jersey. Instead of signing them individually, she combined them in the group she called The Sugar Hill Gang, and in 1979 the trio released a single called "Rapper's Delight," the first rap song to crack *Billboard* magazine's Top 40 chart. Introducing themselves one by one, the three MCs—known as "Wonder Mike" Johnson, "Big Bank Hank" Johnson, and Guy "Master Gee" O'Brien—conjured up a fantasy world very different from their real lives on the street, in which their prowess at rapping and getting people to dance made them sexually irresistible—"the women fight for my delight"—and afforded them a lavish lifestyle complete with fancy cars and clothes, private pools, and "more money than a sucker could ever spend."

As Sugar Hill Records signed up more acts, Sylvia Robinson began recruiting for a house band to play backup during recording sessions and warm up crowds at live performances. She turned to a group of musicians who had paid their dues performing in clubs around Hartford, Connecticut. One was drummer Keith LeBlanc, who had grown up in nearby Bristol. LeBlanc had first become fascinated with drums as a young boy, when he watched Ringo Starr and the Beatles perform on *The Ed Sullivan Show*. He played in the school orchestra and student rock bands, and by the age of fourteen was starting to get professional gigs. In his late teens, he met a drummer named Harold Sargent, who had formed a soul and funk group called Wood, Brass and Steel with two fellow Black musicians, guitarist Skip McDonald and bass player Doug Wimbish. When Sargent left the trio, he recommended LeBlanc as a replacement, and soon Keith was also joining McDonald and Wimbish at Sugar Hill Records studio sessions.

Among the rappers LeBlanc accompanied for the label was a group that Joseph Saddler, the legendary South Bronx DJ, had formed with a band of fellow rappers called Grandmaster Flash and the Furious Five. Saddler had been raised in foster homes in upstate New York and in the violent Bronx neighborhood policed out of a station house known as Fort Apache. The group's lead MC, Melvin Glover, known as Melle Mel, and his brother Nathaniel, nicknamed Kidd Creole, grew up in a Bronx housing project. In 1979, the group produced another commercial hit for Sugar Hill Records, but it had a very different tone from the breezy, boastful "Rapper's Delight." Called "The Message," the song described the harsh reality of life in the ghetto, where young people dreamed of the big time but were more likely to end up unemployed, on drugs, or in prison. The lyrics were also marked more by subtle internal rhymes than clever couplets, reflected in the refrain: "It's like a jungle sometimes/ It makes me wonder how I keep from going under."

LeBlanc was just as struck by another of Grandmaster Flash's innovations. Hanging around the Sugar Hill studios, he saw Flash experimenting with putting excerpts of dialogue—or "spoken word," as it was called in hip hop lingo—into his mix of samples. One came from a Flash Gordon movie, and found its way into Flash's 1981 dance hall hit "The Adventures of Grandmaster Flash on the Wheels of Steel." Another came from the movie *Dirty Harry*, when the ruthless police detective Harry Callahan says to a wounded Black suspect who is about to reach for a gun: "You gotta ask yourself one question. Do you feel lucky? Well do you, punk?"

As it happened, Joe and Sylvia Robinson had compiled several albums of Malcolm X's speeches, which LeBlanc found lying around the studio. Before then, he recalled, "I didn't know much about Malcolm X except that my parents told me that Martin Luther King was good and Malcolm was bad." But when he started listening to the records, LeBlanc thought Malcolm sounded like a rapper, with his biting social commentary and use of rhythm and rhyme. To learn more, he reached out to his drummer friend Harold Sargent, who gave him more Malcolm records and encouraged him to read the *Autobiography*. On his own time, LeBlanc began slipping into the Sugar Hill studios to put a drum machine beat and bass and rhythm guitar accompaniment behind bits of Malcolm's speeches, among them "The Ballot or the Bullet" and the speech he gave after his Queens house was firebombed.

When Betty Shabazz finally called LeBlanc's mother's house, she said she liked "No Sell Out" and granted permission to use Malcolm's words. Her only request was that LeBlanc take out the sound of gunfire. In return, LeBlanc offered to give Betty half of any profits from the record's sales. But because the Robinsons were notoriously stingy, and had never paid Betty royalties for their records of Malcolm's speeches, LeBlanc took the project to Tom Silverman, the white founder of the Tommy Boy Records label. Silverman embraced the project and invited Shabazz to write the liner notes. In November 1983, Tommy Boy released a 12-inch single with a pensive, black-and-white photo of Malcolm on the front cover, and Betty's moving endorsement on the back. "This recording documents Malcolm's voice," she wrote, "at a time and space in history some nineteen or more years ago. Its meaning is just as relevant today as it was then. His belief is that people must constantly monitor behavior, refine goals, and direct their objectives to insure that the right to life and work is a reality. Ultimately, our goals should be peace and brotherhood. After all, the universe belongs to all its inhabitants."

Peace and brotherhood didn't prevail with Sugar Hill Records, however. When the Robinsons found out that LeBlanc had taken "No Sell Out" to another label after using their records and taping in their studio, they sued him and Tommy Boy for copyright infringement. In a twist of fate, the case ended up in court before Judge Herbert J. Stern, the former assistant district attorney who had represented the D.A.'s office in the Malcolm X murder trial. After seeing Stern give Betty Shabazz a friendly courtroom greeting, the Robinsons realized the case wasn't likely to go their way, and agreed to a settlement that gave Tommy Boy control of the record but offered Sugar Hill a small cut of royalties. But then Joe Robinson turned around and used his influence with Black radio stations to persuade them not to play the record.

Even so, "No Sell Out" became a hit in Europe and on college radio stations. It was chosen as "single of the week" by several music magazines that covered the world of rap, and even earned a brief review in *People* magazine, whose critic wrote that it "succeeds in reminding the listener of the challenging directness of Malcolm's rhetoric." Yet the record's greatest impact wasn't on those old enough to be reminded of Malcolm; it was on a new generation of rap enthusiasts young enough to be discovering him for the first time. In particular, it put Malcolm's bracing words and message in the minds of a second wave of hip hop pioneers, who were about to steer the music in a more overtly political direction—starting with a group that came together in 1985 on Long Island, some twenty miles east of the South Bronx, and called itself Public Enemy.

While the plight of the South Bronx got far more national media attention in the 1970s, a different but parallel story was unfolding in and around the suburban town of Roosevelt, on the South Shore of Long Island. In the early twentieth century, Roosevelt had been so thoroughly white that local "sundown laws" required visiting Blacks to leave town by nightfall, lest they be subject to arrest or attack by a local contingent of the Ku Klux Klan. But after the construction of the north–south Meadowbrook Parkway in the mid-1930s—masterminded, like the highways through the Bronx, by the all-powerful urban planner Robert Moses—towns to the west of the highway grew progressively more integrated, while towns to the east remained almost exclusively white. Real estate firms accelerated the racial disparity by "blockbusting," or manipulating anxious white home owners into unloading their homes at a discount, then turning around and selling those same homes at a markup to Blacks looking to escape the city or move north in the Great Migration. In the 1960s, a wave of busing and other school integration plans in Roosevelt and surrounding towns attracted more Black home-buyers looking to improve educational opportunities for their children, while causing growing numbers of white families to flee. In that one decade alone, the population of Roosevelt went from 82 percent to

32 percent white, and from 17 percent to 67 percent Black—a racial trend line that would continue for the next fifty years, until whites accounted for less than 2 percent of Roosevelt's population.

Yet like the South Bronx, Roosevelt became an incubator for Black talent and creativity in the midst of increased segregation and economic decline. Basketball great Julius Erving would grow up in Roosevelt, as would the comedy and movie star Eddie Murphy. In the annals of hip hop, the Roosevelt area would become known as the home of two rappers who revolutionized the sound and the social content of the new music. Born in Queens, Carlton Douglas Ridenhour moved to Roosevelt at age eleven, attended the local public high school, and enrolled at nearby Adelphi University, where he met a Roosevelt native and resident of nearby Freeport named William Drayton Jr. Together, they would form the rap group Public Enemy under the distinctive names and contrasting stage personas of Chuck D, the earnest radical, and Flavor Flav, his comedic sidekick.

Ridenhour's father, Lorenzo, was an ex-Marine who quit his job as warehouse manager for a fabric company to start his own trucking company. Carlton's mother, Judy, ran Roosevelt's community theater. Both were avid jazz and R&B listeners and outspoken political activists. They filled their home with the sounds of scores of musicians who would later serve as sources of inspiration and "sampling" for their son—from James Brown and Sly and the Family Stone, to John Coltrane and Nina Simone. They also talked politics and current events with their three children, and sent Carlton to a school program in Black history at nearby Hofstra University that was also attended by several of his future bandmates.

If Public Enemy's political message seemed fresh in the 1980s, Ridenhour would later argue, it was because its founders, unlike many of their musical peers, had been born in an era of social consciousness that predated rap. "You have a group of people, they grew up, their first ten years, in the turbulent 1960s as kids," Ridenhour noted. "The assassinations that took place in the 1960s, they stuck. . . . The assassination of Malcolm X, when I was five. Dr. Martin Luther King, when I was eight. Then you had the destruction—COINTELPRO, J. Edgar Hoover, the Black Panther Party. So coming up in the Sixties made us see a different world than somebody who was born in 1970 and saw the Seventies."

When Ridenhour first enrolled at Adelphi University, however, he had his sights set on becoming a graphic artist. Looking for work, he offered to design flyers for a sound system business called Spectrum City DJ, which provided music for dance parties in parks and other venues across southern Long Island. The founder, Hank Boxley, turned down the offer, but later remembered Ridenhour when he saw him address an open mic party on campus. Impressed, Boxley invited Ridenhour to MC for Spectrum City DJ, and he was an instant success. Of medium height but athletically built, Ridenhour commanded the party venues with his confident stride, thrusting boxing jabs, and booming baritone. It was a voice that resonated with influences ranging from his father's lectures to the basketball play-by-play of New York sportscaster Marv Albert. As Bill Stephney, an Adelphi student who hosted a show on the campus radio station, WBAU, put it, Ridenhour came across as "part radio announcer, part stadium announcer, part Southern Black preacher, part . . . sassy, brassy New Yorker."

Stephney, who was also WBAU's program director, offered Ridenhour and Boxley their own weekly show, called *The Spectrum City Mix Hour*. At the station, they befriended another budding radio host, named William Drayton. Referring to himself as "DJ MC Flavor," Drayton was a wiry bundle of energy, with a rubbery face, expressive eyes, and a mouth of gold-capped teeth that stretched easily into a wide grin. "Personality walks, personality talks, personality smiles!" was Drayton's philosophy of life, as he put it. But beneath the playful façade, he was a serious musician who was fluent on the piano and had mastered several other instruments as well. In a higher register, Drayton also had a vocal delivery that in its own way was just as distinctive as Ridenhour's, peppered with infectious exclamations like "Yeeah, boyee!"

For Ridenhour, Boxley, and Drayton, playing the latest rap records on WBAU provided a crash course in the existing hip hop repertoire— and a realization of how limited it still was. So to fill all the airtime on their shows, the three began gathering with other friends in the basement of Boxley's house to come up with their own music. They dubbed their makeshift group Spectrum City, passed around business cards with a spaceship-inspired logo drawn by Ridenhour, and quickly developed a reputation around the greater New York rap scene for their unique chemistry. Ridenhour, now calling himself "Chuckie D," brought a sense of gravitas, while Drayton's "MC Flavor" provided just the opposite. As Ridenhour put it, "Flavor is the dude who presents disorder, dissonance, spontaneity, the gift of gab and anything goes." Meanwhile, with years of live production under their belts, Hank Boxley and his brother Keith had the expertise and ambition to push instrumental accompaniments beyond the predictable sounds of beat mixes and drum machines.

On Monday nights at the time, WBAU aired a show called *The Operating Room*, hosted by another Long Island DJ named André Brown. His nickname was Doctor Dré—not to be confused with a more famous Dr. Dre who emerged in the West Coast rap scene soon after. On a competitive dare from Brown, Ridenhour composed a song to promote *The Operating Room* that he titled "Public Enemy #1." The song started with MC Flavor teasing Chuckie D that he had developed such a fearsome reputation as a rapper that he was being called a "public enemy," setting up Ridenhour to deliver a sly and forceful variation on the familiar hip hop braggadocio, all set to a funky James Brown beat. One of *The Operating Room*'s regular listeners was Rick Rubin, the white record producer who several years earlier had cofounded the Def Jam record label with his Black business partner, Russell Simmons. Rubin had put Def Jam on the map by signing early rap stars such as LL Cool J and the Beastie Boys. When Rubin heard "Public Enemy #1" on WBAU, he became determined to sign "Chuckie D" to a record contract.

Initially, Ridenhour wasn't interested, having had a bad experience recording a forgettable single record with Spectrum City. He only agreed to a meeting with Rubin after Bill Stephney went to work for Def Jam. At first, Rubin and Stephney offered a deal only for Chuckie D, and had no interest in signing the clownish MC Flavor. But Ridenhour insisted on bringing along his friend—sensing correctly that Flavor's higher-pitched voice and theatrical antics would serve to make his own hard-edged lyrics and delivery more palatable to a broad audience. "I wanted the group to be serious, I didn't want Flavor in the group,"

Stephney recalled to the hip hop journalist and historian Jeff Chang. "Flavor was like a comic cut-up, so my thing was, 'Here we're trying to do some serious shit, how are we gonna fit this guy in?'" However, Stephney later admitted his error. "They were completely right," Stephney said, referring to Ridenhour and Boxley. "With Chuck being serious, with the stentorian tones, you needed a break, you needed someone to balance that or else it would have been too much."

From the start, Chuck D, as Ridenhour now called himself, had two clear intentions for the group that he renamed Public Enemy. One was that its message be as important as its music. Chuck borrowed from numerous Black heroes in evoking that ethos, but none more than Malcolm X. He liked to tell the story of the day he and Hank Boxley were putting up flyers with Malcolm's picture on them to advertise one of the group's early concerts. A young fan approached them and asked who "Malcolm the tenth" was. "We looked at each other," Chuck recalled, "and said, 'Well, we've got to do something about that!'" He also talked about wanting to give young Blacks a sense of political leadership and awareness that had been lost with the assassinations of the 1960s. "Our generation didn't see anyone filling the shoes of Martin Luther King and Malcolm X," Chuck said. "The music filled the vacuum."

A second intention was that Public Enemy be seen as a "posse," as he described it, and not just a star vehicle for him. Chuck brought all his collaborators from Spectrum City to Def Jam and encouraged them all to take on distinctive new identities. MC Flavor became "Flavor Flav." The Boxley brothers became Hank and Keith "Shocklee." An expert in electronic music named Eric Sadler was nicknamed "Vietnam." Together, he and the Shocklees became known as "the Bomb Squad" for their explosive backup mixes and instrumentals. A turntable specialist named Norman Rogers, who had DJ'd for Spectrum City, was given the handle "Terminator X." To provide protection—and a provocative stage presence—the group allied itself with a concert security crew formed by another Black Roosevelt resident named Richard Griffin. A self-styled Black nationalist and follower of Louis Farrakhan, the new leader of the Nation of Islam, Griffin became known as "Professor

Griff." With their berets and camouflage uniforms that harked back to
the Fruit of Islam and the Black Panthers, his foot soldiers were called
"Security of the First World," or "S1W."

Def Jam supported this vision but didn't offer much money—only
$5,000 to record a debut single. So Chuck had to come up with ideas for
songs and lyrics while driving around Long Island working as a delivery
man for a photography store. Hank Shocklee rented production space
in the middle of the night to get a discount. But because Chuck was
so prolific, and the Bomb Squad could produce all the backup music
the group needed using their own records and mixing equipment, the
group managed to come up with enough music to fill an album while
staying within the Def Jam budget. Recorded in the summer of 1986,
Yo! Bum Rush the Show offered a strong first taste of what would make
Public Enemy unique, with aggressive beats and lyrics that made reference to gun violence and the crack epidemic. The album cover introduced a new logo designed by Chuck—a Black figure in the crosshairs
of a gun—and featured a moody image of the group gathered around a
turntable in a dark room lit by only one overhead light.

Because of production delays, however, *Yo! Bum Rush the Show*
wasn't released until early 1987. Soon after it came out, two Long Island rappers, Eric Barrier and William Griffin Jr., known as "Eric B. &
Rakim," released an album titled *Paid in Full*. Several songs on the
album, including the title track and another, called "I Know You Got
Soul," had a jazzy, syncopated feel that all of a sudden made the metric
sound of the rhythm and raps on the Public Enemy album seem stiff
and dated. Meanwhile, reviews harped on how loud the album was
compared to most rap of the era. In *The Village Voice*, John Leland,
a young white critic, wrote a review titled "Noise Annoys"—a reference to a song by the British punk rock band Buzzcocks. Although
Leland also had some good things to say, Chuck took the headline as
an affront—and a challenge. As quickly as possible, he vowed to record new songs that would allow Public Enemy to again "dominate the
streets," as he put it.

Starting in the summer of 1987, the group made good on that boast
by releasing two groundbreaking new singles. The first, "Rebel Without a Pause," looped the squealing saxophone intro to a record called

"The Grunt" by James Brown's backup band to produce a siren-like noise that would become a feature of many Public Enemy songs from then on. The Bomb Squad also accelerated the speed of its accompaniment, from the then standard 90 beats per minute to 109 beats, a rhythm that created a propulsive groove and pushed Chuck to come up with more intricate and unpredictable rhymes. Six months later, Public Enemy released another single, titled "Bring the Noise"—a retort to the headline on Leland's *Village Voice* review—that unapologetically piled sirens on top of scratches on top of electronic loops on top of accelerated drumbeats. To underscore the message of defiance, the group turned to Malcolm X. They spliced together two fragments from his famous 1963 "Message to the Grassroots" speech to lead into the song with Malcolm's voice repeating the words: "Too Black, too strong. Too Black, too strong."

In the summer of 1988, Public Enemy released a second album, *It Takes a Nation of Millions to Hold Us Back*, that included those two singles and matched them with others that sustained the same high level of musical daring and political commentary. With titles such as "Don't Believe the Hype," "Louder Than a Bomb," and "Prophets of Rage," the songs addressed issues ranging from police violence and unequal justice in Black communities to FBI surveillance campaigns against Black leaders. The last song on the album, "Party for Your Right to Fight"—a play on the hit "(You Gotta) Fight for Your Right (to Party!)" by the white rappers the Beastie Boys—crammed a quarter century of Black history and musical allusions into a three-and-a-half-minute track. The Bomb Squad mixed grooves from Funkadelic, James Brown, Sly and the Family Stone, and Bob Marley and the Wailers. Rapping in unison, Chuck D and Flavor Flav made reference to J. Edgar Hoover, Huey Newton, Bobby Seale, Eldridge Cleaver, and Elijah Muhammad.

In the middle of "Party for Your Right to Fight," listeners again heard the voice of Malcolm X. "When the government will not protect or defend us," Malcolm declared to a scratch accompaniment, "or find those who have brutalized us and made us the victims of the last four hundred years, then it is time to do whatever is necessary to defend ourselves." The words came from an appearance that Malcolm made on a Boston radio show in June 1964, at which he took questions from a live audience and responded to a man who asked about his position on nonviolence. For many of Public Enemy's growing millions of young fans in the late 1980s, it may have been the first time they were introduced to the concept encapsulated in Malcolm's most famous saying: "By any means necessary."

———

Three weeks after Public Enemy's *It Takes a Nation of Millions* album was released in the summer of 1988, director Spike Lee began shooting the movie *Do the Right Thing* in the Brooklyn neighborhood of Bedford-Stuyvesant. In the two previous years, Lee had emerged as a major new force in America's independent film world, with his wryly humorous movies *She's Gotta Have It*, about the life of young Black urban bohemians, and *School Daze*, about the rituals and class rivalries at a historically Black college. Now Lee was tackling the broader topic of race relations in America, through the prism of "Bed-Stuy," another once racially mixed community that had become a predominantly Black and Hispanic neighborhood but where whites still owned many of the local businesses.

In Lee's script, simmering tensions between an Italian pizzeria owner and his sons and a delivery boy named Mookie and other local Black youths erupted into a full-scale riot that ended in the destruction of the store and the police killing of an unarmed rap enthusiast, "Radio Raheem." Lee would dedicate the movie to the real-life victims of similar racial incidents that had taken place across New York City in the 1980s, from Morris Heights in the Bronx to Howard Beach in Queens. But in discussing his vision for *Do the Right Thing*, Lee also talked about wanting to illustrate other urban realities. One was how extreme summer heat could inflame passions and ignite violence, which Lee conveyed by setting the entire movie within one twenty-four-hour period on the hottest day of the year. Another was the role music could play, particularly during the idle summer months, in giving urban communities a sense of unity and connection with the outside world.

Once the eight weeks of shooting *Do the Right Thing* were over, Lee set out to commission what he called an "anthem" for his provocative drama. With an eye toward marketing the movie a year later, he also envisioned a "song of the summer" that would become a commercial hit and drive fans to the box office. "I wanted it to be defiant, I wanted it to be angry, I wanted it to be very rhythmic," Lee recalled. "I thought right away of Public Enemy." In the fall of 1988, Lee arranged for a meeting with Chuck D, who brought along Hank Shocklee from the Bomb Squad and Bill Stephney from Def Jam Records. All three men immediately grasped what Spike had in mind, and Chuck agreed to begin work on a new song while Public Enemy was on tour in Europe that winter. "We were all Black in New York," Chuck recalled, "familiar with the interracial problems in neighborhoods that were united by Black radio."

After rejecting Lee's first idea—a rap version of "Lift Every Voice and Sing," known as the Black national anthem—Chuck had the idea for a song called "Fight the Power." He borrowed the title from an R&B dance classic of the 1970s: "Fight the Power (Part 1 & 2)," by the Isley Brothers. That song urged listeners to "fight the powers that be," but mostly in a spirit of youthful self-expression. ("I try to play my music, they say my music's too loud . . ." went a memorable verse.) By contrast, Chuck turned the phrase into a communal call to action, repeating "Fight the Power!" seven times in the refrain, then ending with "We've got to fight the powers that be!" The verses mixed political messages with sly historical and pop culture references, and the Bomb Squad created a backtrack drawing on samples from more than twenty well-known musicians, so as to make the song sound familiar even to those hearing it for the first time.

In the most daring verse, Chuck took aim at two revered icons of white American culture. "Elvis Presley was a hero to most, but he never meant shit to me," Chuck wrote about the rock 'n' roll legend who had made a fortune singing Black music. "Motherfuck him and John Wayne," he had Flavor Flav chime in, referring to the movie star who had once said he was in favor of "white supremacy until the Blacks are educated to the point of responsibility." Decades later, Kevin Powell, an influential Black music and social critic, described the revelatory effect those lyrics had on him as an impressionable twenty-three-year-old. "It was shocking," Powell recalled. "What Chuck was saying was, enough with the white heroes, we want to celebrate other heroes as well. When people talk about Chuck D being Malcolm X, that was the kind of stuff that was Malcolm-esque."

Malcolm's influence was also on full display when Spike Lee shot the music video for "Fight the Power" in the spring of 1989. It was the height of the era when TV music video channels such as MTV and VH1 were as influential as radio—and had belatedly realized rap's reach. Lee decided that his first attempt at a video—setting the song to clips from the movie—wasn't dramatic enough. So on a drizzly day in April, he filled an entire block of Bedford-Stuyvesant with hundreds of local Black residents to simulate a youth march. Signs were handed out showing Black leaders from Dr. King to Medgar Evers, Angela Davis and Frederick Douglass, Jackie Robinson and Harriet Tubman. Chuck D and Favor Flav mounted a huge outdoor platform and performed the song as though they were addressing a political rally. Behind them loomed a huge portrait of Malcolm X, conjuring up the days when he could summon similar crowds from a podium in Harlem.

———

As it happened, *Do the Right Thing* had its world debut a month later, at the Cannes Film Festival, on Malcolm X's birthday. Celebrating the anniversary, Lee wore a T-shirt emblazoned with Malcolm's image and the words "No Sellout" to a press conference following the morning screening. The response from the audience had been enthusiastic, and the early reviews were glowing. "Spike Lee Stirs Things Up in Cannes," read the headline on a story filed by *New York Times* critic Vincent Canby, who touted the movie as an early contender to win the festival's top prize, the Palme d'Or.

Canby called *Do the Right Thing* Lee's "most self-assured film yet." In addition to the acting, he praised the film's color-saturated look, created by cinematographer Ernest Dickerson, set designer Wynn Thomas, and costume designer Ruth Carter. Canby also noted the powerful depiction of the psychic impact of "sheer noise," starting with "a militant rap number performed by Public Enemy." Serving as musical director, Bill Lee, Spike's father, had used "Fight the Power" as a kind of symphonic theme. In the opening credits, actress Rosie Perez did a furious boxing dance to the song. Throughout the film, the song played loudly from Radio Raheem's boombox. Then in the final scenes, Sal the pizzeria owner smashed Raheem's boombox with a baseball bat to stop the song from playing, setting off the last tragic sequence of events.

No sooner had the awards talk started, however, than the attacks on the movie began. A source inside the Cannes jury told Lee that the chair that year, German director Wim Wenders, found the Mookie character "unheroic" for his decision to throw a trash can through the window of Sal's pizzeria after police killed Radio Raheem—an act that led to looting and arson but also created a distraction that arguably saved Sal from a vengeful mob. In the end, the jury awarded the Palme d'Or to the Steven Soderbergh film *Sex, Lies and Videotape*, and *Do the Right Thing* didn't win any Cannes prizes. Back in America, several prominent reviewers suggested that the film might cause Black viewers to riot in real life, and that it would feed a white backlash that could hurt New York City councilman David Dinkins's bid to become the city's first Black mayor in the fall elections.

Then three days after the Cannes debut, *The Washington Times* ran an interview in which Professor Griff of Public Enemy accused Jews of being responsible for "all the wickedness in the world." Although Griff was caught off-guard by a reporter, the remarks reflected the crudely anti-Semitic views that he had absorbed from Louis Farrakhan's reincarnated Nation of Islam. His intemperance also betrayed Griff's anger over his increasingly marginal role in the group. When *The Village Voice* called attention to the interview several weeks later, Jewish groups made the connection to *Do the Right Thing* and called for a boycott of the film when it opened in theaters in June. Slow to respond at first, Chuck D announced that he was firing Griff, then sought to douse the media firestorm by temporarily disbanding Public Enemy.

In the end, however, the controversies didn't prevent "Fight the Power" and *Do the Right Thing* from becoming critical and commercial hits. As soon as the Public Enemy song was released in July, along with Lee's cinematic music video, it climbed near the top of the Billboard R&B and rap charts and stayed there for three more months. Decades later, the influential hip hop magazine *The Source* would rank "Fight the Power" as the fifth-greatest rap song of all time, and the editors of *Rolling Stone* would put it at number seven on their list of top 100 hip hop songs. Shot for only $6.2 million, *Do the Right Thing* grossed $26 million at the box office, made numerous lists of the best movies of the century, and helped inspire Black filmmakers including John Singleton, Lee Daniels, Steve McQueen, and Ava DuVernay. That *Do the Right Thing* did not receive an Academy Award nomination for Best Picture in 1990 came to be seen as a historic oversight, particularly when the sentimental interracial drama *Driving Miss Daisy* won the Oscar.

With the "Fight the Power" anthem playing in the background, Lee also reshaped the way a new generation would think about Martin Luther King Jr. and Malcolm X. Until then, the two men had almost always been portrayed as personal and ideological rivals—the preacher of nonviolence and integration versus the advocate for separatism and armed self-defense. Except to a small segment of the Black community, King was also seen as the more historically significant of the two. But Lee put them side by side, at the same level, and suggested that it wasn't necessary to choose between them, that King's idealism and Malcolm's realism could coexist within the Black consciousness.

In *Do the Right Thing*, Lee first conveyed this new way of thinking about the two Black icons with a visual image. In the opening shot of the movie, a seemingly mentally challenged man whom everyone in the neighborhood calls "Smiley" was shown holding aloft a photograph of King and Malcolm smiling and shaking hands. For the rest of the film, Smiley wandered the neighborhood, trying to sell copies of the photograph that he had decorated with magic marker. Although it was never explained, the photograph was taken during the one time King and Malcolm met, when they came face-to-face while visiting Capitol Hill to observe a debate on the 1964 Civil Rights Act. Malcolm greeted King in a hallway and they exchanged a few words. "Now they're going to investigate you," Malcolm joked to King as they parted ways.

In the theatrical tradition of the "wise fool," everyone in the movie dismissed Smiley's obsession with the photograph. They either shooed him away, or humored him by buying a copy for a dollar. But at the very end of the film, Lee suggested that Smiley had been onto something profound all along, when a long quote from Dr. King scrolled down the screen, followed by another one from Malcolm X. First King's words made the case against using violence to achieve racial justice. "The old law of an eye for an eye leaves everybody blind," they read. "Violence ends by defeating itself. It creates bitterness in the survivor and brutality in the destroyers." Then Malcolm's quote argued for a right to self-defense. In a world where "bad people . . . seem to have all the power" and are "in positions to block things that you and I need," it read, "I don't even call it violence when it's self-defense, I call it intelligence."

Wesley Morris, the Pulitzer Prize–winning cultural critic at *The New York Times*, recalled being "confused" by those two quotes when he first saw *Do the Right Thing* as a Black teenager growing up in Philadelphia. Before then, he noted, he had always seen Malcolm and King "pitted against one another." Then Morris read critiques in the mainstream white media that assumed that, by following King's quote with Malcolm's, Lee meant to take sides with Malcolm. But Morris came to a different conclusion. The white critics "missed the whole point of the movie, which is that it's a complete dialectic," Morris observed about Lee's juxtaposition and the way it was reflected in the film. "There's a one hand, and then there's another hand, and he never ever loses sight of that at any point in the movie. It's almost a perfect philosophical text in that way."

Of all the rap pioneers, few had more in common with Malcolm X's personal odyssey than Lawrence Parker. Born in Brooklyn in 1965, Parker was raised by his mother, who moved repeatedly during his childhood and was involved with a series of abusive men. After running away from home as a teenager, he ended living in a homeless shelter in the Bronx. He fell into a life of petty crime and stints in juvenile detention, much like Malcolm in his youth, but he also snuck into libraries to educate himself and joined the roving bands of graffiti artists who were spray-painting their work across New York City's subways and buses in the mid-1980s. Parker acquired the nickname "Krishna" after volunteering to help members of the Hare Krishna sect who came to dispense food at the shelter. He shortened that nickname to "Kris" and adopted it to create his new graffiti signature: "KRS-One," which he announced stood for "Knowledge Reigns Supreme over Nearly Everyone."

Tall and gangly, Parker was at a dance party one day when the MC made fun of the way he was dressed, and he responded by grabbing the mic and freestyling a comeback. Hooked by the experience, he threw himself into the competitive world of rapping. Then at the homeless shelter, he befriended a youth counselor named Scott Sterling, who DJ'd on the side under the name DJ Scott La Rock. The two teamed up, and soon they were performing and recording music under the name Boogie Down Productions. In 1987, they produced an album, *Criminal Minded*, that foreshadowed the arrival of gangsta rap, with its lyrics about urban violence and a dust jacket cover for which Kris and Scott posed with guns and ammunition belts. But Parker had a change of heart when, shortly after the album came out, La Rock got in the middle of a gang dispute and was fatally shot—making him the first of scores of rappers who would rise to fame only to die violently.

To mark his new direction, KRS-One channeled Malcolm X. He called his next album *By All Means Necessary*—a play on Malcolm's most famous slogan. For the album cover, he imitated the iconic photo in which Malcolm, protecting his house in Queens, peered out through drawn curtains armed with a M1 carbine rifle. (In Kris's re-creation, the firearm was an Uzi submachine gun.) Images of Malcolm flashed on a screen throughout the music video for the song "My Philosophy," in which Kris gave himself a new nickname: "The Teacher." Echoing Malcolm in songs called "Stop the Violence" and "Necessary," he decried self-destructive violence within urban communities while also denouncing outside forces that contributed to it, from economic exploitation to police corruption and drug profiteering. Viewed with admiration by some and irritation by others, KRS-One went on to try to serve as a one-man conscience for the hip hop movement, launching a broader Stop the Violence campaign and a would-be spiritual movement he called the "Temple of Hip Hop."

In the early 1990s, rap stardom took another Malcolm X admirer in the opposite direction: deeper into entanglement with the gangsta lifestyle. Like Malcolm, with his Garveyite parents, Tupac Amaru Shakur grew up around radical activists. He was raised by his mother, Afeni Shakur, a former Black Panther who was once jailed and later acquitted on a bombing charge. Afeni also encouraged Tupac's artistic side, and sent him to arts school in Baltimore before he dropped out in his late teens to move to Northern California and throw himself into the local hip hop scene. He learned the business as a roadie for the group Digital Underground before releasing his first solo album, *2Pacalypse Now*, shortly after his twentieth birthday. In the song "Words of Wisdom," Shakur echoed Malcolm in accusing white society of crimes against Black Americans and planting "chains in our brains" to reinforce a sense of racial inferiority. "No Malcolm X in history text, why that?" the song asked. "Cause he tried to educate and liberate all Blacks."

The same year, an organization called the Malcolm X Grassroots Movement invited Shakur to address a luncheon banquet in Atlanta. Launched two years earlier in Jackson, Mississippi, the Grassroots Movement was a loose federation of chapters across the country dedicated to supporting policies and programs that encouraged Black "self-determination," as one Los Angeles member put it. But Shakur didn't bother to flatter the crowd of older activists, who turned up fashionably dressed in suits and dresses with African-patterned accessories. Wearing a red hoodie, rally cap, and chain jewelry, his wiry frame bursting with righteous energy, Tupac explained why Malcolm was a hero to young Blacks like him, who had grown up in a different era of broken homes, a crack epidemic, and the draconian Reagan-era war on drugs. His generation felt affinity with Malcolm, Shakur told the crowd, because he had lived their reality before he became the Malcolm being celebrated at the banquet. "Before we can be new Africans, we gotta to be Black first," Shakur insisted. "We gotta get our brothers from the street like Harriet Tubman did. Like Malcolm did, the real Malcolm, before the Nation of Islam. You gotta remember: this was a pimp, a pusher and all that. We forgot about all that. In our striving to be enlightened, we forgot about all our brothers in the street, about our dope dealers, our pushers and our pimps, and that's who's teaching the next generation."

Over the next four years, as he rocketed to international fame, Shakur became a modern version of both Malcolms at once. He romanticized and lived the life of a "gangsta" even while writing songs that described its personal toll and destructive impact on Black communities. After climbing the record charts with his next album, *Strictly 4 My N.I.G.G.A.Z . . .* , Shakur rose to the very top with his next release, *Me Against the World*. A third album, *All Eyez on Me*, debuted at number one and sold more than half a million copies in one week. Shakur also embarked on a career as a movie actor, appearing in half a dozen films in just a few years. Yet all the while, he was making headlines for his violent personal life. He was accused of shooting two off-duty police officers, became the victim of a gun attack outside his recording studio, and went to prison on a sexual assault charge for almost a year. When he was released, he signed with a new record label, Death Row, founded by the Black entrepreneur Marion "Suge" Knight, that was embroiled in a nasty feud over mutually perceived disrespect with gangsta rappers based on the East Coast.

Shakur had only just turned twenty-five when that feud cost him his life. He had accompanied Knight to Las Vegas to watch Mike Tyson defend his heavyweight boxing title, and after the fight the two were headed to a nightclub in Suge's black BMW. Off the Strip, a white Cadillac pulled alongside them and gunfire strafed the passenger side of the car, where Tupac was sitting. He was rushed to the city's University Medical Center, where doctors tried in vain to save his life. He was joined there by his girlfriend of four months, Kidada Jones, a daughter of the legendary music producer Quincy Jones. Six days later, Kidada was at Tupac's bedside when he was taken off life support and pronounced dead.

In subsequent years, Quincy Jones invoked Malcolm X in talking about the loss of Shakur. Jones had first become aware of Malcolm when he was a teenage trumpet player touring with Lionel Hampton's big band. He heard stories about a drug dealer called "Detroit Red," who had sold heroin to members of the band before he went to prison. Jones had seen that same man emerge from jail to become Malcolm X, and he had witnessed firsthand a similar capacity for growth in Shakur. Tupac had once publicly castigated Jones for marrying white women, but they found common ground and became close once he started dating Kidada. Jones's son, the hip hop producer Quincy Jones III, also became friends with Shakur at the end, and was convinced that Tupac was on the verge of pivoting away from his gangsta lifestyle to preach a more positive message to his vast following.

Writing a foreword to a commemorative book published by the editors of *Vibe* magazine, the elder Quincy Jones pointed out how much Shakur had achieved at such a young age—and how much more personal evolution he might have undergone had he lived. "The tragedy of Tupac is that his untimely passing is representative of too many young black men in this country," Jones wrote. "If we had lost Oprah Winfrey at 25, we would have lost a relatively unknown, local market TV anchorwoman. If we had lost Malcolm X at 25, we would have lost a hustler nicknamed Detroit Red. And if I had left the world at 25, we would have lost a big-band trumpet player and aspiring composer—just a sliver of my eventual life potential."

In the fall of 1986, two Harvard undergraduates, Dave Mays and Jon Shecter, began hosting a Friday night hip hop show on the campus radio station, WHRB. Called *Street Beat*, the program became a favorite with rap fans around the Boston area, who would phone in to make requests and offer comments. Mays collected the addresses of the callers and began sending them a one-page newsletter of announcements and other rap news that he called *The Source*. By the time they graduated, the newsletter had enough of a following that Mays and Shecter decided to move to New York City and launch a monthly magazine by the same name. Over the next three decades, *The Source* would become the bible of the hip hop world, reaching a total national subscription of more than a half million and spawning a glitzy award show that, among other things, became a venue for the East-West feud that many believed led to the murder of Tupac Shakur and, soon after, of his rapping rival Chris Wallace, otherwise known as "The Notorious B.I.G."

For millions of rap fans, Black and white, *The Source* served as a guide to not just how to listen to hip hop but also to how to think about its role in American culture. Lawrence Ware, a Black professor of philosophy and African American Studies who grew up in a strict Baptist household in Oklahoma, would credit *The Source* with turning him into a critical thinker, eager to debate the relative merits of new rap albums and understand the larger social message of their songs. "That magazine changed music journalism," Ware recalled. "And it turned me into a philosopher." In March 1990, *The Source* also became the first national magazine of that era to highlight the resurgence of interest in Malcolm X, when it put the slain leader on its cover to mark the anniversary of his assassination. "Malcolm X: After 25 Years, Hip Hop Keeps His Message Alive," read the cover line. Inside, articles hailed Malcolm as "the original rapper" and a "cult hero for a new generation of revolutionaries."

The success of *The Source* inspired the creation of dozens of other magazines and websites devoted to covering the hip hop phenomenon. Together, they further contributed to introducing a new generation to Malcolm X, by charting his influence on prominent rappers over the next four decades. On the fiftieth anniversary of his assassination, *The Source* published another cover story, "Malcolm X and the Hip-Hop Generation." *XXL* magazine celebrated "15 Songs That Name Drop Malcolm X," and *Vibe* magazine highlighted "Malcolm X's Most Powerful Quotes." The website of the Black Entertainment Television network tracked visual references to "iconic Malcolm X images" and offered a roll call of rappers who "channel the spirit of Malcolm X." On the list were Chuck D, KRS-One, and Tupac Shakur and also superstars Ice Cube, Common, Nas, and Killer Mike. So was Kendrick Lamar—the soulful rapper who, after winning the 2018 Pulitzer Prize for Music, described his life as having been changed forever by reading *The Autobiography of Malcolm X.*

At the same time, the hip hop press helped defend Malcolm's legacy against the music's growing excesses. In 2014, the provocative rapper Nicki Minaj was preparing to release a single called "Lookin Ass Nigga" that ridiculed men who objectified and showed off for her, and that repeated the "n-word" nonstop. Online, Minaj released an image for the record jacket that superimposed the name of the song over the photograph of Malcolm protecting his house in Queens with an M1 carbine rifle. The outcry from hip hop watchdogs and Malcolm's surviving family was immediate and intense—for placing Malcolm's image next to the "n-word" and making it look he was ogling women from behind the curtains in his house. "Malcolm X frowned on Black self-hatred, anti-intellectualism, and materialism," critic Kevin Powell wrote in a petition demanding that Minaj cease and desist. "He was about the uplifting and empowerment of our communities, and he was a husband and father, not a nigger." Stunned by the outrage, Minaj took down the image and publicly apologized.

By the year 2020, hip hop was nearing the fiftieth anniversary of its birth in the South Bronx. In a sign of how powerful a cultural force it had become, *Saturday Night Live* booked the female rapper Megan Thee Stallion as its musical guest for the season premiere, which marked the show's first live outing after several pretaped episodes during the height of the Covid pandemic. Megan appeared onstage at NBC's headquarters in New York in a zebra-striped leotard, flanked by backup dancers in similar outfits and pink wigs. Together, they began to perform Megan's sexually suggestive hit "Savage."

Midway through the performance, Megan suddenly stopped singing, and the sound of gunshots rang out as images of bullet holes flashed on a screen behind her. Then the voice of Malcolm X filled the studio as his words appeared against the backdrop. "The most disrespected, unprotected, neglected person in America is the Black woman," Malcolm said, in a recording taken from the impassioned speech he gave at the funeral of Ronald Stokes, the Nation of Islam leader killed by Los Angeles police in April 1962. "Who taught you to hate the texture of your hair, the color of your skin and shape of your nose? Who taught you to hate yourself from the top of your head to the soles of your feet?"

Then another voice was heard, condemning Daniel Cameron, the Black Republican attorney general of Kentucky who had refused to press charges against a policeman who fired the shots that killed Breonna Taylor, an unarmed young Black woman in Louisville caught in the middle when officers raided her apartment looking for her boyfriend. Taylor's death came two months before a white policeman was caught on a cell phone camera choking the life out of George Floyd, an unarmed Black man in Minneapolis, igniting weeks of protest across America. "Daniel Cameron is no different than the sellout Negroes that sold our people into slavery," called out the voice, which belonged to a Black activist named Tamika Mallory. Megan Thee Stallion then added her own commentary, before she finished rapping her hit song. "We need to protect our Black women, and love our Black women, cause at the end of the day we need our Black women," Megan declared. "We need to protect our Black men and stand up for our Black men, cause at the end of the day we're tired of seeing hashtags of our Black men."

According to Nielsen ratings released two days later, more than eight million viewers watched the latest rapper to bring Malcolm X back to life. It was the largest audience for an *SNL* season premiere in four years.

ELEVEN

The Movie

After *Do the Right Thing*, Spike Lee directed two more critically acclaimed films: *Mo' Better Blues*, about a self-destructive jazz musician; and *Jungle Fever*, about an ill-fated affair between a middle-class
Black architect and his white, working-class Italian assistant. Like his
previous three films, the movies were financed and distributed by Universal Studios, which gave Lee wide artistic license and was content
with modest returns on relatively small investments. Then in 1990,
Lee read news that stirred an ambition he had harbored ever since
becoming a filmmaker. The revival of interest in Malcolm X among the
hip hop generation—and a sudden leap in sales of *The Autobiography
of Malcolm X* and books of his speeches—had persuaded a Hollywood
studio that the time was ripe for a Malcolm biopic. But that studio
was Warner Brothers, not Universal. And to direct the movie, Warner
Brothers had hired Norman Jewison, the respected Canadian director
whose some twenty Hollywood films included racially charged classics
such as *In the Heat of the Night* and *A Soldier's Story*.

Despite Jewison's distinguished track record, Lee believed that
only a Black director could do justice to Malcolm's story—and that he
should be that director. Born and raised in Brooklyn, Lee had been obsessed with Malcolm X ever since reading the *Autobiography* in junior
high school, and had been infatuated with cinema for just as long. His
father, Bill Lee, was a jazz bassist and composer who disliked going to
the movies because he didn't approve of the way Hollywood depicted

Black characters. So Spike's mother, Jacqueline Shelton Lee, a school-teacher, would take him to the movies as her companion. When Spike enrolled in Morehouse College, his father's alma mater, he majored in communications studies. Home after his sophomore year in 1977, he bought his first movie camera, a Super 8, and roamed the city shooting footage of that summer's blackout. After graduating from Morehouse, he enrolled in New York University Film School, where he won a special Academy Award for best student film for his senior thesis project, *Joe's Bed-Stuy Barbershop: We Cut Heads*. Over the next decade, Lee made six commercially released films and assembled a team of trusted collaborators. By the time he turned thirty-three, Spike was convinced that he was ready for the challenge of bringing Malcolm X's life to the big screen.

Lee launched his campaign by publicly challenging the idea of allowing a white filmmaker to direct the Malcolm film. "I have a big problem with Norman Jewison directing *The Autobiography of Malcolm X*," he told reporters. "That disturbs me deeply, gravely. It's wrong with a capital W. Blacks have to control these films." To his surprise, Lee found a sympathetic ear in Marvin Worth, the white producer who had purchased the film rights to the *Autobiography* in the 1960s and had optioned them to Warner Brothers. Worth was a fan of Lee's previous movies—particularly *Do the Right Thing*—and he offered to arrange a meeting with Jewison and Warner Brothers if Spike toned down his public criticism.

Meanwhile, Jewison was struggling with the movie's screenplay. He had enlisted Charles Fuller, the Black playwright who had written both the stage and film scripts for *A Soldier's Story*, but wasn't happy with the results. Malcolm X was "an enigma to me," Jewison later confessed. "I just haven't licked it." So after meeting with Lee, Jewison agreed to relinquish the project—a gesture for which Spike later saluted him, despite his earlier attacks. "Norman had the gig and he did not have to step aside," Lee recalled. "He gracefully allowed me to take over, and I have to thank him and send him love for doing that."

Marvin Worth had met Malcolm X personally in the 1940s, when Worth was beginning his career booking concerts for the likes of Charlie Parker and Billie Holiday. Still known as "Detroit Red," Malcolm peddled drugs to the jazz musicians on 52nd Street in New York City. "He was selling grass," Worth recalled. "He was 16 or 17 but looked older. He was very witty, a funny guy, and he had this extraordinary charisma. A great dancer and a great dresser. He was very good-looking, very, very tall. Girls always noticed him. He was quite a special guy."

After Malcolm's assassination twenty years later, Worth became fixated with the idea of making a film about his life. Knowing that he would have a better chance of convincing Alex Haley and Betty Shabazz to sell him the film rights to the *Autobiography* if he hired a Black screenwriter, Worth approached James Baldwin, who had been friendly with Malcolm. As it happened, Baldwin had been talking to the director Elia Kazan about writing a stage version of Malcolm's story, but nothing had come of those discussions. So Baldwin accepted Worth's offer, and the producer secured the rights to the *Autobiography* and licensed them to Columbia Pictures.

Worried about Baldwin's reputation for spreading himself thin as a writer and speaker, Columbia insisted that he move to Hollywood to work full-time on the script. So he left his writing lairs in France and Turkey and relocated to a room in the Beverly Hills Hotel. But the social bustle there proved too much of a distraction, so Worth rented a house for Baldwin in Palm Springs and paid for a chauffeur and a cook. Yet in the desert, too, Baldwin found himself passing his days drinking with visitors such as Truman Capote and the actor Billy Dee Williams, whom he was touting to play Malcolm. In early April 1968, Baldwin and Williams were lounging poolside when they received a call with the news that Dr. King had been shot and killed in Memphis. Baldwin immediately dropped everything to attend King's funeral in Atlanta, putting him even more behind in meeting Columbia's deadlines.

Baldwin was further stymied by the threat of legal action from the Nation of Islam, which led him to invent a religious sect called "the Movement" and to leave Elijah Muhammad out of his first script. When he finally had enough of a draft to show the movie executives, they thought it read too much like a play or a novel and wasn't sufficiently cinematic. So the studio brought in a more experienced Hollywood hand to work with Baldwin: Arnold Perl, a white screenwriter who had collaborated with director Ossie Davis on the script for his movie *Cotton Comes to Harlem*. But Columbia still had objections to the 250-page script that the two writers produced together, and Baldwin found the collaboration difficult enough that he withdrew from the project. Some years later, he vented about the experience in *The Devil Finds Work*, a book-length essay about race and Hollywood. "I would rather be horsewhipped, or incarcerated in the forthright bedlam of Bellevue, than repeat the adventure," Baldwin wrote.

By the early 1970s, Worth and Perl had also temporarily abandoned the idea of creating a dramatic version of Malcolm's life. Instead they produced a feature-length documentary, *Malcolm X: His Own Story as It Really Happened*, that mixed footage of his public speeches with passages from the *Autobiography*, narrated by Ossie Davis. Released shortly after Perl died of a sudden heart attack, the film was nominated for an Academy Award but soon disappeared from movie theaters. Baldwin, meanwhile, published his original screenplay as a short book, *One Day When I Was Lost*, that took enough liberties with the story lines and time sequences of the *Autobiography* to suggest why the Columbia executives had doubted that it would make a successful mass-market film.

Over the next two decades, numerous other attempts to bring the Malcolm X story to the screen came and went. In 1981, Woodie King Jr., the founder of the off-Broadway New Federal Theater in New York City, made an hour-long television drama called *Death of a Prophet*, ostensibly about the last day of Malcolm X's life. Introduced with real-life recollections from friends of Malcolm's such as Ossie Davis and Yuri Kochiyama, the TV movie then shifted to a highly fictionalized portrayal of Malcolm by the actor Morgan Freeman. Once Columbia let the option for the *Autobiography* lapse and Warner Brothers entered the picture, scripts were written by the Black novelist David Bradley and by the white playwrights and screenwriters David Mamet and Calder Willingham. Another treatment was commissioned by director Sidney Lumet. After Lee took control, he read all the previous screenplays and concluded that the early version written by James Baldwin and revised by Arnold Perl was still the best. It vividly conjured up Malcolm's hoodlum years in Boston and Harlem, with flashbacks to his childhood, and his conversion to the Nation of Islam.

The script's weakness, Lee thought, was in its "third act," starting with Malcolm's break with Elijah Muhammad and ending with the assassination. Lee attributed the flaws to the fact that Muhammad was still alive when the script was written, and that Baldwin and Perl had been afraid to antagonize him or his followers. But by 1990, Muhammad was dead, and there was also a clearer picture of who had carried out the assassination—thanks to the new testimony that Talmadge Hayer had given in the late 1970s, and the work that William Kunstler and Peter Goldman had done in bringing that new evidence to light.

At NYU Film School, Lee had met Ernest Dickerson, the cinematographer who worked on all his early movies, and both had fallen in love with the films of David Lean, the director of *Lawrence of Arabia*, *Doctor Zhivago*, and *The Bridge on the River Kwai*. Just as the two were beginning pre-production planning for the Malcolm X project, a remastered version of *Lawrence* was shown at the Ziegfeld Theatre, the ornate hall in midtown Manhattan with one of the largest movie screens in the country. Lee and Dickerson agreed that their Malcolm film should have the "epic" feel of that Lean classic, which was almost four hours long. They also estimated that making the movie they envisioned would cost close to $40 million. At the time, Warner Brothers was offering to spend only half that amount, and insisting that the film be closer to two hours. Lee believed that even the studio knew that wouldn't be enough to do the biopic justice, but he chose to start reworking the script and leave the battles over budget and length for later. "Marvin and I still thought we should move forward, the thinking being that there's no such thing as half-pregnant," he recalled. "But everybody knew the dreadful day would come when something bad was gonna happen."

Warner Brothers had made one invaluable decision before Spike Lee signed on to the Malcolm X project: the studio had cast Denzel Washington in the lead role. When Columbia Pictures had the rights to the story in the late 1960s, it had toyed with hiring Sidney Poitier or James Earl Jones for the part, and there was even a rumor that someone suggested Charlton Heston in blackface. During his brief involvement in the 1980s, Lumet envisioned Richard Pryor as Malcolm X and Eddie Murphy as Alex Haley. But by 1990, Washington had emerged as the hottest young Black male dramatic talent in Hollywood, after critically acclaimed performances in the films *Glory*, *A Soldier's Story*, and Lee's *Mo' Better Blues*. He also had the advantage of having played Malcolm onstage, in a 1981 production of a one-act play called *When the Chickens Came Home to Roost*, an imagined meeting between Malcolm and Elijah Muhammad during which both men realize they are headed for a rupture.

Although darker skinned and not as tall, Washington had key life experiences and personal traits in common with Malcolm. His father, Denzel Sr., was also a minister, in the Pentecostal church, and Denzel Jr. himself was a man of deep personal faith. He and his two siblings had also been left to be raised by their mother, Lynne, after their parents divorced when Denzel was fourteen. By coincidence, Washington grew up in Mount Vernon, the New York City suburb where Betty Shabazz settled with her daughters after Malcolm was killed, and Betty had even been a customer at Lynne Washington's hair salon. Most important for his on-screen likeness, Denzel was extremely handsome and charismatic, with an ability to project great strength in public settings but also quiet intelligence and sensitivity in more private moments. Reviewing the one-act play for *The New York Times*, theater critic Frank Rich noted the difficulty that many actors had in playing real historical figures, and applauded Washington's ability to capture Malcolm's greatness and his humanity at the same time. "It's much to the credit of Denzel Washington's firm, likable performance," Rich wrote, "that this Malcolm is honorable and altruistic without ever becoming a plaster saint."

To play Malcolm again, Washington put in months of research and physical preparation. He interviewed Betty Shabazz and two of Malcolm's siblings, participated in a two-week training course for Nation of Islam converts, and studied Arabic and the Koran as well as video and audiotapes of Malcolm's speeches and media appearances. As filming neared, Washington shed ten pounds, and stopped drinking alcohol or eating pork according to NOI teachings. He also didn't cut corners when it came to getting his hair "conked" for several pivotal scenes in the movie. He submitted to the same noxious mixture of lye and raw eggs that Blacks used to straighten their hair at the time, and to multiple experiments to find the right shade of hair color for the period when Malcolm was known as Detroit Red. "I must have had my hair fried 30 times, dyed thirty times, or some kind of patchwork, streaks, tips," Washington recalled. "We'd test this, then that. It comes out on the reddish side, but it's not the color of Malcolm's. He not only had red hair, he was red-boned. I end up with red hair."

In the winter of 1991, Spike Lee embarked on more than six months of his own research as he revised the script and prepared to begin filming in the fall. As a historical consultant, he hired Paul Lee (no relation), a Detroit native who had become obsessed with Malcolm as a teenager and had amassed voluminous files documenting every phase of Malcolm's life. Paul Lee helped point Spike to William Kunstler and to Mujahid Halim (the convicted shooter formerly known as Talmadge Hayer), who was now in a work release program that allowed him to spend several days a week outside prison. They gave Spike their accounts of an assassination plot planned and carried out by an NOI hit squad from Newark. At a hotel in New York City, Spike met with Benjamin Karim—the former Benjamin 2X Goodman, who had introduced Malcolm on the day of the murder. Using a floorplan of the Audubon Ballroom, Lee reviewed how the Newark hit would have unfolded and asked Karim what he thought of that scenario. Karim hesitated for a moment, then said: "If it did come down that way, it would have had to come as an order from the officials in Chicago. They could have never done that without their actions. They would've never done that."

In the screenplay that Lee was adapting, Baldwin and Perl had paid special attention to two female characters in the *Autobiography*. One was "Laura," the pseudonym for an innocent-seeming young Black woman Malcolm befriended when he first arrived in Boston. The other was "Sophia," the older and more worldly white woman for whom Malcolm left Laura. In his interview with Spike, Karim confirmed that Malcolm had continued to feel guilty about his treatment of the real-life Laura, who sank into drug use and prostitution after they broke up. He had "wrecked her life," Malcolm told Karim. At the same time, Karim tried to warn Lee away from showing Malcolm "doing drugs or running around with white women," lest he tarnish his legacy and invite angry and even violent backlash from members of Louis Farrakhan's reconstituted Nation of Islam. "For your sake, whatever you do, don't do it," Karim urged after asking Lee to turn off his tape recorder.

Spike didn't respond, knowing full well that he planned to follow Baldwin's lead in making Malcolm's interracial romance a major plot line in the movie. The real-life Sophia was a Boston-area native of Armenian ancestry named Beatrice "Bea" Caragulian, whom Malcolm met at a dance club in Roxbury. She later followed him to Harlem, and then back to Boston after he ran afoul of a hoodlum and numbers runner nicknamed West Indian Archie. Bea and her younger sister Joyce assisted Malcolm and his friend Malcolm Jarvis—on whom "Shorty" in the *Autobiography* was mostly based—in the robberies that eventually got all four of them arrested and sent to prison. In the movie, the sultry blond actress Kate Vernon would play Sophia—and be at Denzel Washington's side and in his bed for much of the first "act" of the film, before Malcolm goes to jail and embraces the Nation of Islam.

Over the following months, Lee interviewed dozens of other sources with insights into Malcolm's life and personality. They included Kenneth Clark, the psychologist who had debated him on television; David Du Bois, the son of W. E. B. Du Bois, who had met Malcolm during his travels in Africa; and several siblings and other longtime aides and allies. From a historical point of view, Lee's most groundbreaking interview was with Captain Joseph X, the former head of security for Mosque No. 7 in Harlem, who now went by the name Yusuf Shah. When Lee asked Shah point blank if he had ever received an order to kill Malcolm X, he replied: "I won't answer that question." After accusing Malcolm of having his own house firebombed at the time, Shah now conceded that NOI "zealots" were responsible. He similarly described the Audubon Ballroom assassins as "zealots." When Lee asked if the hit men came from Newark, and read off the names of the accomplices named by Mujahid Halim, Shah chuckled. "That's about all of them," he said. "You're something, Mr. Lee."

Lee and Washington also gained access to FBI audiotapes of the murder scene, as well as of phone wiretaps from the days and weeks before. In the movie, Lee would show FBI agents listening in as Malcolm spoke to Betty Shabazz, and use the tapes as the basis for dialogue he wrote for Denzel and for Angela Bassett, who played Betty. Another FBI tape captured the speech Malcolm gave at the Audubon Ballroom two days after the firebombing of his house, at the end of which an audience member could be heard shouting something that seemed intended to create a distraction. Lee recognized it as a "dry run," as he put it, and he worked that scene into his script as well. In the movie, he would show five Black men meeting in a dark room to test their weapons, inspecting the Audubon Ballroom for exits during a dance the night before the murder, and then driving back there from out of town the next morning. In the shooting script and in the credits for the movie, the five would be identified clearly as Thomas Hayer, Ben Thomas, Leon Davis, Wilbur Kinley [sic], and William X.

When the movie came out a year later, Lee included the results of his research and reporting in a companion book, *By Any Means Necessary: The Trials and Tribulations of the Making of Malcolm X.* After reading the book, the civil rights historian David Garrow published an op-ed piece in *The New York Times* under the headline "Does Anyone Care Who Killed Malcolm X?" Garrow credited Lee with making the most significant contribution to the understanding of Malcolm's murder since Halim's affidavits and Peter Goldman's reporting in the late 1970s, and added his voice to their calls for revisiting the convictions of Muhammad Aziz and Khalil Islam, who by then had been paroled from prison but were struggling with getting their lives back on track under the burden of felony murder records. "Malcolm's assassination deserves thorough historical attention, irrespective of whether or not the legal question of his death ever returns to the courts," Garrow argued. "Spike Lee merits considerable respect for addressing issues that almost everyone has long avoided."

After a decade of making films professionally, Lee also prided himself on having become a master of marketing. As he saw it, it was a task directors couldn't afford to leave to the movie studios—particularly if they were Black. "See," Lee explained, "I realized that being a Black filmmaker, I'm never going to have the same amount of money spent to market my films as I would if I was a white filmmaker with the same number of notches on his gun." That lesson had been driven home as Lee watched fellow Black graduates of the NYU Film School struggle to find an audience for their films.

Soon after Lee had his first box office success with *She's Gotta Have It*, he had begun directing commercials for Nike's Air Jordan sneakers. In the ads, Lee cast himself as the character he played in that movie, Mars Blackmon, interacting with the basketball legend Michael Jordan. The collaboration contributed to the runaway sales of the shoes—and to spreading awareness of Lee and his movies. In another stroke of inspired marketing, Lee came up with an idea for how to supercharge the resurgence of interest in Malcolm X in 1990, even before he had won the battle to direct the film. He designed a black baseball cap with a plain silver X on it, and started selling copies in the shop he had opened in Brooklyn, called Spike's Joint. Lee began wearing the X cap in public, and persuaded Jordan and other celebrity friends to do the same. Soon other companies were making knockoffs and variations, and X caps suddenly seemed ubiquitous, particularly in urban neighborhoods across America. By the summer of 1991, as Lee recalled it, "It's raining caps, X this, X that, sometimes without the wearers knowing the story behind the X. The word of mouth is beginning to pick up on this already."

As Lee was reworking the script that August, the movie received another marketing windfall of the "any publicity is good publicity" variety. Just as Lee had protested hiring a white director to tell Malcolm's story, a group of critics started to complain publicly that Spike was the wrong kind of Black artist to make the movie. Leading the attack was Amiri Baraka, the onetime pioneer of the Black Arts Movement. Baraka announced the formation of a group called United Front to Preserve the Legacy of Malcolm X and staged a rally in Harlem at which he urged attendees to write letters to Lee telling him "not to mess up Malcolm's life." "We will not let Malcolm X's life be trashed to make middle-class Negroes sleep easier," Baraka proclaimed to the crowd. His argument was that Lee was too much a product of the Black elite to do justice to Malcolm's radical message or the positive legacy of the Nation of Islam. "Based on the movies I've seen," Baraka sniped, "I'm worried of seeing Spike Lee make Malcolm X. I think Eddie Murphy's films are better."

Approached for comment about Baraka's campaign, Lee fired back with a combination of indignation and mocking humor. "Where's his book on Malcolm?" Lee quipped. "When Malcolm was on this earth Amiri Baraka was LeRoi Jones running around the Village being a beatnik. He didn't move to Harlem until after Malcolm X was assassinated." Lee also chided other members of the Black Power generation who had taken Baraka's side. "A lot of these guys—not all—weren't even down with Malcolm when he was around," Lee scoffed. "I was seven years old at the time so I had an excuse. I had to be home by dark."

Jumping on the story, The New York Times and Newsweek described the spat as a sign of how strongly Blacks felt about Malcolm, as a man and as a representative of the race. Some admirers didn't want to see the film play into negative stereotypes by focusing on Malcolm's criminal past, the publications observed, while others were concerned the movie would suggest that their radical hero had become a toothless moderate at the end of his life. "There are various constituencies within the black community that feel as if they own Malcolm X," Harvard scholar Henry Louis Gates Jr. told the Times. "So anyone is going to be attacked who does something with Malcolm they don't agree with." Reached by Newsweek, Alex Haley echoed the futility of pleasing all Malcolm's admirers. "Probably no scriptwriter alive could write a script that would satisfy the diverse groups who feel an ownership of Malcolm," Haley said.

As the reporters dug deeper, however, they discovered that Baraka had other reasons to be feuding with Lee. Lee had grown close to one of his daughters, Lisa Jones, and she had collaborated with him on several writing projects. Baraka was also still steaming over Lee's decision not to publish a piece he wrote for a collection of essays about the director's previous film, Mo' Better Blues. Lee had made the offer, but then had second thoughts and sent Baraka a kill fee when he saw how critical the essay was about all his movies. "He wrote a piece that was 100 percent negative," Spike recalled. "Not everybody [who contributed to the book] is saying Spike Lee is great, great. But this was so negative, I said, 'I ain't running this.'"

Newsweek invited Lee to write his own piece about the spat, and he took the opportunity to take another sardonic swipe at his critics while cleverly building more anticipation about what he would do with Malcolm's story. "In four weeks I will begin directing my sixth feature film, 'Malcolm X,'" Spike wrote. "They [Baraka and his supporters] have appointed themselves as the ministers of Black Culture, and it is they who decide what is politically correct art, and which art isn't. This is my problem with them: I know I never voted to put them into office. Who did? When was the election? . . . Whose Malcolm is it anyway? Malcolm belongs to everyone and everyone is entitled to their own interpretation. African-Americans as diverse as Supreme Court nominee Clarence Thomas, Minister Louis Farrakhan, Jesse Jackson and Chuck D of Public Enemy all claim him. I reserve my right as an artist to pursue my own vision of the man. . . . I'm through with this. No more public spats. No more defending ourselves. And no more discussions. As my great grandfather used to say, 'DEEDS NOT WORDS.'"

The filming of *Malcolm X* began in mid-September 1991 on a block in the Williamsburg neighborhood of Brooklyn that had been made to look like Dudley Square in the heart of Roxbury, the Black section of Boston where Malcolm moved as a teenager and fell into the life of a hustler. After several contentious meetings with Warner Brothers, Lee had instructed his line producer, Jon Kilik, to cut his shooting budget to under $30 million, which was still more than the studio had committed to spending. But Lee was determined not to stint on the first minutes of the movie, in which he wanted to establish the feel of a cinematic epic.

As much as one million dollars, therefore, went into creating the opening scene in Roxbury. World War II–style subway cars were built and towed along an overhead rail line. Storefronts were remade in the style of the era, and scores of actors and extras were dressed in period costumes. To establish the panoramic look he was after, Lee spent an entire day shooting the first two brief outdoor scenes: when Malcolm's

friend Shorty, played by Lee, gets his shoes shined before heading to
a barbershop to conk Malcolm's hair for the first time; and when the
two emerge onto the bustling streets of Roxbury wearing extravagant
zoot suits and hats.

Lee took even longer—three days in all—on the second major scene
in the movie, meant to take place in Boston's fabled Roseland Ballroom,
where Malcolm shined shoes and later entered dance competitions and
romanced the women referred to in the book as "Laura" and "Sophia."
The actual shoot took place in the ballroom of the Hotel Diplomat,
an affordably seedy dinosaur off Times Square. Harking back to the
Hollywood era of Fred Astaire and Ginger Rogers, Lee staged a Black
version of their glamorous dance numbers that one critic would call
"the single greatest dance scene in the history of cinema in regard to
Swing Dancing or Lindy Hopping or Jitterbugging or whatever else
it's labeled."

For the music, Lee chose a recording of the Lionel Hampton big
band classic "Flying Home." To ensure a look of authenticity, he hired
professional musicians to play the parts of Hampton and his band members. One of the sidemen was Javon Jackson, a twenty-six-year-old saxophonist who acted out Illinois Jacquet's famous solo. Like hundreds
of other minor players in the movie, Jackson recalled it as "an honor"
just to be part of a film about Malcolm X, who had been one of his heroes since he read the *Autobiography* in college. He was also struck by
how obsessed Lee was with getting every detail right, up to personally
coaching Jackson, whom Spike playfully nicknamed "Flying Home,"
even though Javon was only shown in the background and didn't have
a speaking part.

In three short months, Lee shot dozens of scenes spanning the
thirty-nine years of Malcolm's life, all at locations within or driving distance from New York City. Flashbacks to the Ku Klux Klan attacks on
Malcolm's childhood home in Omaha were filmed in upstate Peekskill.
His hoodlum phase in New York was re-created at the Lenox Lounge
in Harlem. A scene of Malcolm and Shorty burglarizing a wealthy Boston family before they are arrested and sent to prison was shot in an
apartment on Park Avenue. Malcolm's jailhouse conversion to the Nation of Islam was conjured up at Rahway State Penitentiary in New

Jersey. Denzel Washington delivered the fiery speeches of Malcolm's NOI ministry on the street corners of Harlem and the campus of Columbia University, and had a first date with Angela Bassett's Betty at the American Museum of Natural History.

With characteristic whimsy, Lee invited several well-known figures who had interacted with or been inspired by Malcolm to make cameo appearances. Black Panther leader Bobby Seale and activist Reverend Al Sharpton played fellow Harlem street speakers. William Kunstler, the lawyer who had tried to exonerate the two men wrongfully convicted of killing Malcolm, was cast as the Boston judge who sentences Malcolm to prison.

By the second week of December, Lee was finally ready to shoot the climactic scene of Malcolm's assassination. At first, he had his heart set on filming at the Audubon Ballroom itself, which had been turned into a Spanish-language movie theater after Malcolm's death and then shut down and left deserted. But after an early scouting trip, Kilik's line production team discovered that the building's interior was crawling with asbestos that would require a million dollars to remove. Months were spent configuring a more limited footprint, then it turned out that even that scenario would involve prohibitively expensive environmental cleanup. So with less than two weeks left in the preparation schedule, Lee sent his construction crews back to the Hotel Diplomat to create a semblance of the Audubon interior, leaving only exterior shots of the assassination scene to be filmed at the original building.

A focused, upbeat atmosphere had prevailed on the set until then, with everyone involved determined to "bring their A game," as Lee put it. But the mood darkened as the week-long assassination shoot began. Lee compared it to a soaring line on a stock market chart that suddenly takes a bearish plunge. In addition to the physical problems the shoot presented, Lee had also set himself a daunting psychological challenge. He wanted to make the movie audience feel something that Betty Shabazz herself had confided in him during their interviews: that Malcolm had a premonition he was going to die that day.

Working around the limitations of the location, Lee created that haunting impression with a combination of dialogue, music, and camera work. Taking a page from the climax of *Godfather II*, he filmed three cars converging on the Audubon Ballroom. One car carried the killers from New Jersey; a second, Betty and her daughters being chauffeured from Queens; and a third, Malcolm driving alone from the New York Hilton, where he had spent the night. Lee chose "A Change Is Gonna Come," the soulful Sam Cooke classic, to play in the background—sending an ominous message both of personal danger and social prophecy. Once inside, during the tense waiting period before his speech, a weary Malcolm talks to and then hugs his close aide, Brother Earl Grant, as though it's the last time he will see him. "It's time for martyrs now," Malcolm says.

Two more memorable artistic choices underscored Lee's thesis about Malcolm's fatalistic state of mind. One was his use of the "double dolly shot," a camera trick that Spike and Ernest Dickerson had experimented with in film school and used in two previous films. By placing both Washington and the camera filming him in close-up on a moving dolly outside the ballroom, Lee created the impression that Malcolm was floating through space, in a trance of stoic anticipation. The second effect was the look Malcolm would have on his face when he saw the hit man who is about to kill him. With a subtle widening of his eyes and smiling curl of his lips, Denzel Washington conveyed a sense not of fear but of relief—that the martyrdom Malcolm had so long envisioned had finally come.

Wrapped in time to give the production movie crew a Christmas break in 1991, the Audubon Ballroom shoot marked the end of the domestic phase of the filming of *Malcolm X*. All that was left were a few scenes depicting Malcolm's journeys overseas in the last year of his life. In January 1992, Lee and Washington planned to travel to Egypt to capture Malcolm visiting the Pyramids and to use mosques there to shoot interior scenes of his historic pilgrimage to Mecca. Meanwhile, a small second unit would travel to Saudi Arabia to film exterior shots of millions of faithful making a real-life hajj—the first time an American movie crew had been permitted such access. From there, Lee planned to make a quick trip to South Africa to shoot a modern-day ending he envisioned for the film featuring Nelson Mandela, the legendary Black independence leader who recently had been released after twenty-seven years in prison.

By then, however, the movie was already running over budget. After months of wrangling, Warner Brothers had agreed to spend no more than $20 million on the film. Foreign rights had been sold to a distribution company called Largo International for $8 million. Yet between what Lee's team had already spent and the money they needed for foreign filming and for editing and other post-production work, they calculated the final cost would be $33 million. Faced with the $5 million disparity, Warner Brothers could have opted to give Lee more money and waited to get it back at the box office. Instead, the studio demanded that the cost of any further production be borne by the Completion Bond Company, a firm that sold insurance policies to movie studios for uncompleted or severely over-budget films.

Shortly before the Christmas break, a representative from the bond company named Mack Harding began visiting Lee's sets and trying to dictate how to finish the film. Fond of large fedora hats, Harding was mockingly described by the film crew as "Indy"—short for "Indiana Jones"—or "the Terminator." He suggested that the foreign travel be canceled and that the remaining scenes be shot in New Jersey. Lee exploded. "Now, how the fuck are you going to shoot fucking Cairo or the Sahara desert and Mecca in fucking January at the fucking New Jersey shore?" he thought. Lee ignored the meddling and went ahead with the planned trips, only to return in February to demands for a rough cut of the movie by the end of the month. That was "crazy," Lee thought, given the months of editing, sound mixing, and scoring still needed to make a polished film. When Spike ignored that deadline, too, the bond company tried to shut down post-production entirely. In mid-March, Lee's editors all received certified letters informing them that "their services were no longer needed," as Spike acidly described it.

Lee knew it was a bluff. Neither Warner Brothers nor the bond company would get any of their money back if the film wasn't finished, so eventually one or both would have to relent. But as Spike saw it, he didn't have time to wait for the brinkmanship to play out. Fittingly, he found an answer to his dilemma by thinking about Malcolm X, after attending a ceremony held on the anniversary of his death. "Self-determination" is what Malcolm had always taught, Spike told himself—that Black folks should organize themselves financially and politically and not expect charity or justice from white society. Lee knew more than a few major Black celebrities who had "bank," as he put it. So he decided to ask those wealthy friends for help.

Lee made his first two calls to Bill Cosby and Oprah Winfrey, and they both immediately agreed to write checks. Next Spike went down a list that included Prince, Janet Jackson, the singer Tracy Chapman, and philanthropist and art collector Peggy Cooper Cafritz, a descendant of one of the wealthiest Black families in Alabama. Everyone agreed to chip in, even after Lee explained that he needed gifts and not loans, and that the donations wouldn't be tax-deductible. Spike was "begging," as he later put it. He stressed the importance of bringing Malcolm's story to a new generation. He confided that he had put his own skin in the game, giving up two thirds of his own $3 million deal to make the numbers work. He even played mind games by saving the last call for his competitive friend Michael Jordan, so he could let slip that he had already received a big check from Magic Johnson.

Once Warner Brothers learned that Lee was raising his own money, it called off the bond company. Lee was given until April to show a rough cut to the studio's top executives, Terry Semel and Bob Daly, before they left on a long trip to Asia. Their response was favorable, although they still thought the film was too long at three hours and fifty minutes. By then, however, the studio's leverage in the battle over length had been undercut by the release of another of its films, Oliver Stone's *JFK*. For most of the previous year, Lee had been arguing that his film should be at least as long as Stone's—who was also a personal friend—and Warner Brothers had insisted that they were also holding the line on the John F. Kennedy biopic. But now that movie was out, and it was three hours and eight minutes long.

By the time Lee screened the movie for Semel and Daly a second time—on May 4—news had also intervened to justify its new length of three hours and twenty-two minutes. The day before, in the Los Angeles suburb of Simi Valley, an all-white jury had acquitted the police officers caught on a civilian video camera savagely beating the unarmed motorist Rodney King. Just a few miles from the screening room, violence had erupted in South Central L.A. and was spreading across the city. "This film is needed now, more than ever," Lee announced before the screening began, and when it was over no one in the hushed, impressed audience could disagree.

Two weeks later, on Malcolm X's birthday, Lee held a press conference at the Schomburg Center for Research in Black Culture in Harlem to publicly thank the rich celebrities who had bailed him out. "These are black folks with some money who came to the rescue of the movie," Spike said. "As a result, this film will be my vision. . . . I will do the film the way it ought to be, and it will be over three hours." Although he had privately taken to calling Warner Brothers "the Plantation," Spike seized the occasion to shoot down press reports that the studio was still unhappy with his film. "The trouble began when the bond company took over the financial part and we couldn't write checks anymore," he explained. "Warner Brothers has seen the film twice and they're behind it."

As Lee finished his final edit over the summer, the turmoil in Los Angeles also gave him a new idea for how to start the movie. Denzel Washington's angry voice would be heard, delivering one of Malcolm's stinging indictments of the treatment of Blacks in America, while news footage played of Rodney King's beating and the rioting that followed the Simi Valley verdict. Then an American flag would fill the screen and start to burn down, until only the singed shape of an "X" remained.

Just as he had done in *Do the Right Thing*, however, Lee would end the movie on a gentler note, focusing on the less strident and more inspiring legacy of Malcolm. As Ossie Davis, now seventy-five years old, read his famous eulogy, images of the real man would appear, flashing his dazzling smile and looking every bit as much a movie star as Denzel Washington. Then a series of young Black children, first in Harlem and then in South Africa, would be seen rising from school desks, embodying Malcolm's calls for racial pride and education. "I am Malcolm X!" each child would declare.

Finally, Nelson Mandela would appear at the front of the South African classroom, delivering a passage from Malcolm's 1964 speech announcing the formation of the Organization of Afro-American Unity. "As Brother Malcolm said," Mandela told the schoolchildren, "we declare our right, on this earth, to be a man, to be a human being, to be given the rights of a human being, to be respected, as a human being, in this society, on this earth, in this day, which we intend to bring into existence . . ." Then, just as Mandela was about to finish, the camera would cut away. No longer a political prisoner and now a potential candidate for president of South Africa, Mandela had told Lee that he couldn't afford to be shown uttering the ending of the passage from the OAAU speech lest it be used against him by the white apartheid government. So Lee decided to end the film with a clip of Malcolm X, in real life, uttering his most famous four words: ". . . by any means necessary!"

After all the drama surrounding the making of *Malcolm X*, its release in November 1992 was surprisingly subdued. No violence broke out in theaters, as some had feared, particularly after the shootings that took place a year before at early screenings of another Warner Brothers movie, the gang war drama *New Jack City*. The early reviews were mixed, and even the positive ones came with qualifications. Vincent Canby, the *New York Times* critic who had raved about *Do the Right Thing*, credited Lee with having produced "an ambitious, tough, serious biographical film" that looked "as authentic as any David Lean film." But Canby also described the movie "simultaneously awe struck and hard pressed" in its attempt to do justice to the historical Malcolm, and falling into "a kind of reverential narrative monotone." Other reviewers called the movie "Lee's most conventional film to date" and, more archly, "Malcolm X for Beginners."

Box office returns also fell far short of the $100 million that Lee had boastfully predicted. The movie had a solid opening week but went on to gross less than $50 million worldwide. Some entertainment reporters concluded that Lee had alienated moviegoers with his theatrics, including a demand that news organizations send only Black journalists to interview him during the press tour. But executives at Warner Brothers concluded that the length of the movie had proved to be a turnoff after all, limiting the number of showings per day and intimidating many potential ticket buyers.

Praise for Denzel Washington's performance was near universal, however, and he was touted as a contender to win an Academy Award, particularly after he took home a Best Actor prize at the New York Film Critics Circle Awards. For the rest of the cast and crew, the hopes for Washington rose even higher once the movie failed to get Oscar nominations for Best Picture or Best Director, and was recognized in only one other category, for Ruth Carter's costume design. But on Oscar night, Denzel lost to Al Pacino for his role as a bitter blind Vietnam War veteran who rediscovers his zest for life in *Scent of a Woman*. Later, Washington would say that he was glad that he didn't deprive Pacino of his first Oscar after the legendary actor had been passed over for his memorable roles in *The Godfather Part II*, *Serpico*, and *Dog Day Afternoon*. But Lee scoffed that Pacino had benefited from a "makeup call"—the sports term for a questionable ruling made by a referee to compensate for a blown call earlier in the game.

Nine years later, the same thing would be said when Washington finally won a Best Actor Oscar for his role in the police drama *Training Day*: that Academy voters were retroactively honoring him for *Malcolm X* as well. With time, Lee would also see the sting of the Best Picture snub eased by future film history rankings. At the end of the decade, film critic Roger Ebert would rate *Malcolm X* as one of the ten best movies of the 1990s. Two decades later, *Time* magazine named it the best movie made in 1992.

Academic and journalistic experts on Malcolm's life had more substantive quibbles. Historian Manning Marable, then just beginning work on an in-depth biography of Malcolm, lamented the lack of attention to his political agenda, and to the nationalist influence of his Garveyite parents. The veteran Harlem journalist Herb Boyd regretted the scant references to the global pan-Africanism of Malcolm's final year. The feminist author bell hooks recalled the criticism that Lee had received for his depiction of women and male-female relationships in previous films, and accused Spike of still being obsessed with "jungle fever" in devoting so much screen time to Malcolm's dalliance with the fictional "Sophia."

In a symposium on the movie published in the film journal *Cineaste*, meanwhile, Black television pioneer Jacquie Jones chided Black intellectuals for expecting too much from a mass-market movie. "These critics, I think, are suffering from an elemental delusion with regards to Hollywood and its capabilities and some pretty off-base assumptions about contemporary African-American popular culture, in which the cinema is the most coveted vehicle," Jones wrote. "The charge of Hollywood has never been to produce functional political documents. And were the point of Lee's sixth feature film to capture faithfully the meaning and the resilient spirit of Malcolm in a manner that would satisfy the needs of every person of African descent in the United States, it would have remained as unmade as it has been for the past two decades."

If *Malcolm X* seemed tamer than many of its critics expected or wanted, there was another explanation that went largely undiscussed at the time. Lee was determined that as many young people as possible see the movie. As the film was about to open in New York City, he even suggested that teachers declare a school holiday. Warner Brothers arranged for special student screenings, and sent a study guide to the movie to classrooms in America's hundred largest cities. With young people in mind, Lee made a number of artistic concessions to secure a PG-13 rating. He minimized the use of swear words, and only fleetingly alluded to Malcolm's teenage drug use, cutting away quickly from a shot where he tries cocaine for the first time. If Lee disappointed his more cerebral critics by depicting a "mythic" Malcolm rather than a radical organizer, it was because he never considered them his most important audience.

Whether Lee was simultaneously encouraging young people to view Malcolm as a commodity, however, became a topic of worried discussion. By the time the film debuted, Lee had opened two more boutiques in Los Angeles, in addition to his Brooklyn store, to sell X hats and other Malcolm memorabilia. So many other retailers were trying to get in on the action that Betty Shabazz hired a management company to demand licensing fees for the use of Malcolm's likeness and words, and at least five lawsuits were filed. At Michigan State University, the manager of an Afrocentric bookstore refused to stock X caps because he predicted that students who saw the movie would be more interested in Malcolm "merch" than in his message. Harvard's Henry Louis Gates Jr. despaired of seeing "a lot of people running around with X caps who ain't read the autobiography and ain't going to read the autobiography. They've emptied [Malcolm] of his complexity."

Yet interest in exploring Malcolm's complexity hadn't gone away. Once the hoopla over the film version died down, attention shifted back to the political Malcolm—to arguments over whether he was at heart a social conservative or a political radical, and then to impassioned debate over Marable's voluminous biography when it was finally published. Despite its lackluster performance at the box office, polling data also showed that Lee's movie and the marketing surrounding it had laid the groundwork for those debates by increasing popular awareness of Malcolm, and by continuing to shift his image away from the frightening, one-dimensional figure depicted in much of the media during his lifetime.

On the eve of the movie's premiere, *Newsweek* magazine published a cover package titled "The Meaning of Malcolm X" that included the results of a telephone survey of 501 Black Americans conducted by the Gallup organization. Asked "Do you consider Malcolm X a hero for black Americans today?" 59 percent of respondents said yes, including 84 percent of those between the ages of fifteen and twenty-four. Sixty percent of the respondents no longer associated Malcolm with the term "Black separatism," and a mere 29 percent connected him with the idea of "Violence as a means to black goals." By contrast, 74 percent admired Malcolm for promoting "Black self-discipline," 82 percent saw him as "A strong black male," and 84 percent agreed that he stood for "Blacks helping one another."

TWELVE

Hero to the Right and Left

I n 1987, Clarence Thomas, then head of the Equal Employment Opportunity Commission, was profiled by journalist Juan Williams for
the *Atlantic* magazine. The position made Thomas, at thirty-eight, the
second-highest-ranking official in the Reagan administration, but it
was an unusual fit. Created as part of the Civil Right Act of 1964, the
EEOC was tasked with ensuring that private companies didn't discriminate in hiring, firing, or other business practices on the basis of race
or gender. Yet while he was African American himself, Thomas didn't
believe that government should take action on behalf of social groups.
He had directed the agency to intervene only in favor of individuals
who could prove that they had been the specific victims of unfairness
or mistreatment. Sitting for a long interview in his Washington office,
where an American flag and a flag emblazoned with the words "Don't
Tread on Me" hung behind a huge oak desk, Thomas explained that he
opposed all government-mandated programs aimed at helping Blacks
as a group, from affirmative action to school busing.

So many readers of the *Atlantic* article were surprised to learn that
Thomas took inspiration from Malcolm X. At one point during the
interview, he quoted a long passage from the *Autobiography*, summa-
rizing a case Malcolm made for Black economic self-help in the early
1960s, when he was still a spokesman for the Nation of Islam. "The
American black man should be focusing his every effort toward building his own businesses, and decent homes for himself," Thomas said,

recalling Malcolm's words from memory. "As other ethnic groups have done, let the black people, wherever possible, however possible, patronize their own kind, and start in those ways to build up the black race's ability to do for itself. That's the only way the American black man is ever going to get respect."

Asked how he came to his views on Black self-reliance, Thomas cited his grandfather, Myers Anderson, who had raised him from the age of seven. Until then, Thomas's childhood was geographically remote and emotionally unstable. His parents, M. C. Thomas and Leola Williams, were subsistence farmers in Pin Point, Georgia, a rural backwater where the Black community still spoke Gullah, a local dialect. After M.C. abandoned the family, Thomas and his two siblings were shuffled back and forth between his financially strapped mother and an aunt. Only when Leola remarried and the children went to live with their grandparents in Savannah was a strict sense of order imposed on their lives.

Although all but illiterate, Anderson was a forbidding task master who had managed to acquire property and build a successful business delivering ice, coal, and oil. A convert to Catholicism, he enrolled his grandchildren in an all-black Catholic school run by white nuns. After school, if they weren't studying at a local Black library funded by Andrew Carnegie, their grandfather required the children to help out with the business. Although active in the local NAACP, Anderson had a dim view of the government programs advocated by the organization's national leaders. Thomas recalled his grandfather's derisive account after visiting relatives in the North who were living in a housing project and dependent on welfare checks. As Thomas described it, "He'd say, 'Damn welfare, that relief—Man ain't got no business on relief as long as he can work.'"

After graduating from an integrated Catholic high school, Thomas spent a year in seminary school before giving up thoughts of becoming a priest and transferring to the College of the Holy Cross near Boston. There, he read *The Autobiography of Malcolm X*, hung a poster of Malcolm in his dorm room, and joined the handful of other Black students on campus in embracing the ethos of Black Power. "Young and hot-blooded and ill-tempered," as he later put it, Thomas grew an Afro and a goatee and took to wearing a black leather jacket. He served as secretary of the Black Student Union, and helped a local chapter of the Black Panthers organize a free breakfast program for local schoolchildren.

As the rhetoric of Black Power grew more extreme and violent, however, Thomas came to see it as at odds with the lessons of stoic self-discipline he had learned from his grandfather. Over the next decade, he grew steadily more conservative in outlook and dress as he attended Yale Law School and took jobs working for the Monsanto company and for the state of Missouri and its Republican senator, John Danforth. After joining the Republican Party himself, Thomas attended a conservative conference where he caught the eyes of recruiters staffing the Reagan administration.

Yet all along, Thomas continued to collect record albums of Malcolm X's speeches. Listening to them, he found himself still agreeing with another strain in Malcolm's ministry—his critique of the false promise of racial integration. Thomas's own experience had taught him that "there is nothing you can do to get past black skin," he told Williams. "I don't care how educated you are, how good you are at what you do—you'll never have the same contacts or opportunities, you'll never be seen as equal to whites." Like Malcolm did in his day, Thomas saw programs promoting integration as mostly benefiting middle-class Blacks, while programs aimed at helping the less well-off did little to improve their standing in society while eroding their dignity and cultural support systems. Malcolm "was hell on integrationists," Thomas reminded Williams. "Where does he say black people should go begging the Labor Department for jobs? Where does he say that you should sacrifice your institutions to be next to white people?"

In 1991, Thomas was named to the Supreme Court by President George H. W. Bush, filling the seat of the retiring civil rights pioneer Thurgood Marshall. When liberals read profiles of the court's new lone Black justice and learned that he claimed kinship with Malcolm X, they were aghast. In her widely read essay "Clarence Thomas, Man of the People," law professor Patricia J. Williams speculated that Thomas might have been attracted to Malcolm's association with Black "manhood," or that he had fetishized Malcolm in the way that his former colleague Anita Hill, in her testimony during his tumultuous confirmation hearings, had talked about his interest in pornography.

Whatever the attraction, Williams suggested, Thomas's embrace rested on a gross distortion of what Malcolm really stood for. "Clarence Thomas is to Malcolm X," she scoffed, "what 'Unforgettable. The Perfume. By Revlon' is to Nat King Cole." Williams also quoted a letter that she received shortly after Thomas's confirmation from an irate female friend. "Thomas invokes a mythical image of Malcolm X to serve his own needs," the friend wrote. "Thomas's use of X is the theft of a religious icon from a people whose religious and spiritual [ties come not from triptychs or cathedrals, but] memories. . . . In short, Thomas is a thief in the temple."

But other legal experts disputed the accusations of bad faith. One was Stephen F. Smith, a former clerk for Thomas who went on to teach law at Notre Dame. In 2009, Smith wrote a paper for a symposium held at NYU's law school, "The Unknown Justice Thomas," in which he argued that his former boss had been entirely sincere and consistent in following the lessons that he drew from Malcolm X. "It is false to say, as many of Thomas's critics in the black community do, that Justice Thomas 'thinks white,' and has forgotten that he is black," Smith argued. "To anyone who cares to listen, Justice Thomas's opinions thunder with the strong black-nationalist voice typically associated with one of Thomas's personal heroes, Malcolm X. . . . So, if we care to know who the 'unknown' Justice Thomas is, the answer is as provocative as it is obvious from his opinions. He is, quite simply, Clarence X—a jurist who is not only a constitutionalist, but a black nationalist as well."

Thomas's opinions in three areas demonstrated his Malcolm X–style Black nationalism, Smith argued. The first was whether white supremacists should enjoy the protections of the First Amendment. In Thomas's very first term, the Court overturned the death sentence of David Dawson, a Delaware inmate who had robbed and brutally murdered a couple after escaping from prison. In the majority opinion, Chief Justice William Rehnquist found that Dawson's free speech rights had been violated when prosecutors argued that his membership in the racist Aryan Brotherhood should be taken into account in his sentencing. Thomas issued a lone dissent, maintaining that the Brotherhood wasn't merely a vehicle for Dawson's "abstract beliefs," as Rehnquist had written, but a "singularly vicious prison gang" founded out of "hostility to black inmates," and that membership in the group was sufficient evidence of "bad" character to have factored in Dawson's death penalty verdict.

A decade later, in a case known as *Virginia v. Black*, the Supreme Court reviewed two convictions involving modern-day incidents of cross-burning. The state of Virginia was appealing its prosecution of a Ku Klux Klan leader named Barry Black, who had burned a cross at a Klan rally in full public view, and two white teenagers who set fire to another cross in the backyard of a Black family with whom they had a dispute. The defendants had been found guilty under a Virginia law that barred cross-burning as a prima facie threat of physical violence, but an appeals court ruled that the statute violated the First Amendment protection of symbolic free speech.

Still known for barely speaking during oral arguments, Thomas stunned court watchers by vehemently interrupting the state deputy solicitor general arguing on behalf of the Virginia law. Thomas asked why the lawyer wasn't making an even stronger case that cross-burning evoked a "reign of terror" and "a hundred years of lynchings." Thomas's impassioned questioning shamed the other justices into acknowledging the evils of cross-burning, but all eight nonetheless found the Virginia statute unconstitutional to various degrees. Only Thomas issued an outright dissent supporting the prima facie standard. "Just as one cannot burn down someone's house to make a political point and then seek refuge in the First Amendment," he wrote, "those who hate cannot terrorize and intimidate to make a point."

A second area where Thomas echoed Malcolm X was in his skepticism toward school desegregation. Like Malcolm, Thomas viewed the Supreme Court's *Brown v. Board of Education* decision as having brought about far less racial progress than it promised, while not recognizing the enduring value of historically Black colleges and universities. In his first year on the court, Thomas made his priorities clear when the court took up a case called *United States v. Fordice*, involving a federal order to Mississippi to take stronger action to integrate state colleges and universities that had remained virtually all-white. A lower court had struck down the federal order, but in an eight-to-one decision, the justices vacated that ruling.

Thomas joined the majority but wrote his own concurrence. He warned against doing anything to shut down or weaken Mississippi's virtually all-Black HBCUs, which he described as instilling "pride" and "hope" in Blacks who couldn't or didn't want to attend integrated schools. Beginning his opinion with a quote from W. E. B. Du Bois—"We must rally to the defense of our schools"—Thomas concluded that "it would be ironic, to say the least, if the institutions that sustained blacks during segregation were themselves destroyed in an effort to combat its vestiges."

Thomas showed outright hostility in a third area—the battle over affirmative action—but for reasons that were more Malcolmesque than most of his critics appreciated. Unlike many other conservatives, Thomas didn't oppose programs favoring minorities in college admissions or corporate hiring primarily because he believed in the dream of a color-blind society. As he would continue to argue throughout his career, "our society is not, nor has it ever been, colorblind." Like Malcolm, he rejected racially preferential measures as tokenism, existing to make whites feel more virtuous about themselves and their institutions, while giving them license to ignore the more intractable problems of millions of Blacks with no hope of qualifying for special treatment.

In 2003, the Supreme Court revisited its 1978 *Bakke* decision upholding affirmative action when it reviewed lawsuits claiming reverse discrimination by two white students who had been rejected by the University of Michigan. In a dissent to the majority opinions in favor of Michigan, Thomas focused less on the rights of the white applicants than on the hypocrisy of the university. He accused it of resorting to affirmative action to improve "classroom aesthetics" and maintain an image of selectivity—what he called the "self-inflicted wound of this elitist admissions policy." Recalling the way he was made to feel at Yale Law School, Thomas also argued that affirmative action had the paradoxical effect of promoting the perception of white superiority by suggesting that Blacks couldn't compete without special help.

By the 2020s, Thomas had served for three decades on the Court, making him the longest-serving active justice. In that time, he had gone from the lonely dissent of his early years to writing or joining more and more majority opinions as the overall makeup of the court grew

increasingly conservative. In a 2019 essay on Thomas's racial jurispru-
dence for *The New Yorker*, Brooklyn College professor Corey Robin
noted that his "politics are selective"—and that was an understatement.
Critics would argue that his positions limiting voting rights, opposing
gun control, and eliminating abortion access provided in *Roe v. Wade*
all had disproportionately negative consequences for Black people. Reports of the undisclosed gifts Thomas received from rich conservative
supporters also undermined public confidence in the court's independence, and had the potential to feed the kind of negative stereotypes
about Black people against which Thomas had so long railed.

Yet for all that, Robin agreed with Stephen F. Smith that Thomas
had articulated a "radical vision of race" that owed much to Malcolm X—and that stood to influence legal decisions and policy debates
for decades to come. Over his thirty years on the bench, Thomas had
written an average of thirty-four opinions per term. His influence
could further be measured by those who have clerked for him. Eighteen former clerks had gone on to serve as federal, state, or military
judges, and numerous others had argued cases before the Supreme
Court and served in Republican administrations. "On the Court,
Thomas continues to believe—and to argue, in opinion after opinion—
that race matters," Robin wrote, "that racism is a constant, ineradicable
feature of American life; and the only hope for black people lies within
themselves, not as individuals but a separate community with separate
institutions, apart from white people. This vision is what sets Thomas
apart from his fellow conservatives on the bench, who believe that
racism is either defeated or being diminished . . . [and his] beliefs are
coming closer, each term, to being enshrined into law."

Four years after Robin made that comment, it was borne out when
the Supreme Court banned affirmative action in college admissions
entirely in the case known as *Students for Fair Admissions v. Harvard*.
The ruling was made possible by the new six-to-three conservative "su-
permajority" on the court, and Chief Justice John Roberts wrote the
majority opinion finding that admissions policies favoring minority
students at Harvard and the University of North Carolina violated the
Fourteenth Amendment. But unlike the other five justices joining the
majority, Thomas was in a unique position to do more than merely

point out why affirmative action did harm to Asian and other applicants. Repeatedly quoting from his previous minority opinions, Thomas reiterated his long-held arguments why affirmative action also did harm to Blacks in the long run—by failing to expand overall minority access to higher education; by allowing schools to favor already well-off Blacks merely for the sake of "social aesthetics"; and by diluting a standard of meritocracy by which "those who have the most to prove can clearly demonstrate their accomplishments—both to themselves and to others."

At the end of his historic concurrence, Thomas returned to the themes of Black excellence and self-determination reminiscent of Malcolm X, by extolling the record of historically Black colleges and universities. He cited a United Negro College Fund study showing that, as of 2021, HBCU's produced 80 percent of all Black judges, 50 percent of Black doctors, and 50 percent of Black lawyers, in addition to a higher percentage of Black students who graduated with STEM degrees than predominantly white schools. "Why, then," Thomas concluded, "would this Court need to allow other universities to racially discriminate? Not for the betterment of those black students, it would seem."

In 1990, Shelby Steele, an English professor at San Jose State University, became another new face of Black conservatism when he published a provocative collection of essays called *The Content of Our Character: A New Vision of Race in America*. Together, Steele's meditations painted a picture of an America where the very real progress achieved during the civil rights era—putting the country "on the downward slope" toward Dr. King's "promised land," as Steele put it—had been obscured by the perverse new psychology of race. Finally acknowledging America's racist past, Steele argued, whites were bending over backward to support affirmative action and other programs of racial preference to reassert their "innocence," and thus encouraging Blacks to preserve an outdated posture of "victimhood" in order to extract the benefits. Although critics faulted Steele for lacking strong historical or sociological proof for his assertions, the book was original and timely enough to win one of publishing's most coveted prizes—the National Book Critics Circle Award for General Nonfiction.

Like Clarence Thomas, Steele had arrived at his idiosyncratic views on race partly under the influence of Malcolm X. His parents were an interracial working-class couple who had settled in a town on the edge of Chicago's South Side. His father, Shelby Sr., drove a truck, and his mother, Ruth, was a social worker. Both were early members of the Congress of Racial Equality (CORE) and raised their children in that group's spirit of racial idealism. But by the time Shelby was a teenager, he had suffered enough racial slights to be receptive to Malcolm and his unapologetic dual message to Black people—to find fault with whites, and to love themselves.

When Steele enrolled at Coe College, a small liberal arts school in Iowa, he was one of the few Blacks on campus. "At night in the dorm," he recalled, "my black friends and I would turn off the lights for effect and listen to [Malcolm's] album of speeches, *The Ballot or the Bullet*, over and over again. He couldn't have all that anger and all that hate unless he really loved black people, and, therefore, us. . . . With Martin Luther King, by contrast, there were conditions. King asked blacks—despised and unloved—to spread their meager stock of love to all people, even those who despised us. What a lot to ask, and of a victim. With King, we were once again in second place, loving others before ourselves. But Malcolm told us to love ourselves first and to project all of our hurt into a hatred of the 'blue-eyed' devil who had hurt us in the first place."

As he entered adulthood, Steele grew out of this "cathartic" separatist phase, as he described it, and embraced the universalist vision espoused in his award-winning book. Even then, however, he understood the powerful pull that Malcolm X's memory had on so many Black Americans. Steele also had a novel explanation for that attraction. Shortly after Spike Lee's movie came out, Steele wrote a cover story for *The New Republic* in which he argued that the resurgence of interest in Malcolm was due not to his militancy but to his conservatism. Privately, he pointed out, Malcolm was a model of sobriety and self-discipline. Publicly, as Steele put it, Malcolm resembled a Black version of Henry Kissinger in his belief in realpolitik; of Ronald Reagan, in his insistence on negotiating from a position of strength; and of David Duke, in his appeals to racial chauvinism.

It was Malcolm's conservatism, Steele maintained, that accounted for two unique aspects of his continued popularity. One was his resonance with Blacks on both sides of a widening social divide—with a Black middle class that had more opportunities than ever, but also with a Black underclass that was still mired in poverty and beset by violence and crime. "In times when the collective identity is besieged and confused," Steele argued, "groups usually turn to their conservatives, not to their liberals; to their extreme partisans, not to their open-minded representatives. The last twenty-five years have seen huge class and cultural differences open up in black America. . . . Black identity no longer has a centrifugal force in a racial sense. And in the accompanying confusion we look to the most conservative identity figure."

The other marvel of Malcolm, Steele pointed out, was how beloved he was even by those who didn't share many of his views, because they received from him what children might get from a strict but adoring father. As Steele put it:

Malcolm X was one of the most unabashed conservatives of his time. And yet today he is forgiven his sexism by black feminists, his political conservatism by black and white liberals, his Islamic faith by black Christians, his violent rhetoric by nonviolent veterans of the civil rights struggle, his anti-Semitism by blacks and whites who are repulsed by it, his separatism by blacks who live integrated lives, and even the apparent fabrication of events in his childhood by those who would bring his story to the screen. Malcolm enjoys one of the best Teflon coatings of all time.

I think one of the reasons for this is that he was such an extreme conservative, this is, such a partisan of his group. All we really ask of such people is that they love the group more than anything else, even themselves. If this is evident, all else is secondary. In fact, we demand conservatism from such people, because it is a testament to their love. Malcolm sneered at government programs because he believed so much in black people: they could do it on their own. He gave up all his vices to intensify his love. He was a father figure who distributed love and hate in our favor. Reagan did something like this when he called the Soviet Union an "evil empire," and he, too, was rewarded with Teflon.

═══

One measure of Malcolm's Teflon-coating, as Steele described it, was how rarely his name came up during this period in the widespread media coverage of Louis Farrakhan. By the 1980s and 1990s, Farrakhan had consolidated his position as the new head of the Nation of Islam, and had also assumed the role Malcolm once played as the NOI's most public spokesman. His calls for Blacks to address the crises of drug use and crime in their own communities and to start their own businesses were reminiscent of the self-help messages that made Malcolm a hero to Black conservatives, and in some polls as many as two thirds of Black Americans rated Farrakhan as an "effective leader" who was "good for the Black community" and said "things the country should hear."

But Farrakhan was rarely described as Malcolm's heir, either inside or outside Black America, for several reasons. One was that he never came close to rivaling Malcolm as a public speaker, despite a fiery delivery and a mellifluous voice that had once made him a popular calypso singer. Another reason was Farrakhan's overt and persistent anti-Semitism. Although Malcolm had sometimes been described as anti-Semitic, his attitude toward Jews was more nuanced than that term implies. He often said harsh things about Jewish businesses in Black neighborhoods, and about the conduct of Israel in its conflict with the Arab world, but he admired Jews as a group for their ethnic pride, solidarity, and ability to acquire economic and political power on their own. Most of the white professionals Malcolm came to trust and like on an individual level were Jewish, among them attorney William Kunstler and journalists Mike Wallace, M. S. Handler, Peter Goldman, and Helen Dudar.

Farrakhan, by contrast, openly attacked Judaism as a religion, and repeatedly invited negative publicity with the ugly language he used about Jews. In 1984, he backed Jesse Jackson's presidential bid, then defended Jackson when it was reported that he privately referred to New York City as "Hymietown." Amid the furor that ensued, Farrakhan declared that "if you harm this brother, I warn you in the name of Allah, this will be the last one you harm"—a remark that was widely seen as a threat of violence to Jackson's Jewish critics. A few months later, the *Chicago Sun-Times* reported that Farrakhan had made a speech that was broadcast on a local radio station in which he called the founding of Israel an "outlaw act" and denounced Jews for "using the name of God to shield your gutter religion." Although it turned out that Farrakhan had used the word "dirty" and not "gutter," the word was widely repeated in the press and led mainstream civil rights leaders and politicians of both parties to strongly condemn and distance themselves from Farrakhan.

Any question of comparing the two men was also clouded by Farrakhan's denunciation of Malcolm after he left the Nation of Islam—and by persistent questions about whether he might have played a role in Malcolm's death. At the very least, Farrakhan had helped put a target on Malcolm's back with a piece in *Muhammad Speaks* that appeared under his byline after the split. "The die is set and Malcolm shall not escape," the article read. "Such a man is worthy of death." On the day of Malcolm's assassination, Farrakhan was also visiting the Newark mosque—a coincidence that looked more suspicious once Mujahid Halim revealed that the murder plot was hatched in Newark. Although Farrakhan repeatedly denied any involvement in the killing, he continued to make statements that suggested Malcolm got what he deserved as late as 1992, when he engaged the crowd at the NOI's annual Savior's Day rally in the following call-and-response exchange:

"Did you clean up Malcolm?" Farrakhan thundered, referring to those outside the NOI.

"No!" the crowd shouted back.

"Did you put Malcolm out before the world?" Farrakhan continued.

"No!" the crowd shouted again.

"Was Malcolm your traitor or was he ours?" Farrakhan asked.

"Ours!" the crowd shouted.

"And if we dealt with him like a nation deals with a traitor," Farrakhan seethed, "what the hell business is it of yours?"

Two years later, the question surrounding Farrakhan's links to Malcolm's death unleashed a chain of tragic events for the surviving Shabazz family. In 1994, on his weekly television show, New York political reporter Gabe Pressman asked Betty Shabazz if she thought

Farrakhan had played a role in the murder. "Of course, yes," Betty replied. "Nobody kept it a secret. It was a badge of honor. Everybody talked about it, yes." Malcolm's second daughter, Qubilah, became obsessed with the same suspicion—and with a desire to take revenge. Bright but troubled, Qubilah had dropped out of Princeton University and moved to Paris, where she became involved with an Algerian man and gave birth to a boy she named Malcolm. After moving back to the United States with her son and settling in Minneapolis, Qubilah contacted a childhood friend named Michael Fitzpatrick and offered to pay him to kill Farrakhan. But Fitzpatrick turned out to be an FBI informant, and Qubilah was arrested and indicted on federal murder conspiracy charges. With William Kunstler acting as her attorney, she accepted a plea deal that spared her prison in exchange for agreeing to undergo psychiatric counseling and treatment for substance abuse.

Cannily, Farrakhan seized the opportunity to win public sympathy and incur a personal debt from the Shabazz family. He announced that he considered Qubilah innocent, and offered to help Betty raise money to pay her legal bills. The overture led to a rally at the Apollo Theater in Harlem at which a large crowd paid up to $100 per ticket to sit through a long series of speeches that ended with Farrakhan making a vague public apology to Betty, who looked down impassively from a box above the stage. "Members of the Nation of Islam" whose "zeal and love" had been "manipulated" had been responsible for Malcolm's death, Farrakhan confessed, although he denied any personal involvement.

While Qubilah moved to Texas to undergo her court-ordered treatment, Betty cared for her grandson Malcolm, now twelve, in the Yonkers apartment to which she had moved after her daughters had grown up and moved out of the house in Mount Vernon. But Malcolm had his own troubles, and one night he apparently grew upset with his grandmother. After Betty went to bed, Malcolm poured gasoline in the hallway outside the apartment, lit a match, and fled. Malcolm would later insist that he only wanted to scare Betty, and expected her to call the fire department when she smelled smoke. But instead she walked into the hallway and was consumed by flames that left her with third degree burns over 80 percent of her body. Three weeks later, Betty died from her wounds, an unspeakably sad end to a life that had already been full of so much loss and pain.

Farrakhan wasn't among the dignitaries who attended a wake at a Harlem funeral home or Betty's funeral service at an Islamic cultural center, before her body was laid to rest at Ferncliff Cemetery next to her husband's. But in 2000, he made another ritual show of contrition in a televised interview with Mike Wallace of *60 Minutes*. Malcolm had initially viewed Wallace with suspicion, after the airing of the 1959 documentary *The Hate That Hate Produced*. But the two men developed a relationship once they were introduced by Louis Lomax and Malcolm chose Wallace to confide his accusations about Elijah Muhammad's sexual misconduct. Since the assassination, Wallace had remained friendly with Malcolm's family. When he learned that the eldest daughter, Attallah, and Farrakhan had stayed in contact after Betty Shabazz's death, Wallace persuaded the two of them to sit down with him for a filmed interview at the Phoenix mansion that had once been the second home of Elijah Muhammad.

Wallace's CBS producer, Jay Kernis, recalled the tense atmosphere surrounding the long shoot. Fruit of Islam security guards frisked the camera crew and insisted on taking apart their equipment for inspection. The three participants sat around a large wooden table while Wallace confronted Farrakhan with evidence that seemed to point to his knowledge of the murder plot against Malcolm. Wallace pressed about the article in *Muhammad Speaks* in which Farrakhan declared that Malcolm was "worthy of death," and the fact that Farrakhan had been present at the Newark mosque on the day of the assassination.

For more than four hours Farrakhan gave windy, evasive answers to Wallace's questions, attributing Malcolm's death to the "envy" of other NOI members and suggesting that the FBI had been involved. Finally, his eyes misting, Farrakhan uttered enough of a semi-apology to make news. He conceded that his public attacks on Malcolm had made him "complicit" and expressed "regret that any word that I have said caused the loss of life of a human being." As soon as the story aired, Farrakhan took to *The Final Call*, the NOI newspaper that replaced Muhammad Speaks, to insist that he had only been at the Newark mosque on the day of the murder as a substitute preacher and to denounce *60 Minutes* for focusing on the complicity angle and not his attempts to reconcile with the Shabazz family. Tellingly, however, Attallah refused to forgive

Farrakhan on camera, and only gave Wallace a statement to read at the end of the segment. "He has never admitted this publicly until now. . . ." she said of Farrakhan. "I thank him for acknowledging his culpability and I wish him peace."

By then, Farrakhan had further complicated his controversial public image with an impressive feat of national organizing. In 1995, race relations in America had reached another flash point after the not-guilty verdict in the O. J. Simpson trial and tough talk in both political parties about the prevalence of crime, welfare dependency, and the rise of unwed pregnancies in Black communities. Farrakhan responded by inviting Black men from across the country to travel to Washington, D.C., to affirm their commitment to behaving as responsible husbands, partners, and fathers. Farrakhan labeled the event the Million Man March, and on a sunny day in October, between a half and three quarters of that ambitious number descended on the Washington Mall— well more than the quarter million who had attended the March on Washington in 1963. But unlike Dr. King's short and soaring "I Have a Dream" speech, Farrakhan's address to the crowd that day turned into a two-hour diatribe, full of attacks on critics and discursion into numerology before he called on the sea of men to raise their hands and forswear use of weapons, physical force, or "the B-word" in their domestic relationships.

Reporting on the day's events on the popular *Nightline* news program that evening, Ted Koppel of ABC News suggested that Farrakhan "may now have to be called one of the most influential leaders in Black America." But in the subsequent months and years, Farrakhan fell back into warring with his detractors, defending anti-Semitic outbursts from his followers, and inviting fresh controversy by traveling to meet with dictators in Libya, Iraq, and Iran. Surveys of the Million Man marchers also showed that it wasn't allegiance to Farrakhan that had drawn most of them to Washington. Asked what factors had been "very important" in their decision, less than a third credited the "initiation by Louis Farrakhan." More than four-fifths of the marchers said they made the trip to show their belief in the kind of "conservative" values that Malcolm X had preached: "self-determination," "building broad-based Black unity," and "improving and affirming moral values in the Black community."

Another school of admirers, meanwhile, continued to argue that Malcolm was much more of a radical than conservatives imagined, or than Haley portrayed in the *Autobiography*. In the immediate aftermath of the assassination, Malcolm had been painted as no less than a budding Marxist by George Breitman, a founder of the Socialist Workers Party (SWP) and editor of its newspaper, *The Militant*. In 1965, Breitman edited a book of speeches, *Malcolm X Speaks*, for a small Trotskyite publishing house that later became part of the SWP imprint, Pathfinder Press. Over the next few years, Pathfinder published two more books by Breitman, *The Last Year of Malcolm X: The Evolution of a Revolutionary* and *By Any Means Necessary*, in which he mined Malcolm's speeches for evidence that before his death he was paving the way for a political alliance between the OAAU and white socialist and left-wing labor union movements.

Malcolm was fast evolving into "a revolutionary—increasingly anti-capitalist and pro-socialist as well as anti-imperialist," Breitman contended, even though Malcolm had never used any of those terms to describe himself. In the 1990s, two books on the assassination purported to prove that Malcolm was killed to prevent him from undermining the Cold War struggle with the Soviet Union by bringing the plight of American Blacks before the United Nations. In *Conspiracys: Unravelling the Assassination of Malcolm X*, Baba Zak Kondo, a young Black community college professor, explored the evidence first presented by Talmadge Hayer, William Kunstler, and Peter Goldman that five Newark gunmen carried out the murder. At the same time, Kondo contended that the hit men were abetted by two overlapping conspiracies: by the FBI and the CIA, to fan the feud between Malcolm and the Nation of Islam; and by officers from the NYPD and its intelligence wing, to leave Malcolm unprotected on the day of the murder. Karl Evanzz, a Black freelance investigative journalist, made a similar three-part case in his book, *The Judas Factor: The Plot to Kill Malcolm X*—although neither author ever managed to establish a direct link between the Black hit men and the law enforcement and intelligence agencies.

Like Breitman's, those two books were published by small

independent presses and never found a broad audience. Around that
same time, however, another Black historian began work on what
would become the most widely read and discussed study of Malcolm's
life and thinking since the *Autobiography*. Born in 1950, William Marable, known by his middle name, Manning, grew up outside Dayton,
Ohio. His parents were both graduates of Central State University, the
historically Black college in nearby Wilberforce. James Marable taught
high school math and science, and June Marable became an ordained
minister, and both were active supporters of the civil rights movement.
When Dr. King was assassinated in 1968, Manning's mother encouraged her son to travel to Atlanta to witness his funeral, and the high
school senior arranged to cover the story for the *Dayton Express*, a local
Black newspaper. "With King's death, my childhood abruptly ended,"
he recalled. "My understanding of political change began a trajectory
from reform to radicalism."

Manning Marable entered Earlham College in Indiana the following
year, at the height of the Black Power movement, and quickly ceased
to be a "King man," as he put it. He joined a Black activist group, wrote
militant columns for the student newspaper, and hosted a campus radio
program called *The Black Magazine*. He also read *The Autobiography
of Malcolm X* for the first time. "The full relevance and revolutionary
meaning of the man suddenly became crystal clear to me," he recalled.
Setting his sights on becoming a "public historian and a radical intellectual," as he described it, Marable earned a master's degree from the
University of Wisconsin and a PhD from the University of Maryland,
but also kept his hand in activist politics. In 1980, he helped organize a
short-lived initiative to form a new left-wing Black political party, and
later served as vice chair of the Democratic Socialists of America and
editor of its journal, *Third World Socialism*.

With the new field of Black Studies sweeping the country, Marable
also became one of its most visible pioneers. He went from college
to college launching or chairing Black Studies programs—at Smith,
Colgate, Ohio State, and the University of Colorado at Boulder. As
he added the *Autobiography* to his reading lists, Marable came to see
the book from the perspective of a professional historian rather than
an impressionable student, and was increasingly struck by how Alex

Haley had shaped Malcolm's story to conform with his own integrationist, liberal Republican worldview. At Ohio State, Marable began working with his students to create a detailed timeline of Malcolm's life, and that project had evolved into plans to write a full-scale biography by the time Columbia University came calling in 1993. Eric Foner, Columbia's renowned white scholar of Reconstruction, was leading a search for the director of a new center called the Institute for Research in African-American Studies (IRAAS), and he persuaded Marable to leave his post at Boulder to take the position.

Over the next decade, Marable devoted himself to building up IRAAS and also launching Columbia's Center for Contemporary Black History. Finally determined to finish the Malcolm book, he stepped down as head of IRAAS and signed a contract with Wendy Wolf, a top editor at Viking Press, to publish a biography that would be accessible to the general public as well as to scholars. At Columbia, he assembled a team of graduate students who helped gather documents and video footage, mine FBI files, gain access to Nation of Islam archives, and record oral histories and interviews with people who had known or reported on Malcolm. Early to recognize the power of the internet and interactive media, Marable oversaw the creation of an online database called the "Malcolm X Project," as well as content for kiosks that would greet the public when the Audubon Ballroom was renovated and turned into a museum called the Malcolm X and Betty Shabazz Memorial and Educational Center.

All the while, however, Marable was battling a grave personal health crisis. Since his mid-thirties, he had suffered from a rare disease called sarcoidosis, which caused inflammation in his lungs. By his late fifties, he had to bring an oxygen tank to many of his meetings and interviews. In the summer of 2010, he underwent a double lung transplant just as he was finishing the Malcolm X manuscript in time to meet Viking's publication schedule. The chosen publication day was April 4, 2011—midway between the anniversary of Malcolm's assassination on February 21, and his birthday on May 19, and also the date of Martin Luther King's murder in 1968. But a week before the rollout, just as Viking was shipping hardcover copies to bookstores and lining up a book tour, Marable entered the hospital with pneumonia that had overcome his fragile immune system. On April 1, he passed away at the age of sixty, before he could witness the commercial success and prestigious awards that would greet the book Marable had titled *Malcolm X: A Life of Reinvention*—or answer the firestorm of criticism it also provoked.

===

As tragic as it was, Marable's sudden death served to heighten anticipation for the biography. The following day, *The New York Times* published a front-page story on the poignant timing, describing the book as its author's "life's work" and "full of new and startling information and insights." With plans for a *Today* show appearance and other book tour events in the works, prominent Black academics who were friends with Marable, including historian Michael Eric Dyson and Princeton historian Melissa Harris-Perry, stepped up to handle press appearances. Within days of publication, mostly glowing reviews appeared in the nation's leading newspapers. *Malcolm X: A Life of Reinvention* debuted at number three on the *New York Times* bestseller list for hardcover nonfiction and stayed on that prestigious list for three weeks. In the fall of 2011, the book was shortlisted for the National Book Award. Six months later, it was named a finalist for the 2012 Pulitzer Prize in Biography and then recategorized and awarded that year's prize in History by the Pulitzer board, which hailed Marable for producing a "stunning achievement" and a "definitive work."

Announcing his intention to go "beyond the legend" created by the *Autobiography*, Marable challenged the long-accepted narrative presented by Alex Haley in three significant areas. The first was his interpretation of Malcolm's personal influences. Marable documented just how deeply involved Malcolm's parents, Earl and Louise Little, were in Marcus Garvey's Universal Negro Improvement Association during their son's early childhood, first in Oklahoma and then in Wisconsin and Michigan. Those records suggested that Malcolm began inheriting his Black nationalist worldview and talent as a dynamic speaker and proselytizer well before he joined the Nation of Islam. From interviews and previous books, Marable also assembled ample evidence that Malcolm and Haley exaggerated the criminal activities of the teenage "Detroit Red," so as to make his prison conversion to the NOI and salvation by the teachings of Elijah Muhammad seem all the more dramatic. As suggested by the subtitle of the book, Marable argued that this and other "reinventions" in Malcolm's life were the products not only of spiritual growth but also of calculated brand management, the better to win over the converts he was courting. "Self-invention was an effective way for him to reach the most marginalized sectors of the black community," as Marable put it, "giving justification to their hopes."

Marable's second revision of Haley's account involved Malcolm's split with the Nation of Islam. He maintained that Malcolm was so shaken to learn about the female assistants whom Elijah Muhammad had gotten pregnant largely because one of them, named Evelyn Williams, was a woman Malcolm had fancied before he met his wife, Betty. Yet like Peter Goldman—whom he interviewed at length for the book—Marable concluded that the deeper tension was over Malcolm's hunger to play a bigger part in the civil rights struggle. Muhammad wanted the Nation of Islam to stay out of national politics, ostensibly because of his disdain for the corrupt white world but also out of a desire to maintain the NOI's tax-exempt status as a religious organization. Behind the scenes, the Messenger repeatedly clashed with Malcolm over the latter's political forays—when he pushed to take on the Los Angeles police over the murder of Ronald Stokes in 1962, for instance, or insisted on attending the March on Washington in 1963. In a fascinating reconstruction of the "Chickens coming home to roost" speech, Marable argued that even before ad-libbing those fateful words about the assassination of President Kennedy Malcolm had already defied Elijah Muhammad by delivering remarks that turned "from eschatology to racial politics" and seemed calculated to "push the NOI toward a more militant posture."

Marable's third challenge to the *Autobiography* came in his depiction of Malcolm's final ideological turn. In his account of Malcolm's last year, Haley highlighted the spring pilgrimage to Mecca and the epiphany that not all whites were devils. That emphasis suggested that Malcolm had started inching in the direction of Dr. King and his hopes for racial reconciliation. By contrast, Marable put a new spotlight on Malcolm's longer trip across Africa, the Middle East, and Europe in the late summer and fall of 1964, during which he lobbied heads of state to support his plan to bring the United States before the UN Commission on Human Rights, and was received more as a globe-trotting diplomat than a wide-eyed tourist. Drawing on a diary that Malcolm kept during that trip, Marable portrayed him as evolving not into an integrationist but into a global pan-Africanist, with a vision of American Blacks finding new unity and strength in solidarity with sympathetic allies across the developing world.

Marable devoted the last hundred pages of the biography to the threats on Malcolm's life, and in some media accounts he was credited with revealing for the first time that the man who fired the fatal gunshot blasts at the Audubon Ballroom was named William Bradley and came from Newark. In fact, Bradley's identity had surfaced three decades earlier, in Mujahid Halim's affidavits and in Peter Goldman's reporting, and Marable merely provided the update that Bradley had since changed his name to Al-Mustafa Shabazz, had served time for armed robbery, and was now free and helping to run a boxing gym in Newark. Marable's source for this information was Abdur-Rahman Muhammad, an Arlington National Cemetery tour guide and amateur historian who served as a researcher for the book and would later star in the Netflix documentary *Who Killed Malcolm X?* A full year before Marable's book was published, in April 2010, Muhammad had made his discoveries about Bradley's new identity public in a blog post featuring an image of a white-bearded Al-Mustafa Shabazz taken from a commercial for then Newark mayor Cory Booker.

More newsworthy in Marable's account were week-to-week details of the NOI's thuggish campaign of harassment against Malcolm and his family in the period leading up to the assassination, and of how closely the FBI and the NYPD were also surveilling him. This portrait of the walls closing in provided new context to the previous portraits by Haley, Goldman, and Spike Lee of Malcolm as a hunted, haunted man in his final days. Yet it wasn't those compelling hundred pages that would get most of the attention in the public discussion of Marable's biography that followed. It was a dozen or so pages that the late historian devoted to two more personal topics: Malcolm's teenage ties to an elderly white man in Boston, and the private details of his marriage to Betty Shabazz.

As it happened, the early 2010s were also the time when blogging began to democratize the world of book reviewing. With the spread of easy-to-use digital publishing tools and widgets that allowed readers to leave comments, the phenomenon known by the shorthand for "web logging" was no longer mostly the province of techies with programming skills sharing their arguments and enthusiasms. Now authors, critics, and experts on a wide variety of subjects could create their own blogs, attract communities of followers, and weigh in with their take on new books almost as fast as print newspapers and magazines could publish assigned reviews. So it was that, on April 13, 2011, just nine days after Marable's biography was published, the freelance journalist Karl Evanzz created a sensation among Malcolm obsessives with a post on his personal blog, *Paper Tiger: Manning Marable's Poison Pen.* Evanzz didn't mince words. "*Malcolm X: A Life of Reinvention* is an abomination," he began. "It is a cavalcade of innuendo and logical folly, and is largely 'reinvented' from previous works on the subject."

Evanzz clearly had a personal axe to grind. Two decades earlier, he had written both his book about Malcolm's assassination and a biography of Elijah Muhammad, and Marable had appeared to take a shot partly directed at both works in his introduction. "In reading nearly all of the literature about Malcolm produced in the 1990s," Marable wrote dismissively, "I was struck by its shallow character and lack of original sources." Yet now, Evanzz charged, it was Marable who had cribbed from his and other books and recycled titillating rumors without offering any new evidence. Providing no additional proof, for instance, Marable repeated suggestions in other books that Earl Little left his first wife without divorcing her, and that Malcolm carried on an affair with a female follower up until the night before the assassination. Marable also credited his "years of research" with uncovering the "missing" chapters that Alex Haley left out of the *Autobiography*, when they had very publicly been sold at auction in 1992.

Beyond his own critique, Evanzz's attack opened a floodgate of criticism from other obsessive students of Malcolm's life. They included well-known activists such as Amiri Baraka and Maulana Karenga; young Black academics such as Jared Ball, Todd Burroughs, and Baba Zak Kondo; and veteran journalists such as Black newspaper legend Herb Boyd and Peter Bailey, a former editor of *Ebony* magazine who had joined the OAAU in his youth and was present at the Audubon Ballroom on the day of the murder. Within months, these critics rushed out a volume of essays attacking Marable's book, while other scholars debated its shortcomings in academic journals.

Two of Marable's story lines in particular angered the critics. In a chapter on his Boston hoodlum days in the *Autobiography*, Malcolm had written about a mulatto waiter he called "Rudy" who became part of his petty larceny ring and who had a lucrative "hustle" on the side. "Once a week," Malcolm wrote, "Rudy went to the home of this old, rich Boston blue blood, pillar-of-society aristocrat. He paid Rudy to undress them both, then pick up the old man like a baby, lay him on his bed, then stand over him and sprinkle him all over with talcum powder. Rudy said the old man would actually reach his climax from that." In revisiting this tale, Marable identified the unnamed Boston man as an elderly former hotel manager named William Paul Lennon, who had employed Malcolm as a part-time butler and housekeeper and who later visited him in prison. "Circumstantial but strong evidence" also suggested, Marable wrote, that it was Malcolm himself who had the talcum powder hustle.

Numerous reviews of *A Life of Reinvention* treated this detail as a bombshell, but it wasn't new. In another one of those 1990s books that Marable dismissed in his introduction, a psycho-biographer named Bruce Perry had identified Lennon as the unnamed elderly white man. According to Perry, he interviewed Malcolm "Shorty" Jarvis, Malcolm's main partner in the Boston robbery ring, who told him that Lennon paid Malcolm to sprinkle talcum powder over him and "massage him until he reached his climax." In the essays attacking Marable, a number of male critics accused him of deliberately reviving the Lennon story to create publicity for the book and to call into question Malcolm's image as the epitome of Black masculinity. But in the *Journal of American Studies*, Cornell historian Margaret Washington had more scholarly objections. She faulted Marable for not providing "a single footnote" to indicate if his information came from Perry or from some other sources, and for treating such a creepy paid service, "whether this is true or not," as if it were a "sexual encounter" of any meaningful significance.

Marable's detractors were even more disturbed by his depiction of Malcolm's marriage. Challenging the impression of a deep love affair conveyed by the *Autobiography* and Spike Lee's movie, Marable cited NOI sources who suggested that Malcolm only wed Betty Shabazz because marriage was expected of a minister—and by Elijah Muhammad. This portrait of a loveless marriage of convenience was supported by the fact that Malcolm proposed from a phone booth while traveling, Marable argued, and by the three times Betty became so upset with Malcolm that she left the Queens house and took her children to her hometown of Detroit. Yet Marable's sources for the marital strife stories all had questionable motives, the critics charged. And it was Louis Farrakhan who provided Marable with the catty suggestion that Malcolm had never stopped being in love with Evelyn Williams, the young NOI follower who became pregnant by Elijah Muhammad.

Marable's most graphic evidence of marital discord came from a letter that Malcolm wrote to Elijah Muhammad in March 1959, four months after Betty gave birth to their first daughter, Attallah. Malcolm complained to his mentor that Betty had been "miserable during her expectancy," and that "the main source of our trouble was based upon SEX. . . . One day she told me that we were incompatible sexually because I had never given her any real satisfaction." Yet that letter had only surfaced in 2002, leading some skeptics to wonder if it was fabricated or maliciously leaked by the NOI. A 2005 biography of Betty Shabazz by Dartmouth historian Russell Rickford—a former student of Marable's—also cited the letter to Elijah Muhammad, but put it in a more sympathetic context. In Rickford's telling, Betty was indeed frustrated in the early years of her marriage, after giving up her plans for a nursing career to raise a family largely on her own. But she gradually earned Malcolm's love and respect and proved an invaluable source of support and advice, particularly once he broke with Elijah Muhammad.

Unlike Marable, Rickford interviewed the adult Shabazz children for his book. The daughters testified to the deep affection they witnessed between their parents by the time they were old enough to have memories. Attallah recalled the two taking long walks together, dancing romantically in the den of the Queens house, and her father calling Betty by flirtatious nicknames such as "Brown Sugar," "Apple

Brown Betty," and "Girl." Gamilah, who was still an infant when her
father died, described how physically excited her mother became
when she talked about Malcolm decades later. "What they had must
have been so intense that she kept him around," Gamilah told Rickford.

As an avowed democratic socialist in the 1990s, Marable had set
out to write a biography that would rescue Malcolm X from Alex Haley's moderate Republican gloss and place him in the company of history's revolutionaries. But by the time he was finishing his book, Barack
Obama had been elected president, and Marable seemed at pains to
reconcile his conclusions about Malcolm with that moment of apparent racial progress. In the conclusion of his book, Marable pointed out
that Malcolm never stopped being a fighter for his people, or an advocate for structural social change. But he also argued that what Malcolm ultimately stood for—Black self-determination—could no longer
be seen as best achieved by the separatism or the uncompromising
militancy that he had preached for so long. "If legal racial segregation
was permanently in America's past," Marable wrote, "then Malcolm's
vision today would have to radically redefine self-determination and
the meaning of black power in a political environment that appeared
to be 'post-racial.'"

Marable's detractors also attacked him for buying into this Obama-
era "post-racial" talk. They accused him of the same thing that Marable
had condemned in Alex Haley: of shaping Malcolm's story to conform
with the political fashion of the day so as to appeal to as wide a commercial audience as possible. But if anything, the debate over Marable's
version of Malcolm X demonstrated the narrowness of intellectuals
trying to claim him as a champion for only their own beliefs. For as the
new century unfolded, Malcolm was once again in the heads not just of
biographers and critics but of real-world actors who were shaping new
chapters in American history. They included Barack Obama himself,
as he made his improbable rise to the White House; young Black Lives
Matter leaders, whose movement culminated in a seismic summer of
racial protest in 2020; and some of the nation's leading cultural gate-
keepers, who turned to Malcolm to breathe new life into institutions
as old as the postage stamp and the opera.

THIRTEEN

From Obama to
Black Lives Matter

F or Malcolm X's grown daughters, the last century ended with news
that would have once seemed unthinkable: their father's face was
going be on a U.S. postage stamp. In late 1998, the Postal Service announced that Malcolm had been chosen as the twenty-second historical figure to be commemorated with a Black Heritage Stamp, a series
created to integrate a recognition that for 130 years was awarded only
to prominent whites. Clarence Irving, a Black electrical plant manager
and amateur history buff from Queens, led the campaign to extend
the honor to people of color, and Harriet Tubman was chosen as the
first honoree in 1978. Martin Luther King Jr. came next, followed by
a series of well-known figures including civil rights leaders Whitney
Young and A. Philip Randolph, cultural icons Jackie Robinson and
Scott Joplin, and trailblazers Ida B. Wells and Madame C. J. Walker.

Yet even three decades after his murder, word of Malcolm X's
addition to this philatelic pantheon was startling enough to make
national headlines. In the lead paragraphs of newspaper stories
across the country, Malcolm was identified with descriptions such
as "one of the most controversial figures of the 1960s." Reached for
comment by the *Los Angeles Times*, Maxine Waters, the outspoken
congresswoman from a predominantly Black and Hispanic district
of the city, heralded the choice as a major symbolic breakthrough.
"Far too often, society does not recognize leaders who have been

controversial, that are important specifically to black Americans. Honoring Malcolm X breaks that kind of thinking."

Some Malcolm admirers were suspicious, seeing the honor as an attempt by the white establishment to soften Malcolm's public image and undercut the power of his message. In a syndicated newspaper column, activist Yemi Touré described the strategy as: "We have crushed his body, and that did not stop his influence, so now let us co-opt his words and images." In another op-ed, "Bulk Rate Treatment of a First Rate Man," Paul Lee, the historical adviser to the Spike Lee movie, noted the irony of Malcolm being celebrated by the same Postal Service that cooperated with the FBI and CIA in surveilling him while he was alive. Paul Lee also pointed out that the Postal Service had misidentified the photo reproduced on the stamp, showing a bearded Malcolm talking to reporters with his hand raised thoughtfully to his cheek. The photo wasn't taken in New York after Malcolm returned from Mecca and repudiated his earlier attacks on white people, Lee noted, but at a press conference in Cairo where Malcolm voiced support for Egypt's left-wing leader, Gamal Abdel Nasser.

Even more misleading, Lee argued, was the assertion in the Postal Service's press release that after leaving the NOI Malcolm had "supported a more integrationist solution to racial problems." In fact, Lee noted, Malcolm had never bought into the possibility or desirability of assimilating into a racial melting pot. Just a month before his assassination, he had told a British journalist that "we do not want integration—not in the way white people mean it, at least. . . . They want my people to forsake their identity and merge. But they can never do that. The only way we can live together is in a brotherhood of equals."

Yet Malcolm's daughters and other close friends chose to see the honor as a positive sign that mainstream America had changed enough to finally acknowledge Malcolm's historical significance. The day before the stamp's release in January 1999, those intimates gathered for a public celebration at Harlem's Apollo Theater. The ceremony began with a film tribute featuring a recording of Ossie Davis's eulogy playing over footage of Malcolm's speeches and interviews and photos depicting his private life with Betty and their daughters. Then the lights went up and Davis and his wife, Ruby Dee, walked onto the stage. "What a privilege to witness the radical become respectable in our time," Ruby proclaimed, addressing the crowd first. "We in this community," Ossie followed, "look upon this commemorative stamp finally as America's stamp of approval."

Harry Belafonte appeared next, taking over as master of ceremonies. After pointing out that "a stamp is among the highest honors that our country can pay to any of its citizens," Belafonte introduced *60 Minutes* star Mike Wallace, who described how his impression of Malcolm changed when he finally met him in person after the airing of *The Hate That Hate Produced*. "Not long after the broadcast, which caused a considerable stir," Wallace recalled, "Louis Lomax invited me to sit down for breakfast for my first meeting with Malcolm, and strangely and rather swiftly after that morning a curious friendship began to develop, and slowly a trust. And on my part a growing understanding and eventually an admiration for a man with a daring mind and heart. And gradually it became apparent to me that here was a genuine, compassionate, and far-seeing leader in the making. A man utterly devoted to his people, but at the same time he was bent on reconciliation between the races in America."

Percy Sutton, Malcolm's lawyer, drew knowing nods from the audience as he harked back to the days when the Black establishment shunned Malcolm. "I can remember a Minister Malcolm that nobody wanted to be near," Sutton recalled. "Lawyers, accountants, persons of consequence to the black community . . . were afraid to be identified with him, afraid to be seen with him." Randall Robinson, the president of TransAfrica, a forum for study of U.S. policy toward Africa and the Black Caribbean, followed, evoking what Malcolm had meant to him and his generation of young Blacks growing up in Richmond, Virginia. "I am one of the unfortunate millions who never knew or met Malcolm X," Robinson said. "So perhaps I can presume to speak for those millions like me, then and now, when I say that Malcolm X was a shining model for a new, whole and proud black personhood. Before we in the South could see through the mean veil of Southern segregation, there was Malcolm X. Before we could function beyond the humiliation of Southern bigotry, there was Malcolm X. Before we would come to know Africa's glorious past, there was Malcolm X. Before we could find our self-esteem and self-respect, there was Malcolm X. And we owe him so dearly in ways our young must never be allowed to forget."

Finally, Malcolm's six daughters—Attallah, Qubilah, Ilyasah, Gamilah, and the twins born after his death, Malaak and Malikah—joined Belafonte onstage. Shedding a tear as she addressed the crowd, Attallah drove home the theme of the day: that the establishment hadn't co-opted Malcolm so much as caught up to him. "Malcolm is not a changed man, it is a changing America," Attallah observed. "Malcolm was on time. We were late." With a huge image of the new stamp projected on a screen behind them, the Boys' Choir of Harlem ended the ceremony with "We Are Heroes," their signature anthem. "Black boys are born of heroes," the choir sang, "ancient heroes, biblical heroes, historical heroes, present-day heroes, explorers, scientists, navigators and such, all Black boys are born of heroes."

As a new century began, Barack Obama had just been elected to his second term in the Illinois State Senate. Still only thirty-nine, Obama was already well along in his own remarkable life of reinvention. His Kenyan father, Barack Obama Sr., had met his white American mother, Ann Dunham, while they were both graduate students in Hawaii, but the two had divorced and Obama Sr. had returned to Africa when their son was still a toddler. An anthropologist, Dunham spent much of Barack Jr.'s youth doing field research in Asia, sometimes taking him and his younger stepsister along with her but often leaving them to live with her parents in Honolulu. A bright but sometimes aimless high school student who liked to play basketball and smoke marijuana, Obama received a scholarship to study at Occidental College in Los Angeles, then after two years transferred to Columbia University, where he became serious about his studies but lived an otherwise lonely existence in off-campus rental apartments.

After college, Obama moved to Chicago to work as a community organizer. But he eventually became frustrated with the limited impact he could have in that role and decided to earn a law degree. Admitted to Harvard Law School, Obama started to come out of his reclusive shell and was elected the first Black editor of the school's prestigious law review. Upon graduating, he returned to Chicago and met and married Michelle Robinson, another impressive young Black attorney who had grown up in the city. Uninspired by corporate legal work, Obama started teaching constitutional law but soon became restless again and decided to enter politics. After winning his first State Senate race in 1996, he mounted an unsuccessful challenge to Bobby Rush, the former Black Panther who represented the South Side of Chicago in the U.S. House of Representatives, before returning to the Illinois legislature in 2001.

Throughout this early journey of ambition and self-discovery, Obama turned to Malcolm X as a touchstone. He had first read the *Autobiography* in high school, and he described the profound effect the book had on him in the memoir Obama wrote in his mid-thirties, *Dreams from My Father*. Seeking to figure out his identity as a mixed-race teen being raised in remote Hawaii, Barack—then known as Barry—devoured dozens of fictional and nonfictional coming-of-age stories by well-known Black writers. In most of them, he found poignant depictions of the Black existential condition but no compelling prescription for how he himself could make his way in the world. "I gathered up books from the library—Baldwin, Ellison, Hughes, Wright, Du Bois," Obama recalled. "At night I would close the door to my room, telling my grandparents I had homework to do, and there I would sit and wrestle with words, locked in suddenly desperate argument, trying to reconcile the world as I'd found it with the terms of my birth. But there was no escape to be had. In every page in every book, in Bigger Thomas and invisible men, I keep finding the same anguish, the same doubt; a self-contempt that neither irony nor intellect seemed to deflect."

In Malcolm, by contrast, Obama found a man of action as well as eloquence, who offered a model of self-respect, daring, and discipline even when espousing separatist ideas with which Barack didn't agree. "Only Malcolm X's autobiography seemed to offer something different," he wrote. "His repeated acts of self-creating spoke to me; the blunt poetry of his words, his unadorned insistence on respect, promised a new and uncompromising order, martial in its discipline, fired through sheer force of will." The biracial Obama found particular solace in Malcolm's journey from a boy who declared hatred for every drop of white blood in his body— the heritage of Louise Little's white father—to the man who returned from Mecca with a changed mind and heart about the prospect of racial coexistence. "If Malcolm's discovery toward the end of his life, that some whites might live beside him as brothers in Islam, seemed to offer some hope of eventual reconciliation, that hope appeared in a distance future, in a far-off land," Obama wrote. "In the meantime, I looked to see where the people would come from who were willing to work toward this future and populate this new world."

The year after Obama graduated from Harvard Law and returned to Chicago, he began to dip his toe into electoral politics by taking a position as executive director of Project Vote, an initiative aimed at registering 150,000 new voters in the city's Black and Hispanic communities. The Spike Lee biopic *Malcolm X* had just come out, X hats and T-shirts were everywhere, and Obama began invoking Malcolm as a way to break through to potential young voters. "Our biggest problem is the young, the 18-to-35 group," Obama explained to Vernon Jarrett, the veteran Black columnist for the *Chicago Sun-Times*. "Today, we see thousands of young blacks talking 'black power' and wearing Malcolm X T-shirts, but they don't bother to register and vote. We remind them that Malcolm once made a speech titled 'The Ballot or the Bullet,' and that today we've got enough bullets in the streets but not enough ballots."

In their bid to recruit and train eleven thousand registrars, Obama's staff came up with a catchy slogan: "It's a Black Power Thing!" One of the aides was Carol Anne Harwell, a savvy community activist who would become Obama's guru in the Byzantine ways of Chicago politics and later serve as his first campaign manager. In an interview with David Remnick for his biography *The Bridge: The Life and Rise of Barack Obama*, Harwell recalled how Project Vote appropriated the trendy Malcolm fashion look. "We took the 'X' from Malcolm, put it on some kente paper, and made posters and T-shirts with the slogan 'It's a Power Thing' that were so popular that we ended up trademarking them," Harwell said. "Of course, people in the African-American community knew that the 'X' referred to Malcolm, but we also had white girls going around wearing them, and one told us, 'Look at this! I'm Number Ten!'"

In 2004, Obama gave the keynote address at the Democratic National Convention in Boston, a dazzling performance that set the stage for everything that came after: his election to the Senate later that year, and then his challenge to Hillary Clinton for the 2008 Democratic nomination and his victory over Republican John McCain in the general election. With its churchlike cadences and lofty appeals to American ideals that transcended race, Obama's Boston address reminded many listeners of Dr. King, as did many other memorable speeches that Obama delivered on his path to the White House and during his eight years as president. But when called for, Obama also knew how to channel Malcolm X, particularly in addressing Black audiences.

During the 2008 primary race, for example, Obama arrived in the make-or-break state of South Carolina after beating Clinton in the Iowa caucuses, then losing to her in New Hampshire. All of a sudden, South Carolina voters started getting anonymous emails falsely accusing Obama of being a practicing Muslim, an assertion that seemed aimed at associating him with the terrorist attacks of September 11, 2001. Barnstorming in predominantly Black areas around the state, Obama added some new lines to his standard stump speech. "Don't let people turn you around because they're just making stuff up," he told the crowds. "That's what they do. They try to bamboozle you, hoodwink you."

Campaign reporter Carrie Budoff Brown of *Politico* noted the new language and its similarity to a memorable Malcolm riff in Spike Lee's film. "You've been had," Denzel Washington, playing Malcolm, told a crowd on the streets of Harlem, as he described the brainwashing of Blacks by white society. "You've been took. You've been bamboozled. Led astray. Run amok." It wouldn't be the last time Obama strategically echoed Malcolm on the campaign trail. He began using the "bamboozled" language again in 2016, repeatedly and with relish, as he worked to get out the Black and youth vote for Hillary Clinton in her ill-fated race against Donald Trump.

As president, of course, Obama governed mostly as a cautious moderate. So when David Remnick brought up Malcolm X during a White House interview, Obama took pains to insist that he had never agreed with his political ideas. "I think that I find the sort of policy prescriptions, the analysis, the theology of Malcolm full of holes, although I did even when I was young," Obama said. "I was never taken with some of his theorizing." Yet even then, at the height of his political powers, Obama still emphasized the psychological appeal that Malcolm had for him and for so many other Black people, and the importance of that message of self-belief through the ages.

"I think that what Malcolm X did, though," Obama told Remnick, "was to tap into a long-running tradition within the African-American community, which is that at certain moments it's important for African-Americans to assert their manhood, their worth. At times, they can overcompensate, and popular culture can take it into caricature—blaxploitation films being the classic example of it. But if you think about it, of a time in the early nineteen-sixties, when a black Ph.D. might be a Pullman porter and have to spend much of his day obsequious and kowtowing to people, that affirmation that I am a man, I am worth something, I think was important. And I think Malcolm X probably captured that better than anybody."

On February 26, 2012, just as Obama was beginning his run for re-election, seventeen-year-old Trayvon Martin was shot and killed in a gated community in Sanford, Florida. Wearing a hoodie on a cool winter night just after sundown, the Black teen was on his way back to the home of his father's fiancée after buying a snack of Skittles and iced tea at a local convenience store when a neighborhood watchman named George Zimmerman started following him. Zimmerman first called 911 to report "a suspicious person," then took it upon himself to confront Martin, resulting in a struggle during which Zimmerman fired fatal gunshots. When police arrived, they declined to arrest Zimmerman when he claimed he had acted in self-defense. But three weeks later, the story became national news when tapes of the 911 call revealed that Zimmerman had ignored instructions to stay in his car, and that cries of "Help! Help!" were heard before his gun went off. Federal authorities stepped in to investigate, and Obama made a rare statement describing his personal reaction as a Black parent. "When I think about this case, I think about my own kids," Obama told reporters. "If I had a son, he would look like Trayvon."

Zimmerman was charged with manslaughter but then acquitted by a Florida jury in 2013, setting off a wave of protests across the country. In Oakland, California, a local political activist named Alicia Garza took to Facebook to voice her anguish, coming four years after she had witnessed a white policeman go free after killing an unarmed Black man named Oscar Grant at San Francisco's Fruitvale Station subway stop. "I continue to be surprised at how little Black lives matter," Garza wrote at the end of the post. "Stop giving up on black life . . . black people. I love you. I love us. Our lives matter." Patrisse Cullors, an L.A.-based activist and a friend of Garza's, turned the phrase into a Twitter hashtag—#BlackLivesMatter—and a third, Brooklyn-based friend Opal Tometi, built social media platforms around the slogan. A year later, #BlackLivesMatter became a national rallying cry when two more unarmed Black men died at the hands of police: a teenager named Michael Brown, who was shot during a chase in Ferguson, Missouri; and a Staten Island resident named Eric Garner, choked by police who were trying to arrest him for the trivial offense of selling loose cigarettes.

The Black Lives Matter movement also brought another surge of renewed interest in Malcolm X. This time, it was because he was the Black leader who, more than any other of his generation, had made a crusade out of protesting police brutality in Black communities. In 1957, Malcolm had first come to the attention of many non-Muslims in New York City when he led a march to demand medical treatment for Johnson X Hinton, a Nation of Islam member who tried to stop cops from roughing up a Black couple on the streets of Harlem. A patrolman named Mike Dolan turned on Hinton, beating him with a nightstick, resulting in bleeding in the brain and multiple lacerations on his scalp.

As a crowd gathered outside the police station where Hinton was booked, Malcolm demanded to see the wounded suspect and arranged for him to be taken to Harlem Hospital. When Hinton was returned to the station, the crowd had grown to several thousand, but Malcolm dispersed them with a wave of his hand after receiving assurances that Johnson wouldn't be further mistreated. "No man should have that much power," an awestruck white policeman told James Hicks, the Black reporter covering the story for the *New York Amsterdam News*. The NOI subsequently filed three lawsuits against the police and won an award of $70,000 for Hinton from an all-white jury, the largest settlement New York City had ever paid in a police misconduct case up to that point.

The Hinton incident also marked the beginning of the surveillance of Malcolm by the NYPD and its special intelligence unit, BOSSI. Later the following year, two police detectives showed up at the door of the Queens house that Malcolm and his wife, Betty, pregnant with their first daughter, Attallah, then shared with two other NOI couples. Malcolm wasn't there, but the other NOI members tried to block the detectives, who stormed the house from the front and back, firing their guns in the air. Betty and the two other NOI couples were arrested and charged with assaulting police officers. During a three-week trial in early 1959, the NOI filled the courthouse with supporters and assigned its own photographer and stenographer to ensure an accurate recording of the proceedings. In the end, an all-male jury of nine whites and three Blacks handed down acquittals on most of the charges and deadlocked on the others, and the city eventually made a small settlement to Betty. Attending the trial every day, Malcolm made news by linking the case to more widely publicized civil rights battles in the South. "Negroes in Mississippi," he told reporters, "could not have their civil rights as openly violated and stomped upon any worse than has been done here in Queens County Courthouse."

In April 1962, what came to be known as the Ronald Stokes case started when Los Angeles cops confronted two NOI members who were selling suits out of a car trunk outside Mosque No. 27, questioning whether the suits were stolen. When the police used racial slurs and tried to put one of the men in a chokehold, other NOI members emerged from the mosque to intervene, and the LAPD rushed seventy more cops to the scene. The police then entered the building, where Stokes, a twenty-nine-year-old Korean War veteran who served as the mosque's secretary, approached them with his arms raised, pleading for calm. Instead, an LAPD officer named Donald Weese opened fire, killing Stokes and wounding four others, including a worshipper named William X Rogers, who was left paralyzed. The police arrested fourteen NOI members on charges of resisting arrest and attempt to commit murder—leading to a trial in which four would be convicted by an all-white jury—and Mayor Sam Yorty and Chief of Police William H. Parker issued statements blaming the entire confrontation on the Nation.

Malcolm had first met Stokes years before, when he was establishing the NOI mosque in Boston, and the two had remained close. Personally distraught by his friend's death, Malcolm found himself caught between enraged members of the Fruit of Islam who wanted to go to war with the LAPD, and Elijah Muhammad, who advised him not to create a spectacle. Defying Muhammad, Malcolm flew to Los Angeles and proceeded to do just that. He made the case a national media story by holding a press conference at the Statler Hilton to condemn the attack on the mosque and to dispute Yorty and Parker's description of the events. In further defiance of NOI headquarters, Malcolm briefed reporters from Black newspapers across the country and reached out to other civil rights leaders, even eliciting a telegram of support from Roy Wilkins of the NAACP. Asked at the press conference about the rare show of Black establishment solidarity with the NOI, Malcolm responded: "Negro leaders are against police brutality, no matter who it is against."

At a rally held at the Second Baptist Church, three thousand protesters passed unanimous resolutions calling for local, state, and national investigations into excessive police violence in Los Angeles. When Malcolm was spotted in the crowd, a call went up for him to take the stage, and he foreshadowed his calls for Black racial and religious alliances once he split from the NOI in 1964. "Today, it is our temple," he told the audience, "but tomorrow it will be your churches, your lodges and your synagogues." Coming a year after Yorty had won support from Black voters with promises to rein in the police, the Stokes case left the city's Black community deeply bitter about the tough-talking mayor and the militaristic tactics of police chief Parker—a simmering distrust that would boil over three years later during the historic Watts Rebellion of 1965.

As the Black Lives Matter movement spread in the 2010s, videos of Malcolm X went viral. On YouTube, one of the most watched clips came from the speech Malcolm gave at Ronald Stokes's funeral, in which he condemned Los Angeles as a "police state" and turned the description of the NOI as a hate group on its head by arguing that it was white society that had conditioned Black people to doubt their own value. "Who taught you to hate the texture of your hair?" Malcolm asked. "Who taught you to hate the color of your skin? To such extent that you bleach, to get like the white man? Who taught you to hate the shape of your nose and the shape of your lips? Who taught you to hate yourself from the top of your head to the soles of your feet? Who taught you to hate your own kind?"

In another widely shared video clip, taken from a 1960 speech, Malcolm coined one of his most memorable phrases in describing how Blacks end up being blamed, or worse, for confrontations initiated by police. "Every case of police brutality follows the same pattern," Malcolm argued. "They attack you, bust you all upside your mouth and then take you to court and charge you with assault. . . . This is American justice. This is American democracy and those of you who are familiar with it know that American democracy is hypocrisy. Now if I'm wrong, put me in jail, but if you can't prove that democracy is not hypocrisy then don't put your hands on me."

Historians also recalled Malcolm's early opposition to two controversial police tactics that became flash points again in the Black Lives Matter era. In March 1964, Governor Nelson Rockefeller signed the first "no-knock" and "stop-and-frisk" bills into law in New York State, permitting police to search the homes and bodies of suspects without warrants or explanation. When Malcolm and his supporters began holding planning meetings for the OAAU in the home of follower Lynn Shifflett, protesting the Rockefeller laws became their "primary action target," as Garrett Felber of the University of Michigan put it. The OAAU founders set up a twenty-four-hour hotline to field reports of police misconduct, planned a mock funeral with a casket on the streets of Harlem to announce their "intention to bury the 'No Knock' law," and joined the Harlem Lawyers Association and local branches of the NAACP and CORE in mounting legal challenges to the Rockefeller statutes.

During his presidential campaign in 2016, Donald Trump voiced support for the stop-and-frisk tactic, and argued that the stance would win him favor with Black voters who were often the primary victims of inner-city crime. Felber noted that Rockefeller made the same case in introducing his bills in 1964—and that Malcolm X ridiculed the governor's patronizing claim in his OAAU speech at the Audubon Ballroom that June. "Where this police brutality also comes in—the new law that they just passed, the no-knock, the stop-and-frisk law, that's an anti-Negro law," Malcolm told the crowd. "That's a law that was passed and signed by Rockefeller. Rockefeller with his old smile, always he has a greasy smile on his face and he's shaking hands with Negroes, like he's the Negro's pappy or granddaddy or great-uncle. Yet when it comes to passing a law that is worse than any law that they had in Nazi Germany, why, Rockefeller can't wait till he got his signature on it. And the only thing this law is designed to do is make legal what they've been doing all along."

═══

In addition to connecting him with a new generation of political activists, the end of the 2010s brought three major new developments in the historiography of Malcolm X—or the way familiar versions of his story were enhanced or reinterpreted. The first was the resurfacing of a so-called missing chapter from the *Autobiography*. After Alex Haley died in 1992, a collection of his papers was put up for auction to pay debts owed by his estate. They were purchased for $100,000 by a Detroit lawyer and collector named Gregory Reed, who at various times had represented Rosa Parks and a number of Motown artists. For the next twenty years, Reed tantalized historians with hints that among the papers were several analytical chapters that were written for the *Autobiography* but rejected by the editors at Doubleday because they didn't fit the structure or message they favored for the book. Manning Marable was so intrigued that he agreed to fly to Detroit and meet Reed in a restaurant, where the lawyer allowed him fifteen minutes to scan a number of the mysterious pages. At another point, Morgan Entrekin, the ambitious publisher who had taken over Barney Rosset's

Grove Press, traveled to Detroit in an unsuccessful attempt to negotiate a purchase, coming away mystified by Reed's odd behavior.

In 2010, Reed came to New York to participate in an event at the
Audubon Ballroom, after the venue had been turned into a museum
honoring Malcolm and Betty Shabazz. He read brief excerpts from
the missing chapters, then projected images on a screen of several
pages marked "Urgent" in red ink. In the audience, Komozi Woodard,
a Malcolm X scholar at Sarah Lawrence College, grew hot with frustration. "He had been holding this stuff hostage for decades," Woodard
recalled. "I had to restrain myself from asking, 'What part of urgent
don't you understand?'"

Finally, in 2018, Reed himself was forced to declare bankruptcy
and to put the Haley trove up for auction again. Although he had let
it be known that he possessed three missing chapters, only one—an
essay called "The Negro"—was in a condition to be of interest to bid-
ders. The document was a twenty-five-page carbon copy in blue ink
on onionskin. At the top of the first page was marked "Chapter Nine,"
indicating the order in which it was supposed to appear at the time
it was written. That numbering confirmed accounts of how the *Autobiography* had evolved—starting as a series of polemical arguments
prefaced with short biographical sketches about Malcolm and Elijah
Muhammad, and gradually morphing into a full-fledged narrative as
Haley coaxed more personal memories out of Malcolm during their
late-night interviews in Greenwich Village. At the time "The Negro"
was typed up and shown to editors at Doubleday—October 1963—the
book was apparently still a hybrid, with seven or eight chapters recounting Malcolm's early life and conversion to the Nation of Islam at
the beginning, and a number of analytical chapters at the end.

The Schomburg Center for Research in Black Culture—the renowned branch of the New York Library system in Harlem—snapped
up "The Negro" for $7,000, then paid another undisclosed sum for a
manuscript of the *Autobiography* annotated with handwritten comments by both Malcolm and Haley. When scholars were finally able
to see the full text of the missing chapter, the first thing that jumped
out to them was the vividness of Malcolm's language. The widespread

assumption had been that the Doubleday editors rejected "The Negro" because it detracted from the arc of Malcolm's personal story. Yet the language was a reminder that Malcolm's polemical talent was an essential part of who he was—indeed, perhaps his most memorable trait.

In using "Negro" in the title, Malcolm wasn't simply employing the outmoded term for American Blacks, scholars noted. He was making a conscious association with the linguistic root "necre," for death, as in "necrology." That, in turn, alluded to Malcolm's description of the Nation of Islam's mission of "raising the dead," or returning passive and self-sabotaging Blacks to a consciousness of their historical roots and cultural worth. On the first page of the chapter, Malcolm launched into a biting critique of how white America had brainwashed and manipulated Blacks into this psychologically and economically somnolent state:

> The Western world is sick. The American society—with the song of Christianity providing the white man with the illusion that what he has done to the black man is "right"—is as sick as Babylon. And the black man here in this wilderness, the so-called "negro," is the sickest of them all.
>
> The black man here is the world's only race of people that tries to get social, and civil, and economic equality by begging for it.
>
> The black man here is the nation's only large minority that has gone for one hundred years as the biggest drain on social welfare, as the forever ghetto-dweller, the forever most-unemployed, the forever most-ununited race.
>
> The black man here, man for man, is the forever biggest consumer at the same time that he is the biggest non-producer. And when you have got that combination, you have got—automatically—a man that somebody else has got to produce and provide for.
>
> The so-called "Negro" here is the perfect parasite image—the black tick under the delusion that he is progressing because he is riding on the back of the fat, three-stomached cow that is white America.

While "The Negro" added new context to the story of the *Auto-biography*, it didn't offer simple answers to those looking for evidence of where Malcolm might have stood on the political debates of the early twenty-first century. On the one hand, much of the middle of the chapter was devoted to a blistering critique of "liberal incrementalism," as Garrett Felber put it. Malcolm also associated the word "Negro" with mainstream Black leaders who approached politics from a position of supplication, or what he contemptuously described as "sittin-in and kneeling-in at the bottom of the ladder, looking up and hollering, 'I'm just as good as you.'" At the same time, Malcolm ended the essay with an appeal to "bloc voting," arguing that flexing political muscle—and withholding support from candidates who didn't support Black causes—could "overnight, take hold of the black man's destiny in America."

Close students of Malcolm's chronology pointed out that this defense of electoral politics came six months before the famous "The Ballot and the Bullet" speech of April 1964. "A ballot is like a bullet," he declared in that address. "You don't throw your bullets until you see a target, and if that target is not within your reach, you keep your ballot in your pocket." Malcolm also submitted "The Negro" several months before he split with the Nation of Islam, and even suggested in the essay that Elijah Muhammad was "advising the black masses to activate America's greatest untapped source of political bloc strength." However, no other evidence existed at the time that Muhammad had abandoned his long-held position that the NOI should stay out of politics. As Manning Marable and Peter Goldman both suggested in their accounts of the tense relationship between the two men by late 1963, Malcolm was more likely engaging in a last-ditch lobbying campaign to win Muhammad over to his growing desire for political engagement.

Whether it was in or out of the electoral arena, scholars took "The Negro" as proof that Malcolm remained a believer in history made from the bottom up, rather than the top down. The essay showed, they argued, that Malcolm had been inaccurately associated with the "great man theory of history"—a construct that the young social activists of the new century largely rejected. First, that framework had been imposed by Haley's focus on Malcolm's individual story. Then, it had been reinforced by the trend toward placing Malcolm X on a pedestal with Martin Luther King Jr. as the two commanding and indispensable figures of modern Black history. As Felber put it in challenging that notion: "By reanimating the autobiography's original aim to tell the story of a people, not just a single person, the newly discovered materials let the air out of the persistent myth that we should look—and, by implication, wait—for this generation's King or Malcolm. This was always a convenient fiction, relying on the marginalization of women and grassroots activists. 'The movement made Martin,' as [the legendary civil rights leader] Ella Baker pointed out, 'rather than Martin making the movement.'"

The second major development in the historiography of Malcolm X was this revised portrayal of him as Martin Luther King Jr.'s equal—and in some ways, his implicit partner—in the struggle for racial justice. The shift was remarkable, given that the two men were almost universally viewed as antagonists while they were alive. For years, Malcolm courted media attention by attacking Dr. King as a "House Negro" and a "modern Uncle Tom." He mocked King's dream of racial integration, and suggested that his Christianity-infused gospel of nonviolent resistance was detrimental both to Black safety and to Black pride. As Malcolm once put it, with typical rhetorical relish: "The white man pays Reverend Martin Luther King, subsidizes Reverend Martin Luther King, so that Reverend Martin Luther King can continue to teach the Negroes to be defenseless." While refusing to engage in tit-for-tat name-calling—or agree to a public debate—King, the Southerner, patronized Malcolm as a bright but misguided victim of racism and poverty in the North. "Malcolm was clearly the product of the hate and violence invested in the Negro's blighted existence in this nation," King said after hearing of the murder at the Audubon Ballroom. "He was too young for the Garvey Movement, and too poor to be a Communist . . . and yet he possessed a native intelligence and drive which demanded an outlet for expression."

The disparity in media coverage of the two men's assassinations also reflected the very different historical ranks the two men occupied at the time of their deaths. When Malcolm was killed in 1965, *The New York Times* treated it as a local story. "Malcolm X Shot to Death at Rally Here," read the headline over a piece that ran in the middle of the front page. Below, Malcolm was described tersely as "the 39-year-old leader of a black militant faction." By comparison, when Dr. King was killed three years later, the *Times* gave the story the kind of treatment usually reserved for wars, presidential elections, or breakthroughs in space travel. "MARTIN LUTHER KING IS SLAIN IN MEMPHIS; A WHITE IS SUSPECTED; JOHNSON URGES CALM," read a two-line banner headline across the front page. For decades afterward, even as Malcolm's legend endured within parts of Black America, most Americans of both races viewed Dr. King as the far more consequential figure, one who not only gave memorable speeches but helped end Jim Crow and get the Voting Rights Act passed. As Thurgood Marshall, the first Black Supreme Court justice, was quoted as saying of Malcolm: "Tell me one thing he did to free black people, or lift the level of their lives."

Periodically, a significant thinker would make the case that King and Malcolm had more in common than the conventional wisdom suggested. In 1972, James Baldwin wrote his elegiac piece for *Esquire* magazine, "Malcolm and Martin," in which he described learning of King's death as he was trying to write his Malcolm X screenplay in Palm Springs. As Baldwin attended King's funeral in Atlanta, he meditated on how the two leaders were united in a joint struggle that outweighed their differences and cost both of them their lives. "Malcolm and Martin," he wrote, "beginning at what seemed to be very different points—for brevity's sake, we can say North and South, though, for Malcolm, South was south of the Canadian border—and espousing, or representing, very different philosophies, found that their common situation (south of the border!) so thoroughly devastated what had been seen to be mutually exclusive points of view that, by the time each met his death there was practically no difference between them."

In 1991, Yale religious scholar James H. Cone published *Martin & Malcolm & America: A Dream or a Nightmare*, a scholarly study of how each man, coming from a different faith tradition, contributed to the rise of "Black liberation theology." On the screen, Spike Lee turned the photo taken of Malcolm and King on Capitol Hill into a visual leitmotif for *Do the Right Thing*, then ended the film by scrolling quotes that suggested what a new generation could learn from both men. For several decades before her death, Betty Shabazz's appearances with Coretta Scott King bolstered the perception of common cause between their husbands, as did a theater project in the 1980s jointly produced by Attallah Shabazz, Malcolm's eldest daughter, and King's daughter Yolanda.

In the Black Lives Matter era, however, the joint historical studies took a new turn. Instead of merely pointing out what King and Malcolm had in common, they argued that the two men had directly influenced each other's beliefs and actions in their final years. The foremost proponent of this school of thought was historian Peniel E. Joseph of the University of Texas at Austin, previously known for his expertise on the Black Power movement. In his 2020 book, *The Sword and the Shield: The Revolutionary Lives of Malcolm X and Martin Luther King Jr.*, Joseph described Malcolm X as Black America's sword and Dr. King as its shield, and maintained that each contributed to the other's effectiveness. A case in point was Malcolm's remark to Coretta Scott King when both spoke at the Brown Chapel AME Church in Selma in early February 1965, after Dr. King was arrested and taken to a local jail. "Mrs. King, will you tell Dr. King that I'm sorry I won't get to see him," Malcolm said. "I want him to know that I didn't come to make his job more difficult. I thought that if the white people understood what the alternative was they would be willing to listen to Dr. King."

After Malcolm was assassinated a few weeks later, Joseph argued, King felt compelled to become more of a sword as well as a shield. An additional "mountaintop moment," as Joseph put it, was the Watts Rebellion in August 1965, just days after President Johnson signed the Voting Rights Act. King flew to Los Angeles and was badly shaken not only by the destruction he saw but also by the less than enthusiastic welcome he received from Black protesters. The experience showed King that the civil rights battlefield was about to shift to the North, and to the issues that Malcolm had long highlighted such as policing, housing, and jobs. In an essay, "Beyond the Los Angeles Riots," King began to lay out a more aggressive vision, as Joseph put it, of "nonviolent civil disobedience as a peaceful sword that paralyzes cities to produce justice that goes beyond civil rights and voting rights."

Still preaching racial separatism in 1963, Malcolm X would soon split from the Nation of Islam, start backing away from his anti-white rhetoric, and seek a role in the civil rights struggle.

After Malcolm was gunned down at the Audubon Ballroom in upper Manhattan on February 21, 1965, his body was rushed to a nearby hospital where he was pronounced dead.

3

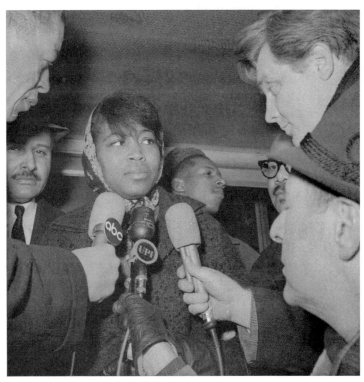

A shattered Betty Shabazz, Malcolm X's widow, told reporters that she blamed the New York City police for leaving him unprotected.

4

5

Nation of Islam leader Elijah Muhammad denied involvement in the assassination but suggested that Malcolm had it coming.

Ghostwriter Alex Haley was left to finish *The Autobiography of Malcolm X*, which won critical acclaim and became an enduring classic.

6

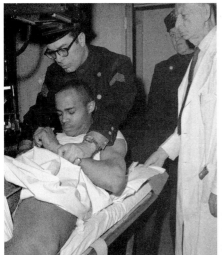

Talmadge Hayer (later Mujahid Abdul Halim), the guilty gunman who was apprehended at the Audubon Ballroom.

7

Norman 3X Butler (later Muhammad Abdul Aziz), one of two innocent men who went to prison for Malcolm X's murder.

8

9

The other wrongfully convicted suspect, Thomas 15X Johnson (later Khalil Islam), on the day of his booking.

William 25X Bradley, who fired the fatal shotgun blasts, became Al-Mustafa Shabazz and lived openly in Newark, New Jersey.

In 1966, Bobby Seale and Huey Newton studied Malcolm X's speeches before launching the Black Panther Party for Self-Defense in Oakland, California.

11   12

Malcolm inspired Black Arts Movement leaders including Maya Angelou.

Free Jazz innovators such as John Coltrane also paid homage to Malcolm.

Malcolm X with his protégé Muhammad Ali, then Cassius Clay, days after Clay won the heavyweight boxing crown in 1964 and before Elijah Muhammad drove the two men apart.

Kareem Abdul-Jabbar (then Lew Alcindor), credited *The Autobiography of Malcolm X* with changing his life.

15

14

Behind the 1968 Olympics protest in Mexico City were two Malcolm followers: sprinter John Carlos (far right) and sociologist Harry Edwards.

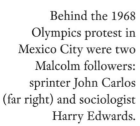

Hip hop pioneers such as Public Enemy introduced Malcolm X to a new generation by "sampling" his speeches and evoking his image on album covers.

Spike Lee's 1992 *Malcolm X* biopic spurred a fashion craze.

Denzel Washington gave a riveting performance as Malcolm.

19

Historian Manning Marable wrote a
prizewinning biography that focused
on Malcolm X's pan-African message.

20

Supreme Court Justice
Clarence Thomas insisted
that Malcolm should be seen
as a hero to conservatives.

21

When Malcolm X was honored with a commemorative U.S. postage stamp, his
daughter Attallah proclaimed: "Malcolm was on time. We were late."

Malcolm X and Martin Luther King Jr. met only once, on Capitol Hill in 1964, but their visions are now viewed by historians as having grown increasingly close in their final years.

Journalist Peter Goldman got to know Malcolm well and wrote one of the first in-depth books on his life and death.

After four decades of protesting the wrongful convictions, Goldman congratulated Muhammad Aziz on his exoneration.

Another way of looking at their dual roles, Joseph wrote, was that Malcolm X acted as Black America's "prosecuting attorney," and King served as its "defense attorney." Malcolm indicted white America for historic and present-day crimes, while King made the case for the moral innocence of Black Americans—and for whites who supported racial justice. Yet "after Malcolm's assassination," Joseph argued, "one of the biggest ironies and transformations is that King becomes Black America's prosecuting attorney." Both King's tactics and his tone became more militant in the battles of his last three years—over housing in Chicago, opposition to the Vietnam War, preparations for a Poor People's March on Washington, and support for the sanitation workers' strike that brought him on his fateful trip to Memphis in April 1968.

In 2023, white author Jonathan Eig published *King: A Life*, the first major biography of Dr. King in more than thirty years. Eig undertook the project in part to mine newly available FBI files and other documents, as well as interviews with still living sources who knew King personally. But Eig also wanted to assert King's relevance to the Black Lives Matter era, by showing that he was a more radical figure than the sanitized figure of school textbooks. In reevaluating King's legacy, Eig, too, concluded that King was influenced by Malcolm's example in his last years, particularly once he witnessed the toll of Watts and the violent backlash to his fair housing campaign in Chicago. "But if King didn't change Chicago, or Los Angeles for that matter, Chicago and Los Angeles changed King," Eig wrote. "He began to strike more anti-capitalist themes, saying that America, despite its great wealth, still struggled with poverty and still muddled through with endless wars. He sounded more like Malcolm X, in some ways, calling America a morally sick society."

In the course of his research, Eig also made a startling discovery that shifted the understanding of King's attitude toward Malcolm. For decades, a piece of evidence held up to illustrate their antipathy came from King's *Playboy* interview with Alex Haley in the January 1965 issue. In the interview—the longest he ever gave to a journalist—King sounded harshly critical of Malcolm. "And in his litany of articulating the desire of the Negro without offering any positive, creative alternative, I feel that Malcolm has done himself and our people a great disservice," King was quoted as saying. "Fiery, demagogic oratory in the black ghettos, urging Negroes to arm themselves and prepare to engage in violence, as he has done, can reap nothing but grief." While searching through archives at Duke University, Eig found an original transcript of the interview that suggested Haley misidentified or fabricated much of that quote. King condemned "fiery, demagogic oratory in the ghetto" in general, but not in relation to Malcolm personally. The phrases "great disservice" and "nothing but grief" also didn't appear in the transcript.

King did express some criticism in the transcribed *Playboy* interview. He said he "totally" disagreed with many of Malcolm's political and philosophical views, and "wished that he would talk less of violence, because I don't think that violence can solve our problem." Instead of saying Malcolm did Black people a disservice, King said "he falls into a rut sometimes." But he also praised Malcolm as "articulate" and conceded that he might have had the superior grasp of some issues. "I don't want to seem to sound as if I feel so self-righteous, or absolutist, that I think I have the only truth, the only way," King said. "Maybe he does have some of the answer." At the very least, the transcript showed that King was still searching for new ways to serve his people, and that he saw Malcolm as a valuable point of reference. As Eig put it, King "was not afraid to criticize Malcolm, but he was also willing to listen to him, and he was not ruling him out as a crackpot, as a violent wild card. He was thinking about Malcolm and where he belonged on the team of people fighting for justice."

A third historiographic breakthrough came in 2020 with the publication of the most deeply reported of all the biographies of Malcolm X. The author of *The Dead Are Arising: The Life of Malcolm X* was veteran journalist Les Payne, assisted with research by his daughter, Tamara. Born in Alabama, Payne had spent his childhood years in segregated Tuscaloosa, in an era when Blacks were forced to use separate public facilities and to refer to all whites as "sir" and "ma'am." At the edge of town, a sign welcomed visitors to "The Home of Robert Shelton, Imperial Wizard of the Ku Klux Klan." Worried for their future, Payne's single mother moved Les and his two older brothers north to live in Hartford, Connecticut, when he was twelve, and he started to attend predominantly white public schools. Les did well in his studies and won admission to the University of Connecticut as one of fewer than sixty Black students on its Hartford campus. But even there, his self-doubts were reinforced by a white guidance counselor who discouraged him from majoring in engineering, and by a white English professor who thought one of his papers was so well written that it must have been plagiarized. On the verge of adulthood, Payne recalled, he had "never met a white person, South or North, who did not feel comfortably superior to every Negro, no matter the rank or station. Conversely, no Negro I'd met or heard of had ever felt truly equal to whites."

Then on June 5, 1963, Malcolm X came to speak at Hartford's Bushnell Memorial Hall. Sitting with a white roommate in the half-filled auditorium, Payne felt that Malcolm was speaking directly to him as he delivered a fiery lecture that marshaled history, linguistics, and psychology to show how whites had instilled a "false sense of inferiority" in Blacks. "The lightning Malcolm X unleashed that night scored a direct hit on my own psyche," Payne recalled. "By the end of the lecture, I felt—and knew—that something within me had changed again, this time irretrievably. . . . My own group birthright, so indelibly stamped upon the souls of black folks in America, was difficult to remove as a tattoo. It was finally stripped away by Malcolm's acid bath of racial counter-rejection, tough-love logic, and bottom-up primer on American history. Since Tuscaloosa, I had carried deep within me the mark of the conditioned Negro, the most despised—and self-despising—creature in America. Up until this June night I had been lost, but all praises be to Malcolm X, my dungeon shook, and, as the poet said, my chains fell off. I entered Bushnell Hall as a Negro with a capital 'N' and wandered into the parking lot—as a black man."

Payne graduated with a degree in English, served six years in the Army Rangers, and then embarked on a four-decade career as a reporter, columnist, and editor at *Newsday*. He shared a Pulitzer Prize as part of a team that traced the trail of heroin from Turkey to Long Island, and was a finalist for another Pulitzer for his dispatches from South Africa. But Payne never forgot his life-changing exposure to

Malcolm X, and in the early 1990s he leapt at the chance to meet one
of Malcolm's surviving brothers, Philbert Little. The introduction
was made by Walter Evans, a Detroit physician who was friendly with
Payne and who would go on to become one of America's leading private collectors of Black art and historical memorabilia. Around the
same time, Payne also became friends with Faith Childs, a young Black
literary agent in New York City. They began meeting over lunch to
discuss possible book projects, and when Childs heard about Payne's
interest in Malcolm and his entrée to Philbert she suggested that he
think about writing a biography. Not since the *Autobiography* became
such a sensation, Childs pointed out, had a major independent study
of Malcolm's life been undertaken by a Black writer with the kind of
reporting skills that Payne had, or the potential access to family members and other sources who might never open up to a white author.

Childs negotiated a book deal with Doubleday, and for the next
few years Payne spent much of his free time working on the Malcolm X biography. From in-depth interviews with Philbert Little and
his brother Wilfred, he gained vivid new details of Malcolm's childhood, and telling insights into how he was influenced by each of his
parents. While Earl Little doted on Malcolm and took him on pros-
elytizing trips, the brothers recalled, Louise Little doled out verbal
discipline and occasional spankings and drummed the importance of
education into her quick-witted son. Before her breakdown, the proud
Caribbean native also imbued in all the children a "self-assured pride
and equanimity," as Payne put it, that caused them to be viewed as
"uppity" young Negroes at the time but went a long way toward explaining the adult Malcolm's preternatural confidence and poise.

At the same time, Wilfred gave Payne an explanation of Earl Little's
bloody death that was at odds with Malcolm's conspiratorial account.
First in Alex's Haley's *Playboy* interview and then in the *Autobiography*,
Malcolm had charged that white supremacists from the Black Legion
killed Earl and left his body on the Lansing trolley tracks—a brutal
scenario that had deepened Malcolm's hostility toward white people.
But Wilfred, who was eleven at the time, recalled overhearing the conversation his mother had with an earnest young white police officer
who brought Louise back to the Little farm in the middle of the night

after she had gone to the hospital and learned that Earl was dead. The officer said that Earl had still been alive when police arrived at the scene, and that he described having slipped and fallen on the tracks while running to catch the last trolley of the evening. Payne also found a copy of Earl's death certificate, which described injuries consistent with the policeman's account.

Payne tracked down at least a half-dozen Black and white friends who knew Malcolm as a restive young teen in Lansing, before he dropped out of school and went to live with his half sister, Ella Collins, in Boston. (Malcolm's nickname had been "East Lansing Red," Payne discovered, but he became known as "Detroit Red" when he moved to Boston because no one there had heard of Lansing.) Payne conducted in-depth interviews with Malcolm Jarvis, the running buddy, immortalized as "Shorty" in the *Autobiography* and Spike Lee's film, who shared Malcolm Little's hustling days in Boston and Harlem and was arrested and went to prison with him for petty larceny. Fleshing out the first years after Malcolm got out of jail and joined the Nation of Islam, Payne interviewed dozens of NOI converts who watched him build up the mosques in Detroit and Philadelphia before he was put in charge of Mosque No. 7 in Harlem. He spent so much time reporting on the several months in 1955 during which Malcolm established an NOI outpost in Hartford, Payne's hometown, that the first draft of a chapter on that small mosque ran to more than a hundred pages.

Marable, Goldman, and other biographers had reported the basic facts of one of the most bizarre episodes in Malcolm's years with the NOI: the assignment he was given by Elijah Muhammad in 1961 to conduct talks with representatives of the Ku Klux Klan about securing a large plot of land in Georgia to establish a Black separatist colony. But Payne got cinematic, fly-on-the-wall details of those negotiations from Jeremiah X Shabazz, the then minister of the NOI mosque in Atlanta at whose kitchen table the encounters took place. The talks began with comically forced niceties: the Klansmen joked that they had never shaken hands with "niggras" before, and Malcolm wryly asked whether an alliance would make him eligible for a white robe. But the negotiations broke down as the Klan leaders showed more interest in enlisting the NOI's help in a common war against Jews and in cooperating in a plot to assassinate the man they referred to as "Martin Luther Coon."

Payne's biggest reporting scoops involved the run-up to and the aftermath of Malcolm's assassination. He managed to secure a series of interviews with Captain Joseph X, the former chief of security in the Harlem mosque, before Joseph died in 1993 of complications from diabetes. In one interview, conducted on the streets of Harlem, Joseph recounted a secret meeting of NOI ministers and Fruit of Islam heads convened by Elijah Muhammad in Michigan in September 1964 at which the order went out to inflict "terminal bodily harm" on Malcolm. A day before he passed away, Joseph called Payne to confirm that he had personally supervised the firebomb attack on Malcolm's home in Queens, and that NOI headquarters in Chicago had ordered it.

Shortly before his own death from congestive heart failure in 1998, Jeremiah X Shabazz told Payne that he and other ministers received a deadline by which Chicago wanted to see Malcolm dead: February 26, 1965, Savior's Day. For the first time, Payne also found sources who connected the Audubon Ballroom hit squad to the leadership of the NOI mosque in Newark. A former member of the mosque identified by the pseudonym "Talib" told Payne that the Newark minister, James 3X Shabazz, was in direct contact with the hit squad organizers and had provided assistance in drawing up their escape plans. Talib insisted that one of the rewards received by the four hit men who got away was a trip to attend the Savior's Day celebration in Chicago a week later. Payne also reported new details about William Bradley, the burly ex–Green Beret who fired the fatal gunshot blasts. Around the Newark mosque, Bradley had been known as William 25X. And he was so feared that, after serving a prison term for armed robbery, he was said to have demanded and received a piece of the Italian mob's illegal operations in northern New Jersey.

Before he died, Jeremiah X Shabazz even gave Payne an answer to the mystery of what Louis Farrakhan was doing at the Newark mosque on the day of the assassination. Farrakhan didn't have advance knowledge of the Audubon Ballroom plot, Shabazz insisted, even though he had described Malcolm as "worthy of death" in *Muhammad Speaks* months earlier. Rather, Shabazz maintained, Elijah Muhammad was still so suspicious of the fact that Farrakhan had once been a protégé of Malcolm's that he wanted to compromise him by placing him near the scene of the crime. Shabazz believed Muhammad wanted "to ensure [Farrakhan's] silence, if not his trustworthiness," as Payne put it. "The Messenger was like that," Shabazz told Payne.

By the late 1990s, Payne had done a wealth of reporting on Malcolm but still hadn't written much. At their regular lunches, he would regale Faith Childs with his new discoveries but have no pages to show. Eventually, Doubleday became so frustrated that it canceled Payne's book contract for nondelivery. Another decade went by, and Payne forged on obsessively, chasing down new leads and amassing piles of notebooks and files in his Harlem brownstone, in a top-floor home office whimsically decorated with a barber chair. When the Manning Marable biography came out in 2011, Childs worried that it might kill interest in another one. But then she read the Marable book and realized how much exclusive material Payne was still sitting on. "After my initial sense of gloom, I felt we were very much on target and we should stay the course," she recalled. "No question."

By the mid-2010s, Childs thought that the time was ripe again, once the hoopla and controversy over the Marable book had subsided and the Black Lives Matter movement had revived interest in books about racial justice. By this point, Payne had written enough that he had "the spine, the central nervous system and all the important organs of the biography," as Childs put it. She began shopping for a new publisher and found one in Bob Weil, a veteran editor at W. W. Norton who ran its Liveright imprint. Weil had a strong interest in African American history and had published, among others, an acclaimed book on the family of Sally Hemings, the Black mistress of Thomas Jefferson, by another Childs client, the legal scholar and historian Annette Gordon-Reed. Payne signed a new contract with Liveright, and began working with Weil, who was captivated by Payne's reporting on Malcolm's life and death but wanted to situate the story against a more sweeping backdrop of the Depression, the Great Migration, and the struggles of Black Americans after World War II. Payne was hard at work making those additions when, in March 2018, he died suddenly of a heart attack.

Childs got a call on the night of Payne's death and was "devastated," she recalled. "It was just so unjust in so many ways." But she encouraged Tamara Payne to finish the biography with Weil's help, and it was finally published in the fall of 2020, catching a huge wave of interest and sales of books about Black history that accompanied that summer's nationwide protests over the police murder of George Floyd. Hailed for the depth of detail that Payne had mined from hundreds of hours of interviews with dozens of intimate sources, *The Dead Are Arising* won the National Book Award for Nonfiction in 2020, and the Pulitzer Prize for History in 2021—posthumously gaining Payne the individual Pulitzer (shared with Tamara) that friends said he always coveted. When Childs heard about the prize, she was overcome by emotion all over again. "I wept," she recalled. "I couldn't believe it. We'd come this long, long distance." Others talked about the timeliness of a new Malcolm X biography in that year of "racial reckoning," but Childs knew the full story. "It wasn't just the moment, it was [Payne's] unassailable research, and the faith that powered that," she said.

Before the Payne and Marable biographies, before Black Lives Matter and the Obama presidency, before Public Enemy's hits and Spike Lee's movie, three young members of an accomplished Black family of artists and intellectuals created an opera about Malcolm X. Jazz pianist and composer Anthony Davis and his younger brother Christopher, an actor and director, were the sons of Charles Twitchell Davis, a literary scholar who became the first chair of African American studies at Yale. Their second cousin Thulani Davis was a poet and journalist raised in Hampton, Virginia, where her parents taught at Hampton University and her great-grandparents had been among the founders of the historic Black settlement in that region. As a student at Swarthmore College in the 1970s, Christopher had read the *Autobiography* for a course on Black memoir, and was struck by all the music it conjured up, from the sound of the big bands that Malcolm danced to in his Boston hustler days to the modern jazz that played on Black radio stations that hosted him in the 1960s. He suggested to Anthony that Malcolm's story could be made into a musical, and he raised the possibility again several years later when the two were living in New York, where Christopher appeared in a revival of a Black Arts Movement–era theater piece titled *El Hajj Malik: A Play About Malcolm X.*

Anthony had an even more ambitious idea: to turn Malcolm's story into an opera. Fascinated by a wide variety of musical forms—from the free jazz he played in clubs around New York City, to the percussive sound of South Indian and Indonesian gamelan music he had studied as a music major at Yale—Anthony had also long been a fan of classical opera. Living with his family in Italy as a teenager, he had read *The Birth of Tragedy*, by Friedrich Nietzsche, the literary hero of German composer Richard Wagner. Anthony started listening to Wagner operas and imagining that he might write his own one day. By the early 1980s, he was also being encouraged to try his hand at opera by the director of a New York avant-garde art hub known as the Kitchen. As Anthony reflected on Malcolm's life, he saw a story full of the dramatic tension between passion and order that Nietzsche described as symbolized by the Greek gods Dionysus and Apollo—a pull that Anthony was eager to experiment with musically. "This binary between the Dionysian and the Apollonian was very interesting to me," Anthony recalled, "because it kind of mapped onto my thinking, at the time, as the improvised and the composed. There's also a binary between European music and the music of the African diaspora that is reflected in American music. I thought that would play very well with Malcolm's story."

Davis also saw in Malcolm's story another classic operatic theme: a looming sense of mortality. He pictured an aria in the first act, in which Malcolm's mother would mourn his father's death, that contained musical themes that returned as the last act built toward the assassination. "As a composer, you try to plant seeds, musically, that will pay off in the end," Davis recalled thinking. "I wanted to capture the feeling of Malcolm being haunted by the past, of thinking that violence was behind him, with revelation at Mecca, only to have it all culminate with the Audubon Ballroom."

The brothers agreed that Anthony would compose a score and that Christopher would break down Malcolm's life into dramatic scenes for the stage. For the libretto, they turned to their cousin Thulani, a graduate of Barnard College who was writing poetry and lyrics for experimental productions at the Public Theater while holding down a day job at *The Village Voice*. Over the next year, the three worked separately—Anthony in midtown Manhattan, Christopher in Greenwich Village, and Thulani amid a community of young Black artists living in Fort Greene, Brooklyn—then brainstormed over the phone or met at a diner to review their progress. After a successful workshop and debut performance in Philadelphia, the Davises were thrilled to learn that the New York City Opera, then run by the retired soprano Beverly Sills, had chosen the opera for its 1986 season. But to avoid legal trouble or bad word of mouth, the trio were advised, they would need to get approval from Betty Shabazz, who had responded negatively to the project when Thulani tried to interview her while writing an aria for her character.

David Dinkins, then Manhattan borough president, offered to host a meeting to make peace between Betty and the Davises. At first, Anthony recalled, their inclination was to "let the Black people work it out." But when Sills heard about the meeting, she asked to attend. As Anthony put it, they "couldn't say no" to the legendary diva who was busy raising the more than $300,000 needed to stage the production.

As soon as Betty walked into Dinkins's office in Harlem, Sills turned on the charm. "Have you picked out a dress for opening night?" she asked.

Betty brightened. "No, I'm looking at that," she said.

Watching the two formidable women hit it off so quickly, Anthony thought: "That's it. We're in."

Betty gave her blessing to the opera and Sills invited her and her daughters to attend the premiere. Betty also "blew my mind," Anthony recalled, when she told Sills how much she and Malcolm had enjoyed watching her sing on *The Carol Burnett Show*. Later, Betty even arranged for Beverly to become an honorary member of her Black sorority, Delta Sigma Theta.

In the fall of 1986, the City Opera production of *X* opened to impressive reviews. "This is not a 'jazz opera,' tuneful and cheerfully unthreatening," music critic John Rockwell wrote in *The New York Times*.

"It's a serious work making serious claims to a place in the operatic tradition." Opening night drew a standing-room-only crowd of nearly three thousand, some half of it Black. But from Sills's perspective, the rest of the run proved to be a financial disappointment, because it didn't attract the white season ticket holders who were the City Opera's economic mainstay at the time.

Over the next few decades, a wave of new operatic works based on current events—referred to by some as "CNN operas"—gained critical acclaim and started to enjoy regular revivals. They included John Adams's *Nixon in China* and *The Death of Klinghoffer*, as well as an opera about Harvey Milk, the San Francisco gay activist murdered by a fellow white city councilman. Anthony Davis went on to compose several more operas and to win the 2020 Pulitzer Prize for one of them, *The Central Park Five*. But in all that time, X was performed again only once, in a stripped-down version accompanied by synthesizers rather than a full orchestra at the Oakland Opera House in 2006. For a time, Davis recalled, most American opera companies still didn't have enough Black singers—or musicians who could handle the passages of improvisation called for in his score—to do the production justice. Then after the terrorist attacks of 9/11, opera directors and funders balked at supporting a work that featured Muslim characters and depictions of Islamic prayer.

During the Covid pandemic, however, Davis found himself at home without any new commissions, and he started to tinker with X again. He composed a more dramatic overture, as well as a duet between Malcolm and Betty that was inspired by a new movie that had just come out called *One Night in Miami*. Adapted from a play by the director and actress Regina King, the movie imagined the night in early 1964 when Muhammad Ali won the heavyweight crown from Sonny Liston and then went back to a Black hotel in Miami to celebrate with Malcolm, fullback Jim Brown, and singer Sam Cooke. At one point, Malcolm left the group to phone Betty and tell her that he had decided once and for all to break with Elijah Muhammad and the Nation of Islam. Watching that conversation on-screen, Davis thought that turning the exchange into a quiet musical moment with only Malcolm and Betty onstage would be a powerful new way to end the opera's second act.

Then, just as the pandemic began to ease, Davis was contacted by Yuval Sharon, the Chicago-born son of Israeli immigrants who had become renowned in the classical music world for his innovative stagings of operas and symphonies. Sharon had been named artistic director of the Michigan Opera Theatre, and he told Davis he wanted to revive *X* for the theater's first season under a new name, the Detroit Opera. About the same time, the Metropolitan Opera in New York was reopening after a pandemic shutdown with a new opera, *Fire Shut Up in My Bones*, by the Black jazz trumpeter-turned-composer Terence Blanchard. Based on a memoir by journalist Charles Blow about his childhood sexual abuse by a male relative, the production had been chosen by Met general manager Peter Gelb in a nod to the Black Lives Matter racial protests of 2020. Much was made of the fact that Blanchard's opera was the first by a Black composer to be performed at the Met in its 138-year history. But *Fire* also turned out to be a commercial hit, drawing younger and more diverse crowds than the Met had seen in decades. That success led Gelb to look for other contemporary operas that might attract similar crowds, and once he learned about the new production of *X* planned for Detroit, he invited Davis to bring the opera to New York in 2023.

To direct the new production, Sharon brought on another innovator—Robert O'Hara, the Black playwright and director known for such daring creations as *Insurrection: Holding History*, a play about a young gay Black man who time travels back to Nat Turner's Rebellion. For *X*, O'Hara had another bold idea: to land a spaceship on the stage at the beginning of the opera, as though aliens were delivering Malcolm to earth and staying to watch over him. In his production notes, O'Hara described the spaceship as a reference to the Black Star Line, the shipping company that Marcus Garvey, the separatist leader who played such a large role in Malcolm's childhood, advertised as a means of escape to a new Black homeland. On a more practical level, the device also gave O'Hara a way of tying Malcolm's story to America's long history of racial violence, by projecting the names of Emmett Till and other Black murder victims on the side of the hovering spacecraft.

In Detroit, Malcolm was played by young bass-baritone Davóne Tines, who gave a "steady, calm and committed" performance, as *New*

York Times critic Zachary Woolfe described it. But for the Metropolitan Opera production, the role went to Will Liverman, the baritone who had become a box office draw with his performance in *Fire Shut Up in My Bones*. Visually, the casting was a bit jarring, since the short, dark-skinned Liverman looked nothing like Malcolm, with his light skin and commanding height. But Anthony Davis was more concerned with what his operatic Malcolm sounded like than how he looked. In jazz terms, Davis thought of Martin Luther King's voice as resembling John Coltrane's saxophone, soaring and passionate. But he thought of Malcolm as sounding more like Miles Davis's trumpet—piercing and rhetorical, with playful spurts of humor.

Although reviewers were divided over Liverman's performance, the overall power of the opera's singing, genre-mixing score, and visionary staging led *The New York Times* to conclude that the Davises' opera had achieved the status of "an American classic." Unlike the original production, this one managed to escape getting dragged into the political battles of the day. In the 1980s, amid furor over Louis Farrakhan's anti-Semitic rants and his defense of Jesse Jackson for calling New York City "Hymietown," City Opera had been attacked by some critics who still saw no difference between Malcolm X and Farrakhan. This time, however, there was little discussion of Malcolm's pro-Palestinian views on the Middle East, even though the Met production debuted less than a month after the October 7 Hamas attack on Israel and launch of the war in Gaza. The lack of controversy suggested that the public had come to see Malcolm as a symbol of the yearning for self-determination by all peoples, regardless of race and region. Driving home that point, the Met production crescendoed to a scene in the third act in which Malcolm returns from his travels abroad and sings: "I have learned so much in Africa/ We are part of something big/ A movement spanning the globe/ We are freedom fighters all!"

With Robert O'Hara's spaceship backdrop and the science fiction–inspired ensembles, created by costume designer Dede Ayite, worn by the chorus, the *X* revival was also hailed as associating Malcolm with the Afrofuturist movement. "I had never thought of it in terms of Malcolm X, but when Robert said he wanted to add this aspect I was very excited," Anthony Davis recalled. Davis himself was a science fiction enthusiast and fan of the work of authors Samuel Delany and Octavia E. Butler, two pioneers of Afrofuturism. He had even written an opera, *Under the Double Moon*, that took place on another planet. "It put a frame on the opera that was not just a retelling of something from the past but that was also saying, 'Wait for the future,'" Davis observed. "You look at the costumes and you think that could be our African past or it could be the African-American future. It provides a sense of continuity, of putting these tragic events in the longer context of history."

With the Afrofuturistic twist, the sometimes arcane world of opera also became a vehicle for making Malcolm newly relevant to the "Black Panther" generation, as some called young people raised on the super-hero comic books and hit movies. On a rainy Sunday before the New York premiere in November, scores of them showed up at the Metropolitan Opera House to participate in a day-long group reading of *The Autobiography of Malcolm X*. Five days later, hundreds were among a sold-out opening night crowd more than half of whom, by the Met's estimation, was under the age of forty. In the long tradition of dressing up for Met premieres, many came arrayed in flamboyant Afrofuturistic outfits and hairdos.

"This is fantastic!" Anthony Davis recalled thinking as he surveyed the diverse, festive crowd. "You know, it was an event. It was a happening. It was like the audience was reflecting what was going on onstage."

Almost sixty years after Malcolm X's death, it was also a sign that a new generation was ready to carry his legacy decades into the future and beyond.

PART FIVE

EXONERATION

2017–2021

FOURTEEN

The Reinvestigations

f William Kunstler's legal appeals and Peter Goldman's magazine articles failed to get the murder cases of Muhammad Aziz and Khalil Islam reopened in the late 1970s, they only sharpened Aziz's hunger for freedom. In the early 1980s, Aziz (the former NOI enforcer known as Norman 3X Butler) reached out to Edward Bennett Williams, the legendary criminal defense lawyer who had appealed his conviction in 1966, to ask what might make Manhattan district attorney Robert Morgenthau reconsider. Williams handed off the request to an associate at his Washington, D.C., law firm, Williams & Connolly, who in turn contacted a young lawyer friend named Mark O'Donoghue, who worked at the New York firm Curtis, Mallet-Prevost, Colt & Mosle. There, O'Donoghue had become a protégé of Peter Fleming, a former assistant D.A. in Morgenthau's office who also had a colorful history as a criminal defense attorney representing high-profile clients including John Mitchell, Richard Nixon's attorney general, and boxing promoter Don King.

O'Donoghue agreed to look into the case, and to get up to speed, he read Peter Goldman's *The Death and Life of Malcolm X*. Although Goldman hadn't challenged the guilty verdict in his first edition, O'Donoghue thought the reporting showed the case had been deeply flawed from the start. He also read Goldman's 1979 *New York Times Magazine* article, with its evidence pointing to the hit squad from Newark. With the addition of the new affidavits from Mujahid Halim, Gene Roberts, and

Benjamin Karim, O'Donoghue thought, there was more than enough evidence to warrant a reinvestigation. When he briefed Peter Fleming, Fleming agreed on the merits, but warned that Morgenthau would see reopening the closed Malcolm file as a political loser. Morgenthau had inherited the case from his predecessor, Frank Hogan, and wouldn't want to antagonize political leaders in Harlem who still mourned Malcolm and had little sympathy for the men convicted of killing him, no matter what the facts. Sure enough, when Fleming and O'Donoghue reached out to Morgenthau and a meeting was set up at an Italian restaurant near the D.A.'s office, Morgenthau listened to their pitch and then told them he would need more evidence to change his mind.

When Mike Wallace taped a story for *60 Minutes* in early 1982 titled "Who Killed Malcolm X?," airing all the new questions that had surfaced about the murder convictions, Aziz held out hope that it might lead somewhere. But Wallace's piece came and went with little pickup or commentary in the rest of the media. Then in 1983, Democrat Mario Cuomo took office as New York's governor, and Aziz wrote a letter to Albany pleading for executive clemency. He got back a postcard from Cuomo's office rejecting the plea, but word of his petition piqued the interest of William F. Buckley, the conservative editor and host of the television interview show *Firing Line*.

Finding the clemency letter "eloquent," Buckley traveled to Sing Sing in January 1984 to tape an hour-long conversation with Aziz. They talked about everything from Aziz's claim of innocence to his role as a prison imam and his understanding of his Islamic faith. Accompanying Aziz for the interview was Warren Herendeen, an English professor from nearby Mercy College, which ran a study program for Sing Sing inmates through which Aziz had earned a bachelor's degree with honors in behavioral psychology. Buckley came away impressed with Aziz's thoughtfulness and sincerity—so much so that he agreed to write a letter recommending Aziz for a weekend work release program in the nearby city of Newburgh.

Finally, in February 1985—twenty years after his arrest—Aziz became eligible for parole. By then, Mark O'Donoghue had come to know and like him personally, as well as to believe in the justice of his cause, so he agreed to represent Aziz in the parole process. Usually, eligible prisoners had to admit guilt in order to have any hope of winning release on their first try, but Aziz had no intention of doing that. So O'Donoghue helped support a lobbying campaign begun by an activist ally of Aziz's. Benjamin Ward, the former state prison commissioner who had just become New York City's first Black police chief, agreed to write a letter of support. So did Kenneth Clark, the psychologist famous for his research on the impact of school segregation on children, and two of the state's most powerful Black elected officials: assemblymen Albert Vann of Brooklyn and Arthur Eve of Buffalo.

Peter Goldman also wrote to the parole board to commend Aziz. He described the man he had come to know in his visits to Sing Sing, and in their letters and once frequent phone calls. He testified to Aziz's keen intelligence and thirst for knowledge, which after he earned the college diploma led him to take correspondence courses for a master's degree in religion from the New York Theological Seminary. He also wrote of the high regard in which Aziz was held by fellow inmates and prison officials as a religious counselor and mediator.

In December 1984, Aziz and his supporters received good news: a three-member parole board panel had approved his release. But two months later, something strange happened. A second review panel, which in most cases served as a rubber stamp, reversed the first panel's decision and ruled two-to-one that Aziz should stay in jail for two more years.

Of the two parole board members who opposed the release, the most adamant was Black—a former Buffalo policeman named Theodore Kirkland. A fervent admirer of Malcolm X, Kirkland still believed Aziz was guilty and had disdain for the fact that he had white sympathizers—beginning with Peter Goldman. "We're not going to let some white man free one of the people who shot down our hero," Kirkland responded upon reading the letter, according to another member of the parole board who called Goldman to apologize.

During the review hearing, Kirkland openly challenged Aziz about his white supporters. "Do you think that all those folks would be recommending you for parole if you had killed a white person of similar status?" he asked.

"I don't really know," Aziz replied.

"In America?" Kirkland snickered. "You really don't know?"

At another point, Kirkland compared the Attica prison revolt and another one at Sing Sing to slave rebellions and likened Aziz to a Black informant against Nat Turner. "Malcolm was a great statesman," Kirkland lectured. "He was a leader. You have done nothing to match him. So don't paint too many roses on your chest. . . . The death of Malcolm has set folks back 100 years. I want you to remember that."

After Aziz was transferred from Sing Sing to the Arthur Kill prison on Staten Island to serve another two years, a reporter reached him for comment on Kirkland's hostile line of questioning. "He's asking me why all these white people are helping me," Aziz replied. "There are no blacks in a position to help me. The only people in a position to help me are white people."

As one of those white people helping Aziz, O'Donoghue recognized that Kirkland's public display of racial bias might provide grounds for getting the parole board to reconsider the reversal. He found an ally in the chairman of the State Senate's committee on crime and corrections, a Republican named Christopher Mega. Taking up Aziz's cause, Mega issued statements to the press accusing Kirkland of "prejudice" against whites, and called for another hearing. The parole board agreed, and this time three different officials chosen by lot all concluded that Aziz's immediate release was warranted.

Wearing a green bell-bottom suit and white tie, Aziz walked out of the Arthur Kill prison at a quarter past nine on a June morning in 1985, with O'Donoghue by his side. "He's going to get a job and earn a living," O'Donoghue assured reporters. But after twenty years behind bars, Aziz struggled to find work that he considered commensurate with the education he received in prison, with the leadership role he played there, or with his ambitions to run his own business. There had been a promise of a job managing a limousine service, but that didn't pan out. Aziz also worked in a retail sales, and in a homeless shelter, but none of those positions proved a satisfying fit. A relationship with a woman that started while he was incarcerated broke up, and he married another woman who died of cancer. Of his six children, Aziz was able to reestablish ties only with a daughter from a brief out-of-wedlock relationship in his teens. He had no luck with four sons who were adults now, some with families of their own. "They didn't want to hear anything I had to say," Aziz recalled.

For a while, Goldman and Aziz stayed in touch with letters and phone calls. "He called me one day soon after he got out saying things were really looking up," Goldman recalled. "He was going to be selling Dick Gregory's Bahamian diet drink. He really thought that was going to be the pot of gold at the end of a very dark rainbow." But that stint selling a canned nutritional powder developed by the activist Black comedian didn't work out, and the only steady work Aziz could find was working as a counselor at a Harlem drug clinic. Then in the early 1990s, Goldman heard that Aziz had gone back to work for the Nation of Islam, and was mystified enough that he stopped trying to maintain contact.

Now running the NOI in Chicago, Louis Farrakhan had offered Aziz a post as head of security at the Harlem mosque, which had moved to West 127th Street. A new minister had recently taken over the mosque: Benjamin F. Muhammad, previously known to the world as Ben Chavis, a former national chairman of the NAACP. As part of the job offer—which also included overseeing security at mosques up and down the East Coast—the NOI agreed to proclaim Aziz's innocence in the Malcolm case, something that it had never done during his murder trial or his twenty years in prison. "Muhammad Aziz did not kill Malcolm X," Benjamin Muhammad declared at a press conference. "Muhammad Aziz was falsely accused, wrongfully convicted and unjustly imprisoned for 20 years, and to this day is unfairly the target of racial hatred, fear, ignorance and misinformation." For the NOI, meanwhile, the appointment bought Aziz's loyalty and silence at a time when Betty Shabazz's horrific death and the bizarre events leading up to it had raised fresh questions about Farrakhan's complicity in Malcolm's murder.

If returning to the NOI offered a paycheck and some structure to Aziz's life after a period of drifting, by the 2000s he had recommitted himself to the code of independence and self-mastery that had seen him through two decades in prison. He quit the security post and plunged deeper into a life of religious study, writing, and lecturing. In 2009, Aziz published a book, *The New Song*, whose inspiration came from Abraham, the patriarch claimed by Muslims, Jews, and Christians alike. Aziz sold the book online through Amazon, which also owned the publishing house that printed copies on demand. In his online biography, Aziz said nothing about the famous name to which fate had linked him, but there were unmistakable echoes of Malcolm X in his sales pitch. "I propose the former slaves stop asking Caucasians to change their thinking and instead to do the changing of their own thinking and behavior from within, using this book and 'the New Song,'" Aziz wrote. Then he added: "I know of this injustice personally."

By the time Khalil Islam (the former Thomas 15X Johnson) came up for parole in 1985, he, too, was a changed man. When Islam had entered prison after being convicted for participating in Malcolm's murder, he was still a street-hardened brawler with a head full of the bizarre teachings of Elijah Muhammad. He believed there really was a half-mile-wide space platform called the "Mother Wheel" hovering above the earth, carrying bombs that would one day rain down on white civilization. He also took it as gospel that Wallace Fard Muhammad, the mysterious door-to-door silk salesman who had first recruited Elijah Muhammad into the Nation of Islam in Detroit, was directly descended from the Prophet Muhammad, and that the convoluted numerology he touted held the keys to understanding. In the prison yard one day, Islam asked a fellow inmate who was adept at math for help in solving an equation that the NOI founder had said could unlock the power of atomic particles. "The mathematician looked at my figures and laughed," Islam recalled in an interview with journalist Mark Jacobson. "It amused him, me trying to solve this unsolvable problem. I almost punched the guy out. Who was he to insult Fard Muhammad, put down my religion?"

As Johnson moved from prison to prison, however, fellow inmates began to initiate him into the tenets and practices of traditional Islam. He began to read the Koran seriously, and to say daily prayers according to orthodox custom. At the maximum security facility in upstate Auburn, New York, the prison imam gave Johnson a copy of the *Metaphysical Bible Dictionary*, an exploration of the roots of scriptural words and concepts by Charles Fillmore, the nineteenth-century founder of the Unity Church. Transferred to Attica, Johnson was introduced to

the writings of the Russian mystics P. D. Ouspensky and Madame Blav-
atsky. Like Malcolm X in his prison years, Johnson memorized Shakespeare. He would strain his eyes reading by the low-watt bulbs in his
jail cells, often skipping meals because he was so engrossed.

Another spiritual turning point for Johnson came in 1976, when
Wallace D. Muhammad visited Attica. Elijah Muhammad had died the
previous year, and Wallace had repudiated his father's separatist doctrine and begun to root out the self-dealing and thuggish violence that
had grown rampant within the NOI. "The Nation had become corrupt, the ministers just a bunch of money-skimming pimps," Johnson
recalled hearing. As one of Attica's imams, Johnson was appointed to
greet Wallace, who had adopted the Muslim name of Warith and called
on NOI followers to embrace the orthodox faith. As soon as Wallace
was introduced to Johnson, he recalled, "he told me to look him in the
eye and tell him whether or not I had anything to do with killing Malcolm X. I knew they were friends, so he wasn't asking just as a leader
but also as a man. I told him I didn't do it. That's when he gave me my
new name, Khalil Islam, which means 'friend of God.'"

When Islam was transferred to the notoriously harsh Dannemora
prison, he quickly became "the captain of the joint," as he put it. He
negotiated with the warden to get Muslim prisoners the right to pray
and to be served meals that conformed with their dietary laws. He also
helped broker peace agreements between prison gangs of all faiths and
colors. "If there was any trouble with the white power nuts or the Panthers, I sent out my strike teams, because in a place like Dannemora,
you can't let nothing slide," he recalled.

Like Aziz, Islam had letters of support from prison officials when
he first applied for parole. He also had the negative results of a poly-
graph test that had been paid for by Muhammad Ali, for whom Islam
had once provided security when the boxer visited the Harlem mosque.
But like Aziz, Islam ran afoul of a parole board officer who thought
anyone convicted of killing a figure as great as Malcolm X deserved to
serve more than twenty years in jail. In this case, the naysayer was the
parole board commissioner, Gerald Burke, who during Islam's hearing
went on about what Malcolm might have achieved had he lived. "You
changed history, do you understand?" Burke told Islam. "Malcolm was

an awakened spirit. . . . It's no essential difference . . . between Malcolm X and Gandhi for a segment of the population. . . . We don't know where we would be today, twenty years later, if he still had been around. . . . We would talk about Kennedy. We would talk about Sadat. . . . I'm trying to tell you, you got convicted of a heavy crime."

Listening to the lecture, Islam couldn't believe that, twenty years after Malcolm's death, a white parole board commissioner was comparing Malcolm to Mahatma Gandhi, JFK, and Anwar Sadat, the Egyptian leader assassinated for making peace with Israel. "They couldn't wait to bury Malcolm," he thought, "and now he's this great hero."

Islam was sent back to prison for two more years and didn't win parole until 1987. Once released, he found work as a drug counselor and as a religious teacher in the Bronx, but he also struggled to hold jobs for long. Then his health started to fail. He began suffering from diabetes and shortness of breath, and required a triple heart bypass operation. By the 2000s, he had moved into a seniors home in Harlem with his third wife, Helen Greene Johnson, who several times had to administer CPR to keep him alive. Yet throughout, Islam remained the stoic and realist he had always been, through twenty-two years in prison and even as far back as the murder trial, when he told Talmadge Hayer that changing his testimony wouldn't do anyone any good unless he was prepared to name names. As for Malcolm X, Islam maintained that all the speculation about what he might have achieved was moot, because by the time he arrived at the Audubon Ballroom his death had become inevitable. "He was a sitting duck," Islam told Jacobson. "God would have had to come down and pull that man out of there. That's the only way he would have survived. Everyone's got their destiny. He had his, I have mine. Our paths crossed, and we both suffered."

Islam passed away in 2009, at the age of seventy-four, just a year before Mujahid Halim (the former Talmadge Hayer) himself was finally freed from prison. Two decades earlier, Halim had been moved to a minimum security facility in Harlem and approved for a partial release program that allowed him to live and work outside for five days a week. During that time, he had made a home in the Sunset Park neighborhood of Brooklyn with a new wife and children and held down a job in a fast-food restaurant. But Halim was rejected nineteen straight times for full parole until his life sentence was reduced after forty-five years. During his decades in prison, Halim gave several interviews to reporters—starting with Peter Goldman in 1979, and including a taped exchange with the New York City broadcast journalist Gil Noble in the 1980s. But after his release, Halim made a point of not talking to the media—even as events unfolded that would at last bring justice to the two convicted men who never had anything to do with Malcolm X's murder.

In late 2017, documentary filmmaker Rachel Dretzin was looking for her next project. Over the previous decade, Dretzin had done a series of successful collaborations with Henry Louis Gates Jr., the dynamic chairman of the African American Studies Department at Harvard University. The two had made several documentaries about Black history for PBS and launched *Finding Your Roots*, a show in which Gates uses DNA samples to trace the ancestry of celebrities. Dretzin's husband, Barak Goodman, was also a documentary filmmaker, and the couple had started a small production company in Brooklyn called Ark Media. So Dretzin was intrigued when a young colleague at Ark, Hannah Olson, came to her with an idea for a new documentary: to go in search of the man who killed Malcolm X.

Olson had read Manning Marable's biography, and been struck by what Marable revealed about William Bradley, the ex–Green Beret identified in the book as the New Jersey hit man who fired the fatal gunshot blasts that cut Malcolm down in the Audubon Ballroom. After the assassination, Marable wrote, Bradley had gone on to commit a series of bank robberies and had served a long jail sentence. After he emerged from prison in 1998, however, he turned his life around. Now known by a Muslim name, Al-Mustafa Shabazz, Bradley married a well-known Black community activist in Newark named Carolyn Kelly. Shabazz helped Kelly run a boxing gym and day care center she owned, called the First Class Championship Center, and became a mentor to local youth and a respected figure in the Newark mosque and around the city. A former high school baseball star, Shabazz had been inducted into the Newark Athletic Hall of Fame, and had even appeared in a 2009 campaign video supporting the reelection of Newark's then mayor, Cory Booker.

Olson's "story concept" intrigued Dretzin, and the two began to do more digging. They discovered that Marable's information about Bradley's post-prison life came from Abdur-Rahman Muhammad, the Arlington National Cemetery tour guide and amateur historian who first disclosed what he knew about Al-Mustafa Shabazz in a 2010 blog post. While working on other civil rights documentaries, Dretzin had also come to know David Garrow, the Pulitzer Prize–winning author of the 1986 Martin Luther King Jr. biography, *Bearing the Cross*. She found the *New York Times* op-ed piece that Garrow had written in 1993, after Spike Lee's biopic came out, titled "Does Anyone Care Who Killed Malcolm X?" When Dretzin consulted Garrow about the idea of revisiting that question in documentary form, he also pointed to Abdur-Rahman Muhammad. Although not a professional historian, Garrow noted, Muhammad had been on a decade-long mission to learn everything he could about Bradley and the other four Newark hit men now widely believed by scholars to have carried out the assassination of Malcolm.

Dretzin zeroed in on a potential outlet and source of funding for the documentary: Fusion, an English-language cable TV network that had been launched in the early 2010s in a joint venture between ABC and Univision. Fusion was looking for original programming that would appeal to its target audience of urban millennials, and Gates conveniently sat on the network's advisory board. For a presentation to Fusion's executives, Ark produced a "sizzle reel": a four-minute film clip laying out the elements of the documentary. Included were brief introductory interviews with Abdur-Rahman Muhammad and Muhammad Abdul Aziz, who had been tracked down and persuaded to talk, after some reluctance, by another young Ark producer, Emily Chapman, who won Aziz over by reading his book. The reel also featured still photographs of Al-Mustafa Shabazz as he appeared at the time—rotund and bearded, like a Black Santa—with earlier fearsome-looking mug shots and archival images of Malcolm X and the Audubon Ballroom assassination. To help make the sale, Dretzin also brought on Phil Bertelsen, a longtime collaborator and fellow veteran of previous Henry Louis Gates Jr. projects, as coproducer.

Once Dretzin and Bertelsen received a green light and a modest budget from Fusion, they assembled a small team that included two gifted young producers, Shayla Harris and Nailah Sims, and a skilled archival researcher, Wyatt Stone. Together, the filmmakers immersed themselves in all the previous journalistic and legal work that had been done to expose the flaws in the original Malcolm X murder trial and convictions. They got back to Muhammad Aziz, who agreed to more interviews. They contacted the family of William Kunstler, who supplied notes that Kunstler had taken as an observer at the 1966 murder trial, and pointed to a TV appearance he had made when he was trying to get the case reopened in the 1970s. The producers had two lunches with Peter Goldman, who passed on an offer to serve as a consultant on the project because he was suspicious of their initial preoccupation with "state conspiracy theories," as he called them. But two of Manning Marable's former graduate students and book researchers, Zaheer Ali and Garrett Felber, agreed to sit for interviews. So did Baba Zak Kondo, the Malcolm obsessive who had criticized Marable's book but done so much of his own research about the assassination. After initially refusing, because he wanted to save his Malcolm scoops for his own book, Les Payne also agreed to an interview. But on the morning a film crew was scheduled to meet him, the producers learned that Payne had suffered a fatal heart attack the night before.

Abdur-Rahman Muhammad, the lay historian, was eager to participate, and he offered the prospect of a dramatic narrative arc and ending to the documentary. After years of tracking down information about the former William Bradley, Abdur-Rahman would travel to Newark, find Bradley living under his new name, Al-Mustafa Shabazz, and personally confront him with evidence of his past. But Dretzin and Bertelsen knew that relying on Muhammad to "carry" the documentary involved challenges. He was a passionate but inexperienced interview subject, so they did multiple screen tests to determine what parts of the story he could narrate himself, and what they would need to tell with their own interviews and archival footage. To establish credibility with professional historians, they persuaded Garrow to testify on camera to his respect for Abdur-Rahman's research. The biggest unknown was what they would find when they sent cameras into inner-city Newark with Muhammad to search for people who might know Al-Mustafa Shabazz, and to see how many were aware of the allegations against him.

Because Muhammad was a practicing Muslim, he was able to attend prayers at the Newark mosque and start asking around. It quickly became clear that Shabazz was well known and widely liked within the community, but almost no one wanted to talk about his past. Some of the local mosque members refused to appear on camera, and those who did tried to wave Abdur-Rahman off. "Malcolm's assassination? We don't dwell on that. That's a waste," he was told by Earl Siddiq, a former member of Mosque No. 25. "It's in the history books. Leave it there. Move on."

Interviewed by Dretzin and Bertelsen, Newark mayor Ras Baraka— the son of the late Black poet and activist Amiri Baraka—acknowledged that he had seen Shabazz "in the community" and knew of his reputation as the "shotgun dude." But Baraka preferred not to hear more. "Some of that stuff can be dangerous," he said. "That's why I don't like to deal with gossip." The producers also interviewed Cory Booker, now a U.S. senator, and showed him the video of Shabazz in his campaign ad. "I know him well," Booker responded. But he seemed genuinely surprised to learn that Shabazz was alleged to have been among Malcolm's assassins. "You are breaking news to me," Booker said, before saying carefully that he hoped the producers would "get to the truth . . . but not jump to conclusions about anybody."

After a year of slowly putting pieces together, however, the filmmakers believed they had amassed enough evidence to demonstrate to viewers that Al-Mustafa Shabazz had been William Bradley, and that Bradley was Malcolm's killer. They had found footage shot outside the Audubon Ballroom after the murder that appeared to show a shadowy figure with Bradley's dark skin and stocky build walking away without anyone noticing. They had gathered archival material to tell Bradley's life story, from his high school yearbook picture, to newspaper stories about his arrests and later good deeds. They had filmed the shuttered boxing gym that Al-Mustafa had helped run and the home where he now lived in Newark, a two-story brick house with a small yard and a towering white metal gate. Using phone cameras to remain inconspicuous, the producers had even captured fresh footage of Shabazz. With a long white beard but still barrel-chested in his seventies, he came to the gate of his house to pick up a Postal Service package, dressed in jeans and wearing a dark green leather baseball cap with the insignia of the Tuskegee Airmen.

But then in October 2018, just as the producers were about to film their planned ending—an on-camera encounter with Abdur-Rahman Muhammad—Al-Mustafa Shabazz died of undisclosed natural causes. The producers realized they needed a new focus and ending for the documentary. So instead of merely the search for a killer, they decided to tell the broader story, largely ignored since the efforts of William Kunstler and Peter Goldman in the late 1970s, of how two innocent men had been wrongly convicted for Malcolm's murder. "If there's any kind of linchpin to what made the series a success, it was actually [Al-Mustafa Shabazz's] death," Bertelsen recalled. "We set out to find the man who killed Malcolm X. We were going to track him down and ultimately confront him, but he dies on our watch. Consequently, our film turns from who killed Malcolm X to who didn't. Because we had amassed all his evidence about who had done the crime, and who didn't, and nobody was doing anything about it. All this evidence was hiding in plain sight, much like the killer. But no one was really connecting the dots."

If Dretzin and Bertelsen were going to widen the focus of their documentary, they needed more time, and that meant more money. But by late 2018, the Fusion network was on the verge of financial collapse. The only leverage the producers had was that Fusion had sold the rights to re-air the documentary, after its initial run on the network, to the then rapidly growing streaming service Netflix. For Fusion to receive this "second window" payment, the documentary had to be completed. "It really got to the point where we were trying to get blood from a stone," Bertelsen recalled, "because Fusion was on death's door, and they were only leaving the lights on for us." So Gates offered to set up a meeting with Fusion's executives and the producers so they could make their case. The three arrived first, and Gates instructed Dretzin and Bertelsen to let him take the lead. After everyone helped themselves to a buffet lunch, Gates guided the conversation, allowing the producers to make their plea but making sure that no final answers were demanded. Watching the artful dance, and then hearing shortly afterward that Fusion had agreed to "a little more time and a little more money," Bertelsen was reminded why Gates had such a formidable track record raising money both inside and outside the world of academia. "It was like a lesson in diplomacy," Bertelsen recalled. "I'll never forget it."

Once Al-Mustafa Shabazz was dead, the shadowy wall of silence that had protected him became more visible to the filmmakers. They knew Shabazz had reinvented himself as an influential figure in Black Newark, but they had no idea how influential until the day of his funeral. A huge crowd showed up for the memorial service, and afterward the coffin was transported in a glass horse-drawn carriage to the stately Glendale Cemetery on the outskirts of the city. There, elegantly dressed admirers took turns shoveling dirt into a grave before it was covered by a large headstone. Filming the day's proceedings from a distance with his iPhone, Bertelsen noticed black town cars with government license plates and strapping men with radio earpieces milling about. He realized that New Jersey lieutenant governor Sheila Oliver—the highest-ranking Black official in the state—was attending the funeral. When the producers reached out to Oliver later for an interview, she admitted knowing about Shabazz's connection to Malcolm's assassination and conceded that it was an "open secret" around Newark, but she defended his hero's send-off nonetheless. "In death," Oliver said, "people remembered what he had done for so many people and families."

After Shabazz's passing, longtime members of Mosque No. 25 also began to speak more freely to Abdur-Rahman Muhammad. They suggested that people in the Muslim community of Newark had stayed silent about Bradley and the other hit men at the time of the assassination because many still revered Elijah Muhammad and thought that Malcolm had been foolish and disloyal to turn against him. After keeping his distance at first, Walid Muslim, one of the original founders of the Newark mosque, agreed to a filmed interview at a local diner. "I knew [Malcolm] had a big head, you know," Muslim said. "But I never thought he would go against the Honorable Elijah Muhammad. And, you know, this is the kind of town where you don't play with that. . . . You do, there's a price to pay."

At the same time, the veterans of the Newark mosque continued to praise and defend Elijah Muhammad, insisting that he had nothing to do with Malcolm's murder. They also suggested that a hit squad made up of members of the Fruit of Islam would not necessarily have had orders from the Newark minister, James Shabazz, even though he had publicly denounced Malcolm as a "chief hypocrite" who deserved to be silenced. "Knowing how the Nation moves . . . I would think that if there was anybody who was involved, in the contrary, you want to move independent of the minister," explained Q. Amini Nathari, another former mosque member. "FOI would never do anything that would come back on Nation leadership."

Beyond the cover-up in Newark, Dretzin and Bertelsen also expanded their focus to explore the long-swirling questions about the role of law enforcement in the Malcolm X case. The first was why there was such a minimal police presence at the Audubon Ballroom. The producers had come across a 1972 documentary, *Red Squad*, in which a crew embedded with BOSSI, the intelligence unit of the NYPD. It featured a detective named Tony Bouza, who had previously been in charge of BOSSI's surveillance of Malcolm. Now retired and in his seventies, Bouza at first didn't want to participate in the new project, but he agreed after the producers of *Red Squad* vouched for their fellow documentarians. Bouza may have come to regret that decision, after Dretzin interviewed him and elicited some remarkable admissions about BOSSI's cavalier attitude toward Malcolm's safety just a week after his house had been firebombed.

"You knew he was in grave mortal danger?" Dretzin asked, referring to Malcolm.

"No question," Bouza responded.

"Didn't you see yourselves as duty-bound to protect this man from an imminent death threat?" Dretzin asked.

"I wouldn't say 'I didn't see that,'" Bouza said. "All I could see was the expense. That's really all I could see. We can't afford it. It's twenty-four-seven, cops, detectives. Can't do it."

Then Bouza confessed to playing what he called "my cleverest note." He knew Malcolm didn't want an extra police presence at the Audubon Ballroom because he worried it would scare away followers. But Bouza offered the protection to Malcolm's aides anyway, so their refusal could be documented in police records.

"It was a cynical gesture, for sure," Bouza said. "Me offering him something I knew he would refuse, and that I expected and wanted him to refuse."

"Why did you know he would refuse it?" Dretzin asked.

"I knew Malcolm!" Bauza replied.

The second law enforcement question was why the prosecution focused so narrowly on convicting the trio of Hayer, Butler, and Johnson (the future Mujahid Abdul Halim, Muhammad Abdul Aziz, and Khalil Islam), relying only on ballistics evidence and the fragmented testimony of eyewitnesses to the chaotic murder scene. In another booking coup, Dretzin tracked down Herbert J. Stern, the district attorney who had overseen the case and was now in private practice after a long career as a judge. Agreeing to an interview in the moody setting of a dimly lit New Jersey restaurant, Stern testily defended the limited scope of his prosecution. "There was no physical evidence to be found," Stern recalled. "People can pick over that all they want, but that's all there was to it."

Yet as the filmmakers discovered, Stern and the other prosecutors didn't have access to all the information that had been gathered by law enforcement. The producers resurfaced the revelation from the early 1970s that Gene Roberts, the bodyguard who had tried to resuscitate Malcolm, was a BOSSI informant, but that BOSSI didn't volunteer him as a witness in order to preserve his cover. A retired FBI agent named Arthur Fulton, who worked in a unit devoted to surveilling Malcolm, also cooperated with the filmmakers. Although Fulton declined to be interviewed on camera, he gave an audio account of how he recruited Black informants inside and around the Harlem mosque, and how he met them to exchange information in basement garages and dark movie theaters. Fulton boasted that the FBI had as many as nine informants inside the Audubon Ballroom on the day of the assassination, but suggested that some of their identities were never shared with the NYPD.

In his interview with Dretzin, Tony Bouza confirmed the FBI withheld information from the NYPD. "Getting information from the FBI was always difficult for us," he recalled. "They played at compliance. They were very pleasant, but they'd never give us anything." Bouza described how FBI agents would pay routine visits to the NYPD intelligence unit's offices to go through their files, but offer nothing in return. "It was a one-way street," he recalled. "There was no sharing. Sharing implies give and take. This was all take, no give."

That raised a third question: *What might the FBI have known that it never shared with prosecutors or with the NYPD?* When Dretzin and Bertelsen began making requests for declassified FBI files that mentioned the Newark mosque, they found some explosive answers. In early March 1965, weeks after Malcolm's assassination, an FBI agent in Boston had interviewed a former NOI member named Leon 4X Ameer. Ameer described attending Malcolm's funeral and running into an acquaintance from Mosque No. 25 who told him that the killer had been a lieutenant in the Newark Fruit of Islam. According to the FBI report, Ameer said his source described "the Negro who handled the shotgun as a lieutenant in the Newark Temple," and revealed that the gunman was "tall" and "dark-skinned" and "shot from the hip and appeared to be an expert in the handling of this type of gun."

Once Al-Mustafa Shabazz was dead, the producers were also able to request FBI files relating to him individually under the rules of the Freedom of Information Act. Sure enough, within the overall "Malcolm Little" file they discovered reports showing that by the time of his murder, FBI agents in Newark had identified a "William 25X Bradley" as an "officer at MM 25" and "a Lieutenant of the FOI at the mosque." Bradley was described as having a "dark brown" complexion and "stocky" build. The reports also showed that no one at the FBI was in a hurry to share information about Bradley or the Leon Ameer tip with police or prosecutors in New York City. In April, a memo directly from the office of J. Edgar Hoover instructed his New York agents to find out if Ameer had talked to the NYPD—and, if not, to refrain from sharing any information relating to his Newark intelligence "without first receiving Bureau authority." By August, Newark agents informed the director's office that the investigation into their Newark suspect had been closed, or "RUC" ("Reviewed Upon Completion") in bureau jargon. In that last memo, the name of the suspect had been "redacted," or blacked out.

In the finished documentary, Abdur-Rahman would suggest that all this evidence raised the question of whether Bradley was an FBI informant. Based on the newly uncovered FBI files, the same could be asked about Leon 4X Ameer. Born Leon Lionel Phillips, Ameer was a short, pudgy thirty-one-year-old with a brash tongue who had served as a bodyguard for Malcolm X and as a spokesman for Muhammad Ali when Malcolm was advising the boxer. After Malcolm's split with the NOI, Ameer was sent to establish an outpost of the Organization of Afro-American Unity in Boston, where he was beaten bloody by a local Fruit of Islam gang after he publicly criticized the NOI leadership in Chicago. Following Malcolm's murder, Ameer was the most vocal of his followers to vow revenge against the NOI—going so far as to issue a death threat to Elijah Muhammad that appeared in the story that Peter Goldman wrote for *Newsweek* that week. "We are going to repay them for what they did to Malcolm; I don't know if he'll live out the month," Ameer raged, referring to Elijah Muhammad.

Three weeks later, a chambermaid found Ameer dead in his room at the Sheraton Biltmore in Boston. A medical examiner ruled that he had slipped into a coma brought on by an epileptic fit or an overdose of sleeping pills. But if there was no foul play involved, Ameer's death certainly came at a convenient time both for the NOI and the FBI. For also included in the FBI report from Boston that the filmmakers uncovered was the disclosure that Ameer was placed in "protective custody" during his trip to New York for Malcolm's funeral, with the information about who had provided that protection blacked out.

With all the interviews, documents, and archival material they had amassed, Dretzin and Bertelsen now had to figure out how to put the story together in the editing room. One of their editors, Brian Funck, had worked on a *Frontline* documentary in which an American journalist whose brother perished in the 1988 Libyan bombing of Pan Am Flight 103 over Lockerbie, Scotland, went in search of the lone terrorist convicted for that attack. Funck created a similar feel of a lonely detective story, with lots of shots of Abdur-Rahman wandering pensively around Newark and Washington, D.C., and poring over documents in police and FBI archives and the Pittsburgh home of David Garrow. Although the approach took liberties with the actual sequence and means by which much of the information was discovered, it gave the documentary a compelling narrative momentum.

The final piece of the storytelling puzzle was to decide how to end the series, now that the original goal of having Abdur-Rahman confront the former William Bradley was no longer possible. Once Dretzin and Bertelsen switched their focus to who didn't kill Malcolm X, they realized that an ideal end point—for the documentary, and for the cause of justice—would be to get legal authorities to reopen the murder case based on the evidence they had unearthed. Manhattan's district attorney Cy Vance had run for office in 2009 promising to do more to correct wrongful convictions, and once elected he had set up a ten-person unit within the D.A.'s office called the Conviction Integrity Program (CIP). So the producers decided to submit a formal petition to the CIP to revisit the Malcolm case.

To proceed, however, they needed the cooperation of Muhammad Aziz, and he was deeply skeptical. In May 2019, the producers filmed Abdur-Rahman as he sat on a park bench and presented Aziz with a copy of the petition.

"I just don't believe in these people," Aziz said. "I've got twenty years of my life to demonstrate that I shouldn't believe in them."

"I believe there's a benefit in correcting the historical record," Abdur-Rahman said. "The history of your family. The history of who you were. That's an injustice that follows you forever."

"I agree with all that," Aziz replied. "I hear you. . . . It's just hard for me to believe, because these are lying people."

Shrugging his shoulders, Aziz finally agreed to let Abdur-Rahman move forward.

"How would you feel?" Abdur-Rahman asked, imagining a favorable outcome.

"I have no idea," Aziz responded. "It's got to show up first. And when it shows up, I'll let you know."

In the three months left before the documentary was scheduled to air on Fusion, nothing did show up. One of the producers on the film, Nailah Sims, ran into an acquaintance who worked for the Conviction Integrity Program and asked if the letter had been received, but there was no official response. Dretzin and Bertelsen also put out feelers to law firms that specialized in wrongful conviction cases, but none of them showed immediate interest. "We don't take cases we can't win," an attorney for one prominent firm told Bertelsen—a blunt admission of how lawyers get paid in the wrongful conviction business, by bringing suits for financial settlements after their clients are exonerated.

But one lawyer did take the chance to reopen the case seriously: Mark O'Donoghue, the white-shoe attorney who had represented Aziz for thirty-five years. O'Donoghue had heard about the documentary and the CIP petition, and over the summer of 2019 he began his own search for a lawyer who might represent Aziz in a wrongful conviction review. In August, O'Donoghue met with Dretzin and Bertelsen, and they invited him to a premiere of their film hosted by the Fusion network at Harlem's Schomburg Center on the night of September 27. The documentary received a standing ovation, and afterward Henry Louis Gates Jr. moderated a discussion with the filmmakers, Aziz, and Abdur-Rahman Muhammad. Malcolm's daughter Ilyasah Shabazz also attended—a sign to the politically savvy O'Donoghue that the world of family loyalists was getting behind the film and might not object to seeing Aziz get a new hearing. O'Donoghue had also watched the law profession change over the decades, becoming more honest about the country's long history of wrongful convictions, and sensitive to the need to correct the past in order to maintain credibility in the present. After all this time, O'Donoghue thought, the winds might finally be shifting in Aziz's favor.

=====

Two nights later, on September 29, O'Donoghue attended a dinner to celebrate Rosh Hashanah, the Jewish New Year, hosted by his friend Peter Aschkenasy, a veteran city parks administrator and restaurant owner. He was on the board of an organization that O'Donoghue chaired called the Fedcap Group that worked to train and secure jobs for people with disabilities. At the dinner, O'Donoghue sat next to Madeline "Maddy" deLone, the executive director of the Innocence Project, the pioneering wrongful conviction organization. For almost two decades, deLone had run the day-to-day operations of the Innocence Project for its founders, Barry Scheck and Peter Neufeld, the lawyers who had become famous for helping defend O. J. Simpson and for winning exoneration for the so-called Central Park Five, the young Black and Hispanic men sent to prison for raping a white jogger in a case that made national headlines in the late 1980s. O'Donoghue had never met deLone, but he found himself describing Aziz's case and all the exculpatory evidence that would be exposed in the *Who Killed Malcolm X?* documentary. Wrongful conviction work wasn't his specialty, O'Donoghue explained, and he was planning to retire from the firm soon, but he was hoping to find a lawyer to represent Aziz if Cy Vance's office agreed to reopen the case.

DeLone sounded intrigued but pointed out that the Innocence Project specialized in investigations that involved DNA evidence, of which O'Donoghue admitted there was none in the Malcolm murder case. DeLone also indicated that she herself was planning to retire from the Innocence Project soon. Still, O'Donoghue came away from the conversation encouraged. He continued to make inquiries with defense attorneys he had met in another public service sideline in the 1990s: vetting candidates for federal judgeships and U.S. district attorney jobs for Senator Chuck Schumer, before Schumer made recommendations to President Clinton.

One person who had come up in O'Donoghue's search for a lawyer to represent Aziz was David Shanies, a young white attorney who had made a name for himself challenging wrongful convictions in the Brooklyn courts. When the two lawyers finally met in early October, Shanies expressed interest in taking on Aziz's case but pointed out the huge effort that it would involve, given the lack of DNA or other physical evidence. Lawyers would have to reexamine decades-old police work; to revisit the testimony of scores of witnesses, most of whom were now dead; and to scour through thousands of pages of records in the files of the NYPD, the police intelligence unit BOSSI, and the FBI. So Shanies suggested reaching back out to Barry Scheck to propose a joint effort that would spread the work and also give the investigation the credibility and media attention that the Innocence Project could bring.

Once Shanies signed on and Scheck agreed to assist, things moved rapidly. In January 2020, Shanies and Scheck met with Vance and Charles King, the head of the D.A.'s Conviction Integrity Program, to make their pitch. The lawyers offered to work jointly with the CIP to conduct an investigation, given the huge workload involved. By that time, word of the evidence unearthed in the *Who Killed Malcolm X?* documentary had also started to filter through the D.A.'s office, so Vance grasped the urgency as well as the merits of the request. Within weeks, he decided to authorize a new investigation, and King offered to get personally involved. Shanies and Scheck were also heartened when King agreed to bring on Peter Casolaro, a forensics specialist who had become renowned for his work in winning exoneration for the Central Park Five.

The lack of surviving physical evidence, and the amount of time that had elapsed since the assassination, presented steep hurdles for the investigators. Any hope of preserving fingerprints or DNA evidence from the original crime scene had been eliminated when, incredibly, the police allowed the Audubon Ballroom staff to clean the premises and host a dance on the night of the murder. The bullet-ridden rostrum behind which Malcolm had stood was moved to the ballroom's basement, where it remained unexamined for decades. Although police at the time found the 12-gauge shotgun used in the murder, wrapped in a coat and stashed in a room off the ballroom stage, all traces of that weapon had disappeared by 2020. So had any sign of the .45 automatic pistol seized by Ronald Timberlake, the FBI informant who took it home and later arranged for it to be turned over to the NYPD. The missing third weapon—the 9mm Luger—had never been located, and the three Malcolm bodyguards who were said to have had custody of the gun at one time or another were all dead.

Key police and prosecution records had gone missing, or never existed in the first place. There were no photographs of police lineups, or accounts of what witnesses were shown or told before they were asked to identify Aziz and Islam. (In his interview with the investigators, Aziz would recall never being placed in a formal lineup, only kept in the room with a mirror.) Nor was there any indication that the suspects were informed of their right to have legal representatives present during any identification procedures, which would become the law of the land the following year with the Supreme Court's 1967 decision in *United States v. Wade*. In a case that turned almost entirely on eyewitness testimony, most of the people who had testified at the trial were dead, as were the prosecutors and defense attorneys. Key players involved in the attempt to get the case reopened in the 1970s had passed away, too, including William Kunstler and the two men who rejected his legal petitions: Manhattan district attorney Robert Morgenthau and Judge Harold Rothwax.

Then the Covid pandemic struck, slowing down the entire process and complicating attempts to interview sources who were still alive. Although dozens of lawyers and researchers were involved in one way or the other—including a group of young attorneys from the law firm WilmerHale, who provided services pro bono—six principals led the investigation: Shanies and his colleague Deborah Francois; Scheck and Vanessa Potkin from the Innocence Project; and King and Casolaro from the D.A.'s office. If the six needed to plot strategy or review progress, they now had to meet on Zoom. Shanies and Francois conducted scores of interviews online or on the phone, but some sources were important or sensitive enough that they still wanted to meet with them in person. So before vaccines became available, they took elaborate precautions to fly, travel, and safely mask for face-to-face interviews.

One of those interviews was with a witness who never testified during the trial but who offered new corroboration of Aziz's alibi that he was at home in the Bronx on the day of the assassination. The source, who would be identified in the findings of the investigation with the initials "J.M.," was an NOI member who had volunteered to man the phones at the Harlem mosque on the day of the murder. Shortly after news started to spread that Malcolm had been shot, Aziz phoned the mosque, the source recalled. He asked to speak to Captain Joseph X, the NOI security chief. The man on phone duty then took down Aziz's number in the Bronx and called it back minutes later after tracking down Captain Joseph X.

Shanies also made several trips to interview Peter Goldman at his apartment in Gramercy Park. Retired now and spending his days writing detective novels, Goldman had been living alone ever since his beloved wife, Helen Dudar, died of breast cancer in 2002. Peter shared memories of the interviews that he and Helen had conducted with Malcolm before the assassination, and let Shanies review notebooks containing scores of interviews for his book. For Shanies, Goldman's notes and memories helped paint a picture of the personalities and mindsets of detectives, prosecutors, and defense attorneys who were no longer around to be interviewed. They also confirmed how attached the rank-and-file NYPD cops and prosecutors were to the narrow explanation of a turf war between Malcolm and the Harlem mosque—and how blind or willfully ignorant they were to evidence that BOSSI, the NYPD intelligence unit, and the FBI had gathered pointing away from Aziz and Khalil.

As far as Goldman was concerned, FBI files available by then proved that Elijah Muhammad was responsible for the assassination, even if he hadn't directly ordered the hit. With the assistance of Paul Lee—the Malcolm expert who had done extensive research for Spike Lee and later for Les Payne—Goldman had made that argument in an expanded preface to a third edition of *The Death and Life of Malcolm X*, published in 2013. In June 1964, the Messenger's son Elijah Jr. convened the meeting of Fruit of Islam chiefs at which he invited the participants to "cut the nigger's tongue out" and bring it to the Messenger. Then in August, Elijah Sr. presided over a marathon gathering in Chicago called the Laborers Meeting, at which he delivered the same message personally, if more elliptically. "If I'm attacked, you should attack the attacker," he instructed. "As the Holy Qu'ran plainly teaches us, mere belief counts for nothing unless carried into practice." Then in December, FBI agents reported, the Messenger himself wrote the infamous article in *Muhammad Speaks* that was attributed to the future Louis Farrakhan. According to the agents, Muhammad told Farrakhan that he should consider it an "honor" to deliver what amounted to an official kill order: "The die is set and Malcolm shall not escape. Such a man is worthy of death."

Shanies and the reinvestigation team were looking for evidence that might have changed the outcome of the murder trial, however, and they found it in numerous FBI files pointing toward New Jersey. On February 22, 1965—the day after the assassination—an internal FBI memo reported that "the killers of Malcolm X were possibly imported to NYC." The same report described the hit man who wielded the shotgun as "a negro male, age twenty-eight, six feet two inches, two hundred pounds, heavy build, dark complexion, wearing a gray coat." That profile didn't fit the light-skinned, medium-built Khalil Islam (the former Thomas 15X Johnson), who was pegged as the man who fired the shotgun during the trial. It more closely matched William Bradley, whose name and description could be found in reports from the FBI bureau in Newark dating back to 1963. Another FBI memo, dated March 4, two weeks after the murder, described the NYPD as looking for an accomplice nicknamed "Turk," then confirmed that Newark agents believed that person to be Leon Davis, from the Paterson mosque.

The reinvestigation team unearthed new evidence that J. Edgar Hoover personally intervened to keep the FBI from sharing the New Jersey intelligence with New York police and prosecutors. Like the *Who Killed Malcolm X?* filmmakers, they found that Hoover had instructed his New York agents to keep the NYPD in the dark concerning Leon Ameer's tip about the involvement of a "lieutenant from the Newark temple." An FBI special agent named August "Gus" Micek was also dispatched to go through the NYPD intelligence unit's files to search for any evidence of William Bradley. When Micek didn't find any, he was told not to share any of the FBI's intelligence about Bradley.

The FBI continued to conceal what it knew about Bradley into the late 1970s, when William Kunstler and Peter Goldman tried to get the murder case reopened, the reinvestigation team found. By then, the existence of the FBI's extensive campaign to surveil and sabotage Black civil rights groups, known as COINTELPRO, had been exposed in televised congressional hearings led by Idaho senator Frank Church. Yet when the FBI was asked if it had any information about the New Jersey suspects named by Mujahid Halim in its still classified or redacted files, a special agent named Steven Edwards told New York prosecutors no such records existed.

District Attorney Robert Morgenthau then relied on Edwards's assurances in rejecting Kunstler's petitions. "There is nothing in any of these unredacted FBI documents which in any way supports any of the defendants' contentions or allegations," Morgenthau insisted. "Specifically, there is no mention or indication of the name of, or reference to, any of the persons identified by [Halim] in his affidavits as having been his accomplices in the murder of Malcolm X." Based on Morgenthau's finding, Judge Rothwax ruled that revisiting the convictions wasn't warranted because the newly named suspects "were never the object of suspicion despite the thorough efforts of local, state and federal law enforcement officials."

Between the suppressed clues to the Newark connection, the fresh corroboration of Aziz's alibi, and a trail of error in police procedure, after twenty-two months Shanies and the reinvestigation team had given the Conviction Integrity Program more than enough evidence to compile a forty-three-page report recommending that the convictions of Muhammad Aziz and Khalil Islam be overturned. By the fall of 2021, a deadline to file the motion also loomed. In early November, prosecutor Alvin Bragg won the election to succeed Cy Vance as Manhattan district attorney. If Vance was going to support the exonerations and show public remorse on behalf of the justice system, he had only weeks to do so before he left office.

FIFTEEN

An Apology

The events that unfolded in lower Manhattan on the warm, sunny fall day of November 18, 2021, would hardly put an end to the questions surrounding the assassination of Malcolm X. A year later, the city and state of New York would acknowledge the role that their police and prosecutors played in the undeserved fates of Muhammad Aziz and Khalil Islam, and would agree to pay financial damages to Aziz and to Islam's family together totaling $36 million. But when David Shanies sued the U.S. government over the FBI's role in 2023, the Department of Justice would immediately move to dismiss the case. The feds would argue that the statute of limitations had run out, and that the alleged harm wasn't covered by the Federal Torts Claims Act, a long-shot law that allows individuals in very limited cases to seek redress from the federal government. Meanwhile, the daughters of Malcolm X would retain the services of Ben Crump, the media-savvy Black personal injury and wrongful conviction attorney, in hopes of one day finding the long-imagined smoking-gun evidence that would prove that the police and the FBI had a direct hand in Malcolm's murder and would lead to a monetary settlement for the decades of loss and distress suffered by the Shabazz family.

For now, however, history had arrived at a drab, drafty courtroom inside the cavernous Manhattan Criminal Courthouse at 100 Centre Street. Outside, television news crews waited for a glimpse of Muhammad Aziz, who was semiretired now and had married a social worker from Baltimore named Paula McLellan. Finally a black town car pulled up and out stepped Aziz, along with Paula and lawyer David Shanies. Aziz was dressed in a waist-length dark green Islámic jubba jacket, and wore tinted glasses and a gray beard that elegantly balanced his shaved head. Two grown sons of Khalil Islam also arrived to represent their father, who had died twelve years too early to experience vindication.

Inside the courtroom, television producers set up more cameras in a corner, whispering under their breath about how to sneak angles that hadn't been approved by hovering guards. A new outbreak of Covid required everyone present to wear masks, but it hadn't kept away the key participants in the two investigations that had made the day possible. At a wooden desk in the front of the room sat District Attorney Cy Vance and Charles King of the Conviction Integrity Program, along with D.A. General Counsel Carey Dunne. An another table sat Aziz, flanked by David Shanies and Deborah Francois on one side, and Barry Scheck and Vanessa Potkin of the Innocence Project on the other. In the audience, along with Paula Aziz, sat lawyer Mark O'Donoghue and the documentary filmmakers Rachel Dretzin and Phil Bertelsen, and Abdur-Rahman Muhammad.

The clerk called the court to order and announced the hearing to consider "indictment number 871 of 1965"—the original docket number for the Malcolm X murder case. Ellen Biben, the New York County Supreme Court administrative judge, came into the room, wearing a purple mask and taking the bench behind a protective barrier. Biben asked all the lawyers before her to identify themselves, and then Cy Vance stood to summarize the exoneration motion and to deliver an earnest statement of remorse. "I want to begin by saying to Mr. Aziz, and his family, and the family of Mr. Islam, and the family of Malcolm X, that I apologize for what were serious, unacceptable violations of law and the public trust," Vance said. "I apologize on behalf of our nation's law enforcement for this decades-long injustice, which has eroded public faith in institutions that are designed to guarantee equal protection under the law. . . . Your Honor, we can't restore what was taken away from these men and their families, but by correcting the record perhaps we can begin to restore that faith."

The lawyers for Aziz and Islam's family spoke next. David Shanies thanked everyone involved in the twenty-two-month investigation, along with the documentary filmmakers and Al Vann, the former city councilman and state senator who had cried foul about the convictions for four decades. Barry Scheck pointed out that if the FBI's cover-ups in the Malcolm X case had been uncovered at the time, it might have helped expose the notorious COINTELPRO program of disruption and dirty tricks that continued to be unleashed against Black activist leaders and groups into the 1970s. Vanessa Potkin and Deborah Francois stressed the damage done to the families of Aziz and Islam, which would later be cited as justification for the huge financial settlements sought from the city and the state.

Finally Aziz rose to speak, reading words he had carefully written out on paper but had been in his heart for more than a half century. "The events that brought us to court today should never have occurred," he said.

> Those events were, and are, the result of a process that was corrupt to its core, one that is all too familiar to Black people in 2021. While I do not need this court, these prosecutors or a piece of paper to tell me that I'm innocent, I'm very glad that my family, my friends and the attorneys who have worked to support me over these years, are finally seeing the truth that we have all known officially recognized. I'm an 83-year-old man who was victimized by the criminal justice system, and I do not know how many years of creative activity I have. However, I hope that the same system that was responsible for this travesty of justice will also take responsibility for immeasurable harm caused to me during the past fifty-five, or fifty-six, years. Thank you, your Honor.

All eyes turned to the bench as Judge Biben delivered her ruling. She began slowly and densely, with a long explanation of the court's limited powers and citations of legal precedent indicating how sparingly it should be used. But then suddenly Biben's language turned eloquent and to the point. "There can be no question that this is a case that cries out for fundamental justice," she said. "To Mr. Aziz and your family, and to the family of Mr. Islam, I regret that this court cannot fully undo the serious miscarriages of justice in this case, and give you back the many years that were lost. Dismissal of the indictment is the full extent of this court's authority. But for the reasons set forth in the joint application and based on the record that has been made today, this court's mandate requires that the judgments of convictions be vacated and that the indictment against Mr. Aziz and Mr. Islam be dismissed. The joint motion is hereby granted."

With those words, loud applause broke out in the courtroom. Aziz nodded his head slightly, then leaned back in his chair as his chest lifted in what looked ever so much like a sigh of relief. Shanies reached out to pat Aziz on the shoulder, while Scheck grabbed his arm to shake his hand. Potkin whispered her congratulations into Aziz's ear, and Francois wiped a tear from her eye.

In the two years that Shanies had been working with Aziz, he had never seen his client appear anything but stoic. Aziz always exuded the sense of discipline he had learned in the Navy and that had seen him through twenty years behind bars, all the time thinking of himself as a prisoner of war. But as the two men filed out of the courtroom and Aziz greeted his wife and children, Shanies saw what looked like happiness on his client's face for the first time. Ever since the two met, Shanies had aways sensed that Aziz never really needed what he saw as a corrupt justice system to confirm what he already knew. But now he saw just how important it was to Aziz for his children and grandchildren to know the truth about their father and grandfather, and to have it publicly acknowledged before the world.

Outside the courtroom, Aziz took off his mask and smiled wide for the television news cameras and posed with the lawyers and film producers, and with his children and grandchildren with whom he was still in the long process of reconciling after so many lost years. But the Aziz family resisted the calls from the reporters to come to the microphones, instead leaving it to Khalil Islam's more voluble sons to give the journalists the quotes that were wanted for the evening news broadcasts and next day's newspapers. After a few minutes, Aziz and his entourage climbed into waiting town cars and headed to a Middle Eastern restaurant uptown where the lawyers had booked an upstairs room for a private celebration.

A year away from turning ninety, with a weak heart and a fear of Covid, Peter Goldman had resisted the temptation to attend the exoneration hearing. But he had accepted an invitation from Shanies to attend the private celebration at the restaurant. A car service dropped Goldman off, and he shuffled inside and announced that he was there to see Muhammad Aziz. When Aziz got the word that Goldman had arrived, his face lit up. Shanies went downstairs to escort Goldman up, but Peter confessed that he didn't think his "bum ticker," as he jokingly put it, was strong enough to climb the stairs.

Shanies went back up to explain the situation, and Aziz immediately volunteered to go downstairs and meet with Goldman privately. "That really showed me how meaningful that relationship was," Shanies recalled. "Because Muhammad doesn't react to most people the way he reacted to Peter. It was just very clear to me how much Peter's presence and support over this entire period meant to Muhammad. They definitely shared a very special moment."

As soon as Aziz saw Goldman waiting at the bar, he reached out to him, and Peter reached up to his much taller friend. "We bro hugged!" Goldman recalled. Then they sat and reminisced about their long journey together. Goldman apologized for losing touch after Aziz got out of prison and rejoined the Nation of Islam. Aziz told Peter that he had just taken the job as a "favor" to old friends in the NOI, and that he regretted the interruption in their friendship, too.

The two bro-hugged again, and then the car service took Goldman back to his Gramercy Park apartment, where he spent the rest of the day thinking of Helen and wishing she could have been there to see this day. Aziz went back upstairs to the private room to keep celebrating with the children and grandchildren he once thought he had lost. The challenges of old age that Malcolm X never lived to see lay ahead for both Aziz and Goldman. But for now, justice had finally shown up, and it felt good.

Epilogue

I n February 1965, Jane Relin and Ellen Friedman were juniors at Barnard preparing for careers in science or medicine. Relin, who had grown up in Rochester, New York, was majoring in chemistry. Friedman, who then went by her maiden name, Wolkin, hailed from Albany and was a zoology major. But both women were also among the students at the predominantly white women's college who wanted to do something to support the civil rights movement, and had become active in a program called Student Exchange. Over winter break each year, the program sent a small group of students to visit two schools in the South, one Black and the one white. Then in the first week of the spring semester, the Barnard students brought a handful of students back from those schools for a week of observing classes, getting tours of New York City, and engaging in group discussions about the contrast between racial conditions in the South and the North.

After Relin became head of Student Exchange that fall, she and her friend Ellen had set out to expand its ambitions. Friedman organized a "Saturday Afternoon Zoo Program" that recruited Barnard students to spend part of their weekends taking kids from Harlem to sites such as the Bronx Zoo, the Columbia University radio station, and the Staten Island Ferry. To educate the students about the housing crisis in New York City, Relin arranged for tours of tenement buildings and interviews with both rent strikers and representatives of slumlords. Once the two Southern schools for that year's program were chosen—the

historically Black Tougaloo College in Mississippi, and white Ogle-
thorpe University in Atlanta—Relin and Friedman also sent out letters
to civil rights leaders, hoping to get one of them to speak on campus
during Student Exchange week. "We decided that we would go for
people in the news," Relin recalled.

To the women's surprise, the first newsmaker to accept the invitation was Malcolm X. In their letter, Relin and Friedman had politely
proposed that Malcolm come to Barnard for "tea," but they immediately recognized what a big draw he would be and announced a public
speech on the evening of February 9. At the last minute, however, they
were informed that Malcolm had received a more pressing offer: to
address the First Congress of the Council of African Organizations in
London. The Barnard speech was rescheduled for February 18, but
then another event intervened that made the students worry Malcolm
might cancel. The night he returned from England, on February 13,
Malcolm's house in Queens was firebombed, and all week long New
York had been buzzing with speculation about more violence to come.

Yet on that brisk Thursday morning, Malcolm kept his word. He arrived on the Barnard campus shortly before the announced time of his
speech—one o'clock in the afternoon—apologizing for the traffic that
had kept him from getting there earlier. "I'm sorry I'm late," he joked to
the delegation of students who received him. "We have to get Mayor
[Robert] Wagner to straighten that out." He wore a dark suit and tie
under his overcoat, and the wool astrakhan winter hat that had become
one of his sartorial trademarks. Behind the familiar eyeglasses, his eyes
were puffy from lack of sleep. He had spent much of the night removing
possessions he wanted to keep from the Queens house before police
arrived to evict him. He had left the doors locked, and when the police
showed up that morning, accompanied by Captain Joseph X from the
Harlem NOI mosque, one of them had kicked in a window to enter the
small brick house that was now empty and reeking of smoke.

The speech took place in the gymnasium, which was packed with an
overflow crowd of at least fifteen hundred. Male students from Columbia had been told that they could attend if they showed university ID,
and for more than an hour they had streamed in from the larger campus
on the other side of Broadway. The president of Barnard, Rosemary

Park, took her place in the middle of the front row, surrounded by dozens of faculty members and hundreds of students. Dozens more sat on the floor in front of the stage. Armed policemen were stationed all around the gym's perimeter. From her place on the stage, as a member of the welcoming committee, Relin looked up and saw something she had never imagined: officers with rifles looking down from an elevated track.

"The atmosphere in the room at the time of his presentation was extremely tense," Relin recalled. "People had no idea what to expect, and were expecting the worst, in some ways, because the press were telling us that here was this violent man." Another Barnard student in the audience recalled the air of trepidation in the hosts' welcoming remarks, advising the crowd that hearing from Malcolm X offered "an opportunity to open our minds . . . to new ideas." But when Malcolm stepped to the rostrum, he spoke warmly and calmly, as though he was explaining himself to a handful of new acquaintances. "We did expect him to be confrontational, but he was educational," recalled Friedman. "He was going to tell us who he was, what his beliefs were, and why he had those beliefs. It was a feeling of a great leader. He could relate to the audience."

Malcolm began by thanking the students for the invitation and apologizing for backing out of the earlier date so he could address the African delegates in London. "They were interested in knowing the progress, or lack of progress, that the black man in America is making in his struggle for human dignity," he explained. Then Malcolm cracked a smile as he made reference to his expulsion from France and the other dangers he had faced during the trip. "So I was there, and couldn't be here," he said. "And at moments during that time I was over there, I almost wasn't over there."

Malcolm continued by assuring the crowd that he hadn't come "as a person representing the religion of Islam" and that he wanted to talk about matters "above and beyond religion." His travels abroad had made him see a bigger picture than the racial battle in the United States, he explained. "It is incorrect to classify the revolt of the Negro as simply a racial conflict of black against white, or as a purely American problem," he said. "Rather, we are today seeing a global rebellion of the oppressed against the oppressor, the exploited against the exploiter."

Malcolm explained his calls for Black pride in terms that the white Barnard and Columbia students could understand—by appealing to their own sense of racial identity. "No matter how dark you are, you're proud of your white blood," he teased. "Why, some of you are darker than I am. There are Italians and Jews who are blacker than some Negroes, and they brag about how white they are." So why should Blacks be denied the embrace of their own history and culture? Malcolm suggested. "Today there is no black man who is not aware of his African ancestry," he noted. "We are proud of our black blood."

The Columbia student assigned to cover the speech for the school's newspaper, the *Spectator*, was waiting to hear what Malcolm would say about nonviolence, and predictably made those remarks the focus of his story the next day. "Negroes Are Willing to Use Terrorism, Says Malcolm X," the headline shouted. In reality, what Malcolm said was that "there are many Negroes, ready, willing, and able" to fight back—against the Ku Klux Klan. More than two years before Martin Luther King Jr. would come out against the Vietnam War, in a speech delivered just blocks away at Riverside Church, Malcolm also drew a round of applause when he linked the urgency of fighting racial injustice at home with bringing an end to that conflict overseas. "If you don't want very bad things to happen, you better put pressure on your parents to put pressure on [President] Johnson," Malcolm urged the students. "I'm not advocating violence but peace—the same approach Johnson does in Vietnam to save the peace."

Yet for everyone in the crowded Barnard gymnasium, one line would be universally remembered from the last speech that Malcolm X ever finished, the one that became prophetic when he was gunned down at the Audubon Ballroom three days later. "I would rather be dead," Malcolm told the students, "than have somebody deprive me of my rights."

Relin and Friedman were spending that Sunday afternoon with another senior, Prudence Poppink, at their rooms in a new off-campus dorm complex known as "616." When they heard the news, they couldn't believe that the man they had just welcomed to campus was dead. "It was like we had lost a friend," Friedman remembered. "It was a shock," Relin recalled. "It was definitely a shock." Not knowing what else to do, the three walked east to Harlem, and joined the hundreds of mourners who poured onto the streets and stayed there all night. Although they were among the few white faces in the crowd, everyone they met made them feel accepted into the outpouring of grief. "We felt part of the community," Relin recalled, "because we had just met him."

Several days later, the three women returned to Harlem to pay their last respects to Malcolm at the funeral home where his body was laid out for viewing. But that week wouldn't be the end of the impact that Malcolm would have on them. Relin, Friedman, and Poppink would all think back on his words and his example of courage and sacrifice as they made their own career choices. "For all three of us," Relin recalled, "it changed the directions of our lives by making us more aware of the problems faced by so many people around us."

Relin would teach chemistry for a while, then switch to social work, focusing on care for the elderly and physically challenged. She moved to Seattle and became clinical director for an organization called Jewish Family Service, before retiring in her seventies and volunteering for the Red Cross. Friedman became a blood cancer doctor practicing in hospitals in the Bronx. As she approached their sixtieth Barnard reunion, she was still treating patients of all colors, training young doctors, and lecturing on rare blood diseases around the country. Poppink moved to the San Francisco Bay Area and became a public interest lawyer and administrative law judge specializing in fair housing and disability rights. Shortly before she died at the age of fifty-six, she was named Public Lawyer of the Year by the California Bar Association.

At a gathering to commemorate the fiftieth anniversary of the speech, Friedman was asked why she thought Malcolm X had come to Barnard that day. Why had he chosen to speak to a crowd of white students, more than half of them women, at a time when his home had just been bombed and he knew he might not have long to live?

"He loved talking to students, and he was actually speaking at many universities," Friedman noted. "However, there were many universities whose administrations refused to allow him to come to campus. It was to Barnard's credit that, once he said he was going to come, they actually allowed us to let him come."

Then Friedman added one more point. "But in fact, he is still talking to students," she said. "He talks to students through his *Autobiography*, which is now a very popular book on campuses and is commonly read. So his words, his thoughts, and his ideals are really still out there for the students to absorb."

ACKNOWLEDGMENTS

My first thanks are to all my former *Newsweek* colleagues who were involved in a cover story I wrote for the magazine more than three decades ago entitled "The Meaning of Malcolm X." Only seven years old when Malcolm was assassinated in 1965, I first became aware of him by reading *The Autobiography of Malcolm X* as a teenager. A biracial kid being raised by a white single mother in a small town in Massachusetts, I was stirred by Malcolm's message of Black pride and captivated by his portrait of inner-city meccas such as Harlem and the Roxbury neighborhood of Boston, not far from where I grew up. But it was when Spike Lee's movie *Malcolm X* came out in 1992, and *Newsweek*'s editors assigned me to write a cover essay, that I discovered how fiercely Black Americans of an older generation were still guarding and wrestling over Malcolm's legacy, while a new generation was discovering him through hip-hop tributes and a craze for X hats and other street garb. From then on, I continued to keep track of signs of Malcolm's posthumous influence, and to read and in several cases to review major news books about him a soon as they came out, even as I held down day jobs as an editor and news executive at *Newsweek* and in television news.

My second thanks go to the Reverend Eugene Rivers III and to longtime Simon & Schuster editor Bob Bender. By 2018, I had left day-to-day journalism to focus on writing books. After publishing a study of the cultural legacy of Black Pittsburgh, I had embarked on a narrative history of the birth of Black Power in 1966—both projects begun under the guidance of my first editor at S&S, the legendary Alice Mayhew. As I became immersed in 1966, I remarked to my friend Gene Rivers how much Malcolm X loomed over that year even though he had been killed in 1965—due to the influence of the *Autobiography*, particularly once it came out in paperback, and to the inspiration Malcolm provided to the pioneers of Black Power, the Black Arts Movement, and Black Studies.

With Gene's encouragement, I started to think about a study of Malcolm's posthumous influence as a separate book. After Alice sadly passed away in 2020, I mentioned the idea to Bob Bender, my new editor. Bob immediately asked me to write a book proposal and signed me up for the Malcolm project well before the last book came out—which is the only reason I had enough of a head start to be able to publish this book on the one hundredth anniversary of Malcolm's birth and three months after the sixtieth anniversary of his assassination.

As a resident of New York City, I was fortunate to have the preeminent Malcolm X archives in my backyard. I'm grateful for the help of everyone at the Schomburg Center for Research in Black Culture in Harlem, and at the Malcolm X and Dr. Betty Shabazz Memorial and Education Center in Washington Heights, housed in the former Audubon Ballroom where Malcolm spoke frequently and met his end. Anyone studying Malcolm's life owes a huge debt to the late historian Manning Marable and his team of graduate students and assistants who assembled "The Malcolm X Project" at Columbia University, a digital guide with links to documents, news stories, and interviews used as sources for Marable's Pulitzer Prize–winning 2011 biography. The chapter on the *Autobiography* was enriched by correspondence between Alex Haley and his publishers housed in the Library of Congress in Washington, D.C., as was the chapter on Black Power by the records of the Student Nonviolent Coordinating Committee collected in the SNCC Digital Gateway and by the San Francisco Bay area–based Civil Rights Movement Archive. The archives of the FBI and the New York Police Department were invaluable in providing a record of how Malcolm was surveilled during his lifetime; a repository of the 1966 murder trial transcript and the legal documents involved in the unsuccessful challenges to the sentencing of two of the suspects in the late 1970s; and proof of the suppressed evidence that allowed those two men to be wrongfully convicted and that was finally fully brought to light in a reinvestigation leading to their exonerations in 2021.

For more than sixty years, Peter Goldman has been known to me and hundreds of other *Newsweek* veterans as a universally revered writer of news stories on politics and civil rights. Yet it was only as I embarked on this project that I learned what a key figure Peter was in the Malcolm X story—as one of the few white reporters, along with his wife Helen Dudar, who got to know Malcolm and to win his respect; as the author of a seminal 1972 book about Malcolm that set a standard for every major study afterward; as the point person, along with lawyer William Kunstler, in the effort to get the wrongful murder convictions overturned in the 1970s; and as the one witness who lived long enough to tell all those stories. At the age of ninety, and at the height of the Covid pandemic, Peter sat for more than ten hours of interviews over Zoom, and either sent or read me key letters and other documents from his files.

Among the scores of other personal interviews and conversations that contributed to this book, I'm particularly grateful to Clarence Jones and Harry Edwards for sharing the details of their last encounters with Malcolm X; to Gene Rivers for describing the insights of his father, Eugene Rivers Jr., aka Eugene Majied, the legendary cartoonist for *Muhammad Speaks*; to Jeannette Seaver, Faith Childs, Bob Weil, Morgan Entrekin, and Farrell Evans for their behind-the-scenes stories of major books about Malcolm; to Javon Jackson for his recollections of the Spike Lee's movie set; to Jay Kernis for his account of Mike Wallace's complicated relationship with Malcolm, his children, and Louis Farrakhan; to Anthony Davis for sharing the origin story of his acclaimed opera, *X: The Life and Times of Malcolm X*; to Phil Bertelsen and Shayla Harris for reconstructing the making of the groundbreaking documentary *Who Killed Malcolm X?*; and to Mark O'Donoghue and David Shanies, the lawyers for Muhammad Abdul Aziz, for retracing his long road to exoneration, and to Aziz for giving them permission to speak to me.

My final thanks go to my early readers and editors. The great scholars Henry Louis Gates Jr., David Levering Lewis and Peniel E. Joseph, and Pulitzer Prize–winning biographer Jonathan Eig all generously offered to review advance copies of the book and give their expert feedback. Bob Bender made incisive comments when the manuscript was half done, then he and Simon & Schuster CEO Jonathan Karp put me in the capable hands of Dawn Davis when Bob retired a year before publication. Dawn finished editing the book with discerning taste, suggested a key tweak to the structure, and pushed for a stronger subtitle on the jacket cover elegantly designed by Rodrigo Corrall. Maria Mendez kept us all on track with our meticulous copy editors—Fred Chase, Sonja Singleton, Rachael DeShano, and Lisa Healy—and Brianna Scharfenberg and Stephen Bedford gave sure direction through the waters of publicity and promotion. Lynn Nesbit, my literary agent, provided her usual warm encouragement and wise advice. As always, I'm grateful most of all for the support of my children Rachel and Matthew and their partners, and to my wife Alexis Gelber for being my first reader, my most patient listener, and the source of love and laugher that make the solitary work of book writing tolerable.

NOTES

PROLOGUE

xi   *street corner sermons:* Sonia Sanchez, in Henry Hampton and Steve Fayer, *Voices of Freedom: An Oral History of the Civil Rights Movement from the 1950s Through the 1980s* (New York: Bantam, 1990), 254.

xi   *"Michaux's":* C. Gerald Fraser, "Lewis Michaux, 92, Dies, Ran Bookstore in Harlem," *New York Times*, August 27, 1976.

xi   *stacks inside:* Nasri Atallah, "The African National Memorial Bookstore (1932–1974)," Facebook, July 30, 2016, https://www.facebook.com /nasriatallah/posts/the-african-national-memorial-bookstore-1932-1974 malcolm-x-spent-many-a-day-insi/10154249605605731/?paipv=0&eav =AfYXpJmRyZn7Rxg5_Tf1WML64UKwB2JrJGJ-4Psq8v05mAiU-zp Jsn7sMSf3Zt_jxEo&_rdr.

xi   *posting a sign:* Peter Goldman, *The Death and Life of Malcolm X* (New York: Harper & Row, 1973), 377.

xii   *delivered a eulogy:* Ossie Davis, "Eulogy for Malcolm X," American Radio Works, https://americanradioworks.publicradio.org/features/black speech/odavis.html.

xii   *copper casket:* Justin Murphy, "Hall, Local Mortician Who Buried Malcolm X, Dies," *Rochester Democrat and Chronicle*, February 22, 2023.

xiii   *$1.25 paperback:* First paperback edition of *The Autobiography of Malcolm X*, for sale on eBay, https://www.ebay.com/itm/265119509679.

xiii   *fourth anniversary:* C. Gerald Fraser, "Malcolm X Memorial Services and Protests Mark Date of Death," *New York Times*, February 22, 1969.

xiii   *C. Gerald Fraser:* Sam Roberts, "C. Gerald Fraser, Longtime Reporter for *The Times*, Dies at 90," *New York Times*, December 9, 2015.

xiii   *"Malcolm X Day":* "St. Malcolm X," *Newsweek*, March 8, 1969.

xiv   *Edwards had met Malcolm:* Author interview with Harry Edwards.

xiv   *"He's dead":* Goldman, *The Death and Life of Malcolm X*, 392.

xvii   *cast ballots:* "The Ballot or the Bullet," George Breitman, ed., *Malcolm X Speaks: Selected Speeches and Statements* (New York: Grove Press, 1965), 23–44.

xvii   *wore T-shirts:* Edward McClelland, "DNC Dispatch, Day 2: Hello,

Cheeseheads," *Chicago*, August 21, 2024; "Nebraska Delegation Roll Call," C-SPAN, August 20, 2024, https://www.c-span.org/video/?c5129103/ne braska-delegation-roll-call.

xvii *college radical:* Chantelle Lee, "'He's a Bundle of Contradictions': Why Clarence Thomas Left the Black Power Movement Behind," *Frontline*, PBS, May 9, 2023, https://www.pbs.org/wgbh/frontline/article/clarence -thomas-black-power-movement/.

xvii *"I don't see how":* Corey Robin, "Clarence Thomas's Radical Vision of Race," *New Yorker*, September 10, 2019.

xviii *Manning Marable:* Manning Marable, *Malcolm X: A Life of Reinvention* (New York: Viking, 2011).

xviii *Les Payne:* Les Payne and Tamara Payne, *The Dead Are Arising: The Life of Malcolm X* (New York: Liveright, 2020).

xviii *"what he was about to do":* "St. Malcolm X."

xviii *"ten different personalities":* Mark Whitaker, "Malcolm X," *Newsweek*, November 16, 1992.

xix *"power of images":* Vikki Tobak, "Style as Subversion: Malcolm X as Revolutionary and Style Icon," *Medium*, May 20, 2017, https://medium .com/@VikkiTobak/style-as-subversion-malcolm-malcolm-x-as-revolu tionary-and-style-icon-c09e4a725870.

xix *"we have not yet overcome":* Whitaker, "Malcolm X."

xx *documentary on Netflix:* Rachel Dretzin and Phil Bertelsen, directors, *Who Killed Malcolm X?*, Fusion, 2019.

xxi *"semblance of justice":* Ashley Southall and Jonah E. Bromwich, "2 Men Convicted of Killing Malcolm X Will Be Exonerated After Decades," *New York Times*, November 17, 2021.

ONE: DEATH IN THE AFTERNOON

3 *form of a cartoon:* "On My Own," cartoon in *Muhammad Speaks*, April 10, 1964.

3 *criticized Kennedy:* "Malcolm X Scores U.S. and Kennedy," *New York Times*, December 2, 1963.

3 *announcing his departure:* M. S. Handler, "Malcolm X Splits with Mu-hammad," *New York Times*, March 9, 1964.

4 *approved by Elijah Muhammad:* Michael Tisserand, "The Cartoonist and the Champ," *Comic Journal*, April 24, 2018, https://www.tcj.com /the-cartoonist-and-the-champ/.

4 *visit his father:* Author interview with Eugene Rivers III.

5 *five-part series:* Video of the hour-long version of *The Hate That Hate Produced*, YouTube, https://www.youtube.com/watch?v=JgWiJ5DK-z8.

6   *panel discussion:* Ibid.

6   *"Malcolm was the Muslims":* Goldman, *The Death and Life of Malcolm X*, 63.

6   *secret murder plot:* "Malcolm X Tells of Death Threat," *New York Amsterdam News,* March 21, 1964.

7   *a long letter:* Photo of Malcolm's letter from Mecca on Moments in Time, https://momentsintime.com/the-most-remarkable-revelatory-letter-ever -written-by-malcolm-x/.

7   *"my previous assumptions":* M. S. Handler, "Malcolm X Pleased by Whites' Attitude on Trip to Mecca," *New York Times,* May 8, 1964.

7   *agenda for the OAAU:* "(1964) Malcolm X's Speech at the Founding Rally of the Organization of Afro-American Unity," *BlackPast,* https://www .blackpast.org/african-american-history/speeches-african-american-his tory/1964-malcolm-x-s-speech-founding-rally-organization-afro-american -unity/.

8   *the Messenger's adultery:* Mike Wallace interview with Malcolm X for *CBS Sunday Morning,* June 9, 1964, YouTube, https://www.youtube.com /watch?v=uUc6o2HlJns.

8   *"I'm David":* Malcolm X, *Autobiography,* 326–27.

9   *eviction order:* Timeline on website for "Malcolm X: A Search for Truth" exhibit at the Schomburg Center for Research in Black Culture, http:// web-static.nypl.org/exhibitions/malcolmx/malcolm.html.

9   *contacted Mike Wallace:* Wallace interview for *CBS Sunday Morning.*

9   *ran into John Lewis:* John Lewis, *Walking with the Wind: A Memoir of the Movement* (New York: Simon & Schuster, 1998), 296–97.

10   *suspicious of NOI musclemen:* Goldman, *The Death and Life of Malcolm X*, 250–51.

10   *Orly Airport:* Ibid., 253–55.

11   *Malcolm was awoken:* M. S. Handler, "Malcolm X Flees Firebomb Attack," *New York Times,* February 15, 1965.

11   *"I just closed my eyes":* Gordon Parks, "I was a Zombie Then—Like All Muslims, I Was Hypnotized," *Life,* March 5, 1965.

11   *"I'm not a racist":* "(1965) Malcolm X. 'Speech at Ford Auditorium,'" *BlackPast,* https://www.blackpast.org/african-american-history/speeches -african-american-history/1965-malcolm-x-speech-ford-auditorium/.

12   *"bullet through my head":* "Malcolm X Speech: There's a Worldwide Revolution Going On (Feb. 15, 1965)," ICIT Digital Library, https:// www.icit-digital.org/articles/malcolm-x-speech-there-s-a-worldwide -revolution-going-on-feb-15-1965.

12   *impromptu interview:* Theodore Jones, "Malcolm Knew He Was a 'Marked Man,'" *New York Times,* February 22, 1965.

13 *Gordon Parks:* Parks, "I Was a Zombie Then—Like All Muslims, I Was Hypnotized."

14 *Clarence Jones:* Author interview with Clarence Jones.

15 *Malcolm checked himself:* Goldman, *The Death and Life of Malcolm X*, 268.

15 *"Better wake up":* Peter Kihss, "Malcolm X Shot to Death at Rally Here," *New York Times*, February 22, 1965.

15 *feeling anxious:* Goldman, *The Death and Life of Malcolm X*, 268–69.

15 *Charles X Blackwell:* Blackwell testimony in trial transcript, *The People of the State of New York v. Thomas Hagan, Thomas 15X Johnson and Norman 3X Butler*, 1602–10.

16 *Outside the entrance:* Goldman, *The Death and Life of Malcolm X*, 268.

16 *a hat had to be passed:* Ibid., 4.

16 *main ballroom:* Photo by Al Burleigh, Associated Press, in Rich Schapiro, "Remembering Civil Rights Icon Malcolm X Fifty Years After His Death," New York *Daily News*, April 9, 2018, https://www.nydailynews.com/new -york/nyc-crime/remembering-malcolm-x-50-years-article-1.2115740.

16 *speakers canceled:* Goldman, *The Death and Life of Malcolm X*, 270.

16 *increasingly testy:* Ibid., 4; Les Payne, "The Day Malcolm X Was Killed," *New Yorker*, August 27, 2020.

17 *dressed elegantly:* Photos in "The Violent End of the Man Called Malcolm X," *Life*, March 5, 1965.

17 *her mother's expression:* Attallah Shabazz interview with local CBS reporter Barbara Rodgers, 1992, YouTube, https://www.youtube.com /watch?v=ivFNrzqztjc.

17 *At the plywood lectern:* The account of the murder is assembled from the transcript of the murder trial, *The People of the State of New York v. Thomas Hagan, Thomas 15X Johnson and Norman 3X Butler*; Goldman, *The Death and Life of Malcolm X*, 273–78; and Payne, "The Day Malcolm X Was Killed."

19 *Malcolm's bloody body:* Photos in "The Violent End of the Man Called Malcolm X."

19 *Yuri Kochiyama:* William Yardley, "Yuri Kochiyama, Rights Activist Who Befriended Malcolm X, Dies at 93," *New York Times*, June 4, 2014.

19 *arrived with a gurney:* Goldman, *The Death and Life of Malcolm X*, 277–78.

19 *"Malcolm X is dead":* Kihss, "Malcolm X Shot to Death at Rally Here."

19 *corpse was transferred:* Ibid.; "Muslim Mosque Burns in Harlem; Blast Reported," *New York Times*, February 23, 1965.

20 *Unity Funeral Home:* Justin Murphy, "Hall, Local Mortician Who Buried Malcolm X, Dies," *Rochester Democrat and Chronicle*, February 22, 2023.

20 *the one gunman:* Goldman, *The Death and Life of Malcolm X*, 276.

21 *Searching the crime scene:* Ibid., 273; "Muslim Mosque Burns in Harlem;

Blast Reported"; Testimony in *The People of the State of New York v. Thomas Hagan, Thomas 15X Johnson and Norman 3X Butler*, 1602–72.

21 *"Things are so confused":* Gay Talese, "Police Save Suspect from the Crowd," *New York Times*, February 22, 1965.

21 *retaliatory attack:* Peter Kihss, "Mosque Fires Stir Fear of Vendetta in Malcolm Case," *New York Times*, February 24, 1965.

21 *rumors spread:* Paul L. Montgomery, "Harlem Is Quiet as News Spreads," *New York Times*, February 22, 1965.

22 *second murder suspect:* Homer Bigart, "Black Muslim Guard Held in Murder of Malcolm X," *New York Times*, February 27, 1965.

22 *Malcolm's funeral:* Paul L. Montgomery, "Malcolm Buried as True Muslim Despite the Unorthodox Ritual," *New York Times*, February 28, 1965; James Booker, "30,000 Mourn Malcolm X," *New York Amsterdam News*, March 6, 1965; E. W. Kenworthy, "Malcolm Called a Martyr Abroad," *New York Times*, February 26, 1965.

23 *"It makes me sick":* Marlene Nadle, "Burying Malcolm X," *Village Voice*, March 4, 1965.

24 *"No white man":* Goldman, *The Death and Life of Malcolm X*, 303.

24 *The undertaker from Unity Funeral Home:* "Slain Malcolm X Is Buried Near New York City," UPI photo and caption, (Zanesville, OH) *Times Recorder*, February 28, 1965; Murphy, "Hall, Local Mortician Who Buried Malcolm X, Dies."

TWO: THE REPORTERS

25 *One of them was Peter Goldman:* Author interviews with Peter Goldman.

26 *Walter Goldman:* Ibid.

26 *Murray Kempton:* Helen Dudar, ed., *The Attentive Eye: Selected Journalism*, (Bloomington, IN: Xlibris, 2002), vi.

27 *scandalous murder trial:* "Crime: End of the Romance," *Time*, October 12, 1959.

27 *"Hey, St. Louis":* Dudar, *The Attentive Eye*, vii.

28 *Willem Van Rie was acquitted:* John H. Fenton, "Van Rie Acquitted in Shipboard Death," *New York Times*, March 3, 1960.

28 *Island Park:* Jennifer Sinco Kelleher, "Helen Dudar, Pioneering Journalist," *Newsday*, October 8, 2022.

28 *speed and accuracy prize:* "Notes from Oceanside," *Newsday*, February 21, 1941.

28 *"Let Prof. Do It":* Kelleher, "Helen Dudar, Pioneering Journalist."

28 *"a demanding, sinewy intelligence":* Merriam-Webster's Collegiate Dictionary, Eleventh Edition (Springfield, MA: Merriam-Webster, 2003), 1163.

29 *driving test:* Helen Dudar, "So You Think You're a Good Driver?," *Newsday*, August 29, 1946.

29 *major prize:* List of Meyer Berger Award winners, Columbia School of Journalism website, https://journalism.columbia.edu/system/files/content/past-berger-winners.pdf.

29 *"the big leagues":* Author interviews with Peter Goldman.

29 *Adams House:* History on Adams House website, https://adamshouse.harvard.edu/house-history.

30 *Harvard course catalog:* Digital copy of the 1960–1961 Harvard course catalog on the Harvard Libraries website, https://iiif.lib.harvard.edu/manifests/view/drs:490292969$33i.

30 *read* Native Son*:* Author interviews with Peter Goldman; Richard Wright, *Native Son* (New York: Harper & Brothers, 1940).

30 *new academic study:* C. Eric Lincoln, *The Black Muslims in America* (Boston: Beacon Press, 1961).

32 *paramilitary guards:* Author interviews with Peter Goldman.

32 *debate with Walter Carrington:* "The Harvard Law School Forum of March 24, 1961," in Archie Epps, ed., *Malcolm X: Speeches at Harvard* (New York: William Morrow, 1969), 115–31.

33 *back-and-forth:* Paul S. Cowan, "Malcolm X Demands States for Negroes, Calls Token Integration 'Mere Pacifier,'" *Harvard Crimson*, March 25, 1961.

33 *"See, I told you about this":* Roger D. Fisher, "Malcolm X—After 31 Years," *Harvard Crimson*, December 3, 1992.

34 *"call Malcolm a Negro":* Ibid.

34 *words that came to mind:* Ibid.

34 *popped the question:* Author interviews with Peter Goldman.

35 *magazine start-up:* "A Regional Magazine: 'FOCUS/Midwest' Makes Bow," *St. Louis Post-Dispatch*, May 20, 1962.

35 *gossip columnist:* "David Felts Column," *Southern Illinoisan* (Carbondale), May 18, 1962.

35 *four separate stories:* Peter L. Goldman, "Black Muslims Fail to Flourish Here," "Racial Harmony Here Stunts Growth of Muslims," "Black Muslim Boss Here Survives Walkout by Rebels," and "Attitude of Negro Leaders Vary on Black Muslims," *St. Louis Globe-Democrat*, January 2, 3, 4, and 5, 1962.

35 *Minister Clyde X:* Goldman, "Black Muslim Boss Here Survives Walkout by Rebels."

36 *NOI's teachings:* Goldman, "Black Muslims Fail to Flourish Here."

37 *compared him unfavorably:* Goldman, "Black Muslim Boss Here Survives Walkout by Rebels."

37 *voice of Malcolm X himself:* Author interviews with Peter Goldman.

38 *luncheonette on the North Side:* Goldman, *The Death and Life of Malcolm X*, 5–8.

38 *"bearing of a soldier, or a priest":* Ibid., 5–6.

38 *soft, plaintive voice:* "A White Man's Heaven Is a Black Man's Hell," YouTube, https://www.youtube.com/watch?v=pNeJxzSRXA8.

38 *the "Charmer":* Richard Lei, "Louis Farrakhan, Calypso Charmer," *Washington Post*, October 14, 1995.

39 *nearly three-hour conversation:* Goldman, *The Death and Life of Malcolm X*, 5–8; Marable, *Malcolm X*, 218–19.

41 *writing tryout:* Author interviews with Peter Goldman.

42 *Hotel Theresa:* "The Muslim Message: All White Men Devils, All Negroes Divine," *Newsweek*, August 27, 1962.

43 *Karl Fleming:* Mark Whitaker, "Reporters at the Barricades," *Newsweek*, December 14, 2012.

43 *Sigma Delta Chi award:* "Witcover Wins Award of Sigma Delta Chi," *St. Louis Globe-Democrat*, April 11, 1963.

43 *March on Washington:* Goldman, *The Death and Life of Malcolm X*, 104–5.

44 *"Mr. Peter Goldman!":* Alex Haley, "Epilogue," *The Autobiography of Malcolm X*, 443.

44 *"kept my big mouth shut":* Goldman, *The Death and Life of Malcolm X*, 120.

45 *Park Sheraton Hotel:* M. S. Handler, "Malcolm X Sees Rise in Violence," *New York Times*, March 13, 1964.

45 *another long private interview:* Author interviews with Peter Goldman; "Malcolm's Brand X," *Newsweek*, March 23, 1964.

45 *five-part series:* Helen Dudar, "The Muslims and Black Nationalism," *New York Post*, April 6, 7, 8, 9, and 12, 1964.

46 *asked him to telephone Dudar:* Haley, "Epilogue," *The Autobiography of Malcolm X*, 434.

46 *considered the piece "fair":* Author interviews with Peter Goldman.

47 *Dudar was blunt:* Jon A. Roosenraad, "Coverage in Six New York Newspapers of Malcolm X and His Black Nationalist Movement: A Study" (MA thesis, Michigan State University, 1968), 77.

47 *spelling out the reasons:* "Death of a Desperado," *Newsweek*, March 8, 1965.

THREE: THE TRIAL

48 *a probe was launched:* Goldman, *The Death and Life of Malcolm X*, 281–88.

49 *"You got everything":* Ibid., 286.

49 *Hayer's fingerprints:* Ibid., 329.

49 *Mosque No. 7:* Ibid., 291–92; Kihss, "Mosque Fires Stir Fear of Vendetta in Malcolm Case."

50 *gruesome ice sculpture:* Photo by Nat Fein, *New York Herald Tribune*, on the cover of *Life*, March 5, 1965.

50 *a phone tip:* Goldman, *The Death and Life of Malcolm X*, 249–50, 293.

51 *Norman 3X Butler:* Ibid., 296–99.

52 *perp walk photo:* Associated Press photo of Butler on page 1 of *The New York Times*, February 27, 1965.

52 *Nation of Islam convention:* Associated Press, "Muhammad Rides Safely into Muslim Convention," *The State* (Columbia, SC), February 27, 1965.

52 *"something we can show":* Ralph Blumenthal and Kenneth Gross, "Muslim Held in Malcolm Case," *New York Post*, February 26, 1965.

52 *Cary 2X Thomas:* Goldman, *The Death and Life of Malcolm X*, 304–5.

53 *stony-faced Johnson:* Associated Press photo on page 1 of *The Sun-Democrat* (Paducah, KY), March 5, 1965.

53 *Herbert J. Stern:* Goldman, *The Death and Life of Malcolm X*, 298, 366, 372, 373.

54 *Judge Charles Marks:* "Charles Marks, Ex-Justice, Dies," *New York Times*, April 3, 1976.

54 *Jury selection:* "Jury Selection Is Lagging in Malcolm X Murder Case," *New York Times*, January 14, 1966; "Jury Selection Completed in Malcolm Murder Trial," *New York Times*, January 20, 1966.

54 *opening statement:* Herman Porter, "D.A. Presents Case in Malcolm X Trial," *The Militant*, January 31, 1966.

55 *Peter Sabbatino:* Ibid.

55 *first witness:* Thomas Buckley, "Witness Recalls Malcolm Killing," *New York Times*, January 22, 1966.

55 *wobbly witness:* Porter, "D.A. Presents Case in Malcolm X Trial."

56 *nine other witnesses:* Herman Porter, "Malcolm X Murder Trial," *The Militant*, March 14, 1966.

56 *surprise witness:* Goldman, *The Death and Life of Malcolm X*, 325–28.

57 *Betty Shabazz:* Thomas Buckley, "Malcolm X's Widow Scores Subjects," *New York Times*, February 18, 1966.

57 *late getting to court:* Goldman, *The Death and Life of Malcolm X*, 348–49.

58 *decided to confess: The State of New York v. Thomas Hagan, Norman Butler and Thomas Johnson*, NYC Department of Records, 3135–80, 3211–42.

63 *Butler took the stand:* Ibid., 3244–408.

65 *closing arguments:* Ibid., 3677–88.

66 *finding all three men guilty:* Thomas Buckley, "Malcolm X Jury Finds 3 Guilty," *New York Times*, March 11, 1966.

67 *"Who ordered the assassination?":* Herman Porter, "Who Killed Malcolm X?," *The Militant*, March 21, 1966.

67 *"I don't think you have a solution here":* Goldman, *The Death and Life of*

Malcolm X, 373; Associated Press, "Three Men Are Convicted in Malcolm X Assassination," (Omaha, NE) *Evening World-Herald*, March 11, 1966.

FOUR: THE AUTOBIOGRAPHY

71 *raised in Chicago:* Douglas Martin, "Barney Rosset Dies at 89; Defied Censors, Making Racy a Literary Staple," *New York Times*, February 22, 2012.

71 *"Malcolm got assassinated":* Harriet Staff, "Interviews with Barney Rosset," Poetry Foundation, February 24, 2012.

71 *Monday morning:* Richard Seaver, *The Tender Hour of Twilight: Paris in the '50s, New York in the '60s: A Memoir of Publishing's Golden Age* (New York: Farrar, Straus & Giroux, 2012), 347–50.

73 *different story:* Tim Warren, "The Rocky Road to Publication of Book on Malcolm X," *Baltimore Sun*, November 16, 1992.

73 *own fiction agency:* "Malcolm Reiss: 1905–1975," Pulp Artists, https://www.pulpartists.com/Reiss.html.

73 *went to Grove Press:* Warren, "The Rocky Road to Publication of Book on Malcolm X."

73 *McCormick, wrote to Haley:* Ken McCormick to Alex Haley, March 16, 1965, Ken McCormick collection of the Records of Doubleday & Co., Manuscript Division, Library of Congress, Box 2, Folder 17.

74 *first hardcover printing:* Seaver, *The Tender Hour of Twilight*, 351–52.

74 *sense of ambition:* Burt A. Folkart, "'Roots' Author Alex Haley Dies of Heart Attack at 70," *Los Angeles Times*, February 11, 1992.

75 *"black man's religion":* Alex Haley, "Epilogue," *The Autobiography of Malcolm X*, 418–21.

75 *pitched the story:* "Alex Haley Remembers," in David Gallen, ed., *Malcolm X As They Knew Him* (New York: Carroll & Graf, 1992), 243–50.

76 *present both sides:* "Mr. Muhammad Speaks," *Reader's Digest*, March 1960.

76 *letter from Muhammad:* "Alex Haley Remembers," in Gallen, *Malcolm X As They Knew Him.*

76 Saturday Evening Post: "Black Merchants of Hate," *Saturday Evening Post*, January 16, 1963.

78 *Murray Fisher:* Myrna Oliver, "Murray Fisher, 69; Shaped Playboy Interview Feature," *Los Angeles Times*, June 5, 2002.

78 *Miles Davis:* "Alex Haley Interviewed by Lawrence Grobel," June 3, 2019, Alex Haley, https://alexhaley.com/2019/05/25/alex-haley-interviewed-by-lawrence-grobel/.

78 *provocative exchanges:* Alex Haley, "Miles Davis: A Candid Conversation with the Jazz World's Premier Iconoclast," *Playboy*, September 1962.

79   *"self-assured executive":* Alex Haley, "The Playboy Interview: Malcolm X," *Playboy,* May 1963.

81   *expressed skepticism:* Haley, "Epilogue," *The Autobiography of Malcolm X,* 421.

81   *Ken McCormick:* Eric Pace, "Publishing's Kenneth McCormick, 91, Dies," *New York Times,* June 29, 1997.

81   *potential for a memoir:* Haley, "Epilogue," *The Autobiography of Malcolm X,* 421–23.

82   *"Memorandum of Agreement":* Marable, *Malcolm X,* 247–48.

82   *internal guidance:* Ken McCormick Collection, Library of Congress, Box 44, Folder 9.

83   *slow and frustrating:* Haley, "Epilogue," *The Autobiography of Malcolm X,* 424–27.

83   *"tell me something about your mother":* Ibid., 427–28.

84   *The memories started:* Malcolm X, *Autobiography,* 3–26.

85   *wrote to Paul Reynolds:* Alex Haley to Ken McCormick, Tony Gibbs, and Paul Reynolds, November 19, 1963, Ken McCormick Collection, Library of Congress, Box 1, Folder 37.

85   *shape of the book:* "Alex Haley Remembers," in Gallen, *Malcolm X As They Knew Him.*

86   *"the new vistas":* Malcolm X, *Autobiography,* 195.

87   *George Sims:* "Alex Haley Remembers," in Gallen, *Malcolm X As They Knew Him.*

87   *"I trust you seventy percent":* Haley, "Epilogue," *The Autobiography of Malcolm X,* 436.

87   *hints of the strain:* Malcolm X, *Autobiography,* 441–43.

88   *draft chapters:* Ibid., 444–46.

88   *criticism of Elijah Muhammad:* Ibid., 446–48.

89   *"the way it was":* Ibid., 449.

90   *advance Malcolm a payment:* Haley, "Epilogue," *The Autobiography of Malcolm X,* 458.

90   *in front of a window:* Niraj Chokshi, "Don Hogan Charles, Lauded Photographer of Civil Rights Era, Dies at 79," *New York Times,* December 25, 2017.

91   *received a phone call:* Malcolm X, *Autobiography,* 468–69.

92   *"sale potential":* Alex Haley to Ken McCormick and Paul Reynolds, March 21, 1964, Ken McCormick Collection, Library of Congress, Box 1, Folder 37.

92   *"financial legacy":* David Remnick, "This American Life: The Making and Remaking of Malcolm X," *New Yorker,* April 18, 2011.

92   *Malcolm's sinfulness:* "Manning Marable's 'Reinvention' of Malcolm X,"

NPR, April 5, 2011, https://www.npr.org/2011/04/05/135144230/man ning-marables-reinvention-of-malcolm-x.

93 *fourteen more printings:* Based on the disclosure in *The Autobiography of Malcolm X*, First Paperback Edition, Grove Press, 1966, that it was the sixteenth edition.

93 *high-profile reviews:* Eliot Fremont-Smith, "An Eloquent Testament," *New York Times*, November 5, 1965; I. F. Stone, "The Pilgrimage of Malcolm X," *New York Review of Books*, November 11, 1965.

93 *greatest sales potential:* Seaver, *The Tender Hour*, 352; Eric Pace, "Alex Haley, Author of 'Roots,' Dies," *New York Times*, February 11, 1992; Warren, "The Rocky Road to Publication of Book on Malcolm X."

94 *"actual yet symbolic journey":* Albert E. Stone, *Autobiographical Occasions and Original Acts: Versions of American Identity from Henry Adams to Nate Shaw* (Philadelphia: University of Pennsylvania Press, 1982), 255.

FIVE: BLACK POWER!

95 *Stokely Carmichael:* Stokely Carmichael, with Ekwueme Michael Thelwell, *Ready for Revolution: The Life and Struggles of Stokely Carmichael (Kwame Ture)* (New York: Scribner, 2003), 22–59.

95 *"step-ladder" speakers:* Ibid., 101–2.

96 *story about Malcolm X:* Ibid., 105.

96 *NAG invited Malcolm:* Ibid., 256–61.

98 *bulletin came across the car radio:* Ibid., 439–41.

99 *"The Ballot or the Bullet":* "The Ballot or the Bullet," in Breitman, *Malcolm X Speaks*.

100 *their own political party:* Mark Whitaker, *Saying It Loud: 1966—The Year Black Power Challenged the Civil Rights Movement* (New York: Simon & Schuster, 2013), 77–99.

100 *two more surprise events:* Ibid., 100–139.

101 *"advantage that Malcolm X never had":* Gene Roberts, "Rights March Disunity," *New York Times*, June 28, 1966.

101 *Meredith Marchers arrived:* Whitaker, *Saying It Loud*, 140–53.

102 *Associated Press account:* James Bossey, "Mississippi Marchers Chant 'We Want Black Power!,'" *Messenger-Inquirer* (Owensboro, KY), June 7, 1966.

102 Ebony *profile:* Lerone Bennett Jr., "Stokely Carmichael: Architect of Black Power," *Ebony*, September 1966.

103 *Ruby Doris Smith Robinson:* Ruby Doris S. Robinson, "Organizational Report," October 21, 1966, crmvet.org, https://www.crmvet.org/docs /661021_sncc_org-rpt.pdf.

103 *give a speech:* Whitaker, *Saying It Loud,* 221–35.

104 *Huey Newton and Bobby Seale:* Ibid., 57–66.

105 *day-long conference*: "Oakland Conclave Is Attracting Top Negro Celebrities," *San Bernardino County Sun,* August 8, 1963.

105 *deeply impressed Newton:* Huey P. Newton, *Revolutionary Suicide* (New York: Penguin Classics, 2009), 71–72.

105 *Air Force veteran:* David Hilliard, with Keith and Kent Zimmerman, *Huey: Spirit of the Panther* (New York: Basic Books, 2006), 12–13.

105 *When Newton got out:* Bobby Seale, *Seize the Time: The Story of the Black Panther Party and Huey P. Newton* (Baltimore: Black Classic Press, 1991), 25–34.

106 *"Ten Point Program":* Whitaker, *Saying It Loud,* 240–46.

107 *greatest influence:* Newton, *Revolutionary Suicide,* 116–18.

107 *resemblance to the speech:* "Malcolm X Repeats Call for Negro Unity on Rights," *New York Times,* June 29, 1964; "(1964) Malcolm X's Speech at the Founding Rally of the Organization of Afro-American Unity," *BlackPast,* https://www.blackpast.org/african-american-history/speeches-african-american-history/1964-malcolm-x-s-speech-founding-rally-organization-afro-american-unity/.

107 *outline for a chapter:* Haley book outline in the Ken McCormick Collection, Library of Congress, 1963, Box 1, Folder 37.

107 *offered ten points:* Newton, *Revolutionary Suicide,* 122–25.

108 *informant for the FBI:* Seth Rosenfeld, "New FBI Files Show Wide Range of Black Panther Activities," *Monterey Herald,* June 9, 2015.

108 *"Shock-a-buku":* Newton, *Revolutionary Suicide,* 129.

108 *forefront of the protests:* Daryl Lembke, "Muslim Trouble Rises in California Prisons," *Los Angeles Times,* May 20, 1962.

109 *Eldridge Cleaver:* Zoe Colley, "The Making of Eldridge Cleaver: The Nation of Islam, Prison Life, and the Rise of a Black Power Icon," *Journal of Civil and Human Rights* 6, no. 1 (Spring/Summer 2020): 61–90; Whitaker, *Saying It Loud,* 249–55.

109 *first Muslim at Folsom:* Eldridge Cleaver, *Soul on Ice* (New York: McGraw-Hill, 1968), 50–61.

110 *Beverly Axelrod:* Ibid., 139–54.

110 *novel strategy:* Peter Richardson, *A Bomb in Every Issue: How the Short, Unruly Life of Ramparts Magazine Changed America* (New York: The New Press, 2009), 68–71.

111 *inviting his widow:* Ibid., 72–74; Hampton and Fayer, *Voice of Freedom,* 365–66.

112 *holiday called Kwanzaa:* Scot Brown, *Fighting for US: Maulana Karenga, the US Organization and Black Cultural Nationalism* (New York: New

York University Press, 2003), 70–71; "Maulana Karenga," *The History-Makers*, https://www.thehistorymakers.org/biography/maulana-karenga-39.

112 *hear Malcolm speak:* David Shaw, "'Negro a Monster Stripped of His Culture'—Malcolm X," *UCLA Daily Bruin*, October 29, 1962; "Maulana Karenga," *The HistoryMakers*.

113 *cousin of Malcolm's:* Brown, *Fighting for US*, 38–42; Douglas Martin, "Alfred Ligon Is Dead at 96; Owned Renowned Bookstore," *New York Times*, August 23, 2002.

113 *profiled by* Newsweek: "Black and White: A Major Survey of U.S. Racial Attitudes Today," *Newsweek*, August 22, 1966.

114 *Panther messaging:* Hampton and Fayer, *Voices of Freedom*, 367; John Kifner, "Eldridge Cleaver, Black Panther Who Became G.O.P. Conservative, Is Dead," *New York Times*, May 2, 1998.

114 *COINTELPRO-BLACK HATE:* Gerald D. McKnight, ed., *Supplemental Detailed Staff Reports on Intelligence Activities and the Rights of Americans, Book III, Final Report of the Select Committee to Study Governmental Operations with Respect to Intelligence Activities, United States Senate* (Ipswich, ME: Mary Ferrell Foundation Press, 1976), 20–22, 188; "COINTELPRO Black Extremist," *FBI Records: The Vault*, Part 1, 3.

115 *a shoot-out:* Brown, *Fighting for US*, 93; Elaine Brown, *A Taste of Power: A Black Woman's Story* (New York: Anchor, 1994), 156–70.

115 *Fred Hampton:* McKnight, *Supplemental Detailed Staff Reports*, 222–23; A. O. Scott, "'Judas and the Black Messiah' Review: I Was a Panther for the F.B.I.," *New York Times*, February 11, 2021.

115 *Newton became enmeshed:* "Huey Newton Killed; Was a Co-Founder of Black Panthers," *New York Times*, August 23, 1989.

115 *Cleaver returned:* Kifner, "Eldridge Cleaver, Black Panther Who Became G.O.P. Conservative, Is Dead."

116 *Karenga went to prison:* Brown, *Fighting for US*, 120–22, 128.

116 *died of prostate cancer:* Michael T. Kaufman, "Stokely Carmichael, Rights Leader Who Coined 'Black Power,' Dies at 57," *New York Times*, December 16, 1998.

116 *might have sought a merger:* Carmichael, *Ready for Revolution*, 440–41.

SIX: THE ATHLETES

118 *Malcolm was a twelve-year-old:* Malcolm X, *Autobiography*, 27–29.

118 *"filthy temptations":* Honorable Elijah Muhammad, "On Sport and Plays," *Final Call*, https://www.finalcall.com/columns/hem/sport_play.html.

119 *meteoric rise:* "Hometown Hero to Global Icon," Muhammad Ali Center, https://alicenter.org/the-timeline/.

119 *discovered the Nation of Islam:* Randy Roberts and Johnny Smith, *Blood Brothers: The Fatal Friendship Between Muhammad Ali and Malcolm X* (New York: Basic Books, 2016), 12–17.

119 *Saxon invited Cassius:* Ibid., 55–56; Malcolm X, *Autobiography*, 332.

120 *Detroit's Olympia Stadium:* Roberts and Smith, *Blood Brothers*, 65–67.

120 *appeared in* Muhammad Speaks*: Muhammad Speaks*, September 15, 1962, https://www.noiwc.info/uploads/1/2/5/7/125752377/sept151962_1.pdf.

120 *"He was so radical":* "Muhammad Ali," in Hampton and Fayer, *Voices of Freedom*, 324–25.

120 *"I liked him":* Malcolm X, *Autobiography*, 332.

121 *Jones fight:* Roberts and Smith, *Blood Brothers*, 88–89; Lincoln Werden, "Spectators Boo Official Verdict," *New York Times*, March 15, 1963.

121 *Malcolm had other reasons:* Roberts and Smith, *Blood Brothers*, 176–77.

122 *Clay invited Malcolm:* Malcolm X, *Autobiography*, 331–35; Muhammad Ali, with Hana Ali, *The Soul of a Butterfly: Reflections on Life's Journey* (New York: Simon & Schuster, 2004), 76.

122 *"know no fear":* David Remnick, *King of the World: Muhammad Ali and the Rise of an American Hero* (New York: Random House, 1998), 186.

122 *George Plimpton:* George Plimpton, "Miami Notebook: Cassius Clay and Malcolm X," *Harper's*, June 1964.

122 *before the fight:* Malcolm X, *Autobiography*, 335–36.

123 *"Eat your words!":* Jack Hand, "I Am the Greatest," Associated Press, February 26, 1964.

123 *After the fight:* Roberts and Smith, *Blood Brothers*, 198–201; "Eyes on the Prize II: Interview with Alex Haley," American Archive of Public Broadcasting, https://americanarchive.org/catalog/cpb-aacip-b545fc6098c.

124 *post-fight press conference:* Robert Lipsyte, "Clay Discusses His Future, Liston and Black Muslims," *New York Times*, February 27, 1964.

124 *reporters approached Clay:* "Clay Says He Has Adopted Islam Religion and Sees It As Way to Peace," *New York Times*, February 28, 1964.

124 *victory tour:* "Clay Talks with Malcolm X," *New York Times*, March 2, 1964.

125 *interview with the* New York Amsterdam News*:* Les Matthews, "The 'Greatest One' Pays a Visit to the Amsterdam News," *New York Amsterdam News*, March 7, 1964.

125 *Malcolm couldn't match:* Roberts and Smith, *Blood Brothers*, 218, 233.

126 *gallantly defended Ali:* "Malcolm X on Cassius Clay & Black Nationalism," YouTube, https://www.youtube.com/watch?v=9E8wWdpSOg0.

126 *face-to-face again:* Lloyd Garrison, "Clay Makes Malcolm Ex-Friend," *New York Times*, May 18, 1964; Maya Angelou, *All God's Children Need*

Traveling Shoes (New York: Random House, 1986), 143–44; Malcolm X, *Autobiography*, 391.

127 *fire broke out:* "Burned Out," *Chicago Tribune*, February 22, 1965; Roberts and Smith, *Blood Brothers*, 297–98.

128 *Savior's Day rally:* "Karate-Guard Protects Elijah," *Boston Globe*, February 27, 1965; Goldman, *The Death and Life of Malcolm X*, 301; Roberts and Smith, *Blood Brothers*, 299.

128 *"I fear no living man, only Allah!":* Norm Miller, "Muslim Reports Bug Cassius," New York *Daily News*, May 23, 1965.

128 *"Whites destroyed Malcolm X!":* *Firing Line with William F. Buckley Jr.: Muhammad Ali and the Negro Movement*, YouTube, https://www.you tube.com/watch?v=NxpuT1SNurU.

129 *appeal to the Supreme Court:* Dave Anderson, "How a Clerk Spared Muhammad Ali from Prison," *New York Times*, June 10, 2016.

129 *imperious treatment: Muhammad Speaks*, April 4, 1969; Dave Kindred, *Sound and Fury: Two Powerful Lives, One Fateful Friendship* (New York: Free Press, 2006), 204.

131 *"I don't hate whites":* Thomas Hauser, *Muhammad Ali: His Life and Times* (New York: Simon & Schuster, 1991), 295.

131 *sense of remorse:* Ali, *The Soul of a Butterfly*, 84–85.

131 Sports Illustrated *had singled him out:* Garry Valk, "Letter from the Publisher," *Sports Illustrated*, October 6, 1969, https://vault.si.com/vault /1969/10/06/letter-from-the-publisher.

132 *expand his mind:* Kareem Abdul-Jabbar, with Raymond Obstfeld, *Becoming Kareem: Growing Up On and Off the Court* (New York: Little, Brown, 2017), 157–63.

132 *sheltered life:* Ibid., 12–22.

132 *"You're acting just like a* nigger*!":* Ibid., 100–102.

132 *covered the 1964 riot:* Ibid., 126–33.

132 The Autobiography of Malcolm X *electrified him:* Ibid., 212–16.

133 *a belief system:* Ibid., 259–67.

134 *confided his conversion:* Ibid., 269–74.

134 *legally changed his name:* Ibid., 282–86.

134 *life-changing invitation:* Ibid., 228–35; Jonathan Eig, "The Cleveland Summit and Muhammad Ali: The True Story," *Andscape*, June 1, 2017.

135 *whether to boycott:* Abdul-Jabbar, *Becoming Kareem*, 252–58.

136 *aware of Malcolm X:* John Carlos, *The John Carlos Story: The Sports Movement That Changed the World* (Chicago: Haymarket Books, 2011), 27–32.

137 *"Man, that can't be Malcolm X":* David Davis, "A Courageous Man: An Interview with John Carlos," *Los Angeles Review of Books*, October 16, 2015.

137   *Malcolm went to the podium:* Carlos, *The John Carlos Story*, 29.

137   *destructive forces:* Ibid., 5–10, 19–26.

137   *"I remember being blown away":* Ibid., 28–30.

138   *steps as a social activist:* Ibid., 33–46.

138   *fateful Sunday:* Ibid., 30–32.

139   *eight days after the murder:* Ibid., 57–61.

139   *welcome mat was rolled up:* Ibid., 63–72.

140   *news arrived from the outside world:* Ibid., 72–76.

140   *Harry Edwards:* Author interview with Harry Edwards; "Harry Edwards," *The HistoryMakers*, https://www.thehistorymakers.org/biography/harry-edwards-41.

141   *planning meeting:* Carlos, *The John Carlos Story*, 79–83.

142   *second thoughts:* Ibid., 89–92.

143   *outlined the plan:* Ibid., 109–10.

143   *as the race started:* Ibid., 115–19; "200m(WR)Smith/Norman/Carlos: 1968 Olympics, Mexico City," AthletixStuff, YouTube, https://www.youtube.com/watch?v=bWI9raEM1-4.

144   *mounted the medal stand:* Ibid., 119–22; "USA Duo Take Stand with Black Power Salute," Olympics.com, https://olympics.com/en/video/usa-duo-take-stand-with-black-power-salute.

144   *fierce backlash:* Joseph M. Sheehan, "2 Black Power Advocates Ousted from Olympics," *New York Times*, October 19, 1968; Carlos, *The John Carlos Story*, 122–42; Davis, "A Courageous Man."

145   *Obama invited the two:* "Iconic Olympic Protesters Honored at White House," *CBS Evening News*, September 29, 2016, YouTube, https://www.youtube.com/watch?v=n9ZSY7JCsxg.

145   *"verbal justification":* Carlos, *The John Carlos Story*, 33.

145   *"ones without regrets":* Ibid., 186.

SEVEN: THE BLACK ARTS MOVEMENT

146   *join a delegation:* LeRoi Jones, "Cuba Libre," in *Home: Social Essays* (New York: William Morrow), 11–62; Amiri Baraka, *The Autobiography of LeRoi Jones* (New York: Lawrence Hill, 1997), 243–47.

146   *"Exaugural Poem":* Baraka, *The Autobiography of LeRoi Jones*, 273; table of contents for *Kulchur* 12, realitystudio.org, https://realitystudio.org/bibliographic-bunker/kulchur/.

147   *local TV shows:* Baraka, *The Autobiography of LeRoi Jones*, 274.

147   *"turning tricks":* Ibid., 274–75.

147   *raised in Newark:* Margalit Fox, "Amiri Baraka, Polarizing Poet and Playwright, Dies at 79," *New York Times*, January 9, 2014.

147 *class structure:* Baraka, *The Autobiography of LeRoi Jones*, 54.

148 *"Only craziness":* Ibid., 134.

148 *joined the Air Force:* Ibid., 137–78.

148 *CIA front:* Michael Warner, "Origins of the Congress of Cultural Freedom: 1949–1950," CIA, Center for the Study of Intelligence, https://www.cia.gov/resources/csi/studies-in-intelligence/1995-2/origins-of-the-congress-of-cultural-freedom-1949-50-cultural-cold-war/.

148 *visited an old friend:* Baraka, *The Autobiography of LeRoi Jones*, 169–70.

149 *met Hettie Cohen:* Ibid., 179–41. In his autobiography, Baraka changed Hettie Cohen's name to "Nellie Kohn" and the name of their publication, *Yugen,* to *"Zazen."* Cohen discussed these changes in her own book, *How I Became Hettie Jones* (New York: Dutton, 1990).

149 *full two-act play:* "Jones' 'Dutchman' Wins Drama Award," *New York Times,* May 25, 1964.

149 *collection of essays:* LeRoi Jones, *Blues People: Negro Music in White America* (New York: William Morrow, 1963).

149 *"the Black Arts":* Baraka, *The Autobiography of LeRoi Jones*, 290.

150 *attending a party:* "8th Street Makes Its Move," *Village Voice,* February 25, 1965.

150 *"Malcolm is dead!":* Baraka, *The Autobiography of LeRoi Jones*, 293–94.

150 *Jones's stay in Harlem:* Ibid., 295–328.

151 *panel discussion:* Jack Newfield, "Gig at the Gate: Return of the White Liberal Stompers," *Village Voice,* March 18, 1965.

152 *story on the controversy:* Hollie West, "'Whitey' Loses to 'Spooks' Nightly in Harlem's Black Arts Theater," *Tucson Daily Citizen,* November 30, 1965.

152 *Paul Harvey:* Paul Harvey, "Your Tax Dollar Used to Encourage Rioting," *Gazette News Current* (Xenia, OH), December 4, 1965.

152 *"confused" politics:* Baraka, *The Autobiography of LeRoi Jones*, 312–14.

152 *similar initiatives:* Larry Neal, "The Black Arts Movement," in John H. Bracey Jr., Sonia Sanchez, and James Smethurst, eds., *SOS—Calling All Black People: A Black Arts Movement Reader* (Boston: University of Massachusetts Press, 2014).

153 *"The idea of the Black Arts":* Baraka, *The Autobiography of LeRoi Jones*, 331–32.

153 *Jones's analysis:* Jones, *Home*, 238–50.

153 *new Islamic name:* Baraka, *The Autobiography of LeRoi Jones*, 375–76.

154 *born in Atlanta:* "Larry Neal: 1937–1981," Oxford Reference, https://www.oxfordreference.com/display/10.1093/oi/authority.20110803100226417;jsessionid=CA7556B99DB5C0302BEC6C8E32DE1B18.

154 *master's degree:* Larry Neal, "The Social Background of the Black Arts Movement," *Black Scholar,* January/February 1987.

154   *Michaux's bookstore:* Larry Neal, "New Space: The Growth of Black Consciousness in the Sixties," in Floyd Barbour, ed., *The Black Seventies* (Boston: Porter Sargent, 1970).

155   *aware of Malcolm X:* Ibid.

156   *present at the Audubon Ballroom:* Ibid.

156   *"always in and out":* Baraka, *The Autobiography of LeRoi Jones,* 297.

157   *suspicions about BARTS's ties:* "FBI Memorandum: To: Mr. Mohr, From: C.D. DeLoach, Subject: Black Arts Repertory Theater," *FBI Records: The Vault,* September 29, 1965.

157   *appeared with a pistol:* Baraka, *The Autobiography of LeRoi Jones,* 328–29. Baraka used pseudonyms for Neal's shooter in the book; an account of the feud using the real names appears in Ishmael Reed, "LeRoi Jones/Amiri Baraka and Me," *Transition,* vol. 114, 1969, 13–29.

157   *defining essay:* Larry Neal, "The Black Arts Movement," *Drama Review,* Summer 1968.

159   *seven-hundred-page collection:* Amiri Baraka and Larry Neal, eds., *Black Fire: An Anthology of Afro-American Writing* (New York: William Morrow, 1968).

159   *male poets:* Bracey et al., *SOS,* 309–26.

160   *come to regret:* Neal, "New Space."

160   *"Larry Neal is important":* Stanley Crouch, "Introduction: The Incomplete Turn of Larry Neal," in Larry Neal, *Visions of a Liberated Future: Black Arts Movement Writings* (New York: Basic Books, 1989), 3–7.

161   *"Frankly, it is tiresome":* Darryl Pinckney, "The Changes of Amiri Baraka," *New York Times,* December 16, 1979.

161   *mixed assessments:* Fox, "Amiri Baraka, Polarizing Poet and Playwright, Dies at 79."

161   *Maya Angelou:* "Maya Angelou: Malcolm X," The National Visionary Leadership Project, YouTube: https://www.youtube.com/watch?v=3kt bLy5euvY.

161   *August Wilson:* Patti Hartigan, *August Wilson: A Life* (New York: Simon & Schuster, 2023), 65–66.

162   *Jimmy Garrett:* "Dr. James 'Jimmy' Garrett," interviewed by San Francisco area high school students, April 27, 2020, crmvet.org, https://www.crm vet.org/nars/garrett_student-20.pdf.

163   *Watts Rebellion:* "From the Streets of LA . . . James Garrett," 2018 University of California, Berkeley, interview, September 30, 2018, crmvet .org, https://www.crmvet.org/nars/1809jimy.htm.

163   *fertile ground:* Ibram Rogers, "Remembering the Black Campus Movement: An Oral History Interview with James P. Garrett," *Journal of Pan African Studies,* June 2009.

164 *"Experimental College":* "Experimental College History," San Francisco State University website, https://ueap.sfsu.edu/exco/history#:~: text=In%20Fall%201965%2C%20Experimental%20College,and%20 over%20300%20students%20enrolled.

165 *meeting with Malcolm X:* Sonia Sanchez interview, in Hampton and Fayer, *Voices of Freedom,* 252–55.

165 *Sanchez's first class:* Fern Gillespie, "Sonia Sanchez: The Literary Power of Herstory and History," *Our Time Press,* September 23, 2022, https://ourtimepress.com/sonia-sanchez-the-literary-powerof-herstory -and-history/.

166 *white students feel guilty:* Terry Spencer and Anthony Izaguirre, "Florida's Rejection of Black History Course Stirs Debate," Associated Press, January 23, 2023.

166 *Malcolm came to town:* Ishmael Reed, "Malcolm and Me," Audible (original production), January 2020, https://www.amazon.com/Mal colm-and-Me/dp/B083MSN2HC/ref=tmm_aud_swatch_0?_encoding =UTF8&qid=&sr=.

166 *new territory:* Colleen "Cosmo" Murphy, "The Story of John Coltrane's 'A Love Supreme,'" *Classic Album Sundays,* https://classicalbumsundays .com/album-of-the-month-john-coltrane-a-love-supreme/.

167 *just to hear Malcolm speak:* Richard Brent Turner, "How Malcolm X Inspired John Coltrane to Embrace Islamic Spirituality," *Literary Hub,* May 4, 2021, https://lithub.com/how-malcolm-x-inspired-john-coltrane -to-embrace-islamic-spirituality/.

167 *"New Super Bop Fire":* Amiri Baraka, "Jazz Criticism and Its Effects on the Art Form," in David Baker, ed., *New Perspectives on Jazz* (Washington, DC: Smithsonian, 1986), 66.

167 *new musical movement:* Nat Hentoff, "The New Jazz—Black, Angry and Hard to Understand," *New York Times Magazine,* December 23, 1966.

168 *widely discussed essay:* Julius Lester, "The Singing Is Over: The Angry Children of Malcolm X," *Sing Out!,* October/November 1966.

EIGHT: A LETTER FROM PRISON

173 *short biography:* Author interviews with Peter Goldman.

174 *another major publishing house:* Bruce Weber, "John Jay Iselin, Public TV Innovator, Dies at 74," *New York Times,* May 7, 2008.

174 *"Bring that book over here":* Author interviews with Peter Goldman.

175 *exuberant and anxious:* Goldman, *The Death and Life of Malcolm X,* 136.

175 *"Silence was not Malcolm's gift":* Ibid., 85.

176 *emerged as a folk hero:* Ibid., 396–99.

177   *Edward Bennett Williams:* Author interviews with Peter Goldman.

178   *conspiracy theories:* Goldman, *The Death and Life of Malcolm X*, 254–55, 287–288.

179   *Gene Roberts:* Ibid., 258–60; Edith Evans Asbury, "Detective Tells Panther Trial of His Attempt to Save Malcolm," *New York Times*, December 8, 1970.

180   *pointed to "higher-ups":* Goldman, *The Death and Life of Malcolm X*, 314–15.

180   *"shiningly eloquent":* Orde Coombs, "The Death and Life of Malcolm X," *New York Times*, January 28, 1973.

181   *single-spaced letter:* Author interviews with Goldman; letter in Goldman personal files.

182   *decade since his conviction:* Peter Goldman interview with Muhammad Aziz at Sing Sing, April 16, 1979; Peter Goldman, "Malcolm X: An Unfinished Story?," *New York Times Magazine*, August 19, 1979.

184   *Kunstler had become friendly:* William M. Kunstler, with Sheila Isenberg, *My Life as a Radical Lawyer* (New York: Birch Lane Press, 1994), 382–85.

185   *recognized defense lawyers:* Richard Pears, "William Kunstler, Fierce Defender of Radical Causes, Dies at Age 76," *Washington Post*, September 5, 1995.

185   *castlelike brick prison:* "The Eastern Story," correctionhistory.org, https://www.correctionhistory.org/easternny100/html/eastory.html.

185   *an affidavit:* Goldman, *The Death and Life of Malcolm X*, 428; Appendix, Michael Friedly, *Malcolm X: The Assassination* (New York: Ballantine, 1995), 215–16.

187   *a letter back:* Author interviews with Goldman; letter in Goldman files.

188   *lengthy response:* Robert Morgenthau filings, New York City Department of Records, https://nycma.lunaimaging.com/luna/servlet/view/search /when/1978%2BJanuary%2B12-July%2B14?q=malcolm+x; https://nycma .lunaimaging.com/luna/servlet/detail/NYCMA~14~14~5699~1223 755:People-s-Responses?qvq=w4s:/when%2F1978%2BJanuary% 2B12-July%2B14;q:malcolm%20x&mi=49&trs=134.

188   *second affidavit:* Appendix, Friedly, *Malcolm X*, 217–18.

188   *Judge Harold Rothwax:* Selwyn Raab, "Herman Rothwax, Stern Criminal Court Judge, Dies at 67," *New York Times*, October 23, 1997.

188   *"No criminal case":* Goldman, "Malcolm X: An Unfinished Story?"

189   *"smelled a rat":* Author interviews with Peter Goldman.

NINE: THREE "PAWN SACRIFICES"

190   *taxi to Sing Sing:* Author interviews with Peter Goldman.

190   *led him to an office:* Peter Goldman interview with Muhammad Aziz at Sing Sing, April 16, 1979.

191 *"playing his last card":* Author interviews with Peter Goldman.

191 *took Aziz back:* Peter Goldman interview with Muhammad Aziz at Sing Sing, April 16, 1979; Goldman, *The Death and Life of Malcolm X*, 420–26.

193 *another interview with Karim:* Goldman, *The Death and Life of Malcolm X*, 421.

193 *shared a story:* Author interviews with Peter Goldman; Goldman, *The Death and Life of Malcolm X*, 414.

194 *Congressional Black Caucus:* Paul Alberta, "Congressional Probe Asked into Death of Malcolm X," *Herald-News* (Passaic, NJ), April 27, 1979.

194 *next issue of* Newsweek*:* Peter Goldman, "Who Killed Malcolm X?," *Newsweek*, May 7, 1979.

194 *face-to-face with Khalil Islam:* Author interviews with Peter Goldman; Goldman, *The Death and Life of Malcolm X*, 422–25; Friedly, *Malcolm X*, 89.

196 *Mujahid Halim:* Author interviews with Peter Goldman; Goldman, *The Death and Life of Malcolm X*, 414–19, 422–27; Goldman, "Malcolm X: An Unfinished Story?"; Friedly, *Malcolm X*, 89.

200 *trouble getting his words out:* Goldman, *The Death and Life of Malcolm X*, 418–19.

200 *changed his testimony:* Goldman, *The Death and Life of Malcolm X*, 422.

201 *"fallen into enemy hands":* Goldman, "Malcolm X: An Unfinished Story?"

201 *"wasted like pawn sacrifices":* Goldman, *The Death and Life of Malcolm X*, 424.

201 *five-thousand-word feature story:* Goldman, "Malcolm X: An Unfinished Story?"

202 *first-person account:* Mujahid Halim with Peter Goldman, "'These Brothers Didn't Kill Malcolm X,'" *Boston Globe*, September 9, 1979.

202 *curt call back:* Author interviews with Peter Goldman.

203 *academic publisher:* Eric Pace, "August Meier, 79, Authority on Black American History," *New York Times*, March 25, 2003.

203 *wistful meditation:* Goldman, *The Death and Life of Malcolm X*, 435.

TEN: THE RAPPERS

207 *Malcolm's grave:* Russell J. Rickford, *Betty Shabazz: Surviving Malcolm X: A Journey of Strength from Wife to Widow to Heroine* (Naperville, IL: Sourcebooks, 2003), 408.

208 *spliced together Malcolm's voice:* Lyrics to "No Sell Out" on Genius, https://genius.com/Malcolm-x-no-sell-out-lyrics.

208 *"This is my life":* JayQuan, "Give the Drummer Some: The Story of Sugar Hill House & Tackhead Drummer Keith LeBlanc," *ThaFoundation*, http://www.thafoundation.com/klblanc.htm.

208 *the South Bronx:* Matt Purdy, "Left to Die, the South Bronx Rises from Decades of Decay," *New York Times*, November 13, 1994.

209 *DJ Kool Herc:* "50 Years of Hip Hop," ABC7 Eyewitness News, https://www.youtube.com/watch?v=VfIzemMk4yc; John Leland, "The Spin Interview: DJ Kool Herc," *Spin*, August 1, 2023, https://www.spin.com/2023/08/the-spin-interview-dj-kool-herc/.

209 *Grandmaster Flash:* John Leland, "Grandmaster Flash Beats Back Time," *New York Times*, August 26, 2016.

210 *"playing the dozens":* Ice-T, director, *Something from Nothing: The Art of Rap*, 2012, YouTube, https://www.youtube.com/watch?v=cbkOz1nkYyw.

210 *Sugar Hill Records:* Stephanie Phillips, "Sylvia Robinson's Legacy as 'the Mother of Hip Hop,'" She Shreds, https://sheshreds.com/sylvia-robinson/.

210 *"Rapper's Delight":* "The Sugar Hill Gang—Rapper's Delight (Official Video)," Sugar Hill Records, YouTube, https://www.youtube.com/watch?v=mcCK99wHrk0.

210 *Keith LeBlanc:* Scott Goldfine, Interview with Keith LeBlanc, *Truth in Rhythm* podcast, YouTube, https://www.youtube.com/watch?v=wwW7UUrPSiA.

211 *Saddler had been raised:* Leland, "Grandmaster Flash Beats Back Time."

211 *"The Message":* "Grandmaster Flash and the Furious Five—The Message (Official Video)," YouTube, https://www.youtube.com/watch?v=gYMkEMCHtJ4.

211 *"spoken word":* "The Adventures of Grandmaster Flash on the Wheels of Steel," Listening to Rap, https://listeningtorap.wordpress.com/2015/07/02/the-adventures-of-grandmaster-flash-on-the-wheels-of-steel-grandmaster-flash/; JayQuan, "Give the Drummer Some."

211 *"I didn't know much about Malcolm X":* JayQuan, "The Malcolm X Effect on Hip Hop," Rock the Bells, https://rockthebells.com/articles/the-malcolm-x-effect-on-hip-hop/.

212 *bits of Malcolm's speeches:* "Malcolm X: No Sell Out," samples on WhoSampled, https://www.whosampled.com/Malcolm-X/No-Sell-Out/; Interview with Zaheer Ali of the Malcolm X Project, August 27, 2001, https://ccnmtl.columbia.edu/projects/ecourse/0402/web/readings/mx_207_ali_f_x.pdf.

212 *Shabazz finally called:* Goldfine, interview with Keith LeBlanc, *Truth in Rhythm* podcast.

212 *sued him and Tommy Boy:* Ibid.; Dan Charnas, *The Big Payback: The History of the Business of Hip Hop* (New York: New American Library, 2010), 102–5.

213 *brief review in* People: Eric Levin, "Song," *People*, February 20, 1984.

213 *suburban town of Roosevelt:* Alex Boyd, "Despite Prejudice, Roosevelt Perseveres," *LI Herald.com*, January 21, 2016.

213 *progressively more integrated:* Olivia Winslow, "Dividing Lines, Visible and Invisible," *Newsday*, November 17, 2019.

213 *white families to flee:* John Kucsera, "New York State's Extreme School Segregation: Inequality, Inaction and a Damaged Future," *The Civil Rights Project*, March 26, 2014, https://civilrightsproject.ucla.edu/re search/k-12-education/integration-and-diversity/ny-norflet-report -placeholder/Kucsera-New-York-Extreme-Segregation-2014.pdf.

214 *racial trend line:* Winslow, "Dividing Lines, Visible and Invisible."

214 *Carlton Douglas Ridenhour:* Robert Christgau and Greg Tate, "Chuck D: All Over the Map," *Village Voice*, October 22, 1991; Lorenzo Douglas Ridenhour obituary, Legacy.com, https://www.legacy.com/us/obituar ies/atlanta/name/lorenzo-ridenhour-obituary?id=16705828.

214 *program in Black history:* Jerry L. Barrow, "The Secret History of Public Enemy's 'Y! Bum Rush the Show,'" OkayPlayer, https://www.okayplayer .com/originals/secret-history-public-enemy-yo-bum-rush-the-show.html.

214 *"made us see a different world":* James Hale, director, *Public Enemy: Prophets of Rage*, 2011, YouTube, https://www.youtube.com/watch?v=x MCvWeWnsJw.

215 *Spectrum City DJ:* Keith Shockley, director, *Spectrum City: How It All Began*, YouTube, https://www.youtube.com/watch?v=xMCvWeWnsJw.

215 *invited Ridenhour to MC:* Barrow, "The Secret History of Public Enemy's 'Y! Bum Rush the Show.'"

215 *"part radio announcer":* Ibid.

215 *"Personality walks":* Hale, *Public Enemy: Prophets of Rage.*

215 *their own music:* Shockley, *Spectrum City: How It All Began.*

216 *"Flavor is the dude":* Hale, *Public Enemy: Prophets of Rage.*

216 *WBAU aired a show:* Barrow, "The Secret History of Public Enemy's 'Y! Bum Rush the Show.'"

217 *"completely right":* Jeff Chang, *Can't Stop, Won't Stop: A History of the Hip-Hop Generation* (New York: Picador, 2005), 247.

217 *"Malcolm the tenth":* Hale, *Public Enemy: Prophets of Rage.*

217 *seen as a "posse":* Ibid.

218 *didn't offer much money:* Barrow, "The Secret History of Public Enemy's 'Y! Bum Rush the Show.'"

218 *album cover:* Picture of original LP cover on eBay, https://www.ebay .com/itm/363847651103.

218 *two Long Island rappers:* "#61: Eric B. & Rakim, 'Paid in Full,'" in *Rolling Stone* ranking of Greatest Albums of All Time, https://www.rollingstone

.com/music/music-lists/best-albums-of-all-time-1062063/guns-n-roses
-appetite-for-destruction-3-1063171/.

218   *"Noise Annoys"*: John Leland, "Noise Annoys," *Village Voice*, April 21, 1987.

218   *"dominate the streets"*: Hale, *Public Enemy: Prophets of Rage*.

219   *"The Grunt"*: "The JB's—The Grunt," YouTube, https://www.youtube
.com/watch?v=L-4VxEtWyRo.

219   *109 beats:* Christgau and Tate, "Chuck D: All Over the Map."

219   *"Bring the Noise"*: Public Enemy, "Bring the Noise," YouTube, https://
www.youtube.com/watch?v=DctKhOn938o.

219   It Takes a Nation of Millions: Ian McCann, "'Nation of Millions': Why
Public Enemy's Masterpiece Cannot Be Held Back," *udiscovermusic*,
June 28, 2023. Critics from Alan Light to Kevin Powell consider *It Takes
a Nation* to be the greatest hip hop album of all time.

219   *musical allusions:* "Party for Your Right to Fight," YouTube, https://
www.youtube.com/watch?v=YDQTZ36lCDA; "Public Enemy: 'Party
for Your Right to Fight,'" WhoSampled, https://www.whosampled.com
/Public-Enemy/Party-for-Your-Right-to-Fight/samples/.

219   *Boston radio show:* "1964 Boston Radio Broadcast," YouTube, https://
www.youtube.com/watch?v=ppV1N5dwJVo.

220   *Lee began shooting:* St. Clair Bourne, director, *Making "Do The Right
Thing,"* 1989, YouTube, https://www.youtube.com/watch?v=ED9p5cv
oKdU.

220   *an "anthem"*: "How Public Enemy's 'Fight the Power' Became an Anthem," PBS, https://www.youtube.com/watch?v=DctKhOn938o.

221   *"I wanted it to be defiant"*: Janice C. Simpson, "Music: Yo! Rap Gets on
the Map," *Time*, February 5, 1990.

221   *"all Black in New York"*: "Public Enemy: The Making of 'Fight the Power,'"
YouTube, https://www.youtube.com/watch?v=m5VGDEab0_0.

221   *"Fight the Power"*: Ibid.; Jeffrey Barrow, "'Fight the Power': The Story
Behind Public Enemy's Searing Classic," *udiscovermusic*, July 4, 2023,
https://www.udiscovermusic.com/stories/public-enemy-fight-the-power
-song-feature/.

222   *"Malcolm-esque"*: Hale, *Public Enemy: Prophets of Rage*.

222   *music video:* "Public Enemy: 'Fight the Power' (Official Music Video),"
YouTube, https://www.youtube.com/watch?v=e-4AtiOjBmg.

222   *world debut:* Vincent Canby, "Critic's Notebook; Spike Lee Stirs Things
Up at Cannes," *New York Times*, May 20, 1999.

223   *attacks on the movie:* Bill Higgins, "Hollywood Flashback: A Snubbed
Spike Lee Trashed Win Wenders in 1989," *Hollywood Reporter*, May 12,
2018; Andrew Pulver, "Spike Lee: Critics Said 'Do the Right Thing'
Would Incite Riots," *The Guardian*, September 11, 2023.

223   *Professor Griff:* Greg Baker, "The Education of Professor Griff," *Miami New Times,* July 11, 1990.

223   *critical and commercial hits:* "151 Greatest Hip Hop Songs According to The Source," Rate Your Music, https://rateyourmusic.com/list/Matica /151_greatest_hip_hop_songs_according_to_the_source/; "7—Public Enemy: Fight the Power," 100 Greatest Hip Hop Songs of All Time, *Rolling Stone,* June 2, 2017, https://www.rollingstone.com/music/music -lists/100-greatest-hip-hop-songs-of-all-time-105784/wu-tang-clan-c-r-e -a-m-2-102425/; "Do The Right Thing (1989)," *American Film Institute Catalog,* https://catalog.afi.com/Catalog/moviedetails/67050.

224   *historic oversight:* "Do the Right Thing, with Sean Fennessey and Wesley Morris," *The Rewatchables* podcast, https://www.youtube.com/watch ?v=cYAbLOKdamg.

224   *King and Malcolm met:* Peniel E. Joseph, *The Sword and the Shield: The Revolutionary Lives of Malcolm X and Martin Luther King Jr.* (New York: Basic Books, 2020), 1–7.

225   *different conclusion:* "Do the Right Thing, with Sean Fennessey and Wesley Morris."

225   *Lawrence Parker:* Hannah Lee, "Reflecting on KRS-One's Legacy in Hip Hop as He Celebrates His 57th Birthday," *Frank151,* August 24, 2022, https://frank151.com/reflecting-on-krs-ones-legacy-in-hip-hop-as -he-celebrates-his-57th-birthday/.

225   *nickname "Krishna":* Ice-T, director, *Something from Nothing: The Art of Rap.*

226   *"My Philosophy":* "My Philosophy" (Official HD Video), Boogie Down Productions, YouTube, https://www.youtube.com/watch?v=h1vKOch ATXs.

226   *Echoing Malcolm:* Anthony DeCurtis, *By All Means Necessary* review, *Rolling Stone,* October 6, 1988.

226   *"Temple of Hip Hop":* Temple of Hip Hop mission statement, https:// thetempleofhiphop.wordpress.com.

226   *Tupac Amaru Shakur:* Jon Pareles, "Tupac Shakur, 25, Rap Performer Who Personified Violence, Dies," *New York Times,* September 14, 1996.

227   *Shakur echoed Malcolm:* Lyrics to "Words of Wisdom," by Tupac Shakur, Genius, https://genius.com/2pac-words-of-wisdom-lyrics.

227   *luncheon banquet:* Video of Tupac's address to the Malcolm X Grass-roots Movement, 1991, YouTube, https://www.youtube.com/watch?v =3m2OUSZ5WR8; Jocelyn Y. Stewart, "Movement Carries On," *Los Angeles Times,* December 3, 1992.

227   *international fame:* Pareles, "Tupac Shakur, 25, Rap Performer Who Personified Violence, Dies."

228   *cost him his life:* Robert Kilburn and Jerry Crowe, "Rapper Tupac

Shakur, 25, Dies 6 Days After Las Vegas Shooting," *Los Angeles Times*, September 14, 1996.

228 *Jones invoked Malcolm X:* Quincy Jones, Foreword, in Alan Light, *Tupac Amaru Shakur: 1971–1996* (New York: Three Rivers Press, 1988); "Quincy Jones, QD3, and More Talk Tupac (2Pac) and How His Music Was Going to Change," YouTube, https://www.youtube.com/watch?v=APlOG6S_1-s.

229 *two Harvard undergraduates:* Chris Hedges, "Public Lives; His Beat Goes On, as a Hip-Hop Empire," *New York Times*, February 20, 2001.

229 *East-West feud:* Paul Cantor, "How the 1995 Source Awards Changed Rap Forever," *Complex*, August 3, 2015, https://www.broadwayworld.com/bwwtv/article/RATINGS-SATURDAY-NIGHT-LIVE-Premiere-Grows-Ten-Percent-20201006.

229 *Lawrence Ware:* Lawrence Ware, "What the Source Taught Me," *New York Times*, August 13, 2018.

230 *slain leader on its cover:* Cover and Table of Contents for March 1990 issue of *The Source* on Worth Point, https://www.worthpoint.com/worthopedia/source-magazine-march-1990-malcolm-1836507382.

230 *another cover story:* "Malcolm X and the Hip Hop Generation," *The Source*, May 18, 2015.

230 XXL *magazine:* Roger Krastz, "15 Songs That Name Drop Malcolm X," *XXL*, May 19, 2015.

230 Vibe *magazine:* Armon Sadler, "Malcolm X's Most Powerful Quotes," *Vibe*, May 19, 2023.

230 *visual references:* "When Rappers Replicate Iconic Malcolm X Images," *BET*, https://www.bet.com/photo-gallery/432du5/when-rappers-replicate-iconic-malcolm-x-images/y1kvhc.

230 *Kendrick Lamar:* Danielle Darling, "Kendrick Lamar Says 'The Autobiography of Malcolm X' Changed Him," hiphopx, November 13, 2014, https://hiphopdx.com/news/id.31402/title.kendrick-lamar-says-the-autobiography-of-malcolm-x-changed-him.

230 *Nicki Minaj:* "Lookin Ass" music video, YouTube, https://www.youtube.com/watch?v=2mwNbTL3pOs; Lily Rothman, "Nicki Minaj Apologizes for Linking Malcolm X to Expletive-Heavy Track," *Time*, February 14, 2014; BKNation.org petition on Change.org: https://www.change.org/p/nicki-minaj-young-money-entertainment-cash-money-records-and-universal-music-group-nickiminaj-youngmoneysite-universal-music-group-umg-stop-disrespecting-malcolm-x-black-history-and-black-people.

231 *Megan Thee Stallion:* Megan Thee Stallion performance of "Savage"

on *Saturday Night Live*, October 3, 2020, https://www.youtube.com
/watch?app=desktop&v=CTpilDQXYr0; "Malcolm X: 'Who Taught
You to Hate Yourself?' May 5th 1962 Los Angeles," YouTube, https://
www.youtube.com/watch?v=l8yNdrPvWjU&t=1480s.

232 *largest audience:* Sarah Jae Leiber, "Ratings: Saturday Night Live Premiere
Grows Ten Percent," *Broadway World*, October 6, 2020, https://www
.broadwayworld.com/bwwtv/article/RATINGS-SATURDAY
-NIGHT-LIVE-Premiere-Grows-Ten-Percent-20201006.

ELEVEN: THE MOVIE

233 *artistic license:* Spike Lee, with Ralph Wiley, *By Any Means Necessary:
The Trials and Tribulations of the Making of Malcolm X* (New York: Vintage, 1993), 29.

233 *hired Norman Jewison:* Liz Smith, "Actor Denzel Washington to Portray Malcolm X," *Los Angeles Times*, December 7, 1989.

233 *obsessed with Malcolm X:* Lee, *By Any Means Necessary*, 3.

234 *Spike's mother:* "Spike Lee Breaks Down His Film Heroes," GQ, YouTube, https://www.youtube.com/watch?v=NfRMe-gnP6s.

234 *first movie camera:* Lee, *By Any Means Necessary*, 8.

234 *best student film:* Lindsey Bahr, "Student Academy Awards—a Launching Pad into Hollywood—Celebrate 50 Years," *Seattle Times*, November 22, 2023.

234 *"a big problem":* "Short Takes: Lee Takes Over Malcolm X Movie," *Los Angeles Times*, January 28, 1991.

234 *sympathetic ear:* Lee, *By Any Means Necessary*, 9–10.

234 *"an enigma to me":* "Short Takes: Lee Takes Over Malcolm X Movie."

234 *"have to thank him":* Jim Hemphill, "'Malcolm X' at 30: Spike Lee Reflects on Winning the Fight to Make His Masterpiece," *IndieWire*, August 18, 2022.

234 *met Malcolm X personally:* Bernard Weinraub, "A Movie Producer Remembers the Human Side of Malcolm X," *New York Times*, November 23, 1992.

235 *Columbia insisted:* James Baldwin, "Malcolm and Martin," *Esquire*, April 1972.

235 *threat of legal action:* D. Quentin Miller, "Lost and . . . Found? James Baldwin's Script and Spike Lee's 'Malcolm X,'" *African American Review*, Winter 2013.

236 *vented about the experience:* James Baldwin, *The Devil Finds Work: An Essay* (New York: Dial Press, 1976).

236 *feature-length documentary:* Weinraub, "A Movie Producer Remembers the Human Side of Malcolm X."

236 *original screenplay:* James Baldwin, *One Day When I Was Lost: A Screenplay Based on Alex Haley's The Autobiography of Malcolm X* (New York: Alfred A. Knopf, 2013).

236 *numerous other attempts:* Woodie King Jr., director, *Death of a Prophet*, remastered (Entertain Me Productions, 2022); Miller, "Lost and . . . Found?"; Lee, *By Any Means Necessary*, 24.

237 *films of David Lean:* Hemphill, "'Malcolm X' at 30."

237 *"no such thing as half-pregnant":* Ibid.

237 *cast Denzel Washington:* Smith, "Actor Denzel Washington to Play Malcolm X."

237 *Charlton Heston in blackface:* David Leeming, *James Baldwin: A Biography* (New York: Alfred A. Knopf, 1994), 297.

238 *one-act play:* Frank Rich, "The Stage: Malcolm X and Elijah Muhammad," *New York Times*, July 15, 1981.

238 *hair salon:* Interview with Spike Lee, Denzel Washington, and Angela Bassett at the Academy Museum of Motion Pictures, September 26, 2021, YouTube, https://www.youtube.com/watch?v=ACNthc-uths.

238 *physical preparation:* Ibid.; Lee, *By Any Means Necessary*, 89–90; Lena Williams, "Playing with Fire," *New York Times*, October 25, 1992.

239 *Paul Lee:* Lee, *By Any Means Necessary*, 28.

239 *William Kunstler:* Ibid., 36.

239 *Benjamin Karim:* Ibid., 33–39.

240 *real-life Sophia:* Marable, *Malcolm X*, 46–47.

240 *Captain Joseph:* Lee, *By Any Means Necessary*, 58–65.

240 *FBI audiotapes:* Interview with Lee, Washington, and Bassett at the Academy Museum of Motion Pictures.

241 *companion book:* Lee, *By Any Means Necessary*.

241 *op-ed piece:* David J. Garrow, "Does Anyone Care Who Killed Malcolm X?," *New York Times*, February 21, 1993.

241 *master of marketing:* Lee, *By Any Means Necessary*, 22.

242 *directing commercials:* Jeff Eisenberg, "Iconic Sports Commercials: Michael Jordan and Mars Blackmon," *Yahoo*, July 17, 2019.

242 *"raining caps":* Lee, *By Any Means Necessary*, 22.

242 *group of critics:* Evelyn Nieves, "Malcolm X: Firestorm over a Film Script," *New York Times*, August 9, 1991; David Ansen, "The Battle for Malcolm X," *Newsweek*, August 25, 1991.

244 *"'DEEDS NOT WORDS'":* Spike Lee, "Spike Lee Takes On His Detractors," *Newsweek*, August 25, 1991.

244 *cut his shooting budget:* Lee, *By Any Means Necessary*, 70–71.

244 *opening scene in Roxbury:* Ibid., 85–89.

245 *Roseland Ballroom:* Ibid., 76.

245 *"greatest dance scene":* M. J. Moore, "Reminiscing in Tempo: On Malcolm X and the Legacy of the Big Band Era," *Honeysuckle*, 2019, https://honeysucklemag.com/reminiscing-in-tempo-on-malcolm-x-and-the-legacy-of-the-big-band-era/.

245 *professional musicians:* Author interview with Javon Jackson.

245 *dozens of scenes:* Lee, *By Any Means Necessary*, 94: "Malcolm X: 1992," Movie-Locations.com, https://www.movie-locations.com/movies/m/Malcolm-X.php.

246 *well-known figures:* Cast of Malcolm X, IMDb, https://www.imdb.com/title/tt0104797/fullcredits.

246 *crawling with asbestos:* Lee, *By Any Means Necessary*, 75–76.

246 *mood darkened:* Interview with Lee, Washington, and Bassett at the Academy Museum of Motion Pictures.

246 *dialogue, music, and camera work:* Ibid.; Spike Lee, director *Malcolm X*, (Warner Brothers, 1992), 2:57:40–3:07:16.

247 *planned to travel:* Lee, *By Any Means Necessary*, 102; Hemphill, "Malcolm X at 30."

248 *running over budget:* Lee, *By Any Means Necessary*, 32, 71.

248 *bond company:* Ibid., 102–3; Hemphill, "Malcolm X at 30."

249 *wealthy friends:* Lee, *By Any Means Necessary*, 138; Hemphill, "Malcolm X at 30"; Spike Lee interview, *Charlie Rose*, June 19, 1992, YouTube, https://www.youtube.com/watch?v=cH3QQDEH2TE.

249 *Stone's JFK:* Lee, *By Any Means Necessary*, 28–30.

250 *"This film is needed":* Ibid., 160.

250 *press conference:* Lena Williams, "Spike Lee Says Money from Blacks Saved 'X,'" *New York Times*, May 20, 1992.

250 *start the movie:* Lee, *Malcolm X*, 00:00–02:43.

250 *end the movie:* Ibid., 3:07:41–3:12:22; Lee, *By Any Means Necessary*, 105.

251 New Jack City: "New Jack City Sparks Violence," Associated Press, March 12, 1991.

251 *Vincent Canby:* Vincent Canby, "Review/Film; 'Malcolm X,' as Complex as Its Subject," *New York Times*, November 18, 1992.

251 *"most conventional film to date":* Jacquie Jones, "Spike Lee Presents Malcolm X: The New Black Nationalism," *Cineaste* 19, no. 4 (1993): 9–11.

251 *"Malcolm X for Beginners":* Introduction to "Malcolm X Symposium: By Any Means Necessary," *Cineaste* 19, no. 4 (1993): 4.

251 *Box office returns:* Renée Graham, "From Sizzle to Fizzle: What Cooled 'Malcolm X,'" *Boston Globe*, February 21, 1993.

252 *Washington's performance:* "Critics' Circle Votes 'The Player' Best Film,"

New York Times, December 18, 1992; Clayton Davis, "Denzel Washington Talks Reinventing Macbeth, Oscars and Who's the Next Denzel," *Variety*, January 6, 2022.

252 *"makeup call"*: Spike Lee interview with Don Bogle at TCM Classic Film Festival, March 28, 2015, YouTube, https://www.youtube.com /watch?v=ozElttlGWI4.

252 *critic Roger Ebert:* "Roger's Top Ten Lists: Best Films of the 1990s," RogerEbert.com, https://www.rogerebert.com/chazs-blog/rogers-top-ten -lists-best-films-of-the-1990s.

252 *best movie made in 1992:* "The 100 Best Movies of the Past 10 Decades," *Time*, July 26, 2023, https://time.com/collection/100-best-movies/62960 84/malcolm-x-1992/.

252 *Manning Marable:* Manning Marable, "Malcolm as Messiah: Cultural Myths vs. Historical Reality in *Malcolm X*," *Cineaste* 19, no. 4 (1993): 7–9.

252 *Herb Boyd:* Herb Boyd, "Malcolm After Mecca: Pan Africanism and the OAAU," *Cineaste* 19, no. 4 (1993): 11–12.

252 *bell hooks:* bell hooks, "Male Heroes and Female Sex Objects: Sexism in Spike Lee's *Malcolm X*," *Cineaste* 19, no. 4 (1993): 13–15.

253 *expecting too much:* Jones, "Spike Lee Presents *Malcolm X*."

253 *as many young people as possible:* Lee interview, *Charlie Rose*, June 19, 1992.

253 *Malcolm as a commodity:* Mark Whitaker, "Malcolm X," *Newsweek*, November 16, 1992.

254 *telephone survey:* "Poll: Malcolm X a Hero for Most Young Blacks," United Press International, November 7, 1992.

TWELVE: HERO TO THE RIGHT AND LEFT

255 *Juan Williams:* Juan Williams, "A Question of Fairness," *The Atlantic*, February 1987.

256 *words from memory:* Malcolm X, *Autobiography*, 300.

256 *cited his grandfather:* Williams, "A Question of Fairness"; Clarence Thomas, *My Grandfather's Son* (New York: HarperCollins, 2007).

256 *"Young and hot-blooded":* Bill Kauffman, "Freedom Now II: Interview with Clarence Thomas," *Reason*, November 1987.

257 *"never be seen as equal":* Williams, "A Question of Fairness."

257 *widely read essay:* Patricia J. Williams, "Clarence Thomas: Man of the People," in Joe Wood, ed., *Malcolm X: In Our Own Image* (New York: St. Martin's Press, 1992), 190–92, 202 (footnote 11).

258 *"Clarence X":* Stephen F. Smith, "Clarence X? The Black Nationalist

Behind Justice Thomas's Constitutionalism," *New York University Journal of Law & Liberty* 4, no. 3 (2009): 583–625.

259   *stunned court watchers:* Linda Greenhouse, "An Intense Attack by Justice Thomas on Cross-Burning," *New York Times*, December 12, 2002.

259   *outright dissent:* Smith, "Clarence X?"

260   *his own concurrence:* Supreme Court opinion in *United States v. Fordice*, supreme.justia.com, https://supreme.justia.com/cases/federal/us/505/717/case.pdf.

260   *outright hostility:* Thomas concurrence in *Students for Fair Admissions v. Harvard*, supreme.justia.com, https://supreme.justia.com/cases/federal/us/600/20-1199/case.pdf.

260   *hypocrisy of the university:* Smith, "Clarence X?"

260   *longest-serving active justice:* Corey Robin, "Clarence Thomas's Radical Vision of Race," *New Yorker*, September 10, 2019.

261   *banned affirmative action:* Supreme Court decisions in *Students for Fair Admissions v. Harvard*, supreme.justia.com, https://supreme.justia.com/cases/federal/us/600/20-1199/case.pdf.

262   *provocative collection of essays:* Shelby Steele, *The Content of Our Character: A New Vision of Race in America* (New York: St. Martin's Press, 1990).

262   *critics faulted Steele:* Patricia J. Williams, "'A Kind of Race Fatigue," *New York Times*, September 16, 1990.

262   *most coveted prizes:* "1990 Winners & Finalists," National Book Critics Circle Awards, https://www.bookcritics.org/past-awards/1990/.

263   *idiosyncratic views:* Samuel Kronen, "American Humanist," *City Journal*, Autumn 2012.

263   *"love ourselves first":* Shelby Steele, "Big Little Man," *New Republic*, December 21, 1992.

265   *"effective leader":* George E. Curry, "Farrakhan, Jesse and the Jews, Part 2," *Emerge*, September 1994.

265   *attacked Judaism:* George E. Curry, "Farrakhan, Jesse and the Jews," *Emerge*, July/August 1994.

266   *a target on Malcolm's back:* Minister Louis X, "Boston Minister Tells of Malcolm—Muhammad's Biggest Hypocrite," *Muhammad Speaks*, December 4, 1964.

266   *Savior's Day rally:* George E. Curry, "The Last Days of Malcolm X," *Emerge*, March 1995.

266   *Pressman asked Betty Shabazz:* "Widow of Malcolm X Suspects Farrakhan Had Role in Killing," Associated Press, March 13, 1994.

267   *plea deal:* Malcolm Gladwell, "U.S., Shabazz Settle Farrakhan Murder Plot Case," *Washington Post*, May 1, 1995.

267   *rally at the Apollo Theater:* Malcolm Gladwell, "Farrakhan Seeks End of
      Rift with Shabazz," *Washington Post*, May 8, 1995.

267   *Betty cared for her grandson:* Trevor W. Coleman, "Betty Shabazz: A
      Mother's Struggle," *Emerge*, September 1997.

268   *Betty's funeral service:* Rachel L. Swarns, "At Funeral for Shabazz, Grief,
      Prayer and Respect," *New York Times*, June 28, 1997.

268   *interview with Mike Wallace:* "Who Killed Malcolm X?," *60 Minutes*,
      May 14, 2000, YouTube, https://www.youtube.com/watch?v=h1VL
      BQxvvjw; Author interview with Jay Kernis.

269   *feat of national organizing:* Michael Janofsky, "The March on Washington:
      The Overview; Debate on March, and Farrakhan, Persists as Black Men
      Converge on the Capital," *New York Times*, October 16, 1995; George E.
      Curry, "After the Million Man March," *Emerge*, February 1996.

270   *George Breitman:* Breitman, *Malcolm X Speaks*; George Breitman, *The
      Last Year of Malcolm X: The Evolution of a Revolutionary* (New York:
      Pathfinder Press, 1968); George Breitman, ed., *Malcolm X: By Any
      Means Necessary: Speeches, Interviews and a Letter* (New York: Path-
      finder Press, 1970).

270   *Baba Zak Kondo:* Baba Zak Kondo, *Conspiracys: Unravelling the Assassi-
      nation of Malcolm X* (Nubia Press, 1993).

270   *Karl Evanzz:* Karl Evanzz, *The Judas Factor: The Plot to Kill Malcolm X*
      (New York: Thunder's Mouth Press, 1992).

271   *another Black historian:* Manning Marable interviews, *The HistoryMak-
      ers*, https://www.thehistorymakers.org/biography/manning-marable-41.

272   *contract with Wendy Wolf:* "Wendy Wolf: The Story Behind 'Malcolm X:
      A Life of Reinvention,'" WBEZ/Chicago, https://www.wbez.org/arts/2012
      /02/07/wendy-wolf-the-story-behind-malcolm-x-a-life-of-reinvention.

272   *"Malcolm X Project":* Website for the "Malcolm X Project," Columbia
      University, https://www.columbia.edu/cu/ccbh/mxp/.

273   *passed away:* William Grimes, "Manning Marable, Historian and Social
      Critic, Dies at 60," *New York Times*, April 2, 2011.

273   *front-page story:* Larry Rohter, "On Eve of Revealing Work, Malcolm X
      Biographer Dies," *New York Times*, April 2, 2011.

273   *prominent Black academics:* Melissa Harris-Perry interview, NPR, April 5,
      2011, https://www.npr.org/transcripts/135144230?storyId=135144230.

273   *mostly glowing reviews:* Michiko Kakutani, "Peeling Away Multiple
      Masks," *New York Times*, April 7, 2011; Macy Halford, "The 2011 Na-
      tional Book Awards Finalists," *New Yorker*, October 12, 2011; 2012
      Pulitzer Prize for History citation, https://www.pulitzer.org/winners
      /manning-marable.

273   *"beyond the legend":* Marable, *Malcolm X*, 1–14.

273 *personal influences:* Ibid., 15–38.

273 *criminal activities:* Ibid., 39–69.

274 *split with the Nation of Islam:* Ibid., 211–68.

274 *like Peter Goldman:* Ibid., 526 (footnotes); author interviews with Peter Goldman.

274 *fascinating reconstruction:* Marable, *Malcolm X*, 269–96.

274 *ideological turn:* Ibid., 297–87.

275 *threats on Malcolm's life:* Ibid., 388–449.

275 *blog post:* Abdur-Rahman Muhammad, "For the First Time in History, the Face of William Bradley; Shotgun Assassin of Malcolm X-El Hajj Malik El Shabazz, in a Public Safety Campaign Commercial for Mayor Cory Booker!," *A Singular Voice*, April 22, 2010, https://singularvoice .wordpress.com/2010/04/22/for-the-first-time-in-history-the-face-of -william-bradley-shotgun-assassin-of-malcolm-x-el-hajj-malik-el-shabazz/.

276 *didn't mince words:* Karl Evanzz, "Paper Tiger: Manning Marable's Poison Pen," Truth Continuum, April 13, 2011, http://mxmission.blogspot .com/2011/04/paper-tiger-manning-marables-poison-pen.html.

276 *appeared to take a shot:* Marable, *Malcolm X*, 490.

277 *a volume of essays:* Jared A. Ball and Todd Steven Burroughs, eds., *A Lie of Reinvention: Correcting Manning Marable's Malcolm X* (Baltimore: Black Classic Press, 2012).

277 *"Rudy":* Malcolm X, *Autobiography*, 152.

277 *"strong evidence":* Marable, *Malcolm X*, 66.

277 *Bruce Perry:* Bruce Perry, *Malcolm: The Life of a Man Who Changed Black America* (Barrytown, NY: Station Hill Press, 1991), 82.

277 *scholarly objections:* Margaret Washington, in "Roundtable" on *Malcolm X: A Life of Reinvention, Journal of American Studies*, February 2013.

278 *marriage of convenience:* Marable, *Malcolm X*, 144–45.

278 *Louis Farrakhan:* Ibid., 516 (footnote to page 145).

278 *wrote to Elijah Muhammad:* Ibid., 149.

278 *biography of Betty Shabazz:* Rickford, *Betty Shabazz*.

278 *deep affection:* Ibid., 84–85.

279 *"in America's past":* Marable, *Malcolm X*, 486.

THIRTEEN: FROM OBAMA TO BLACK LIVES MATTER

280 *Black Heritage Stamp:* "Black Heritage Stamp Series Origins," Smithsonian National Postage Museum, https://postalmuseum.si.edu/exhi bition/freedom-just-around-the-corner-black-heritage-stamp-series /black-heritage-stamp-series#:~:text=U.S.%20postage%20stamps%20 were%20in,introduced%20the%20Black%20Heritage%20series.

280 *Maxine Waters:* Zerline A Hughes, "Black Heritage Stamp to Honor Malcolm X," *Los Angeles Times,* December 27, 1998.

281 *"co-opt his words":* Yemi Touré, "Malcolm's on a Stamp and We Got Licked," *Final Call News,* https://www.finalcall.com/perspectives/mal colmx3-2-99.htm.

281 *misidentified the photo:* Paul Lee, "Bulk Rate Treatment of a First Rate Man," *Newsday,* February 12, 1999.

281 *intimates gathered:* Attallah Shabazz, Foreword, Malcolm X, *Autobiography of Malcolm X* (New York: Ballantine, 1999).

283 *"Malcolm was on time":* Les Payne, "This 'Malcolm' Could Have Been Martin," *Newsday,* January 24, 1999.

283 *Barack Obama:* Details of Obama's early life from profiles and biographies including David Remnick, *The Bridge: The Life and Rise of Barack Obama* (New York: Vintage, 2011).

284 *Malcolm X as a touchstone:* Barack Obama, *Dreams from My Father: A Story of Race and Inheritance* (New York: Crown, 1995), 85–86.

285 *Project Vote:* Vernon Jarrett, "Project Vote Brings Power to the People—Obama," *Chicago Sun-Times,* August 11, 1992.

285 *Malcolm fashion look:* Remnick, *The Bridge,* 223.

286 *"They try to bamboozle you":* Ben Smith, "An Unlikely Echo," *Politico,* January 17, 2008.

286 *again in 2016:* "Obama Stumps for Hillary: 'Don't Be Bamboozled!,'" *Daily Mail,* YouTube, https://www.youtube.com/watch?v=C6LpIjB Q8tY.

287 *psychological appeal:* Remnick, *The Bridge,* 233–34.

287 *Trayvon Martin:* "2012: Florida Teen Trayvon Martin Is Shot and Killed," History.com, https://www.history.com/this-day-in-history/flor ida-teen-trayvon-martin-is-shot-and-killed.

288 *Garza took to Facebook:* Jelani Cobb, "The Matter of Black Lives," *New Yorker,* March 6, 2016.

288 *Johnson X Hinton:* James L. Hicks, "Riot Threat as Cops Beat Muslim; 'God's Angry Men' Tangle with Police," *New York Amsterdam News,* May 4, 1957.

289 *award of $70,000:* Manning Marable and Garrett Felber, eds., *A Man Who Stands for Nothing Will Fall for Anything: The Portable Malcolm X Reader* (New York: Penguin, 2013), 82.

289 *three-week trial:* Ibid., 122–24.

289 *"stomped upon any worse":* "Moslems' Ten Day Trial: Lawyer Breaks Down in Tense Courtroom," *New York Amsterdam News,* March 21, 1959.

289 *Ronald Stokes case:* "Malcolm X Press Conference on Deadly Police Raid

in Los Angeles," UCLA Film & Television Archive, https://www.cin
ema.ucla.edu/blogs/archive-blog/2021/05/04/malcolm-x-press-confer
ence; M. Keith Claybrook Jr., "Remembering Ronald (X) Stokes and
the Politics of Black Solidarity," *Black Perspectives*, African American
Intellectual History Society, April 11, 2022, https://www.aaihs.org/re
membering-ronald-x-stokes-and-the-politics-of-black-solidarity/.

290   *three thousand protesters:* Lois Saunders, "L.A. Negro Community
Unites in Defense of Black Muslims," *The Militant*, May 21, 1962.

291   *Stokes's funeral:* "Hon. Malcolm X: Los Angeles (Ronald Stokes Murder)," YouTube, https://www.youtube.com/watch?v=_VI-iqOuRMo.

291   *"democracy is hypocrisy":* "Malcolm X Speech 'Democracy Is Hypocrisy,'" Educational Video Group, YouTube, https://www.youtube.com
/watch?v=qNfAFfu6VD0.

291   *police tactics:* Garrett Felber, "Fighting 'Stop-and-Frisk' Policing from
Rockefeller to Trump," *Black Perspectives*, African American Intellectual
History Society, September 27, 2016, https://www.aaihs.org/fighting
-stop-and-frisk-policing-from-rockefeller-to-trump/.

292   *purchased for $100,000:* Ben Johnson, "A Lifetime of Haley's Roots Scat-
tered," *Tampa Bay Times*, October 2, 1992.

292   *Marable was so intrigued:* Manning Marable, "Rediscovering Malcolm's
Life: A Historian's Adventure in Living History," *Souls* 7, no. 1 (2005):
20–35.

292   *Morgan Entrekin:* Author interview with Morgan Entrekin.

293   *Reed came to New York:* Jennifer Schuessler, "Missing Malcolm X Writings, Long a Mystery, Are Sold," *New York Times*, July 26, 2018.

293   *twenty-five-page carbon copy:* Ibid.

293   *The Schomburg Center:* Ibid.

294   *first page of the chapter:* Ibid., Jeenah Moon photograph of the manuscript.

295   *critique of "liberal incrementalism":* Garrett Felber, "The Missing Malcolm X," *Boston Review*, November 28, 2018.

295   *"A ballot is like a bullet":* "Malcolm X's Legendary Speech: 'The Ballot
or the Bullet,'" YouTube, https://www.youtube.com/watch?v=8zLQLU
pNGsc.

296   *"the story of a people":* Felber, "The Missing Malcolm X."

296   *"modern Uncle Tom":* "Malcolm X–Dr. King Is an Uncle Tom," Malcolm X interview with psychologist Kenneth Clark, YouTube, https://
www.youtube.com/watch?v=-Rr-aRxItpw.

296   *patronized Malcolm:* Dr. Martin Luther King Jr., "The Nightmare of
Violence," *New York Amsterdam News*, March 13, 1965.

297   *Malcolm was killed:* Kihss, "Malcolm X Shot to Death at Rally Here."

297 *Dr. King was killed:* Earl Caldwell, "Martin Luther King Is Slain in Memphis; A White Is Suspected; Johnson Urges Calm," *New York Times,* April 5, 1968.

297 *"Tell me one thing":* Carl T. Rowan, "Malcolm X—No Hero of Mine," *Washington Post,* September 4, 1992.

297 *elegiac piece:* Baldwin, "Malcolm and Martin."

297 *"Black liberation theology":* James H. Cone, *Martin & Malcolm & America: A Dream or a Nightmare* (Maryknoll, NY: Orbis Books, 1991).

298 *theater project:* Ellen Hopkins, "Yolanda King and Attallah Shabazz: Their Fathers' Daughters," *Rolling Stone,* November 30, 1989.

298 *foremost proponent:* Joseph, *The Sword and the Shield.*

298 *remark to Coretta Scott King:* "Eyes on the Prize; Interview with Coretta Scott King," American Archive of Public Broadcasting, https://american archive.org/catalog/cpb-aacip_151-542j679j5g.

298 *more aggressive vision:* Martin Luther King Jr., "Beyond the Los Angeles Riots," *Saturday Review,* November 13, 1965.

299 *"He sounded more like Malcolm X":* Jonathan Eig, *King: A Life* (New York: Farrar, Straus & Giroux, 2023).

299 *startling discovery:* Gillian Brockwell, "MLK's Famous Criticism of Malcolm X Was a 'Fraud,' Author Finds," *Washington Post,* May 10, 2023.

300 *express some criticism:* "The Playboy Interview: Martin Luther King Jr.," *Playboy,* January 1965.

300 The Dead Are Arising: Les Payne and Tamara Payne, *The Dead Are Arising: The Life of Malcolm X* (New York: Liveright, 2020).

300 *journalist Les Payne:* Les Payne, "The Night I Stopped Being a Negro," in Bernestine Singley, ed., *When Race Becomes Real: Black and White Writers Confront Their Personal Histories* (Chicago: Lawrence Hill, 2002), 37.

301 *four-decade career:* Sam Roberts, "Les Payne, Journalist Who Exposed Racial Injustice, Dies at 76," *New York Times,* March 20, 2018.

302 *friends with Faith Childs:* Author interview with Faith Childs.

302 *Malcolm's childhood:* Payne and Payne, *The Dead Are Arising,* 3–112.

302 *Little's bloody death:* Ibid., 83–84, 545.

303 *restive young teen:* Ibid., 113–43, 546–48.

303 *Malcolm Jarvis:* Ibid., 144–215, 548–52.

303 *dozens of NOI converts:* Ibid., 265–83, 556–59.

303 *outpost in Hartford:* Ibid., 284–12.

303 *more than a hundred pages:* Author interview with Payne's friend Farrell Evans.

303 *Ku Klux Klan:* Payne and Payne, *The Dead Are Arising,* 313–75, 559–62.

304 *Malcolm's assassination:* Ibid., 357–516, 567–570.

304   *Joseph called Payne:* Ibid., 567.

304   *Shabazz told Payne:* Ibid., 567–68.

304   *the pseudonym "Talib":* Ibid., 506–15, 568, 570.

304   *Louis Farrakhan:* Ibid., 503–5.

305   *Doubleday became so frustrated:* Author interview with Faith Childs.

305   *"stay the course":* Ibid.

305   *Bob Weil:* Author interview with Bob Weil.

306   *books about Black history:* Mark Whitaker, "For Publishers, Books on Race and Racism Have Been a Surprising Success," *Washington Post,* June 12, 2020.

306   *"I wept":* Author interview with Faith Childs.

306   *Thulani Davis:* Mary Ellen Gabriel, "When Black History Is Your Own: Professor Thulani Davis Provides a Personal Perspective on Studying the Past," On Wisconsin, https://onwisconsin.uwalumni.com/when -black-history-is-your-own/.

306   *read the* Autobiography: Author interview with Anthony Davis; Zachary Woolfe, "The Family That Turned Malcolm X's Life into Opera," *New York Times,* November 1, 2023; "The Making of Malcolm," Metropolitan Opera, https://www.metopera.org/discover/articles/the-making-of -malcolm/.

307   *fan of classical opera:* Author interview with Anthony Davis.

308   *three worked separately:* "A Conversation with the Creators of X," *Seattle Opera blog,* August 21, 2023, https://www.seattleoperablog.com/2023 /08/a-conversation-with-creators-of-x.html.

308   *New York City Opera:* John Rockwell, "Malcolm X—Hero to Some, Racist to Others—Is Now the Stuff of Opera," *New York Times,* September 28, 1986.

308   *"Have you picked out a dress":* Author interview with Anthony Davis.

308   *impressive reviews:* Rockwell, "Malcolm X—Hero to Some, Racist to Others—Is Now the Stuff of Opera."

309   *Opening night:* C. Gerald Fraser, "A Committed Crowd Supports Premiere of 'X,'" *New York Times,* September 29, 1986.

309   *"CNN operas":* Paul Horsley, "Pat and Dick and Chiang and Mao: The First 'CNN Opera' Finally Appears on Met Gala," *The Independent* (Kansas City), https://kcindependent.com/the-first-cnn-opera-finally -appears-on-the-met-stage/.

309   *2020 Pulitzer Prize:* Pulitzer Prize citation for *The Central Park Five,* https://www.pulitzer.org/winners/anthony-davis.

309   *funders balked:* Author interview with Anthony Davis.

309   *tinker with X again:* Ibid.

310 *Yuval Sharon:* Mark Binelli, "Is the Future of American Opera Unfolding in Detroit?," *New York Times,* July 7, 2022.

310 *Fire Shut Up in My Bones:* James Jorden, "Premiere of 'Fire Shut Up in My Bones' Sets the Reopened Met Ablaze," *New York Observer,* September 28, 2021.

310 *Robert O'Hara:* Chris Jones, "*Insurrection: Holding History,* About the Turner Rebellion, Was Way Ahead of Its Time," *Chicago Tribune,* May 31, 2019.

310 *spaceship on the stage:* Zachary Woolfe, "After 36 Years, a Malcolm X Opera Sings to the Future," *New York Times,* May 15, 2022.

310 *Davóne Tines:* Ibid.

311 *Will Liverman:* "Will Liverman Performs as Malcolm X," *Great Performances at the Met,* PBS, YouTube, https://www.youtube.com/watch?v=P5u7k6va9mE.

311 *Miles Davis's trumpet:* Author interview with Anthony Davis.

311 *"an American classic":* Joshua Barone, "Review: Anthony Davis's Malcolm X Opera Finally Arrives at the Met," *New York Times,* November 5, 2023.

311 *yearning for self-determination:* Kaitlyn Greenidge, "How to Make an Opera About a Revolutionary," *Harper's Bazaar,* November 3, 2023.

311 *Afrofuturist movement:* Channing Hargrove, "A Malcolm X Opera Is Restaged for a 'Black Panther' World," AndScape, December 1, 2023, https://andscape.com/features/a-malcolm-x-opera-is-restaged-for-a-black-panther-world/; Author interview with Anthony Davis.

312 *day-long group reading:* Reggie Ugwu, "Malcolm X's Words, Spoken by a Litany of Fans at the Met," *New York Times,* November 2, 2023.

312 *"This is fantastic!":* Author interview with Anthony Davis.

FOURTEEN: THE REINVESTIGATIONS

315 *hunger for freedom:* Author interview with Mark O'Donoghue; O'Donoghue personal calendar and notes.

315 *Peter Fleming:* Dennis Hevesi, "Peter E. Fleming Jr., 79, Dies; Defense Lawyer Who Relished the Limelight," *New York Times,* January 15, 2009.

316 *interest of William F. Buckley: Firing Line: A Murder Case,* January 18, 1984, YouTube, https://www.youtube.com/watch?v=dT6c_mTey4c.

316 *work release program:* Michael Arena, "Malcolm X Killer Is Denied Parole," *Newsday,* February 21, 1985.

317 *lobbying campaign:* Author interview with Mark O'Donoghue.

317 *Goldman also wrote:* Author interviews with Peter Goldman.

317   *second review panel:* Arena, "Malcolm X Killer Is Denied Parole."
317   *"some white man":* Author interviews with Peter Goldman.
317   *challenged Aziz:* Michael Arena, "Killer of Malcolm X Wins Hearing
       on Parole Appeal," *Newsday*, March 28, 1965; Ronald Smothers, "Panel
       Approves Parole of Killer of Malcolm X," *New York Times*, May 8, 1985.
318   *Christopher Mega:* Marcia Kramer, "He Wants 'Racist' Dumped," New
       York *Daily News*, March 18, 1985.
318   *"He's going to get a job":* Associated Press, "1 of 3 Malcolm Assassins Pa-
       roled," *Daily Record* (Morristown, NJ), June 25, 1985; Author interview
       with Mark O'Donoghue.
319   *stayed in touch:* Author interviews with Peter Goldman.
319   *head of security:* Robert D. McFadden, "An Assassin of Malcolm X Gets
       Islam Post," *New York Times*, March 31, 1998.
319   *published a book:* Muhammad A. Aziz, *The New Song: The Religion of
       Abraham the True in Faith* (BookSurge Publishing, 2009); "About the
       Author" for Muhammad A. Aziz, Amazon.com.
320   *changed man:* Mark Jacobson, "The Man Who Didn't Shoot Malcolm X,"
       New York, September 28, 2007.
322   *passed away in 2009:* Ashley Southall, "Who Are Muhammad Aziz and
       Khalil Islam, the Exonerated Men?," *New York Times*, November 17,
       2021.
322   *Mujahid Halim:* Johan E. Bromwich, Ashley Southall, and Troy Clos-
       son, "56 Years Ago, He Shot Malcolm X. Now He Lives Quietly in
       Brooklyn," *New York Times*, November 22, 2021.
323   *Rachel Dretzin:* Rachel Dretzin biography, Ark Media website, https://
       www.ark-media.net/team/rachel-dretzin.
324   *"story concept":* Author interview with Shayla Harris.
324   *more digging:* Author interviews with Shayla Harris and Phil Bertelsen;
       Garrow, "Does Anyone Care Who Killed Malcolm X?"
324   *Marable's information:* Marable, *Malcolm X*, 475–76.
324   *"sizzle reel":* Author interview with Shayla Harris.
325   *a small team:* Author interviews with Shayla Harris and Phil Bertelsen.
326   *Earl Siddiq:* Rachel Dretzin and Phil Bertelsen, directors, *Who Killed
       Malcolm X?*, Fusion, 2019, Episode 4, "Showdown."
326   *Ras Baraka:* Ibid., Episode 5, "Shotgun Man."
326   *Cory Booker:* Ibid.
327   *fresh footage of Shabazz:* Ibid.
327   *"hiding in plain sight":* Author interview with Phil Bertelsen.
327   *Gates offered:* Ibid.
328   *day of his funeral:* Dretzin and Bertelsen, *Who Killed Malcolm X?*, Epi-
       sode 6, "Legacies."

328   *Sheila Oliver:* Ibid.

328   *Walid Muslim:* Ibid., Episode 4, "Showdown."

329   *Q. Amini Nathari:* Ibid.

329   *Tony Bouza:* Ibid., Episode 5, "Shotgun Man," and Episode 6, "Legacies."

330   *Herbert J. Stern:* Ibid., Episode 5, "Shotgun Man."

330   *Arthur Fulton:* Ibid., Episode 3, "Black Messiah."

331   *Leon 4X Ameer:* Ibid., Episode 6, "Legacies"; Tamara Payne, "Who Killed Malcolm X?," *The Nation*, December 9, 2021.

331   *request FBI files:* Author interview with Phil Bertelsen; Dretzin and Bertelsen, *Who Killed Malcolm X?*, Episode 6.

332   *beaten bloody:* "Member of Clay's Staff Beaten in Back Bay Hotel," United Press International, December 26, 1964.

332   *death threat:* [Peter Goldman,] "Death of a Desperado," *Newsweek*, March 8, 1965.

332   *found Ameer dead:* "Malcolm X Aide Is Found Dead," Associated Press, March 14, 1965.

332   *Brian Funck:* Author interviews with Shayla Harris and Brian Funck.

333   *deeply skeptical:* Dretzin and Bertelsen, *Who Killed Malcolm X?*, Episode 6.

334   *"We don't take cases":* Author interview with Phil Bertelsen.

334   *invited him to a premiere:* Author interview with Mark O'Donoghue.

334   *a dinner to celebrate Rosh Hashanah:* Ibid.

335   *vetting candidates:* Joseph P. Fried, "As Federal Prosecutor Quits, Aspiring Successors Rush In," *New York Times*, June 12, 1999.

335   *David Shanies:* Author interviews with Mark O'Donoghue and David Shanies.

336   *things moved rapidly:* Author interview with David Shanies.

336   *steep hurdles:* Ibid.; "Joint Motion to Vacate Judgments of Conviction and Dismiss Indictment, Indictment No. 871/1965, The People of the State of New York Against Muhammad A. Aziz, Also Known as Norman Butler and Norman 3X Butler, and Khalil Islam, Also Known as Thomas Johnson and Thomas 15X Johnson," Supreme Court of the State of New York, County of New York: Part 99.

337   *Covid pandemic struck:* Author interview with David Shanies.

337   *"J.M.":* "Joint Motion to Vacate Judgments of Conviction and Dismiss Indictment."

338   *interview Peter Goldman:* Author interviews with Peter Goldman and Mark O'Donoghue.

338   *responsible for the assassination:* "A Last Word: 2013," in Goldman, *The Death and Life of Malcolm X*, 2013 Kindle edition.

339   *numerous FBI files:* Author interview with David Shanies; "Joint Motion

to Vacate Judgments of Conviction and Dismiss Indictment," washing tonpost.com.

340 *Bragg won the election:* Tim Balk, "It's Bragg as Next D.A.," New York *Daily News,* November 3, 2021.

FIFTEEN: AN APOLOGY

341 *financial damages:* Marisa Iati, "Men Wrongly Convicted of Killing Malcolm X to Get $36 Million Settlement," *Washington Post,* October 21, 2022.

341 *move to dismiss:* Author interview with David Shanies; Complaint Case No. 23-CV-8504, United States District Court, Eastern District of New York, Muhammad A. Aziz, Plaintiff, Against United States of America, Defendant.

341 *services of Ben Crump:* Emily Mae Czachor, "Malcolm X's Family Announces $100 Million Lawsuit Alleging NYPD and Other Agencies Concealed Evidence in His Murder, CBS News, February 21, 2023.

341 *glimpse of Muhammad Aziz:* Author interview with David Shanies.

342 *Inside the courtroom:* Reuters video of full exoneration hearing posted on Facebook, https://www.facebook.com/watch/live/?ref=watch_per malink&v=954381941829337; Author interviews with David Shanies, Mark O'Donoghue, and Phil Bertelsen.

344 *Outside the courtroom:* "Judge Clears Muhammad Aziz in Malcolm X Killing," Associated Press video, YouTube, https://www.youtube.com /watch?v=MHcqZqR8pNQ.

345 *dropped Goldman off:* Author interviews with Peter Goldman, David Shanies, and Mark O'Donoghue; video of reunion of Goldman and Muhammad Aziz in "X/onerated: The Murder of Malcolm X and 55 Years to Justice," ABC News, February 3, 2021.

EPILOGUE

346 *Jane Relin:* "Jane Relin '66: Malcolm X at Barnard," Barnard College, YouTube, https://www.youtube.com/watch?v=a8MhFuUkL9o&t=82s.

346 *Ellen Friedman:* "Ellen Friedman '66: Malcolm X at Barnard," Barnard College, YouTube, https://www.youtube.com/watch?v=-3Elfh68clQ; *Mortarboard 1966,* Barnard College yearbook, 117.

346 *Student Exchange:* Barbara Rand, "Exchange Formulates Year-Round Plan," *Barnard Bulletin,* September 24, 1964; "Exchange Tours Through Harlem's Housing," *Barnard Bulletin,* October 5, 1964; "Student Exchange Spends 'Sat. Afternoon at Zoo,'" *Barnard Bulletin,* October 19, 1964; "Exchange Receives Answers," *Barnard Bulletin,* November 16, 1964.

347 *"people in the news"*: Abigail Beshkin, "Malcolm X Revisited," *Barnard Magazine*, Spring 2015.

347 *arrived on the Barnard campus*: "Malcolm X–Barnard College, 18th February 1965, clip of final speech," YouTube, https://www.youtube.com/watch?v=y9oQ4qqSwwQ.

347 *the Queens house*: "X Leaves the Spot: Malcolm Moves Out," *Newsday*, February 19, 1965.

347 *overflow crowd*: "Jane Relin '66: Malcolm X at Barnard"; "Ellen Friedman '66: Malcolm X at Barnard."

348 *thanking the students*: "Malcolm X–Barnard College."

348 *"global rebellion"*: Martin Paris, "Negroes Are Willing to Use Terrorism, Says Malcolm X," *Columbia Spectator*, February 19, 1965.

349 *"proud of our black blood"*: "Malcolm X Pleads for Rights Here," *Barnard Bulletin*, February 25, 1965.

349 *say about nonviolence*: Paris, "Negroes Are Willing to Use Terrorism, Says Malcolm X."

349 *Vietnam War*: "Malcolm X Pleads for Rights Here."

349 *"I would rather be dead"*: Ibid.

349 *that Sunday afternoon*: "Jane Relin '66: Malcolm X at Barnard."

349 *"lost a friend"*: Beshkin, "Malcolm X Revisited."

349 *"definitely a shock"*: "Jane Relin '66: Malcolm X at Barnard."

350 *career choices*: "Jane Relin '66: Malcolm X at Barnard"; Gordon Williams, "Age Was No Barrier for Volunteer Jane Relin," American Red Cross, July 20, 2023; "Ellen Wolkin Friedman, M.D.," Albert Einstein College of Medicine, https://einsteinmed.edu/faculty/2007/ellen-friedman; "Poppink, Prudence Kay," obituary, *Rochester Democrat and Chronicle*, November 26, 2000.

351 *"he is still talking"*: "Ellen Friedman '66: Malcolm X at Barnard."

BIBLIOGRAPHY

BOOKS

Abdul-Jabbar, Kareem, with Raymond Obstfeld. *Becoming Kareem: Growing Up On and Off the Court.* New York: Little, Brown, 2017.

Ali, Muhammad, with Hana Ali. *The Soul of a Butterfly: Reflections on Life's Journey.* New York: Simon & Schuster, 2004.

Andrews, William L., ed. *African American Autobiography: A Collection of Critical Essays.* New York: Prentice Hall, 1993.

Angelou, Maya. *All God's Children Need Traveling Shoes.* New York: Random House, 1986.

Asante, Molefe Kete. *Maulana Karenga: An Intellectual Portrait.* Cambridge: Polity, 2009.

Aziz, Muhammad A. *The New Song: The Religion of Abraham the True in Faith.* BookSurge Publishing, 2009.

Baker, David, ed. *New Perspectives on Jazz.* Washington, DC: Smithsonian, 1986.

Baldwin, James. *The Devil Finds Work: An Essay.* New York: Dial Press, 1976.

———. *One Day When I Was Lost: A Screenplay Based on Alex Haley's The Autobiography of Malcolm X.* New York: Alfred A. Knopf, 2013.

Ball, Jared A., and Todd Steven Burroughs, eds. *A Lie of Reinvention: Correcting Manning Marable's Malcolm X.* Baltimore: Black Classic Press, 2012.

Baraka, Amiri. *The Autobiography of LeRoi Jones.* Chicago: Lawrence Hill, 1984.

Baraka, Amiri, and Larry Neal, eds. *Black Fire: An Anthology of Afro-American Writing.* New York: William Morrow, 1968.

Barbour, Floyd B., ed. *The Black Power Revolt.* New York: Collier, 1969.

———. *The Black Seventies.* Boston: Porter Sargent, 1970.

Bloom, Joshua, and Waldo E. Martin Jr. *Black Against Empire: The History and Politics of the Black Power Movement.* Oakland: University of California Press, 2013.

Bracey Jr., John H., Sonia Sanchez, and James Smethurst, eds. *SOS—Calling All Black People: A Black Arts Movement Reader.* Boston: University of Massachusetts Press, 2014.

Branch, Taylor. *At Canaan's Edge: America in the King Years, 1965–68.* New York: Simon & Schuster, 2007.

_____. *Pillar of Fire: America in the King Years, 1963–65*. New York: Simon & Schuster, 1998.

Breitman, George. *The Last Year of Malcolm X: The Evolution of a Revolutionary*. New York: Pathfinder Press, 1968.

_____, ed. *Malcolm X: By Any Means Necessary: Speeches, Interviews and a Letter*. Atlanta: Pathfinder Press, 1970.

_____. *Malcolm X Speaks: Selected Speeches and Statements*. New York: Grove Press, 1965.

Brown, Elaine. *A Taste of Power: A Black Woman's Story*. New York: Anchor, 1994.

Brown, Scot. *Fighting for US: Maulana Karenga, the US Organization, and Black Cultural Nationalism*. New York: New York University Press, 2003.

Carlos, John. *The John Carlos Story: The Sports Movement That Changed the World*. Chicago: Haymarket Books, 2011.

Carmichael, Stokely, with Ekwueme Michael Thelwell. *Ready for Revolution: The Life and Struggles of Stokely Carmichael (Kwame Ture)*. New York: Scribner, 2003.

Carson, Clayborne. *Malcolm X: The FBI File*. New York: Skyhorse Publishing, 1991.

Chang, Jeff. *Can't Stop, Won't Stop: A History of the Hip-Hop Generation*. New York: Picador, 2005.

Charnas, Dan. *The Big Payback: The History of the Business of Hip Hop*. New York: New American Library, 2010.

Cleaver, Eldridge. *Soul on Ice*. New York: McGraw-Hill, 1968.

Cohen, Hettie. *How I Became Hettie Jones*. New York: Dutton, 1990.

Coleman, Brian. *Check the Technique: Liner Notes for Hip-Hop Junkies*. New York: Random House, 2009.

Cone, James H. *Martin & Malcolm & America: A Dream or a Nightmare*. Maryknoll, NY: Orbis Books, 1991.

Curry, George E., ed. *The Best of Emerge Magazine*. New York: Ballantine, 2003.

DeCaro, Louis A., Jr. *On the Side of My People: A Religious Life of Malcolm X*. New York: New York University Press, 1996.

Dudar, Helen, ed. *The Attentive Eye: Selected Journalism*. Bloomington, IN: Xlibris, 2002.

Dyson, Michael Eric. Making Malcolm X: *The Myth and Meaning of Malcolm X*. Oxford: Oxford University Press, 1995.

Eig, Jonathan. *Ali: A Life*. New York: Boston: Houghton Mifflin Harcourt, 2017.

_____. *King: A Life*. New York: Farrar, Straus & Giroux, 2023.

Ellis, Catherine, and Stephen Drury Smith, eds. *Free All Along: The Robert Penn Warren Civil Rights Interviews*. New York: The New Press, 2019.

Epps, Archie, ed. *Malcolm X: Speeches at Harvard*. New York: William Morrow, 1969.

Evanzz, Karl. *The Judas Factor: The Plot to Kill Malcolm X*. New York: Thunder's Mouth Press, 1992.

Fricke, Jim, and Charlie Ahearn. *Yes Yes Y'All: Oral History of Hip Hop's First Decade*. Boston: Da Capo, 2002.

Friedly, Michael. *Malcolm X: The Assassination*. New York: Ballantine, 1995.

Gallen, David, ed. *Malcolm X As They Knew Him*. New York: Carroll & Graf, 1992.

Garrow, David J. *Bearing the Cross: Martin Luther King, Jr., and the Southern Christian Leadership Conference*. New York: William Morrow, 1986.

Garza, Alicia. *The Purpose of Power: How We Came Together When We Fell Apart*. New York: One World, 2020.

Goldman, Peter. *The Death and Life of Malcolm X*. New York: Harper & Row, 1973.

Goudsouzian, Aram. *Down at the Crossroads: Civil Rights, Black Power, and the Meredith March Against Fear*. New York: Farrar, Straus & Giroux, 2014.

Hampton, Henry, and Steve Fayer. *Voices of Freedom: An Oral History of the Civil Rights Movement from the 1950s Through the 1980s*. New York: Bantam, 1990.

Harris, Kamala. *The Truths We Hold: An American Journey*. New York: Penguin, 2019.

Hartigan, Patti. *August Wilson: A Life*. New York: Simon & Schuster, 2023.

Hauser, Thomas. *Muhammad Ali: His Life and Times*. New York: Simon & Schuster, 1991.

Hilliard, David, with Keith and Kent Zimmerman. *Huey: Spirit of the Panther*. New York: Basic Books, 2006.

Jeffries, Hasan Kwame. *Bloody Lowndes: Civil Rights and Black Power in Alabama's Black Belt*. New York: New York University Press, 2009.

Jones, LeRoi. *Blues People: Negro Music in White America*. New York: William Morrow, 1963.

———. *Home: Social Essays*. New York: William Morrow, 1966.

Joseph, Peniel E. *Stokely: A Life*. New York: Basic Civitas, 2014.

———. *The Sword and the Shield: The Revolutionary Lives of Malcolm X and Martin Luther King, Jr*. New York: Basic Books, 2020.

Kindred, Dave. *Sound and Fury: Two Powerful Lives, One Fateful Friendship*. New York: Free Press, 2006.

King, Coretta Scott. *My Life with Martin Luther King, Jr*. New York: Henry Holt, 1969.

Kondo, Baba Zak. *Conspiracys: Unravelling the Assassination of Malcolm X*. Nubia Press, 1993.

Kunstler, William M., with Sheila Isenberg. *My Life As a Radical Lawyer*. New York: Birch Lane Press, 1994.

Lee, Spike, with Ralph Wiley. *By Any Means Necessary: The Trials and Tribulations of the Making of Malcolm X*. New York: Vintage, 1993.

Leeming, David. *James Baldwin: A Biography*. New York: Alfred A. Knopf, 1994.

Lewis, John, with Michael D'Orso. *Walking with the Wind: A Memoir of the Movement*. New York: Simon & Schuster, 1998.

Light, Alan. *Tupac Amaru Shakur: 1971–1996*. New York: Three Rivers Press, 1988.

Lincoln, C. Eric. *The Black Muslims in America*. Boston: Beacon Press, 1961.

Marable, Manning. *Malcolm X: A Life of Reinvention*. New York: Viking, 2011.

Marable, Manning, and Garrett Felber, eds. *A Man Who Stands for Nothing Will Fall for Anything: The Portable Malcolm X Reader*. New York: Penguin, 2013.

Myrie, Russell. *Don't Rhyme for the Sake of Riddlin': The Authorized Story of Public Enemy*. Edinburgh: Canongate Books, 2008.

Neal, Larry. *Visions of a Liberated Future: Black Arts Movement Writings*. New York: Basic Books, 1989.

Newton, Huey P. *Revolutionary Suicide*. New York: Penguin Classics, 2009.

Obama, Barack. *Dreams from My Father: A Story of Race and Inheritance*. New York: Crown, 1995.

Parr, Patrick. *Malcolm Before X*. Boston: University of Massachusetts Press, 2024.

Payne, Les, and Tamara Payne. *The Dead Are Arising: The Life of Malcolm X*. New York: Liveright, 2020.

Perry, Bruce. *Malcolm: The Life of a Man Who Changed Black America*. Barrytown, NY: Station Hill Press, 1991.

Remnick, David. *The Bridge: The Life and Rise of Barack Obama*. New York: Vintage, 2011.

———. *King of the World: Muhammad Ali and the Rise of an American Hero*. New York: Random House, 1998.

Reporting Civil Rights, Part Two, American Journalism, 1963–1973. New York: Library of America, 2003.

Richardson, Peter. *A Bomb in Every Issue: How the Short, Unruly Life of Ramparts Magazine Changed America*. New York: The New Press, 2002.

Rickford, Russell J. *Betty Shabazz, Surviving Malcolm X: A Journey of Strength from Wife to Widow to Heroine*. Naperville, IL: Sourcebooks, 2003.

Roberts, Randy, and Johnny Smith. *Blood Brothers: The Fatal Friendship Between Muhammad Ali and Malcolm X*. New York: Basic Books, 2016.

Rosset, Barney. *Rosset: My Life in Publishing and How I Fought Censorship*. New York: OR Books, 2017.

Seale, Bobby. *Seize the Time: The Story of the Black Panther Party and Huey P. Newton*. Baltimore: Black Classic Press, 1991.

Seaver, Richard. *The Tender Hour of Twilight: Paris in the '50s, New York in the '60s: A Memoir of Publishing's Golden Age*. New York: Farrar, Straus & Giroux, 2012.

Sellers, Cleveland, with Robert Terrell. *The River of No Return: The Autobiography of a Black Militant and the Life and Death of SNCC*. New York: William Morrow, 1973.

Shabazz, Ilyasah, with Kim McLarin. *Growing Up X: A Memoir by the Daughter of Malcolm X*. New York: Random House/One World Books, 2002.

Singley, Bernestine, ed. *When Race Becomes Real: Black and White Writers Confront Their Personal Histories*. Chicago: Lawrence Hill, 2002.

Smethurst, James Edward. *The Black Arts Movement: Literary Nationalism in the 1960s and 1970s*. Chapel Hill: University of North Carolina Press, 2005.

Spencer, Robyn C. *The Revolution Has Come: Black Power, Gender, and the Black Panther Party in Oakland*. Durham, NC: Duke University Press, 2016.

Steele, Shelby. *The Content of Our Character: A New Vision of Race in America*. New York: St. Martin's Press, 1990.

Stone, Alfred E. *Autobiographical Occasions and Original Acts: Visions of American Identity from Henry Adams to Nate Shaw*. Philadelphia: University of Pennsylvania Press, 1982.

Terrell, Robert E., ed. *The Cambridge Companion to Malcolm X*. Cambridge: Cambridge University Press, 2010.

Thomas, Clarence. *My Grandfather's Son*. New York: HarperCollins, 2007.

Thomas, Evan. *The Man to See: Edward Bennett Williams, Ultimate Insider; Legendary Trial Lawyer*. New York: Simon & Schuster, 1991.

Van Deburg, William L. *New Day in Babylon: The Black Power Movement and American Culture, 1965–1975*. Chicago: University of Chicago Press, 1992.

Whitaker, Mark. *Saying It Loud: 1966—The Year Black Power Challenged the Civil Rights Movement*. New York: Simon & Schuster, 2013.

Wood, Joe, ed. *Malcolm X: In Our Own Image*. New York: St. Martin's Press, 1994.

Woodward, Komozi. *A Nation Within a Nation: Amiri Baraka (LeRoi Jones) & Black Power Politics*. Chapel Hill: University of North Carolina Press, 1999.

Wright, Richard. *Native Son*. New York: Harper & Brothers, 1940.

X, Malcolm, as told to Alex Haley. *The Autobiography of Malcolm X*. New York: Grove Press, 1965.

FILMOGRAPHY

Bagwell, Orlando, director. *Malcolm X: Make It Plain*. PBS, 1994.

Dretzin, Rachel, and Phil Bertelsen, directors. *Who Killed Malcolm X?* Fusion, 2019.

King, Regina, director. *One Night in Miami*. Amazon Studios, 2020.

King, Woodie, Jr., director. *Death of a Prophet*. Entertain Me Productions (remastered), 2022.

Lee, Spike, director. *Do the Right Thing*. Universal Pictures, 1989.

———. *Malcolm X*. Warner Brothers, 1992.

Perl, Arnold, director. *Malcolm X: His Own Story As It Really Happened*. Columbia Pictures, 1972.

Wallace, Mike, and Louis Lomax, producers. *The Hate That Hate Produced*. WNTA-TV, 1959.

PHOTO CREDITS

INDEX

INDEX